Salvation and Globalization in the Early Jesuit Missions

This is the first truly global study of the Society of Jesus's early missions. Up to now historians have treated the early-modern Catholic missionary project as a disjointed collection of regional missions rather than as a single world-encompassing example of religious globalization. Luke Clossey shows how the vast distances separating missions led to logistical problems of transportation and communication incompatible with traditional views of the Society as a tightly centralized military machine. In fact, connections unmediated by Rome sprung up between the missions throughout the seventeenth century. He follows trails of personnel, money, relics, and information between missions in seventeenth-century China, Germany, and Mexico and explores how Jesuits understood space and time and visualized universal mission and salvation. This pioneering study demonstrates that a global perspective is essential to understanding the Jesuits and will be required reading for historians of Catholicism and the early-modern world.

Luke Clossey is Assistant Professor of History at Simon Fraser University, British Columbia.

Salvation and Globalization
in the Early Jesuit Missions

Luke Clossey

Simon Fraser University, British Columbia

CAMBRIDGE
UNIVERSITY PRESS

CAMBRIDGE UNIVERSITY PRESS
Cambridge, New York, Melbourne, Madrid, Cape Town, Singapore,
São Paulo, Delhi

Cambridge University Press
32 Avenue of the Americas, New York, NY 10013-2473, USA

www.cambridge.org
Information on this title: www.cambridge.org/9780521887441

First published 2008

Printed in the United States of America

A catalog record for this publication is available from the British Library.

Library of Congress Cataloging in Publication Data

Clossey, Luke, 1975–
Salvation and globalization in the early Jesuit missions / Luke Clossey.
    p. cm.
Includes bibliographical references and index.
ISBN 978-0-521-88744-1 (hardback)
1. Jesuits – Missions.   2. Salvation – Catholic Church.
3. Globalization – Religious aspects – Catholic Church.   I. Title.
BV2290.C56   2008
266′.2–dc22   2007040543

ISBN   978-0-521-88744-1 hardback

v

for

Alda Alari, Andrea Bacianini, 陈志坚, 冯科, 傅捷, 莉迪娅, 李建军, Astrid Meyer, Fabio Micieli, Antonino Nicotra, Andrew Redden, Alisa Roth, 施诚, Paweł Stefaniak

and all the other faraway friends I found
    while doing this research,
for distracting me from this research,
and for reminding me that
you don't have to be a Jesuit to care about distant souls.

Contents

List of Tables and Charts

Tables

Charts

Acknowledgments

The original proposal repeatedly ran up against the warning that this project was too grand for any one person. This warning turned out to be prophetic, and this book has turned out to be the result of the work of what was the finest support network to ever grace the life of a historian.

This would not have been written without the faith and financial support of my benefactors. The trail of these global missionaries' records led me around the world, to research in a dozen countries, and expenses (even for often creative lodging) quickly mounted. I could sympathize with the Jesuit Luis Javier Martín, who wrote (from my *patria* California) in 1762, "Where have we come to be? This is doubtless the very ends of the earth."[†] My time researching and writing was supported by the Susan G. Katz Graduate Fellowship; a Berkeley Fellowship for Graduate Studies; a Fulbright Graduate Fellowship; the UC Berkeley History Department; the Fondazione Lemmermann; the Bavarian State Ministry for Science, Research, and Art Grant; the Andrew W. Mellon Foundation; and a Simon Fraser University President's Research Grant.

This would not have been written without the patient guidance of many experts. Foremost in this regard are the members of my dissertation committee, Thomas A. Brady, Jr., William B. Taylor, and Elizabeth A. Honig, who equalled the dukes of Bavaria in faith and generosity. My gratitude goes to the archivists who assisted me despite their doubts as to the sanity of anyone who searches for Mexican materials in German archives and German materials in Mexican archives, and especially to the late Stefania Cattani, who was too busy being kindly efficient to ever doubt. A special thanks goes to the legions of language teachers, without whom this would have been impossible, for their efforts to hide their horror as they witnessed everything they taught me blend into a Sino-Arabic-Germano-Romantic pidgin. At its various

---

[†] "¿Adónde hemos venido a dar? Esto, sin duda, es la mismísima cola del mundo!" Quoted in Bernd Hausberger, *Jesuiten aus Mitteleuropa im kolonialen Mexiko* (Munich: R. Oldenbourg, 1995), 68.

stages this project has directly benefited from the kind assistance and learned encouragement of Géza Bikfalvi (Budapest), Desmund Cheung (Vancouver), Claudia von Collani (Würzburg), Elisabetta Corsi (Mexico and Rome), Michele Fatica (Naples), Jeanne Grant (Prague), Rita Haub (Munich), Bernd Hausberger (Berlin), Juan Manuel Herrera H. (Mexico City), Sanford Manley (Mejave Mai), Thierry Meynard, SJ (Beijing), S. K. Mhamai (Goa), Kenneth Mills (Toronto), my late *Ersatzdoktorvater* Rainer Müller (Eichstätt), David Mungello (Baylor University), José Jesús Hernández Palomo (Seville), M.P. Рыженков (Moscow), Thomas Reddy, SJ (Rome), Nicholas Standaert (Leuven), Zhu Xiaoyuan 朱孝 (Beijing), Catherine Yvard (Dublin), and in California *Doktormutter* Kathy Brady, Cynthia Col, John Danis, Jan de Vries, Dennis Flynn, David Frick, Arturo Giráldez, Ian Greenspan, George Greiner, SJ, Randolph Head, Kristin Huffine, Gene Irschick, Carina Johnson, Greta Kroeker, Eugenio Menegon, Chris Moustakas, Kenneth Pomeranz, and Randolph Starn, and Michael Watson at Cambridge University Press. At Simon Fraser University, I completed this project in the company of excellent students, especially my intrepid research assistants Brandon Marriott and Kyle Jackson, and my very collegial and very smart colleagues, including John Craig, Alec Dawson, and Nicholas Guyatt, who read a draft and convinced me not to edit out the best parts. In Rome, the anarchist-poet Francesco Pompa proofread, sometimes as I wrote, and Andrew Redden's archival genius continues to inspire. Individual chapters profited from the suggestions of members of the Transatlantic Doctoral Seminar on German History in the Early Modern Era, the University of California (UC) Colloquium on Early Modern Central Europe, the UC Multi-Campus Research Group in World History, the Ritual Workshop at the Katholieke Universiteit Leuven, and the Early Modern World Seminar of Berkeley and Burnaby.

This would not have been written without my parents. In three decades of parenting they made only one mistake, a blunder once characterized as the only error the Irish made in all their dealings with the English – they encouraged me to read. *I'll Teach My Dog a Hundred Words* led to 中國經濟史論叢, and reading in foreign languages led to reading in foreign lands, but I was always glad to return home, or when they brought home to me.

1 Introduction

"Oh, how I sigh, Benito! The missions are not how they paint them to be....."

– Pedro José Cuervo to Benito González Patiño (1766)[1]

Every respectable account of early-modern history spotlights the global range of the missionary orders, especially of the Jesuits, who "preached and argued, taught and counselled everywhere from Prague to Paraguay to Peking."[2] In speed and extent this expansion of Catholicism dwarfed even the explosion of Islam out to Iberia and Transoxania in the century after the death of Muhammad. The Catholic Church was the preeminent international institution of the era, as even contemporaries recognized. One French cynic quipped that the Swedish Queen Christina had converted to Catholicism – under Jesuit influence – only because of that faith's convenience for travellers.[3] Thomas Macaulay later explained why international Catholicism enjoyed strategic advantages over the national churches of Protestantism: "If a Jesuit was wanted at Lima, he was on the Atlantic in the next fleet. If he was wanted at Baghdad, he was toiling through the desert with the next caravan." In contrast, Macaulay held that "the Spiritual force of Protestantism was a mere local militia, which might be useful in case of an invasion, but could not be sent abroad, and could therefore make no conquests."[4] The Jesuits enjoyed what might be

---

[1] P. Pedro José Cuervo, Nonoava, to P. Benito González Patiño, September 25, 1766, quoted in Bernd Hausberger, *Jesuiten aus Mitteleuropa im kolonialen Mexiko: Eine Bio-Bibliographie*, Studien zur Geschichte und Kultur der Iberischen und Iberoamerikanischen Länder 2 (Munich: R. Oldenbourg, 1995), 69.

[2] Eugene J. Rice, Jr. and Anthony Grafton, *The Foundations of Early Modern Europe, 1460–1559*, 2nd ed. (New York: Norton, 1994), 172.

[3] J. S. Cummins, *A Question of Rites: Friar Domingo Navarrete and the Jesuits in China* (Hants: Scolar Press, 1993), 26.

[4] Thomas Babington Macaulay, *The History of England from the Accession of James II* (London: Macmillan, 1913–15), II.713–14; idem, "Ranke's History of the Popes," in *Reviews, Essays, and Poems* (London: Ward, Lock, 1890), 560.

called a system of "compensation" whereby when one mission failed, its missionaries could be transferred to another.

Drawing from world history and from the history of the Catholic Reformation, two histories too rarely associated with each other, this book seeks to describe the reality of this global mission. An equally striking phenomenon, dependent upon but not equivalent to this geographical expansion of the church, was the birth of a sense of global perspective in religion. This introductory chapter outlines how this project approaches the theory of the early Jesuits' global mission, as well as its practice in, around, and between the German lands, New Spain (colonial Mexico), and China.

Historians' Missions

Calls for a world history of Christianity have been, and are being, answered. Recent issues of *Church History* reviewed monographs whose subjects range from Haiti to China, from Michoacán to the Kingdom of Kongo. The agreement on the need for a world history of Christianity is almost universal, as is the disagreement on what a world history of Christianity should include.

One approach considers Christian world history to be all of Christian history, minus Europe. The "world" of this world history is the globe with a gaping abyss north of Africa and west of the Urals, perhaps the result of a hypothetical World War I fought with nuclear weapons. In this understanding, missions in Africa are world historical, but missions in England are not. Of course, defining a world history in terms of Europe, even in terms of Europe's absence, is itself Eurocentric – and is hardly appropriate to the study of a religion historically centred on Europe. A second kind of world history is that which takes place *anywhere* on the planet. Before the moon landing this was comprehensive, and in this view all history becomes world history. An American Historical Association conference panel on "Writing the History of Christianity: Global Issues" included papers which could only be considered global history in that the subject of each occurred somewhere in the world, rather a ways off from all the others. Here we see a Christian history, the nominal unity of which derives from geographical disunity. Scholarship of both these varieties has begun to fill gaps in our understanding, but merely transplants old historical approaches to unfamiliar locales.

A third kind of world history is that which takes place *everywhere* in the world, which trespasses across national and regional boundaries to consider subjects of extended geographical scope. This trend toward global histories has coexisted in recent years, often in the same fields of study, with a flourishing interest in local religious issues, inspired in large part by William Christian's study of sixteenth-century Spain (1981).[5] Global and local approaches offer alternatives to national history, but they also share a more subtle affinity, for scholarship that is considered world historical for its attention to a less-studied geographical area typically restricts the area under study to maintain a local focus. The most expressly world historical studies thus emphasize their subjects' particularity and uniqueness, and so become also the most local studies. Even the ambitious scholarship that encompasses a variety of regions only imperfectly traces out connections among places. Recent projects such as the *World History of Christianity* promise a global view, but again largely consider Christianity as a world-historical phenomenon in discrete chapters for discrete regions. Few pursue world Christianity as a single entity, focussing on its unity rather than on its regional particularities.

Nowhere is this remarkable relation between "world" and "local" Christianity clearer than in mission history. Naturally, a broad geographical range has never been foreign to the history of missions, and few missionaries have pioneered a path into the wilds without later being hounded by an intrepid historian. An impressive scholarship will soon cover every place in the global range of early-modern Catholic proselytizing activity.

These works typically fail to take the early-modern Catholic mission seriously as a macrohistorical phenomenon, that is, as a single world-spanning enterprise. Most historians have treated the Jesuit project as a disjointed collection of homomorphic regional missions directed and supported from centres of power in Rome, Madrid, and Lisbon. China, with an early-seventeenth-century population some hundred times greater than that of New Spain, hosted only dozens of Jesuits as New Spain counted hundreds. Surely the missions there were very different, but in our histories they receive similar treatment. Stephen Neill's one-volume *History of Christian Missions*, the most complete in English, takes the reader along on "our imaginary journey" from one mission station to the next, and any actual connections disappear behind this rhetorical strategy.[6] This same approach appears in the principal multivolume works, K. S. Latourette's *A History of the Expansion of Christianity* (1937–45) and S. Delacroix's *Histoire Universelle des Missions Catholiques* [*Universal History of Catholic Missions*] (1956–59).

---

[5] William A. Christian, *Local Religion in Sixteenth-Century Spain* (Princeton: Princeton University Press, 1981).

[6] Stephen Neill, *A History of Christian Missions*, Penguin History of the Church 6 (New York: Penguin, 1986), 56. The journey seems to disappear as the book progresses, but the presentation of discrete geographical areas does not.

Reaching back before the modern study of missiology, we occasionally unearth, amidst the nineteenth century's cloying missionary biographies and trenchant apologetics, other attempts at global mission history. Patrizius Wittmann's *Die Herrlichkeit der Kirche in ihren Missionen* [*The Glory of the Church in Its Missions*] (1841) tries to synthesize the various regional studies available to him. M. R. A. Henrion's *Histoire Générale des Missions Catholiques* [*General History of the Catholic Missions*] (1844) settles for a method more annalistic than analytic.[7]

These "global" mission histories are essentially anthologies of regional mission histories – long the field's great strength. Several venerable works do cover in encyclopaedic detail the Jesuit missions of the three regions of this book, notably B. Duhr's *Geschichte der Jesuiten in den Ländern Deutscher Zunge* [*History of the Jesuits in the Lands of the German Tongue*] (1907–28), F. J. Alegre's *Historia de la provincia de la Compañia de Jesús de Nueva España* [*History of the Province of the Company of Jesus in New Spain*] (1841–2), Zambrano and Casillas's *Diccionario Bio-Bibliográfico de la Compañia de Jesús en México* [*Bio-bibliographical Dictionary of the Company of Jesus in Mexico*] (1961–77), and J. Dehergne's *Répertoire des Jésuites de Chine de 1552 à 1800* [*Repertoire of the Jesuits in China from 1552 to 1800*] (1974). Since their publication, authors of numerous monographs on various aspects of the missions have built upon these foundations.

Less frequently, scholars have traced connections among these regions. In addition to missionaries' travels,[8] the exchange of personnel has commanded the most attention, especially the overseas work of central-European missionaries. The modern study of the activities of German Jesuits abroad began with Platzweg (1882) and found mature expression in Huonder (1899). Scholars then focussed on German influence in China, as in the works of Münsterberg (1894), Leidinger (1904), Schneller (1914), and Maas (1933). Later works on the German-China missionary connection turned to specific German cities, namely Würzburg (Willeke 1974; Steininger 1983) and Ingolstadt (Treffer 1989;

---

[7] At Robert Streit's suggestion, in 1910 a chair in missiology was established at Münster, to be filled by Joseph Schmidlin. See R. Hoffmann, "Missiology," *New Catholic Encyclopedia* (New York: McGraw-Hill, 1967), IX.902. For a discussion of such early works see Karl Müller, "Katholische Missionsgescichtsschreibung seit dem 16. Jahrhundert," in *Einleitung in die Missionsgeschichte: Tradition, Situation und Dynamik des Christentums*, ed. Karl Müller and Werner Ustorf (Stuttgart: Kohlhammer, 1995), 28–31.

[8] See Joseph Sebes, "Jesuit Attempts to Establish an Overland Route to China," *The Canada-Mongolia Review* 5 (1979): 51–67; Theodore Edward Treutlein, "Jesuit Travel to New Spain (1678–1756)," *Mid-America* 19 (1937): 104–23; Sabine Sauer, *Gottes streitbare Diener für Amerika: Missionsresien im Spiegel der ersten Briefe niederländischer Jesuiten (1616–1618)*, Weltbild und Kulturbegegnung 4 (Pfaffenweiler: Centaurus-Verlagsgesellschaft, 1992).

Wilczek 1993–4) – or to specific people, such as Leibniz (Widmaier 1990).

Occasionally a work of comparison brings together in the historian's mind geographically disparate regions. Abandoning an earlier plan to look at the movement of personnel, Paolo Broggio (2004) has studied the circulation of missionary strategies between Spain and Spanish South America.[9] J. S. Cummins (1978, 1993) and Johannes Beckmann (1964) focus on the missionary connections between China and New Spain. Gauvin A. Bailey's wide-ranging *Art on the Jesuit Missions in Asia and Latin America, 1542–1773* mentions in passing a global exchange of images.[10] Dauril Alden's distinguished *The Making of an Enterprise* presents the history of the Jesuit Portuguese Assistancy, including connections within that administrative unit, and because of the geographical range of the Assistancy, these connections encompass exchanges among Portugal, Brazil, littoral Africa, and Asia.[11]

Apart from Hantzsch (1909) and Stitz (1930), only with World War II did historians shift attention from central Europeans proselytizing in China to their counterparts in America. Sierra (1944) and Blankenburg (1947) followed the Germans, while Odlozilík (1945) and Kalista (1947) wrote on the Czechs. The later works signalled a new trend of looking at non-German Jesuits in America. Stretching back to Hoffmann's (1939) study of Bohemian, Moravian, and Silesian Jesuits abroad, this undertaking endured throughout the Cold War. Thus Štěpánek (1968) continued researching the Czechs, and Bettray (1976) the Austrians, while Prpić (1971), Ryneš (1971), and González Rodríguez (1970) took up the Bohemian, Croatian, and Flemish sides. Even Jaksch's 1957 study of German missionaries restricts itself to the Sudeten Germans. This continued with Grulich (1981) and Kašpar and Fechtnerová (1988, 1991). Six years after the fall of the Berlin wall, Hausberger's (1995) masterful look at Jesuits from all over central Europe in America reintegrated the Germans into this historiography. Among scholars of Latin America, Treutlein (1945), Rey (1970), and Borges Morán (1977) investigated non-Spanish Jesuits in the Americas, many of whom came from central Europe. In any case, these studies trace only the outlines of a global Christianity. These are essential to writing a macrohistory of the Christian missions, but they do not perform that task.

---

[9] Paolo Broggio, *Evangelizzare il mondo: Le missioni della Compagnia di Gesù tra Europa e America (secoli XVI–XVII)* (Rome: Carocci: 2004), 27.

[10] Gauvin A. Bailey, *Art on the Jesuit Missions in Asia and Latin America, 1542–1773* (Toronto: University of Toronto Press, 1999).

[11] See J. Correia-Afonso, "Indo-American Contacts through Jesuit Missionaries," *Indica* 14.1 (1977), 34–37.

This book pairs this global perspective with a willingness to be astonished at the familiar. It explores both the development of the missionaries' global impulses and how their motivations played out on a global stage. Taking up a global perspective allows us to see the existence of a global religion, at the heart of which lies, in the principal argument of this book, the importance of salvific religion and soteriology – the study and technology of salvation.

The Religious Perspective

In recent years mission history, and colonial historiography more broadly, has pursued an increasingly sophisticated understanding of the "other." This usually has meant non-Europeans, as seen through European eyes, although some daring historians have attempted to reconstruct this history by relying on surviving non-European sources. The history of the "other" is fascinating history, but it is not the complete history. The most alarming disadvantage to this approach is the resulting tendency to see the counterpart of the "other," that is, the Europeans, in terms of sameness.

The unspoken but widely lurking prejudice of the Europeans as the "same" leads to two fallacies. The first is essentialism, the idea that all Europeans are the same. In fact, even Europeans had attitudes and goals that could vary widely by profession, social status, national origin, and from individual to individual. As we shall see, the bitterness of the fights among missionaries shows that even Europeans with similar backgrounds and similar goals could hold violently different outlooks.

The second fallacy is anachronism. Europeans are the same as we modern historians, who mostly labour under a Eurocentric historiographical perspective. This fallacy is perhaps more misleading than the first. In their search for exotic mental universes, historical anthropologists rush to the "other," grudgingly making use of the missionaries' sources but deeply uninterested in their mental universes. Still, any historian who has done fieldwork among the early-modern missionaries notices jarringly unfamiliar customs and beliefs. Perhaps most outstanding in this regard is the missionaries' absolutizing fanaticism, a trait largely lacking in modern European religious sentiment. The historian of the missions answers teleological questions dealing with how institutions, and religious attitudes, came to be how they are today, rather than wandering down the dead ends that have died out in the intervening centuries.

Almost a caricature of current concerns about incommensurability, the idea that the meeting of a representative of the "same" and a representative of the "other" necessarily results in cross-cultural dialogue skirts the issue of intention, which is all-important when dealing with missionaries. In the pre-modern period neither representative sought an equal exchange of values. The typical missionary intended religious and cultural values to flow in one direction, and the typical quarry had no interest even in that. The truer reaction might even follow T. S. Eliot's cannibal Sweeney, who responds to impending proselytism by playing on the physical and spiritual meanings of "conversion": "I'll convert *you*! / Into a stew! / A nice little, white little, missionary stew!"[12]

Treating missionaries like modern anthropologists and ignoring intention have led many historians to leave salvation and soteriology out of their studies, which results in missionaries who are inexplicably oblivious to the point of Christian mission. In the extreme cases that make clear a more general trend, we encounter atheistic Jesuits risking their lives to travel to the ends of the earth to embrace multiculturalism, to find themselves, or even to be converted. One historian, unsupported by any evidence, explains the religious elements in Jesuit Joseph Neumann's (1648–1732) *Historia seditionum* [*History of Insurrections*] (1730) merely as a method to appease church censors.[13] Another discovers in Francis Xavier's (1506–52) disapproval of Hinduism proof of the "religious bigotry" of the apostle of the Indies.[14] That "Jesuits stubbornly refused to adopt elements of foreign religion" should surprise no historian of early-modern Christian missions. On the contrary, in these centuries, the exceptions to it should raise eyebrows.[15] As Jonathan Chaves reflects, "How ironic, if we apply anthropological empathy to non-Western religions, only to deny it to Christianity."[16]

With empathy and acumen, K. G. Izikowitz has attracted attention by calling religion – specifically, the feast of ancestors – the "driving force in the entire economic and social life" of the Lamet peasants in northern Laos.[17] This is a key change from previous anthropologists'

---

[12] "Fragment of an Agon" from *Sweeney Agonistes*, in T. S. Eliot, *The Complete Poems and Plays, 1909–1950* (New York: Harcourt Brace & Company, 1980), 80.

[13] Bohumír Roedl, "La Historia de José Neumann sobre la sublevación de los Tarahumaras como fuente historiográfica," trans. Bohumil Zavadil, *Ibero-Americana Pragensia* 10 (1976): 208. He goes on to admit that the work remains important to Latin American historiography, despite Neumann's religious phraseology.

[14] Michael A. Mullett, *The Catholic Reformation* (London: Routledge, 1999), 97.

[15] Bailey, *Art on the Jesuit Missions*, 7. Exceptions appear with any frequency in Christian missions only after the debacle of the First World War stripped Europe of its moral superiority. This liberalism found its most famous expression in *Rethinking Missions*, the 1932 Report of the Laymen's Foreign Missions Enquiry, chaired by the philosopher William Ernest Hocking. See Neill, 455–6.

[16] Jonathan Chaves, "Inculturation versus Evangelization: Are Contemporary Values Causing Us to Misinterpret the 16–18th Century Jesuit Missionaries?" *Sino-Western Cultural Relations Journal* 22 (2000): 59–60.

[17] Karl Gustav Izikowitz, *Lamet: Hill Peasants in French Indochina* (Göteborg: [Elanders boktr.], 1951), 332–3.

condescension, considering "religion as a reflection of a somehow more concrete social reality so that ancestors, for example, are mere symbols of prestige."[18] An explanation of the Jesuits' global mission must take their religious vision just as seriously.

If we try to follow the Jesuits with a modern sensibility, we come to loggerheads even when working out such basic issues as what constitutes victory and defeat. Occasionally, the records offer perplexing assessments of success, so unfamiliar that they suggest the Jesuits' real objectives truly were not of this world. In 1701 one Jesuit superior boasted that the Madura mission was "more flourishing than ever. We have had four considerable persecutions this year. One of our missionaries has had his teeth knocked out."[19]

When we step past this problematic understanding of "same" and "other," we can take up T. O. Beidelman's proposal for the anthropological research of a subject extraordinary in its banality. Instead of focussing on "alien, exotic societies," anthropologists should consider the missionaries themselves as worthy "subjects for wonder and analysis."[20] The Jesuits, too, were anthropologists, secondarily in something like the modern sense, but fundamentally in the older theological sense of the study of man's place in the process of salvation. When we overcome our hesitation to anthropologize the anthropologists, the pagans who were previously "other" often appear more familiar to us than do the missionaries. We discover a missionary mentality just as exotic as the mentalities of the "other," and some surprising, unmodern similarities between them. We discover the Jesuits had their own understanding of "other," distinct from that of modern historians – for their "other" were those to be converted, whether European or not.[21] We discover the missionaries' "cosmovision" – the combination of their "cosmological notions relating to time and space into a structured and systematic worldview" – to be just as alien as the Mesoamericans', and inextricably

[18] Jonathan Friedman, "Religion as Economy and Economy as Religion," *Ethnos* 40.1–4 (1975): 46.
[19] Quoted in Dauril Alden, *The Making of an Enterprise, The Society of Jesus in Portugal, Its Empire, and Beyond, 1540–1750* (Stanford: Stanford UP, 1996), 205. Palafox had also equated persecution with progress, even more strongly than did the Jesuits. See Cummins, *Question*, 141.
[20] T. O. Beidelman, "Social Theory and the Study of Christian Missions in Africa," *Africa* 44 (1974): 235.
[21] Dominique Deslandres, "Mission et altérité: Les missionnaires français et la définition de l' 'Autre' au XVIIe siècle," in *Proceedings of the Nineteenth Meeting of the French Colonial Historical Society, Providence, R. I., May 1993*, ed. James Pritchard (Cleveland: French Colonial Historical Society, 1993), 12.

tied to a global perspective and span.[22] This, then, is a study of missionaries, and it includes their converts only occasionally, and only to better
illuminate the missionaries themselves.

Specifically, this book describes the early Jesuits' participation in Christianity as a global religion, and their construction of Christianity as a universal religion. It is important to distinguish between the concrete, practical global religion and the more theoretical, and more abstract, universal
religion. As John Phelan explains, "The medieval Christian Church was,
of course, always universal in its claims. All men had a common origin
and a common end. But before the Age of Discovery, Christianity was
geographically parochial, confined to a rather small part of the world."
In our period, however, "Christianity for the first time could implement its universal claims on a world-wide basis [and] could be global as
well as universal."[23] The defence of the idea of a universal church serves as
an excellent example of "the contrast between unbounded right and
actual helplessness" by which James Bryce once found medieval Europe
amazingly unperturbed.[24] Because the geographical reality is irrelevant, a
religion limited to a small geographical area might still qualify as a universal religion merely on the strength of its pretensions, just as Frederick
Bronski, the main character in Mel Brooks's *To Be Or Not To Be*, can be
"world famous in Poland."

This "global religion" must be sharply distinguished from the usual
concept "world religion," by which is meant a faith that has enjoyed "great
success in propagating themselves over time and space."[25] Thus any world
religion could have both local and global aspects.[26] Even the great "world

---

[22] The term, and the definition, are from David Carrasco, *Religions of Mesoamerica: Cosmovision and Ceremonial Centers* (San Francisco: Harper & Row, 1990), xix.

[23] John L. Phelan, *The Millennial Kingdom of the Franciscans in the New World* (Berkeley: University of California Press, 1970), 18.

[24] James Bryce, *The Holy Roman Empire* (New York: Macmillan, 1877), 118.

[25] Robert W. Hefner, "Introduction: World Building and the Rationality of Conversion," *Conversion to Christianity: Historical and Anthropological Perspectives on a Great Transformation*, ed. Robert W. Hefner (Berkeley: University of California Press, 1993), 4. Although Hefner refers to the discussion of world religion in Max Weber's 1922 *Sociology of Religion* and in Robert Bellah's 1964 "Religious Evolution," the concept explicitly appears in neither. The equivalent subjects in Weber's and Bellah's works are "religion" (as opposed to magic) and "modern religion," respectively. Max Weber, *The Sociology of Religion*, trans. Ephraim Fischoff (Boston: Beacon Press, 1963); Robert N. Bellah, "Religious Evolution," *American Sociological Review* 29 (3): 358–74.

[26] Terrence Ranger argues that even a traditional (i.e. non-world) religion can include a global perspective. See his "The Local and the Global in Southern African Religious History," in *Conversion to Christianity: Historical and Anthropological Perspectives on a Great Transformation*, ed. Robert W. Hefner (Berkeley: University of California Press, 1993): 65–98.

religions" may lack the global motivation. In medieval England, Jews could actively discourage Christians from converting to their faith, fearing such pyrrhic victories would fuel retribution. In early-modern India, despite the prevalence of regional overland pilgrimages, many Hindus considered merely traversing the ocean to be itself a ritual defilement for the upper castes.[27] Although scholars are increasingly problematizing world religion, Christianity will be included as long as the category exists, for the Jesuits and their colleagues thought universally and acted globally, to make their faith the most popular and widespread religion today.[28]

The Scope of This Study

The preceding comments should differentiate this from a work of multiple area studies, nor is this comparative history. Rather than comparing three missions in Germany, Mexico, and China, this is a non-comparative study of a single transregional phenomenon, three interrelated components of which are singled out for this book.[29] It is perhaps most neatly classified as a work of historical "dromography," a neologism indicating the study of "geography, history and logistics of trade, movement, transportation and communication networks."[30] This is not to say that a comparison of the three areas would not be useful. More ambitiously, a comparison of the Catholic missions with other world missions of the early-modern period would be most instructive.

[27] Charles R. Boxer, *The Portuguese Seaborne Empire, 1600–1800* (London: Hutchison, 1965), 45; Surinder M. Bhardwaj and Pillai Lokacarya, "Hindu Pilgrimage," *Encyclopedia of Religion* (New York: Macmillan; London: Collier Macmillan, 1987), XI.353–54. The *Caturvargacintamani*, the thirteenth-century dharmanibandha by Hemadri, is cited (iii.2:667) in Nicholas Ostler, *Empires of the Word: A Language History of the World* (New York: HarperCollins, 2005), 199. I am grateful to Kyle Jackson for pursuing this reference.

[28] For additional thoughts on approaching global and world religion, see Luke Clossey, "The Early-Modern Jesuit Missions as a Global Movement" (November 16, 2005), UC World History Workshop, Working Papers from the World History Workshop Conference Series 3, http://repositories.cdlib.org/ucwhw/wp/3. For a critical discussion of "world religion" see Joel Tishken, "Lies Teachers Teach about World Religious History," *World History Bulletin* 23 (2007): 14–18.

[29] Although here we are centuries away from independent political entities called "Germany" or "Mexico," these are words used by contemporary Jesuits.

[30] The term derives from the Greek *dromos*, meaning "street or route," and has a closer cousin in "dromograph," an instrument that records the circulation of blood. T. Matthew Ciolek, "Old World Traditional Trade Routes (OWTRAD) Project," May 6, 2004. http://www.ciolek.com/owtrad.html (accessed May 8, 2004). This definition comes from the Ibero-Mundo Regional Atlas Team. "Project Description," 21 November 2001, http://redgeomatica.rediris.es/ecai/atlas_iberomundo/. (accessed May 8, 2004).

Although a resident of Beijing could laugh at Ludwig Pastor's hyperbole in naming Rome the "capital of the world," the papal city directed the early-modern Catholic global mission.[31] Rome's control was dominant, but its dominance was not absolute. In governing the overseas missions, Rome shared its authority with Lisbon and Madrid, allowing Jesuits ample opportunities to play each centre of power off the others. Taking a mathematician's delight in counterexample, this project seeks not to deny the centrality of Rome and the Iberian capitals, but to qualify it. Of the 1,714 Jesuits leaving for the missions from Lisbon before 1725, 1,093 – almost two thirds – were, predictably, Portuguese.[32] This study looks at the unlikely other third.

The natural dimensions of this transnational phenomenon are, of course, global. Selecting only three areas is an evil necessary for making this study feasible and intelligible. I chose these three regions to clash with the ecclesiastical and political situation of the time. The trinity of Rome, Portugal, and China – or better, Spain, Mexico, and the Philippines – would have been a more likely choice, and would have produced more predictable results. In fact, the arbitrariness of place strengthens this project by illuminating the inter-mission connections not normally encountered in standard accounts, thus making the case for a mission globalized beyond the usual political and administrative boundaries.

At times the story irresistibly overflows beyond these three regions. Germany, China, and Mexico were selected as a study in contrast, and not because they provide unmediated connections between each other. No mission historian can connect China to Mexico without the Philippines. The historian of wide-ranging seventeenth-century phenomena cannot avoid the France of Louis XIV. The fact that the history of the missions necessarily spills over my three chosen areas underscores the interconnectedness of the early-modern world, and of the Jesuit mission efforts.

I also refrain from drawing sharp lines around the three areas I have chosen. Often this move reflects a contemporary vagueness. "Germany" for the early-modern period largely coincides with the Holy Roman Empire.

---

[31] Ludwig Pastor, *The History of the Popes: from the close of the Middle Ages*, trans. Ralph Francis Kerr (Nendeln, Liechtenstein: Kraus, 1968–9), VIII.141. In the early sixteenth century, Beijing had some twelve times the population of Rome.

[32] A. Franco, Synopsis Annalium S. J. in *Lusitania ab anno 1540 usque ad annum 1725* (Augustae Vindel.: Sumptibus Philippi, Martini, & Joannis Veith, Hæredum,1726), cited in Anton Huonder, *Deutsche Jesuitenmissionäre des 17. und 18. Jahrhunderts: Ein Beitrag zur Missionsgeschichte und zur deutschen Biographie* (Freiburg im Breisgau: Herder'sche Verlagshandlung, 1899), 9.

In the Society of Jesus at this time, however, the German Assistancy stretched from Lithuania across a continent and an ocean to Maryland,[33] and, as we shall see, Spanish immigration officials had their own ideas of what was German. At least in Spanish, "China" could refer either to what we call China or to the Philippines, and the former was more precisely designated "La Gran China."[34] The sources do not always distinguish clearly between them.

At the core of this study and of the missions themselves were the missionaries. Fifty-three Jesuits are known to have been active in at least two of the three target areas during the seventeenth century.[35] Many of the conclusions presented here regarding the idea of global mission have been derived from their writings. This selection is arbitrary in that a French missionary would, presumably, be just as likely to express global mission ideals as a German. This selection is strategic in that concentrating my research on a limited number of persons has afforded insight into their collective biographies. In fact, the idea of global religion developed in the context of a truly global discourse, and it would be difficult to extract just the German voices, even were that desirable.

The word's dynamic history partially explains this confusion. In the first fifteen centuries of the Christian era, variations on the Latin word *missus* appeared chiefly in Trinitarian theology, and only two "missionaries" were known as such – Christ and the Holy Spirit, both "sent" by God. To indicate those whom we now call missionaries, the earliest writers would use variations on "apostle" (apostolate), which derives from the Greek *apostellein* (ἀποστέλλειν).[36] Innocent VIII, in a bull of 1486, speaks of "orthodoxae fidei propagationem" rather than mission, and well into the sixteenth century papal documents snubbed the word "mission"

---

[33] *Catalogvs Prouinciarum Societatis Iesv, Domorum, Collegiorum, Residentiarum, Seminariorum, & Missionum, quae in unaquaque Prouincia numerabantur Anno 1679* (Rome: Typis Ignatij de Lazaris, 1679), B. Cas., Rome, Miscel. in 8°. v. 565, no. 4, fol. E10r.

[34] Ernest J. Burrus, "Kino's Relative, Father Martino Martini, S. J.: A Comparison of Two Outstanding Missionaries," *Neue Zeitschrift für Missionswissenschaft* 31 (1975): 100.

[35] Insufficient information survives to confirm the hypotheses around the participation of three other Jesuits: The 1692 China catalogue lists a Jacques Barthe, but this could not be the German Jacobus Bartsch, who was still in Europe in 1697. No known documentation substantiates the claim that Philippe Couplet, a Belgian Jesuit missionary working in China, travelled to Berlin in 1687. A father Wilhelm was in Mexico around 1687, but I have no data on his origins. Joseph Dehergne, *Répertoire des Jésuites de Chine de 1552 à 1800* (Rome: Institutum Historicum S. I., 1973), 26; David E. Mungello, *Curious Land: Jesuit Accommodation and the Origins of Sinology* (Honolulu: University of Hawaii Press, 1985), 238; Huonder, *Deutsche Jesuitenmissionäre*, 117. For further information, see the prosopographical appendix in this book.

[36] F. Bordeau, "Le vocabulaire de la mission," *Parole et mission* 3 (1960): 11–12. See also John W. O'Malley, "Mission and the Early Jesuits," *Ignatian Sprituality and Mission: The Way* Supplement 79 (Spring 1994): 3–10.

in favour of "evangelizatio," "propagatio Christianae Fidei," and "Fides propaganda."[37] A variation of this last term, meaning "faith that is to be propagated," appeared in the name of the new (1622) Sacred Congregation for the Propagation of the Faith, called "Propaganda," the methods of which in time would generate the English word "propaganda." Even that Congregation's cardinals initially used "mission" in this sense of "sending out."[38]

In the early-modern period the term "mission" had a very specific meaning. This is underscored by the appearance in contemporary German writings of "missiones" in Latin script, in the midst of gothic letters.[39] What the word specifically denoted, however, was not then, and is not now, agreed upon. Some historians use "missionary" to refer only to Europeans, thus excluding native converts. Those who worked in the Chinese imperial court or in a non-pastoral capacity in Mexico City occasionally find themselves ignored. The word has been restricted to priests, excluding lay brothers, or restricted to regular clergy, thus excluding the seculars.[40]

Historically, the word "mission" only begins to come into common use with the colonization of America. In 1523 Francisco de los Angeles de Quiñones, Franciscan minister general and confessor to Holy Roman emperor Charles V (r. 1519–56, also king of Spain, 1516–56), dispatched twelve Franciscan "missionaries" to the New World. Other expressions for mission still continued alongside "mission." Thus talk of *ire ad infideles* ("to go to the infidels") and the older term of pilgrimage endured: "Following in the footsteps of our glorious father Saint Francis, who sent friars to the lands of the infidels, I resolve to send you, father, to those same lands [in] this hard pilgrimage [*trabajoso peregrinaje*]."[41] Even in the context of incorporating into the church those frontier peoples designated

[37] Adriano Prosperi, "L'Europa cristiana e il mondo: alle origini dell'idea di missione," *Dimensioni e problemi della ricerca storica* 2 (1992): 193–4.
[38] Josef Metzler, "Foundation of the Congregation 'de Propaganda Fide' by Gregory XV," trans. George F. Heinzmann, in *Sacrae Congregationis de Propaganda Fide Memoria rerum* (Rome: Herder, 1971–6), I.96.
[39] For example, A. Amrhyn, Coimbra, to Jacob Rassler, October 23, 1672, BHStA Jes. 607/92, fol. 2.
[40] See *Handbook of Christianity in China*, ed. Nicolas Standaert, Handbuch der Orientalistik: Vierte Abteilung, China, 15 (Leiden: Brill, 2001), I.301, and Johannes Beckmann, "Die Glaubensverbreitung und der europäische Absolutismus," in *Handbuch der Kirchengeschichte*, ed. Hubert Jedin, (Freiburg: Herder, 1965–1979), V.266. The greatest underestimation of secular missionary efforts comes from Robert Ricard, *The Spiritual Conquest of Mexico*, trans. Lesley Byrd Simpson (Berkeley: University of California Press, 1966).
[41] Prosperi, "L'Europa cristiana e il mondo: alle origini dell'idea di missione," *Dimensioni e problemi della ricerca storica* 2 (1992): 197–9.

"Indians"– the stereotypical mission – Spanish legislation does not use the word "mission" until the early seventeenth century.[42] Instead a mission was called a *conversión* or *doctrina*, theoretically depending on how far it had progressed.[43]

The Society spearheaded the new usage of "mission."[44] The Jesuits' first document, which Pope Paul III (r. 1534–49) included in his founding bull *Regimini militantis ecclesiae* (1540), began by attending to the "propagation of the faith," but turned to "mission" before the text's end, without a change in meaning.[45] "Missioned" in the sense of being sent recurs in the seventh part of the Jesuit Constitutions, where the sender is either the pope or the Jesuit general, as well as in the missionary vow *votum de missionibus* and the *Constitutiones circa missiones* (1544–45). Correspondence from the Society's first decades features the words "mission," "journey," and "pilgrimage," apparently with interchangeable meanings. The new expression probably derived from the humanistic reappropriation of the vocabulary of the New Testament.[46] Perhaps the Jesuits' taking up the name of Jesus facilitated taking up the term for a role previously restricted to Christ. "Mission" could encompass any extraordinary mission, whether to Catholics, heretics, Protestants, or pagans. By around 1580 Jesuit sources used "mission" to mean a place where one preaches the gospel.[47] In the next century "mission" became even more dynamic than it appears here. For example, the index of the *Imago primi saeculi*'s [*Picture of the First Hundred Years*] (1640) entry for "missiones" reads, "see Excursiones."[48] As an institutional term within the Society, a *missio*

[42] A. S. Tibesar, P. Borges, E. J. Burrus, et al., "Missions in Colonial America I," in *The Catholic Encyclopedia* (New York: Gilmary Society, 1951), IX.944. For use of the term in Spain itself see Broggio, 87–9.

[43] Charles W. Polzer, *Rules and Precepts of the Jesuit Missions of Northwestern New Spain* (Tucson: University of Arizona, 1976), 4–8.

[44] For an overview, see Michael Sievernich, "Die Mission und die Missionen der Gesellschaft Jesu," in *Sendung – Eroberung – Begegnung: Franz Xaver, die Gesellschaft Jesu und die katholische Weltkirche im Zeitalter des Barock*, ed. Johannes Meier (Wiesbaden: Harrassowitz, 2005), 7–30 and J. López-Gay, "Evolución histórica del concepto de 'Evangelización,'" in *Evangelisation*, ed. Mariasusai Dhavamony, Documenta Missionalia 9 (Rome: Gregorian University, 1975), 161–90.

[45] O'Malley, "Mission," 3. For a discussion of how the pilgrimage-apostolate to the Holy Land transformed into papal service at Rome, see Mario Scaduto, "La strada e i primi Gesuiti," *Archivum Historicum Societatis Iesu* 40 (1971): 323–90, and John C. Olin, "The Idea of Pilgrimage in the Experience of Ignatius Loyola," *Church History* 48 (1979): 395–6.

[46] O'Malley, "Mission," 3–5.

[47] Bordeau, 11–12. Prosperi, "L'Europa," 214, quotes Gabriello Paleotti (1578): "I predicatori che hanno la missione loro ne'luoghi della Diocese dove per l'ordinario sono persone imperite di lettere e che di contunuo stanno occupate nelle fatiche e lavorieri."

[48] *Imago Primi Saeculi Societatis Iesu a Provincia Flandro-Belgica eiusdem societatis repraesentata* (Antwerp: Moretus, 1640), fol. Ffffff2 r.

was the collection of all Jesuits in a political, rather than an ecclesiastical, unit. Thus the *missio hollandica* consisted of all the Jesuits in Holland.[49] Every Jesuit in Spanish America was legally a missionary, a manoeuvre designed to win royal support for his passage over the ocean.

Deriving from the high-profile Jesuit foreign missions, the modern meaning began to congeal in the 1620s, especially in the usage of Propaganda. The new congregation's first letter, in 1622, uses the word "mission" four times in the modern sense.[50] Still, Vincent de Paul (1580–1660) could refer to a local ministry to an abandoned parish as "mission," perhaps influenced by his two companions, both Jesuits.[51]

Because mission retained the original sense of "sending out," Jesuits whose work involved going out to others were more likely to be called "missionaries." Thus arose the distinction between foreign missions to pagans and internal "missions" to Catholics. Missions that involved going out to Catholics became invariably known as such, reaffirming that the characteristic of "mission" referred less to the target (Protestant or Catholic or pagan) than to the target's location (here or there). Alexander Farnese, Duke of Parma and grandson of Paul III, formed in 1587 a group of one or two dozen Jesuits as a "missio castrensis" – perhaps the first standing corps of chaplains.[52] The Infante Isabella brought in Jesuits for the hazardous duty of the *missio navalis* with the northern armada in 1623. By 1685 a Jesuit seminary in Toulon trained missionaries specifically for the *missio* with the French royal navy.[53] Despite its name, the Jesuit *missio moscovitica* dedicated more energy toward the German colonists and Italian merchants in Moscow than toward the Orthodox Russian Christians.[54] Here especially the distance of the location was more important than the target when determining what a "mission" was.

---

[49] John Bossy, "Catholicity and Nationality in the Northern Counter-Reformation," in *Religion and National Identity*, ed. Stuart Mews, Studies in Church History 18 (Oxford: Basil Blackwell, 1982): 286–7.

[50] Bordeau, 12. Kowalsky and Metzler, however, maintain that in 1622 "mission" referred to "any form of extraordinary pastoral care administered to a Catholic milieu." N. Kowalsky and J. J. Metzler, *Inventory of the Historical Archives of the Congregation for the Evangelization of Peoples or De Propaganda Fide*, 3rd ed. (Rome: Pontificia Universitas Urbaniana, 1988), 13.

[51] Bordeau, 12–13.

[52] J. H. Pollen, "History of the Jesuits Before the 1773 Suppression," *The Catholic Encyclopedia*, September 15, 2003, http://www.newadvent.org/cathen/14086a.htm (accessed April 25, 2004).

[53] Alain Cabantous, *Le Ciel dans la mer: christianisme et civilisation maritime (XVᵉ–XIXᵉ siècle)* (Paris: Fayard, 1990), 214–15, 217, 224.

[54] Rudolf Grulich, *Der Beitrag der böhmischen Länder zur Weltmission des 17. und 18. Jahrhunderts* (Königstein: Institut für Kirchengeschichte von Böhmen, Mähren, Schlesien, 1981), 18.

The missionaries active in these three regions belong to a dizzying array of orders, most of which historians have neglected. In addition to the more frequently studied Jesuits, Franciscans, Dominicans, and Augustinians, in New Spain alone we encounter the Mercedarians (such as Bartolomé de Olmedo, who arrived with Cortés), the Hieronymites (arrived ca. 1526), the Brothers Hospitallers of St. John of God (1552),[55] the Discalced Carmelites (1585), the Benedictines (1589),[56] Hippolytans (from 1594), Antonins (1628),[57] Capuchins (1657),[58] Brothers of St. James (*Dieguinos*), Bethlehemites, and Oratorians. Women's orders included the Poor Clares, Capuchins, Carmelites, Conceptionists, Cistercians, Augustinians, and Dominicans.[59] Actually, in the early seventeenth century the Spanish crown authorized only Franciscans, Mercedarians, Dominicans, Augustinians, Capuchins (after 1647), and Jesuits. Other orders were tolerated when not given responsibility for Indians. This point is key to our project, as there was a definite tendency to direct foreign priests to the Indians, leaving the non-Indian ministry to priests born in the Americas.[60]

Several strategic reasons motivated this study to focus on the Society of Jesus. First is the excellent historiographical, bibliographical, and biographical apparatus already in existence.[61] The Jesuits also had a peculiar facility for traveling great distances, even when not acting as missionaries

---

[55] 1602, says Joseph M. Barnadas, "The Catholic Church in Colonial Spanish America," in *The Cambridge History of Latin America* (Cambridge: Cambridge University Press, 1984), I.520.

[56] Ricard, 16; Kenneth Scott Latourette, *A History of the Expansion of Christianity* (New York: Harper & Bros., 1937–45), III.100, 110–1.

[57] Joseph M. Barnadas, "The Catholic Church in Colonial Spanish America" in *The Cambridge History of Latin America* (Cambridge: Cambridge University Press, 1984): I.520.

[58] Johannes Meier, "Die Orden in Lateinamerika: Historischer Überblick" in *Conquista und Evangelisation: 500 Jahre Orden in Lateinamerika*, ed. Michael Sievernich, Arnulf Camps, Andreas Müller, and Walter Senner (Mainz: Matthias-Grünewald, 1992), 10.

[59] Camillus Crivelli, "Mexico," in *The Catholic Encyclopedia*, September 15, 2003, www.newadvent.org/cathen/10250b.htm (accessed April 25, 2004).

[60] Pedro Borges Morán, "Características sociológicas de las órdenes misioneras americanas," in *Evangelización y Teología en América* (Siglo XVI), X Simposio International de Teología de la Universidad de Navarra (Pamplona: Servicio de Publicaciones, Universidad de Navarra, 1990): 620–22.

[61] For over a century this has been the standard justification for a Jesuit focus. See Huonder, *Deutsche Jesuitenmissionäre*, 2. Jesuit literature, however, must be used with special care. Boxer describes Burrus's "200% Jesuit standpoint and his cavalier dismissal of all criticism of the Society, however justified" when that Jesuit accused Cummins of an "'anti-Jesuit animus' solely because he argues here and elsewhere that there may be something to be said for the friars." Charles Ralph Boxer, "Macao as a Religious and Commercial Entrepôt in the Sixteenth and Seventeenth Centuries," *Acta Asiatica* 26 (1974): 87.

in the strict sense.[62] Finally, a horizontal global network will be all the more surprising for an organization famous for its vertically hierarchical organization, centred "in a military fashion" at Rome. To show that this phenomenon is by no means limited to the Jesuits, as a rule I avoid stressing the uniqueness of the Society, and instead point out substantiating trends among other religious orders.

The fifty-three Jesuits at the heart of this book were all missionaries in the strictest sense. Because this study seeks to understand how widely the scope of "mission" actually ranged, it will not lay out an initial definition of mission or missionary. It includes non-missionaries such as the cartographer whose maps would influence missionary thought and the king who would direct the missionaries' attention. Macaulay astutely described Duke Maximilian of Bavaria (r. 1597–1651) as "a fervent missionary wielding the powers of a prince."[63] To trace the extent of this missionary impulse, beyond the traditional categories, this project declines to set out *a priori* definitions of missionary, but rather waits to see who the missionaries really were.

The fluidity of national identity in the early-modern period also demands careful attention. The case of what constitutes a Mexican is the most straightforward, and difficulties will be confronted on an individual basis. Here we adopt the modern notion of Chinese, which does not entirely coincide with that of the late imperial period. Then, in the eyes of the Chinese government (and probably of the people), the Chinese diaspora who abandoned their ancestral graves to live abroad in violation of imperial law were not Chinese at all.[64] The German case is the most complex, and we consider it in detail in Chapters 2 and 7.

As a whole, the project focuses on the time when all three regions see Jesuit missionary activity, that is, after the arrival of Matteo Ricci (1552–1610) in Macao in 1582. Because this project adopts an unusual geographical cluster, the chronological parameters are difficult to specify, and we avoid cataloguing less important changes over time. As an aid to the reader, an appendix synchronizes the most significant events for the network with the most significant rulers' reign dates.[65] The traditional chronologies are, naturally enough, tied to individual places. Only on occasion (the serious world historian chokes on the phrase "by chance")

---

[62] For example, 1675 saw the Prague college's pharmacist post filled by a Scot from Aberdeen. "Catalogus Personarum Collegij Soctis Jesu, Pragae ad S: Clementem. 1675," ARSI Boh.18.133–155.

[63] Macaulay, "Ranke's," 559.

[64] Charles Ralph Boxer, "Notes on Chinese Abroad in the Late Ming and Early Manchu Periods," *T'ien Hsia Monthly* IX (1939): 466.

[65] See Appendix B, Chronological Tables (1540–1722).

do historiographical landmarks of different regions coincide. The most natural approach would be to look at the institutional history of the global phenomenon under examination and notice the natural break that occurs with the almost total suppression of the Society in 1773. The eighteenth century, however, presents so overwhelming a cornucopia of extant sources that any single person would find difficult executing this methodology for that period.

This project, then, follows the story from 1582 through the seventeenth century, including the earliest missionizing of Baja California, which began in 1697. I take 1701, the outbreak of the War of the Spanish Succession, as a benchmark. The war wrecked havoc in the exchange of missionaries and letters, and its resolution in the Peace of Utrecht (1713–1714) marks an important change in the relationship between Spain and the Holy Roman Empire.[66] I hope this study's geographical span will partially compensate for this chronological austerity. I take the relative arbitrariness of this benchmark as license to intrude into the eighteenth century to show several examples which illustrate earlier trends and their trajectories. I also do not hesitate to make use of a post-Utrecht letter written by a missionary active in the seventeenth century.

The chronological limits adopted coincide with several historians' chronologies of the Jesuits, perhaps most precisely with that outlined by Alden, who places a formative period (1540–1615) before "the period of stability" (1615–1704). After these first two eras, which match the years covered by this project, comes the "period of stress" (1704–73).[67] On the other hand, J. F. Bannon sees the middle seventeenth century as the "critical period" in the Jesuit missions of Spanish America, with the increased use of German Jesuits in the New World.[68] R. Grulich finds in the middle of the seventeenth century a turning point characterized by declining Iberian monarchies, rising Protestant powers, the founding of the French missionary society, religious orders forsaking their ideals, and the secular hierarchy losing interest in the mission.[69]

These fifty-three Jesuits most directly active in connecting the German, Mexican, and Chinese missions have left for historians some 1,200 extant texts, mostly letters. Almost half are written in Latin, and almost another quarter in Spanish. A fifth survive only as copies or summaries, mostly

---

[66] For one example, the war prevented the annual fleet from coming to Vera Cruz from Cádiz, thus delaying the new Jesuit provincial, the procurators, and the eight missionaries they had recruited.

[67] Alden, 230.

[68] John Francis Bannon, "The Jesuits in Sonora, 1620–1687," (Ph.D. diss. University of California, Berkeley, 1939), 381.

[69] Grulich, 28.

in German, without an indication of the original language. The rest are in Chinese, Dutch, French, German, Italian, or Portuguese. Only a few hundred of these texts are in the central Roman archive of the Society of Jesus; the rest are scattered in collections around Europe and the Americas. In the last seven years I have managed to consult almost all of these texts, and they form the foundation of this book.

This project, however, largely works against the grain of archival exigency. A document sent to or from the Curia in Rome or the Iberian courts enjoyed an institutional authority which increased the likelihood of its preservation. In addition, its physical presence in Rome or Madrid makes it more likely to be kept in an archive. A letter written from a Jesuit in Sinaloa to another in Fujian would be far less likely to survive. Even when key documents do survive, they often have made their way to unexpected locations, and unlikely archives often overlook (or deny!) their existence, making them all the harder to locate.[70] After 1600 even letters sent to Rome were saved only exceptionally.[71] Because of notarial procedure, many of the letters clearly bearing Rome addresses are actually copies made for circulation in other regions.[72] For all these reasons, the direct ties between Mexico, Germany, and China may be even more profound than the extant documents suggest. For every scrap that survives, countless others have been lost.

[70] Exceptional examples of interest in "misplaced" documents include Josef Franz Schütte, *Documentos del 'Archivo del Japón' en el Archivo Histórico Nacional de Madrid*. Madrid: Raycar S. A., 1978–9; Lino Gómez Canedo, "Fuentes Mexicanas para la historia de las misiones en el Extremo Oriente," in *La expansión hispanoamérica en Asia, siglos XVI y XVII*, ed. Ernesto de la Torre Villar, Fondo de cultura economica (Mexico: 1980), 15–30; Li Yuzhong 李毓中, "Xibanya Saiweiya Yindu zongdang'an guannei suocang youguan Zhongguo shiliao jianmu chubian" 西班牙塞維亞印度總檔案館內所藏有關中國史料簡目初編, *Hanxue yanjiu tongxun* 漢學研究通訊 64 (1997): 476–84.

[71] Edmond Lamalle, "L'archivio di un grande ordine religioso: L'Archivio Generale della Compagnia di Gesu," *Archiva ecclesiae* 24–25 (1981–82): 96.

[72] Josef Franz Schütte, "Wiederentdeckung des Makao-Archivs: Wichtige Bestände des alten Fernost-archivs der Jesuiten, heute in Madrid," *Archivum Historicum Societatis Iesu* 30 (1961): 98.

2 Organizing the Society of Jesus

"Vice-rei vá, vice-rei vem / Padre Paulista sempre tem"
"Viceroys come, viceroys go / But you always have Jesuits"

– Goan jingle[1]

The Birth of the Society

This project studies a Jesuit religious network that helped create, and which itself could only have functioned in, a globalized world. The discovery of new lands across the Atlantic prompted Pope Alexander VI (r. 1492–1503) to issue a series of three bulls in May 1493, usually referred to as *Inter caetera*, the title of two of them.[2] Justified by the Vicar of Christ's unique authority to offer protection to the natives, the bulls drew a meridian one hundred leagues (about five hundred fifteen kilometres) west of the Cape Verde Islands, demarcating the territories of the two Iberian kingdoms. The Treaty of Tordesillas shifted the demarcation line to a position three hundred seventy leagues west of the Cape Verde Islands.[3]

Much of the urgency behind such efforts at organizing the world was soteriological. Whose responsibility were the newfound souls? The pope enjoyed spiritual jurisdiction over Christendom through his bishops. A

---

[1] Boxer, *Portuguese Seaborne*, 74.

[2] The three bulls are *Inter caetera* (May 3, 1493) [Josef Metzler, ed., *America Pontificia: documenta pontificia ex registris et minutis praesertim in Archivo secreto vaticano existentibus.* Atti e documenti/Pontificio Comitato di scienze storiche 3 (Vatican City: Libreria editrice vaticana, 1991–1995), I.71–5], which was essentially restated in *Eximiae devotionis* (May 3[or 4], 1493) [Metzler I.76–78; W. Eugene Shiels, *King and Church: The Rise and Fall of the Patronato Real* (Chicago: Loyola University Press, 1961), 287–89]; and *Inter caetera* [II] (May 4, 1493) [Frances G. Davenport, ed., *European Treaties Bearing on the History of the United States and Its Dependencies to 1648* (Washington, D. C.: Carnegie Institution, 1917–37), I.58–61; Josef Metzler, ed., *America Pontificia: documenta pontificia ex registris et minutis praesertim in Archivo secreto vaticano existentibus* (Vatican City: Libreria editrice vaticana, 1991–95), 79–83; Shiels, 283–287]. For a perceptive discussion of the missionary consequences of these fifteenth-century bulls see Roland Jacques, *Des nations à évangéliser: Genèse de la mission catholique pour l'Extême-Orient* (Paris: Cerf, 2003), 257–336.

[3] Davenport, I.86–93.

bishop's ordinary jurisdiction, however, stopped at the borders of his diocese. Regions outside the territorial limits of any bishopric became mission territories, where the pope alone held jurisdiction. In addition, the idea that all islands belonged to the pope dated back at least to the Donation of Constantine.[4] In the early-modern period, the papacy partially delegated this spiritual jurisdiction, with its rights and responsibilities, to the religious orders, which would include the Society of Jesus. In theory, then, these regular missionaries worked under the jurisdiction of the bishop of Rome alone.[5]

The repeated relocation of soteriological responsibility is astonishing. The missionaries worked to fulfill the duties of the *encomendero*, to whom the crown had assigned Indians (as a source of tribute) in exchange for their being instructed in Christianity. This duty had been conceded to the king as a part of the Spanish *patronato* (patronage) obligations by the pope, who was himself acting on responsibilities inherited from Christ as his Vicar. We shall see in Chapter 7 how patronage affected Jesuit networks.

The key to global integration, and to global soteriology, was thus the expansion of Spain and Portugal and the development of two very different Iberian trading empires. Although both governments sought to regulate their respective trade, the Spanish oceanic commerce was essentially a royal monopoly, while a small group of firms or individuals ran the Portuguese counterpart. In quantity and net worth, Spanish trade totals exceeded the Portuguese. Part of the explanation lies in the nature of the two empires. Outbound Spanish ships carried passengers, like the Portuguese ships, but they also carried flour, oil, wine, agricultural tools, seeds, and domesticated animals – while Portuguese ships left Lisbon in ballast.[6]

These two empires were not the only integrating economic forces. Between 1580 and 1630, the New Christian trading network established key links between what had been mostly separate trading circuits. Moving into Manila and Spanish America after 1580, these merchants congregated in Lisbon, Porto, Medina del Campo, Madrid, Seville, Valladolid, Antwerp, Pernambuco, Lima, Olinda, Mexico City, Cartagena, Macao, Nagasaki, Manila, Goa, and Cochin.[7] The New Christian dealer Manuel

[4] Lewis Weckmann, "The Middle Ages in the Conquest of America," *Speculum* 26 (1951), 131.
[5] Lucien Campeau, *L'Éveché de Québec, 1674: aux origines du premier diocèse érigé en Amérique française* (Québec: Société historique de Québec, 1974), 1–8.
[6] John Horace Parry, *The Spanish Seaborne Empire* (New York: Knopf, 1966), 117–18.
[7] Sanjay Subrahmanyam, *The Portuguese Empire in Asia, 1550–1700: A Political and Economic History* (London: Longman, 1993), 117, 174.

Baptista Peres was involved both in the Atlantic slave trade and the Andean silver mines. His library, inventoried by the Inquisition, which had him burned at the stake in 1639, suggests an appropriately global reader: João de Barros's *Décadas da Ásia* [*Decades of Asia*] and Bartolomé Leonardo de Argensola's *Ystoria de las Molucas* [*History of the Molukas*], a life of Francis Xavier, histories of China and Africa, and several world histories. Such persecution by the Inquisition, however, retarded the outward growth of the New Christian merchant network.[8] The more successful global body would develop with a motivation more parallel, usually, to the Inquisition's: the Jesuits.

On September 27, 1540, with the bull *Regimini militantis ecclesiae*, Paul III sanctioned the formation of Ignatius of Loyola's (1491–1556) Company of Jesus, giving it the Latin name *Societatis Jesu*. The name "Jesuit," like "Lutheran," began as a pejorative term used by opponents but was eventually accepted as a way of self-identification. The Society of Jesus soon commanded a reputation for organization and obedience that endures today. K. S. Latourette wrote of the Jesuits' "army-like organization" and "complete devotion," while historian and soldier Charles Boxer compared them to the United States Marines.[9] The Society has been considered "the prototype of autocracy and monolithic cohesion."[10] This reputation is not undeserved, although Chapter 3 will argue that it is exaggerated and will describe its limits. The present pages rehearse how the Society was supposed to work in theory, and we will pay particular attention to the consequences for global mission, as well as the particular place of Germany, New Spain, and China in the Jesuit network.

The Society's Body and Soul

In 1558 the Society's first congregation approved the Constitutions that had been worked out by Ignatius from 1544 to his death in 1556. Dependent on alms for support, the Society was technically a mendicant order of clerks regular – men who fulfilled the priestly pastoral office while living under a rule with papal approval. Although Jesuits, like Franciscans or Dominicans, take a vow of poverty, in practice scholars rarely apply the adjective "mendicant" to them, nor did their contemporaries, as the Society had a reputation for avarice.

---

[8] Gonzalo de Reparaz Ruiz, *Os portugueses no Vice-Reinado do Peru: (séculos XVI e XVII)* (Lisbon: Instituto de Alta Cultura, 1976), 109; Subrahmanyam, *Portuguese*, 121.
[9] Latourette, *History*, 81; Alden, 9.
[10] G. Lewy cites but does not himself endorse this opinion in "The Struggle for Constitutional Government in the Early Years of the Society of Jesus," *Church History* 29 (1960), 141.

The basic structure of the Society has an elegant simplicity. The fundamental unit is the province; provinces are brought together in broad administrative divisions called "assistancies." The four original assistancies, grouping together the Italian, Spanish, Portuguese, and German provinces, were joined by French (after 1608) and Polish (after 1755) assistancies as the Society grew. Every province had its own missions, sometimes located geographically in another province.[11]

The organization centralized its power in a superior general, appointed for life with wide-ranging authority. The general delegated, but never relinquished, power to a companion (*socio*), a secretary, a procurator-general representing the Society at the papal court,[12] and an assistant for each assistancy. The only elected official in the Society, the general appointed every other officer, at every level. In theory, he decided the dwelling place and occupation of every Jesuit. His power was even constitutionally extra-constitutional, for the Constitutions authorized a general to ignore any of its provisions.[13] The general also evaluated provinces' proposals (*postulati*) advocating alterations in the Constitutions, or in the general's directives and decrees.

The general congregation was separate from, but subordinate to, the superior general. Each provincial congregation would send its head (the "provincial") along with two representative professed members. A general congregation was to set the Jesuits' broadest policies. It would meet roughly every twelve years, either upon the summons of the superior general to confirm his decrees and appointments, or upon his death to choose his successor.[14] At the instigation of the assistants the general congregation could transform into an ecclesiastical court to hear accusations of heresy or serious sin against a sitting general, although no general has ever thus been removed from office.[15]

---

[11] Santos Hernández Angel, *Los Jesuitas en América*, Colección Iglesia Católica en el Nuevo Mundo 5 (Madrid: Editorial MAPFRE, 1992), 203.

[12] Lewy (142) also mentions a counselor (*"admonitor"*) in the person of the general's confessor.

[13] *The Constitutions of the Society of Jesus*, ed. and trans. George E. Ganss (St. Louis: Institute of Jesuit Sources, 1970), 314 [part IX, ch. 3, sec. 8, par. 746].

[14] *Constitutions*, 294–97, 307–308, 320–30 [part VIII, ch. 2–3; part IX, ch. 1, 5, 6]. Ibid., 294 [part VIII, ch. 2, sec. 1, par. 677], advises the general to avoid summoning a congregation.

[15] A two-thirds majority is needed to put the general on trial and remove him from office. Ibid., 295 [part VIII, ch. 2, sec. 2, par. 681], 321–22 [part IX, ch. 5, sec. 4–5, par. 782–85]. In citing the appointment of a vicar-general for Nickel in 1661, Ranke exaggerated the extent to which the general's power was eroded. See Leopold von Ranke, *The History of the Popes during the Last Four Centuries*, (London: G. Bell and Sons, 1913), II.389–90. The constitutional provision for the appointment is at *Constitutions*, 322–23 [part IX, ch. 5, sec. 4, par. 786].

A *Catalogus prouinciarum Societatis Iesu* [*Catalogue of the Provinces of the Society of Jesus*] described the overall arrangement of the Society in 1679: thirty-five provinces and two vice-provinces distributed among five assistancies. The German Assistancy was numerically the largest, with 38.02% of all Jesuits (6,713 of 17,655) – 86.4% more than the Spanish Assistancy, which was the next largest, with 3,601 Jesuits. The Iberian assistancies had, relative to their populations, a disproportionately high number of colleges, missions, residences, and seminaries, perhaps because these provinces were the most widely scattered. Although its geographical range could not compete with that of the Iberian assistancies, the German Assistancy stretched from Lithuania to Maryland. In keeping with contemporary understandings, the *Catalogus* does not distinguish between domestic and foreign mission work, and the German Assistancy counted more missions than the two Iberian Assistancies combined.[16]

The provincial was the principal officer in a province. In addition to presiding over provincial congregations and attending general congregations, he authorized the superior general's personnel decisions and made specific assignments. He regularly inspected the province, and oversaw the provincial press's publications. The provincial could formally seek counsel from a rector, whose primary responsibility was to set policies for the province's college, with an eye to preserving its spiritual and temporal welfare. The general also appointed four *consultores* to advise, and to report on, the provincial.[17]

The basic arrangement between superior general and general congregation was echoed at a regional level with the provincial and the provincial congregation, made up of the province's senior Jesuits and the superior of each house. The provincial congregation was consultative rather than legislative. Although it could offer proposals, its only real power was the selection of procurators and delegates to the general congregation. As we shall see in Chapter 3, because of the vast distances involved in the

---

[16] Although it had more priests than any other assistancy, the German Assistancy had the lowest proportion of priests among its members. For all the assistancies, as the number of Jesuits increase, the proportion of those who are also priests decreases. Listing by increasing population, we have Lusitania (51.6% priests), Gallia (48.45%), Italia (45.68%), Hispania (43.74%), Germania (41.41%). I base my calculations on *Catalogvs Prouinciarum Societatis Iesv, Domorum, Collegiorum, Residentiarum, Seminariorum, & Missionum, quae in unaquaque Prouincia numerabantur Anno 1679* (Romae: Typis Ignatij de Lazaris, 1679), B. Cas. Miscel. in 8°. v. 565, no. 4, fols. A6r, B4r, C7v, D4v, E10v.

[17] Alden, 242; *Constitutions*, 178 [part 4, ch. 2, sec. 5, par. 326], 206–209 [part 4, ch. 10, sec. 5, 9, 10, par. 424, 435, 437], 225 [part 4, ch. 17, sec. 1, par. 490], 289 [part 8, ch. 1, sec. 4, par. 662], and 329–30 [part 9, ch. 6, sec. 14, par. 810].

missions abroad, few provinces in the *ultramar* could call provincial congregations at the prescribed three- or six-year intervals.[18]

The provincial and his province most directly felt the authority of the superior general through the extraordinary appointment of a visitor. The visitor was charged to inspect the various facilities of the province, and he could settle matters with the authority of the general. His power was such that he could remove from office any official, even the provincial, although a visitor could not participate in a provincial congregation.[19]

The leadership was assisted, and the Jesuits' day-to-day life facilitated, by the work of various officers, especially the provincial, college, court, and mission procurators. Provincial procurators coordinated the province's finances among its various colleges and missions, and they collaborated with the provincials on completing the third catalogue, a financial summary prepared for Rome. Provincial procurators directed the movement of correspondence, specie, and supplies.[20] Some enjoyed long tenures and the logistical savvy that comes with time. Manoel de Figueiredo (1589–1663) served as pharmacist and procurator of the Vice-province of China for twenty-four years.[21] Every four or five years, representatives from each province would meet with the general and his assistants in an assembly of provincial procurators. In 1606 the first such meeting of all provincial procurators was convened in response to the Spanish constitutional crisis, which is discussed further in Chapter 3.[22]

As a rule, provinces did not exchange official correspondence. Rather, the general was to forward copies of letters received from one province to any other provinces likely to find the information useful. The Constitutions specified an exception to this: "When there is much interchange between one province and another, as that between Portugal and Castile or between Sicily and Naples, the provincial of the one province may send to the provincial of the other the copy of those letters which he

---

[18] Valignano, Goa, "Summario de algumas cousas que pertencem ao governo da provincia da India" (April 1588), in *Documenta indica*, Josef Wicki, ed., Monumenta historica Societatis Iesu 123, Monumenta historica Societatis Iesu 38 (Rome: Apud "Monumenta Historica Soc. Iesu," 1948), 14.828–98 at 833.

[19] Josef Franz Schütte, *Valignano's Mission Principles for Japan*, trans. John J. Coyne (St. Louis: Institute of Jesuit Sources, 1980–5), 1:44–56 is a detailed, illuminating account of the beginning of Valignano's tenure as visitor (1573–74). See Alden, 232.

[20] See Alden, 305–6, 308–18; Josef Franz Schütte, *Documentos del 'Archivo del Japón' en el Archivo Histórico Nacional de Madrid* (Madrid: Raycar S. A., 1978–79), 24, 28.

[21] Joseph Dehergne, *Répertoire des Jésuites de Chine de 1552 à 1800* (Rome: Institutum Historicum S. I., 1973), 93; BA/JA/49-V-5 n.127. All BA/JA citations are given following Francisco G. Cunha Leão, ed., *Jesuítas na Ásia: Catálogo e guia*, 2 vols. (Lisbon and Macao: Insituto Cultural de Macau/Instituto Português do Património Arquitectónico/ Biblioteca de Ajuda, 1998).

[22] Alden, 231; Ranke, II.132.

sends to the general."[23] The criterion here is geographical, and there was little direct, official correspondence between geographically distant but institutionally close provinces, such as those of Mexico and Spain.

The office of mission procurator was introduced to address difficulties created by distance, and it had a troubled early history.[24] Royal officers originally held these responsibilities, but in 1554 Manuel Godinho took office as the first mission procurator for the Portuguese province. General Everard Mercurian (1573–80) formally institutionalized the office for the two Iberian assistancies in 1573 and 1574, in Lisbon and Seville (later Cádiz).[25] Apparently, mission procurators remained under the assistants, and they certainly did not answer to the provincials, for the Portuguese province's suspicions that the office would allow foreigners greater access to her missions prompted the closure of that office around 1580, with the peninsular procurator taking up its duties.[26] These became so overwhelming that General Claudio Aquaviva (1581–1615) reinstated the post in 1585, though it took two years to find someone willing to accept the position. In the first two decades of the next century, Aquaviva subdivided these two procuratorships so that Brazil, India, and east Asia each had its own procurator.[27]

A mission procurator's responsibilities were indeed intimidating, as General Oliva's 1671 description of the authority of Francisco de Florencia (1619–95) in this role makes clear. Foremost was working with the superior general to organize missionary expeditions. After authorizing recruitment, the general would present the procurator with the names chosen from the pool of Jesuits who had applied directly to Rome. The provincials' roles, however, were equally important. They could themselves provide the procurator with recruits, and they supplied the general with critical background information on those applying through his office. The procurator also shepherded his recruits while they waited to embark, and the details of outfitting these expeditions were his responsibility. He relayed information and gifts from Europe to the missions, and from the

---

[23] *Constitutions*, 292–93 [part VIII, ch. 1, sec. 9, par. 673–75].

[24] Josef Wicki, "Die Anfänge der Missionsprokur der Jesuiten in Lisabon bis 1580," *Archivum Historicum Societatis Iesu* 40 (Jan.–June 1971), 246–322; Felix Zubillaga, "El procurador de las Indias Occidentales de la Compañía de Jesús (1574)," *Archivum Historicum Societatis Iesu* 22 (1953): 367–417.

[25] Alden, 299–300.

[26] See especially Francisco Martins, Alfonsi Pacheco, Gabrielis Afonso[sic], Lisbon, to Mercurian, December 12, 1580, in DI 12:161–63, 165. See also Alden, 300.

[27] See Fr. Jerónimo Cardoso [procurator], Lisbon, to Aquaviva, September 6, 1586, in DI 14:332–33. More weary complaints about the procurators' workload in Fr. Sebastião de Morais [provincial], Lisbon, to Aquaviva, April 26, 1585, in ibid., 14:25–26. See also Alden, 300–1. For Aquaviva's attitudes toward the mission, see Broggio, especially 51–58, 79–85, 250–53.

missions to the general and to other patrons. Other items the procurator brought to Europe were sold, either to cover his own expenses or as a source of income for his province, some of which he used to purchase supplies to bring back to the mission. He collected myriad types of income, and kept the accounts for each college and mission in his jurisdiction.[28] The Society had additional procurators in Madrid to deal with court business of the American and Spanish provinces. Their most important work was intervening to secure permission for the entry of foreign Jesuits, which will be examined in Chapter 7.[29]

Most Jesuits held no such offices, though the Society numbered many remarkable individuals throughout its membership. Even becoming a Jesuit was no mean feat. Physical defects such as blackened teeth or a missing eye sufficed to deny membership to some aspirants.[30] Aquaviva warned against accepting men with impoverished, and therefore dependent, parents.[31] From 1594 until 1945 the Jesuits refused those with Jewish or Moorish blood.[32] Even if he had not been a Jew, his problematic legitimacy of birth and a marked lack of social respectability would have allowed Jesus himself to be admitted to His own Society only as an exception.

Once accepted, individual Jesuits could progress through four categories of membership, following either a spiritual or a temporal track, depending on whether the intended goal included the priesthood. After a two-year probationary novitiate of Spiritual Exercises, hospital work, and preaching, those working toward ordination took simple vows as formed scholastics. This longer scholasticate included the study of languages and humanities, above all theology and Latin. Afterward, these became spiritual formed coadjutors, parallel to the (lay) temporal formed coadjutors who were to fulfill humbler jobs such as cooking and bookkeeping. After taking the traditional vows of poverty, chastity, and obedience, being ordained, and completing an additional year's novitiate, the

---

[28] Pedro Borges Morán, *El envío de misioneros a américa durante la época española* (Salamanca: Universidad Pontificia, 1977), 89–90; Alden, 304–5.

[29] Lázaro de Aspurz, *La aportación extranjera a las misiones españolas del Patronato Regio* (Madrid: Consejo de la Hispanidad, 1946), 187.

[30] For other criteria see *Constitutions*, 127–35 [part I, ch. 2–3]; Thomas V. Cohen, "Why the Jesuits Joined, 1540–1600," *Historical Papers* [Canadian Historical Association] (December 1974), 246.

[31] Aquaviva to Esteban Cavello, October 1596, in Antonio Egaña, ed., *Monumenta Peruana* (Rome: Institutum Historicum Societatis Jesus, 1954–86), 6.220.

[32] Twenty-five of the twenty-seven Jesuits who wrote memorials against the Constitutions in the Spanish constitutional crisis, addressed in the following chapter, were of Moorish or Jewish decent; hence comes this restriction. John W. Padberg, *The General Congregations of the Society of Jesus: A Brief Survey of Their History*, Studies in the Spirituality of Jesuits 6 (St. Louis: Institute of Jesuit Sources, 1974), 18.

spiritual coadjutor became "professed" and entered the Society's core membership. Those of great proficiency in learning, typically measured by proficiency in Latin, could take a fourth vow to God of special obedience to the pope in missionary affairs, and thus become "professed of the four vows." Only these were eligible for the higher offices of the Society.[33]

The care of souls divided the temporal from the spiritual members of the Society. The *Examen Generale*, the foundational document consisting of points to be explained to postulants, defined a temporal coadjutor as "one occupied with the salvation of his own soul." At the same time, however, the Examen affirmed the temporal coadjutors' role in the salvation of others. They "should believe that by helping the Society in order that it may the better attend to the salvation of souls, they are serving the same Lord of all, since they are doing this out of love and reverence for him."[34] Thus the same relation between personal salvation and the salvation of others, discussed more fully in Chapter 6, reappears in the very organization of the Society.

As one would expect, the idea of global mission plays a key role in the core Jesuit documents begun by Ignatius and supplemented by his immediate successors. One climax of the *Spiritual Exercises*, the "Meditation on Two Standards," asks the participant to envision himself with Christ at the head of an army of missionaries: "Consider how the Lord of all the world chooses so may persons, apostles, disciples, etc., and sends them through the whole world to spread His sacred doctrine among all men, no matter what their state or condition."[35] Ignatius even drew up specific directives for travelling, later codified as the *Regulae peregrinatium*.[36] The most important document of all was the Constitutions, and at their core was the Fourth Vow.

Called "our first and fundamental principle" by Ignatius, the Fourth Vow took shape in the Society's foundational papal bulls. As formulated in the first, *Regimini militantis Ecclesiae* (1540), it promised that "whatever the present Roman Pontiff and others to come will wish to command us with regard to the progress of souls and the propagation of the faith, or wherever he may be pleased to send us to any regions whatsoever, we will obey at once, without subterfuge or excuse, as far as in us lies."

[33] *Constitutions*, 136–37 [part I, ch. 4, sec. 3, par. 193–94], 75–85, [General Examen, ch. 1], 128 [part I, ch. 2, sec. 2, par. 148–49]. For the training of China-bound missionaries, see Liam Brockey, *Journey to the East: The Jesuit Mission in China, 1579–1724* (Cambridge: Harvard, UP, 2007), 210–25.
[34] *Constitutions*, 112–13, [General Examen, ch. 5, sec. 8, par. 111; ch. 6, sec. 3, par. 114].
[35] Ignatius of Loyola, *The Spiritual Exercises of St. Ignatius: Based on Studies in the Language of the Autograph*, trans. Louis J. Puhl (Chicago: Loyola University Press, 1951), 28.
[36] Scaduto, 326–30.

The bull underscored the global nature of this vow, and the comprehensive range of missionary targets, by repeating that the pope can send the Jesuit anywhere in the world, to infidels, heretics, schismatics, the faithful Catholics, and "even to the land they call India." Ten years later, Pope Julius III (1550–5) issued a follow-up bull, *Exposcit debitum*, which essentially repeated the original.[37]

The Constitutions further expounded upon the vow's meaning, elucidating in particular two somewhat incongruous points. First, the commentary remarked that the Jesuits, "wishing to make the best choice in this matter," assigned distribution of their missionaries to the pope, as the wisest dispatcher.[38] This indicates that all missions were assigned by the pope. The vow's intent, however, was "to treat the missions from His Holiness first as being most important," suggesting that the Society would also take up missions not commissioned by the pope.

A passage in the Constitutions resolves this vital question of which missionaries go where. The papacy had relegated its authority for sending missionaries to the Society's superiors, although only provisionally, for "these members, wherever they are, will always be at the disposition of His Holiness." This is done out of expedience, and the reader is reminded that the General is merely interpreting the will of Christ. The superiors dispatch missionaries both in order "to be able to meet the spiritual needs of souls in many regions" and for the "greater security for those who go for this purpose." We should not take this "security" to mean a worldly safety-in-numbers, but the personal, spiritual safety afforded by placing one's will wholly under a superior's.[39]

The Constitutions direct the generals to consider two criteria when determining a mission assignment. The first, naturally, is an eye towards "the greater service of God." The second is more revealing. The choices of region, of missionary, of duration, of approach, and of objectives should all be based on the "universal good" – in distinction to those "who make requests more with a view to their own spiritual obligations to their flocks . . . than to those that are common or universal." Thus a limited mission was contrary to the very Constitutions of the Society. A later amendment declares, "The more universal the good is, the more is it divine."[40]

Besides divinity, the Constitutions saw in universality a greater opportunity for ever-increasing expansion. Thus "preference ought to be given

[37] Paul III, *Regimini militantis Ecclesiae*, September 27, 1540; Julius III, *Exposcit debitum*, July 21, 1550 (in *Constitutions*, 63–73).
[38] *Constitutions*, 267–68 [part VII, ch. 1, sec. 1, par. 603, 605].
[39] Ibid., 271–76 [part VII, ch. 2, sec. 1, par. 618–23].
[40] Ibid., 271, 273, 275 [part VII, ch. 2, sec. 1, par. 618, 622d].

to persons and places which, once benefited themselves, are a cause of extending the good to many others who are under their influence or take guidance from them." This would famously translate into the Jesuits' top-down approach to mission. Missions to "important and public" figures such as princes, scholars, and clerics, or to important cities and universities, also partook of this universality, because of the potential to produce further fruit.[41] The great populations the Indies were thought to encompass made those nations especially appealing targets.

Secondary criteria dealt less directly with universality. Simple need, as evidenced by a "lack of other workers" or a people's "danger of eternal condemnation," claimed priority. Special attention was to be directed toward those most eager to accept Catholics and toward those most likely to make enduring progress in the faith. Regions where significant Christian communities already existed, such as Greece, enjoyed a priority for new missions. When a region's residents performed charitable deeds for Jesuits, a sense of indebtedness was also to prompt a mission to that area. Finally, exemplary missions must be sent to strategic regions in order to negate Satan's own campaigns, "particularly where he has spread bad opinion about the Society."[42]

The German Assistancy

We turn now to the three administrative units most closely coterminous with the three places of this study: the Germany Assistancy, the Mexico Province, and the China Vice-province.

The weight of the German lands was recognized early by the Jesuit founder. Ignatius, or his secretary Juan Alfonso de Polanco (1517–76) at his command, called the preaching of Christianity in the German language a "very universal means to help every kind of person."[43] As suggested above, "universal" signified "strategic" rather than "comprehensive." The Jesuit efforts began with the itinerant work of Pierre Favre (1506–46), who arrived in Worms in the fall of 1540. Under papal direction he founded the first Jesuit residence in Germany four years later at Cologne. In 1549 Claude Jay (ca. 1502–52), Peter Canisius (1521–97), and Alfonso Salmerón (1515–85) entered Ingolstadt in response to Duke William IV (1508–50) of Bavaria's appeal to Rome for Jesuits to

---

[41] Ibid.

[42] Ibid.

[43] "Ratio studiorum," in "Anweisung für die nach Ingolstadt entsandten Jesuiten (Sommer 1556)," in Georg M. Pachtler, ed., *Ratio Studiorum et institutiones scholasticae Societatis Jesu per Germaniam olim vigentes collectae concinnatae dilucidatae*, Monumenta Germaniae Paedagogica IX (Berlin: Hofmann, 1890), III. 474.

revitalize his declining university. Eighteen more Jesuits arrived in 1556 to establish a Jesuit college there, and the reputation and influence of the university advanced. Both Maximilian of Bavaria (1587–90) and Ferdinand of Austria (1590) spent time at Ingolstadt as young men.[44] The Jesuits novices of the Upper German province typically studied there after completing their novitiates at Landsberg. Many professors were Jesuits, although the Ingolstadt faculty was never exclusively recruited from the Society. Keen to promote theological studies, Canisius moved on from Bavaria into Austria and Bohemia, and in 1556 he began to establish a college at Prague in an old Dominican monastery. The next century saw twenty new colleges spring up throughout Bohemia and Moravia.[45]

In 1556 Ignatius founded two provinces, Upper Germany (*Prov. Germaniae Superioris*) and Lower Germany (*Prov. Germaniae Inferioris*). The latter's rapid growth prompted further splits already in 1564 to create the Belgian and Rhenish provinces. In 1612 the Province of Belgium was divided into a Province of Flandro-Belgium (*Flandro-Belgica*) administered from Antwerp and a Province of Gallo-Belgium (*Gallo-Belgica*) with a seat at Lille. A decade later the new Rhenish Province also subdivided into Upper and Lower Provinces. The large Upper Germany Province produced an Austrian Province in 1563, but despite impressive growth resisted further attempts at division. The Austrian Province begat a Polish Vice-province (1564–5, which became a full province in 1576 and begat in turn a Lithuanian Vice-province in 1598) and a Bohemian Province (1623). In addition, the Belgian provinces supervised an English mission (*Missio Angliae*), which included the English colony of Maryland in its domain.[46]

A series of visitors, most famously Jerónimo Nadal (1507–80), brought the general's authority to bear in these various provinces. The expansion indicated by these administrative developments did not last. The Thirty Years' War, Louis XIV's advances into the Palatinate (1688–97), the War of Spanish Succession, and episodes of plague all proved extremely disruptive, especially to the Rhineland provinces. The Upper Rhenish

---

[44] G. Treffer, "Iter Sinese: Ingolstadio-Pekinum. Ingolstädter Jesuitenmissionare in China," *Ingolstädter Heitmatblätter* 52 (1989), 2.

[45] See Patrizio Foresta, "Die 'Mission in Germaniam.' Die Wahrnehmung des Apostolats durch den jungen Canisius," in *Sendung – Eroberung – Begegnung: Franz Xaver, die Gesellschaft Jesu und die katholische Weltkirche im Zeitalter des Barock*, ed. Johannes Meier (Wiesbaden: Harrassowitz, 2005), 31–66.

[46] Willem Audenaert, *Prosographia Iesuitica Belgica Antiqua (PIBA), A Biographical Dictionary of the Jesuits in the Low Countries, 1542–1773* (Leuven-Heverlee: Filosofisch en Theologisch College, S. J., 2000), III.302–3; Bernd Hausberger, *Für Gott und König: Die Mission der Jesuiten im kolonialen Mexiko*, Studien zur Geschichte und Kultur der Iberischen und Iberoamerikanischen Länder 6 (Munich: R. Oldenbourg, 2000), 22.

dropped from 434 to 255 members in 22 years (1626–48), and only 147 of these 255 remained stationed in the provinces.

From the colleges, the Jesuits affected a wide program of missionary work, which included education, publishing (including Canisius's catechisms), preaching, hearing confessions, and catechizing. Eventually the Lower Rhenish province extended from Münster and Osnabruck a chain of missions through northern Germany, Denmark, and Sweden: Hamburg, Bremen and Lübeck, Schwerin, Celle, Hannover, Copenhagen, Fridericia, and Stockholm. Another branch reached out from Düsseldorf to include Blankenberg, Elberfeld, and Sollingen, a third from Meppen to Emsland and East Frisia, and a fourth from Büren in Wamberg and Arnsberg. In the south, missions were conducted from Freiburg and Lucerne into Swiss lands.[47] Each mission, typically manned by a pair of Jesuits, worked both with dispersed Catholics and potential Protestant converts.

Encouraged by reforming bishops, the Jesuits conducted *Volksmissionen*, that is, preaching beyond the usual parish bounds. In Bavaria all such missions were most often run by the Jesuits. The sixteenth century saw *Volksmissionen* to the Bavarian Forest and to Regensburg, each usually lasting a half or a full week.[48] Princes financially supported such undertakings, as did the Countess Palatinate Maria Anna (sister of Emperor Leopold and wife of the future Elector Johann William), who founded a *Volksmission* for the Jülich-Berg, Niederrhein, Ruhe and Maas region, with an endowment of ten thousand rhenish florins.[49] The most famous of these missionaries was Philipp Jeningen (1642–1704), who conducted some fifty missions annually from Ellwangen.

In 1677 the new archbishop of Trier, Johannes Hugo von Orsbeck, gave the authority to conduct a visitation, which included the foundation and inspection of local schools, to the Jesuits Nicolaus Alff and Wilhelm Osburg, who came fresh from a nine-year *Volksmission* in Paderborn and would have preferred an assignment in the Indies. Von Orsbeck instructed the local parish clergy that they "should in every possible way, through deed and advice, support the missionaries and under no pretext hinder them in any way." This mission travelled from village to village, giving two to four sermons a day (the last stretching into the night), usually outside of churches, which rarely could hold the immense audiences. Protestants rang bells to drive the two Jesuits off, and civil authorities, such as the officers of ducal Saxe-Eisenach in Altenkirchen, kept them under careful

---

[47] Bernhard Duhr, "Zur Geschichte der deutschen Volksmissionen in der 2. Hälfte des 17. Jahrhunderts," *Historisches Jahrbuch* 37 (1916), 590–613.
[48] Romuald Bauerreiß, *Kirchengeschichte Bayerns* (St. Ottilien: EOS Verlag, 1965), VI.338–9.
[49] Duhr, "Zur Geschichte," 597, 622.

surveillance. During the mission's fourteen-month duration, the Jesuits heard on average some 117 confessions each day. In areas threatened by, or recently won back from, Protestantism there were outdoor altars, music, gun salutes, and processions. Everything theatrical, however, was scorned as "Italian," and in 1718 Elector Maximilian II Emanuel (r. 1679–1726) would forbid such dramatics in Bavaria.[50]

In addition, Jesuits from colleges in Cologne, Münster, and Paderborn took up "military missions" (*Militärseelsorge*) to nearby soldiers and battlefield casualties. The mission to the physically unwell was yet more dangerous. Munich had five Jesuits dedicated to this task alone. In 1597 Fulda lost every Jesuit dedicated to tending the sick. Few records survive about Jesuits devoted to military or infirmary missions.[51]

The most controversial question in most discussions of the German Assistancy is deceptively straightforward: Which Jesuits were German? The German population in Bohemia, the inclusion of Silesia and a part of Saxony in the Bohemian Province, and the domestic need for Bohemian missionaries all led to an unexpectedly high proportion of Germans within the Bohemian Province.[52] The earliest modern scholarship on the central-European Jesuits, dating from the decades around World War I, witnessed bitter catfights over the national identity of their subjects, and these issues continue to inform historical debate today. Anton Huonder claimed to include only those missionaries with non-German names who explicitly were identified and identified themselves as *"Missionarii teutscher Nation,"* but in fact he judged every Bohemian missionary to be German, without exception.[53] Just as often national enthusiasms encourage errors in the other direction, as when historians such as Zdeněk Kalista and Josef Kunský pass off German missionaries as Czechs. The anachronistic practice of Spanish, French, Italian, and English authors to take modern borders as definitive is the worst solution.[54] Even contemporaries ran aground when determining nationalities. Seventeenth-century sources debate whether Walter Sonnenberg (a.k.a. Ignazio de Monte, 1612–80) was Spanish or Flemish. In fact, he

---

[50] Ibid., 594–96. See also Bauerreiß, VII.284–5.

[51] Records from the 1702–4 Bavarian *Militärseelsorge* at Ulm remain at BHStA Jes. 579, fol. 30.

[52] Hausberger, *Jesuiten*, 28; Zdeněk Kalista, "Los misioneros de los países checos que en los siglos XVII y XVIII actuaban en América Latina," *Ibero-Americana Pragensia* 11 (1968), 125, 129.

[53] Huonder, *Deutsche Jesuitenmissionäre*, 4. See Hausberger, *Jesuiten*, 26–27, who further notes that Hassinger's study on Austrians also includes all the Bohemians.

[54] Grulich, 17. For example, Jean-Marie Valentin considers Trigault French. Jean-Marie Valentin, *Le Theatre des Jésuites dans les pays de langue allemande (1554–1680)* (Bern: Peter Lang, 1978), 727.

was born in Lucerne. Relying on surnames as proof of nationality helps little. Often an indication of a missionary's nationality follows his name, as in "P. Christianus Herdtrich Austriacus," for instance; nonetheless some Jesuits with clearly Czech names still referred to themselves as Germans.[55]

Nor are even their original names readily apparent, for central-European Jesuits working in Mexico and China often bore Spanish or Chinese names. Simon Boruhradský became Simón de Castro, and Joachim Calmes (1652–86) became Jin Yujing 金玉敬. Some names became so garbled crossing the ocean that they remain orphaned despite historians' efforts. As is common today, in China renaming was a strategy to ease integration into a new cultural setting, but explanations for name changes in New Spain are more varied. At times German Jesuits adopted new, less threatening, names and origins to thwart Spanish immigration controls, perhaps at the recommendation of the Spanish mission procurator.[56] Before boarding his ship, the Viennese Karl Boranga (1640–84) announced himself as Juan Bautista Perez, "a native of Calatayud, that is, naturalized in Bilbilis in Aragon," and Augustin Strohbach, from Jihlava (Iglau) in Moravia, appears as Carolus Calvanese de Calva, native of Milan – then a Spanish-Hapsburg possession.[57] Name changing occurs mostly in the seventeenth century, the period of greatest suspicion, but perhaps only in the last third of the century was the hispanization of names truly meant to deceive.[58] Certainly the official documents that baldly list a German place of birth adjacent to the new surname prove that sometimes the motivation was more innocent. At times the point may have been simply to sweeten harsh German sounds for sensitive Spanish ears.[59]

Thus deception, laziness, and confusion over German political geography all contributed to name changes. Himself from Amberg, Anton Böhm so feared being excluded from the Indies as a Bavarian that he added "Montipolitanus" to his name – "an Amberger from Innsbruck,

---

[55] "Estado y cualidad de las misiones en China, por Couplet, 1682–3," AHN Jes. 27, n. 43, at fol. 18r.

[56] Huonder, *Deutsche Jesuitenmissionäre*, 22–23.

[57] WB Nr. 2; Josef Jaksch, *Sudetendeutsche in der Weltmission des 17. und 18. Jahrhunderts.* (Königstein i. Taunus.: Sudetendeutsches Priesterwerk, 1957), 15.

[58] Lázaro de Aspurz, 252; Mauro Matthei, "Los primeros jesuitas germanos en Chile (1686–1722)," *Boletín de la Academia Chilena de la Historia* 34, Nr. 77 (1967), 148. See also Štěpánek, who supports Lázaro de Aspurz. Pavel Štěpánek, "Simón de Castro – Simon Boruhradský: un arquitecto checo del siglo XVII en Nueva España – México," *Ibero-Americana Pragensia* 20 (1968), 166.

[59] Hausberger, *Jesuiten*, 41; Lázaro de Aspurz, 252–3, with which Borges Morán agrees (*El envío*, 300).

which is like a Venetian from Munich," his companion chuckled. Böhm's name finally appears, with a tail of varied placenames, as "P. Antonius Adami Bohemi Montipolitanus Ratisbonae in Tyroli natus." Antonius and his cohorts "laughed a good while about this, and were in good spirits. This was itself a mistake, for the Procurator of the Indies recorded all us fathers from one province under the same place, so that he could avoid writing too many different place names." The entire group ended up Tyrolese, to their deep indignation.[60]

Language is no more reliable a criterion than names. In particular, the Bohemian province encouraged bilingualism for German and Czech Jesuits. According to the 1589 report of a novice master, the German novices spent an hour every day refining their Czech, and the Czechs their German. A cursory look at language ability among the Jesuits in Prague and Vienna makes clear the ubiquity of German, even amidst a cosmopolitan variety of other languages. In 1670s Prague more Jesuits spoke German than Czech, though many missionaries from the Prague environs used a German or Latin full of Bohemianisms (Tables 1–3).[61] German missionaries exhibited a strong preference for writing in Latin, but of course they enjoyed no monopoly in this.

Membership in a Jesuit province did not always coincide with birth and nationality. Born in Cologne, Schall von Bell entered the Roman Province, while Joseph Neumann, born in Brussels, joined the Bohemian Province in Olmütz.

Sometimes the reality was too complicated to allow any single index of nationality, or even of any single nationality. Having travelled to the birthplace of Eusebius Kino (1644–1711) in Segno near Trent, the historian H. E. Bolton became so convinced that his subject was Italian that he took personally a contemporary obituary's mention of German nationality: "It was not fair . . . to treat either Kino or the biographer [Bolton] so."[62] In the end, Bolton's resentment was only half justified, for Kino considered himself Italian by birth and German by education and upbringing. His colleagues referred to him as *bávaro* (Bavarian), and he freely admitted being unsure how to identify himself.[63]

---

[60] Quoted in Huonder, *Deutsche Jesuitenmissionäre*, 24.

[61] F. Machilek, "Reformorden und Ordensreformen in den böhmischen Ländern von 10.-18. Jahrhundert," in *Bohemia Sacra: Das Christentum in Böhmen 973–1973*, ed. Ferdinand Seibt (Düsseldorf: 1974), 77; Grulich, 17.

[62] Herbert Eugene Bolton, *Rim of Christendom: A Biography of Eusebio Francisco Kino, Pacific Coast Pioneer* (New York: Macmillan, 1936), 586.

[63] Ernest J. Burrus, ed., *Kino escribe a la duquesa: Correspondencia del P. Eusebio Francisco Kino con la duquesa de Aveiro y otros documentos*, Colección Chimalistac 18 (Madrid: J. Porrúa Turanzas, 1964), 105–15. For example, Eymer, Mexico, to P. Johannes Lober, December 19, 1692, MZA Brno, G-11, 557/6, fol. 45r-45v.

Table 1. *Languages in Jesuit Probation House, Vienna, 1642*

Speakers	Percent	Language
86	80%	German
80	75%	Latin
24	22%	Italian
21	20%	Slovakian
19	18%	Hungarian
7	7%	Slovenian ("carniolicam")
4	4%	Czech
3	3%	Dalmatian*
3	3%	Serbo-Croatian
3	3%	French
1	1%	Daco-Romanian ("vallachia")
1	1%	Moravian

* Dalmatian was a Romance language that largely died out in the nineteenth century.
Source: "Catalogus Primus Domus Prabtionis Viennensis conscriptus Anno 1642" ARSI Austr. 27.310r-319v.

Table 2. *Languages in Jesuit College of Prague, 1675*

Speakers	Percent	Language
188	97%	German
130	67%	Czech (Bohemian)
11	5.7%	Greek
10	5.2%	Polish
7	4%	Italian
4	2%	Latin
3	2%	Hebrew
1	1%	English
1	1%	French
1	1%	Spanish

Source: "Catalogus Personarum Collegij Soctis Jesu, Pragae ad S: Clementem. 1675" ARSI Boh. 18.133–55.

The best solution is the cautious use of multiple criteria while recognizing nationality as an often subjective act of self-identification. Thus "German" can refer to any and all of membership in the German Assistancy, origin in a state of the Holy Roman Empire, or having German

Table 3. *Languages in Jesuit College of Prague, 1678*

Speakers	Percent	Language
173	97%	German
128	72%	Czech (Bohemian)
6	3%	Polish
6	3%	Greek
6	3%	Hebrew
3	2%	Italian
2	1%	French
2	1%	Spanish
2	1%	Syriac (Semitic)
2	1%	Chaldean (Biblical Aramaic)

Source: "Catalogus Personarum Collegij Soctis Jesu, Pragae ad S: Clementem. 1678" ARSI Boh. 19.122–57. (The statistics for Latin ability are remarkable: 75% in Vienna, 2% in Prague (1675), and no listing for Prague (1678). This presumably reflects variations in the methodology of how this data was collected.)

as one's mother tongue.[64] Because issues of nationality are so central to this topic, I did not lay down hard lines at the outset on who is or is not German. Rather this study adopts a loose understanding of German, and observes which contemporary borders appear most salient. Not only is the Germanness of the missionaries not germane, but even the difficulty we find in grappling with questions of nationality itself reveals key realities about the early-modern Jesuits. Roughly, I take "German" Jesuits to be those belonging to a province in the German Assistancy, after France broke off in 1609: Upper German, Austrian, Upper Rhenish, Lower Rhenish, and Bohemian. This project concerns itself less with the work of the missionaries as Germans than with them as being in the "wrong" place – that is, not Spaniards in Spanish America or Portuguese in Portuguese Asia. In this work "German" should be understood to have quotation marks, either explicitly as a direct quotation revealing contemporary attitudes, or implicitly as snigger quotes reminding the reader to consider it loosely.

The Mexican Province

Already in 1538, before the Society had been founded, the imperial ambassador to the papal court attempted to win for the Mexican mission

[64] Hausberger, *Jesuiten*, 31.

some of the men who would become Jesuits.[65] The establishment of an Archbishopric of Mexico in 1548 marked the beginning of an ecclesiastical hierarchy that would develop at far more rapid a pace than its counterpart in Portuguese Asia.[66] The first Jesuits arrived in the New World in 1566, working in the Florida mission, but that campaign received no official approval until Philip II convoked the Junta Magna in Madrid two years later.[67] In 1572 Sánchez de Canales led the first five Jesuits into Mexico City, where he founded the Mexico Province that same year, with himself as provincial. The earliest provincial congregations were held in 1577, 1585, and 1592, the last of which resolved to call a meeting every four years. The next one seems to have been held in 1595.[68] The Mexican province was further developed with the founding of colleges in Mexico (San Pedro y San Pablo, 1573), Puebla, Oaxaca, and Valladolid, a large novice house at Tepozotlán, the seminary San Ildefonso in Mexico City, and residences in Guadalajara, Pátzcuaro, and Vera Cruz. In 1595 a Philippine Vice-province was founded, and it became a full province a decade later.[69]

When the Jesuits began arriving in New Spain, the missionary project had already evolved considerably. The expansion of the colony had lost its first frantic pace, and the evangelization correspondingly lost some of its urgency, to settle into a rearguard stance nurturing the faith of believers already won. Although the Jesuits had obtained royal approval to work among the Mexican Indians already in 1572, they finally did so, near San Luis de Paz, only after a seventeen-year delay. Their missionary vocation included sufficient breadth for the Jesuits both to minister to the urban Spaniards and American-born white creoles and to attend to the education of the children of converted Indians.[70] The urban focus was exactly what the Constitutions considered "universal" – a concentration of efforts to reach the greatest number of people, here through a ministry working for a native educated clergy.

---

[65] Anton Huonder, *Der hl. Ignatius von Loyola und der Missionsberuf der Gesellschaft Jesu.* Abhandlungen aus Missionskunde und Missionsgeschichte 35 (Aachen: Xaverius verlagsbuchhandlung, 1922), 18, 76.

[66] Boxer, *Portuguese*, 232.

[67] Borges Morán, *El envío*, 76.

[68] Francisco Javier Alegre, *Historia de la provincia de la Compañia de Jesús de Nueva España*, ed. Ernest J. Burrus and Felix Zubillaga (Rome: Institutum Historicum, 1956–60), I.555.

[69] Beckmann, "Die Glaubensverbreitung," V.280; Audenaert, III.302.

[70] Borges Morán, *El envío*, 38; A. S. Tibesar, P. Borges, and E. J. Burrus, "Missions in Colonial America I," in *The Catholic Encyclopedia* (New York: Gilmary Society, 1951), IX.944–64.

The mendicant orders' established presence in urban centres, however, as well as Philip II's *Ordenanzas sobre descubrimientos* [*Ordinances on the Discoveries*] (1573) and *del patronato* [*on the Patronage*] (1574), encouraged the Jesuits to seek missions on the frontier. These Ordinances gave primary responsibility for the borderlands to missionaries from the religious orders, possibly with the assistance of modest military garrisons. The assignment was in principle temporary, and when their converted charges had been "reduced" to a settled, agricultural lifestyle, the religious would surrender their duties to secular priests. Advancing the border a step further, the religious would begin the frontline conversion process anew.[71]

This strategy received secular and ecclesiastical approval, and General Aquaviva prohibited the Jesuits from taking on the care of souls of converted Indians already living in parishes and *doctrinas*. This later became a problem in the Philippines, where there were not enough Spaniards to keep the Jesuits occupied. The crown conferred the authority to work specific mission regions on a case-by-case basis. For example, Philip II established the legal basis for the Jesuits' monopoly on missions in the northwest.[72] Similarly, a decree of December 29, 1679, assigned to the Jesuits the mission of the proposed colony of California.[73]

The basic unit of the missionary hierarchy was the mission province, directly under the provincial, who typically delegated his authority to a father visitor, one for each mission province. A mission province consisted of *rectorados*, which in turn subdivided into *partidos* (to be promoted as the converts' faith stabilized into *distritos*), each of which typically had one or two Jesuits residing in a central mission (*cabecera*) but making the rounds to his or their various subordinate missions, the *visitas*. Until the enlargement of the office of visitor general in the early eighteenth century, only the provincial could appoint missionaries, and transfers or deaths could lead to protracted vacancies.[74]

The Mexican Province's first missionary action, undertaken in 1580 at the request of the king, was to the Philippines. The earliest mission province in Mexico proper was the Misiones de Sinaloa (1591). This suffered a demographic and spiritual depression when the Jesuits pushed

[71] Charles R. Boxer, *The Church Militant and Iberian Expansion* (Baltimore: Johns Hopkins University Press, 1978), 72.

[72] Felipe II, Madrid, to [Viceroy] Luis de Velasco el Joven, January 17, 1593, in *Monumenta Mexicana*, ed. Félix Zubillaga (Rome: Monumenta Historica Soc. Iesu, 1946), V.33.

[73] Zephyrin Engelhardt, *Lower California, The Missions and Missionaries of California* (San Francisco: James H. Barry Co., 1908), I.64.

[74] Polzer, *Rules*, 7–10, 25.

further northward to found the Misión de San Luis de la Paz (1594)[75] among the Chichimecs, the Misión de Parras o La Laguna (1594) – mostly abandoned to the seculars at the instigation of the bishop of Durango – and the Misión de los Tepehuanes (1596), where eight Jesuits would become martyrs during a rebellion in 1616. The Misiones de Sonora (1614) subdivided into two *rectorados*, in the west San Javier, and in the east Santos Mártires del Japón, named for those martyred across the ocean. The Misión de Chinipas (1620) extended north from the Sinaloa mission. The unfortunate destiny of the Misión de la Tarahumara Baja (founded 1607) included revolt (1650–52) and plague (1662). A new wave of expansion began with the Misión de la Tarahumara Alta (1674), which suffered famous revolts in the 1690s. 1697 also saw the establishment of the distant desert Misión de California – a location strategic for its potential in controlling trade from China.[76]

The Chinese Vice-Province

In 1534 the Diocese of Goa, then called the "Rome of Asia," was founded with a jurisdiction extending from the Cape of Good Hope across south and east Asia.[77] It was elevated to an archbishopric in 1558, when a Bishopric of Melaka was also created and assigned jurisdiction in China.[78] After the Portuguese assisted the imperial navy against the pirates infesting the South China Sea, an appreciative Beijing allowed Portuguese to reside in Macao, which was soon called "the City of the Name of God." In 1575 Gregory XII issued the bull *Super specula* to establish a bishopric there, suffragan to the Metropolitan See of Goa, that would include all of Japan and China. Only much later, in 1690, did Rome create the Sees of Beijing and Nanjing.[79]

[75] Tibesar, Borges, and Burrus, "Missions," IX.948.

[76] Félix Zubillaga, "Mexico," in *Diccionario histórico de la Compañia de Jesús: biográfico-temático* (Rome: Institutum Historicum, 2001). See Juan de Torquemada, *Monarquia indiana*, Biblioteca Porrua 41–3 (Mexico: Editorial Porrua, 1969), 693 [tom. i, cap. Xlv]. For the importance of California, see Luke Clossey, "Merchants, Migrants, Missionaries, and Globalization in the Early-Modern Pacific," *Journal of Global History* 1 (2006), 43.

[77] Alfons Väth, *Johann Adam Schall von Bell, S. J.* (Nettetal: Steyler, 1991), 45; Boxer, *Portuguese*, 232. Much of the later seventeenth century saw a vacant archbishopric of Goa. See A. D. Wright, *The Counter-Reformation: Catholic Europe and the Non-Christian World* (New York: St. Martin's, 1982), 133.

[78] Josef Wicki, "Die unmittelbaren Auswirkungen des Konzils von Trient auf Indien (ca. 1565–1585)," in *Missionskirche im Orient*, Neue Zeitschrift für Missionswissenschaft. Supplementa 24 (Immensee: Neue Zeitschrift für Missionswissenschaft, 1976), 213.

[79] Geoffrey Francis Hudson, *Europe and China: A Survey of Their Relations from Earliest Times to 1800* (London: E. Arnold, 1931), 233; Latourette, *History*, 124.

The separate Jesuit hierarchy developed more rapidly. The Province of the East Indies (*Indiarum Orientalem*) branched off in 1549 from the Portuguese Province (*Lusitaniae*), itself then only three years old. In the early 1580s another division resulted in an East Indian Province (*Indiae Orientalis*) and a Vice-province of Japan *(Iaponica)*, administered from Macao after the Jesuits' expulsion.

The relationship between the Chinese mission and the Japanese province was often troubled. China mission superior Niccolò Longobardo (1565–1617) was so concerned by the circumstances that, usurping the provincial's prerogative, he appointed the missionary Nicolas Trigault (1577–1628) as procurator and sent him on a new, unauthorized mission – to Europe. The superior had decided that the recent successes of the China mission, coupled with its financial difficulties, made this an advantageous time to seek support from home. His most pressing hope concerned institutional change, as he disliked seeking approval for every request from the Province of Japan, then in exile at Macao. The Japanese mission had enjoyed more tangible success than its younger Chinese counterpart, and resisted diverting too many resources to it. Anticipating opposition, Longobardo sent two letters, of November 21 and 26, 1612, to General Aquaviva, respectively announcing and defending his sending of Trigault, who would play a key role in the creation of the global Jesuit network.[80]

The defence was not gratuitous. Several letters raced Trigault to Rome to denounce his mission before it began. Francisco Vieira, the visitor to Japan, objected to Trigault's inexperience, while Valentino Carvalho, the provincial for Japan, noted the illegality of Longobardo's move and the prematurity of his requests.[81] The most serious objections, however, rested on an early form of nationalism, what General Gonzales would call that "damned national spirit."[82] The following chapter will discuss that damned spirit more fully.

Strongly loyal to his own Portugal, Vieira suspected that Longobardo sought to establish an independent Chinese mission staffed by his fellow Italians. He later disclosed his distrust, not to the new Jesuit General Muzio Vitelleschi (1615–45), who was Italian himself, but to Vitelleschi's assistant for Portugal, Nuno Mascarenhas. Others thought Trigault was naïve about the sensibilities of the colonial powers with respect to foreigners. The Goa procurator, Sebastien Goncalves, warned that Trigault's

[80] Edmond Lamalle, "La propaganda du P. Nicolas Trigault en faveur des missions de Chine (1616)" *Archivum Historicum Societatis Iesu* 9 (1940), 54–5.
[81] Ibid., 54, 56.
[82] George H. Dunne, *Generation of Giants: The Story of the Jesuits in China in the Last Decades of the Ming Dynasty* (Notre Dame, Indiana: University of Notre Dame Press, 1962), 169.

efforts might provoke Lisbon to bar foreign missionaries from Asia. Gabriel de Matos, a Jesuit in the Japan mission, specifically protested the recruitment of non-Portuguese missionaries, reasoning that this would offend Lisbon as a breach of her royal *padroado* (patronage). He added that many of the Jesuits in Nagasaki would prefer that Trigault not return to China at all.[83] It is unclear whether they were motivated by Trigault's supposed anti-Portuguese parochialism or by his pan-European internationalism.

Such protests were in vain, and most of China became an independent vice-province from 1623. The China Vice-province did well in the seventeenth century. Kaspar Castner's (1665–1709) memorandum on China (1703) reported Jesuits in twelve provinces of the empire, distributed among five colleges, thirty-six residences, thirty-eight chief stations (*Hauptstationen*), three hundred churches and chapels, all ministering to 200,000 baptized Christians.[84]

This administrative victory paralleled Curial decisions on other matters brought forward by Trigault, for the resulting resolutions maximized the independence of China. Trigault received authorization for priests to cover their heads during mass, a custom contrary to canon law but in agreement with Chinese decorum. He also had overturned the 1606 order from the general forbidding the Chinese from taking holy orders, and he was granted permission for a translation of the Bible, the celebration of the mass, and the recitation of the canonical hours in classical Chinese. The speed with which the bureaucracy responded to these requests shows the sympathies of Rome. Within three months of his arrival, the petitions had been approved by the Jesuit General, the Jesuit theologians of the Roman College, Pope Paul V (1605–21), and the cardinals. On June 27, 1615 Paul promulgated these concessions in the papal brief *Romanae ecclesiae antistes*.[85] This ensured that the world the Jesuits were forming would include a China distinct from Europe even in its Christianity,[86] a world that would be a stage for divergent ritual traditions.

The Portuguese Jesuits understood the disparity between their small nation and the vast Indies for which she held responsibility. Portugal's delegates to the first General Congregation stressed this, and begged

---

[83] Ibid., 169–70.
[84] Audenaert, III.302. Anton Huonder, *Deutsche Jesuitenmissionäre* [unpublished manuscript of second edition; AMSJ, Munich: Anton Huonder, *Deutsche Jesuitenmissionäre des 17. und 18. Jahrhunderts, 2. Auflage (unveröffentlicht); AMSJ, Abt. 47 (Huonder)*], 1046–7.
[85] Dunne, 164–6.
[86] Zheng Weixin 鄭維信 (1633–1673) entered the Society of Jesus at Rome in 1651, and became the first native Chinese priest in 1664.

for other provinces to contribute missionaries. The response was under-standing but realistic: The rest of the Society would help "as much as possible."[87] Gonçalves da Câmara repeated this request to Nadal, who in 1561 advised General Diego Laínez (1558–65) to send to the Portuguese Indies those physically strong missionaries of a talent too "mediocre" to be useful in Germany.[88]

Despite the high profile maintained by those Jesuits who worked with the Astronomical Bureau, most Jesuits stayed far from the court, working in the provinces and preferring to avoid the scrutiny of Chinese officials.[89] Even those outside Beijing, however, participated in the prestigious scientific exchange. For example, the Polish Jesuit Mikołaj Smogulęcki in Nanjing with his student Xue Fengzuo 薛鳳祚 wrote the revolutionary series *True Course of Celestial Motions* 天步眞原 (ca. 1653).[90]

For some time the missionaries evinced little enthusiasm for Chinese priests. Mercurian, Aquaviva, the visitor Alessandro Valignano (1539–1606), and the Goa provincial Francisco Cabral (1533–1609), and most high civil administrators in the East opposed even the ordination of creoles.[91] The situation evolved slowly in the seventeenth century. In 1606 Aquaviva ruled that the Chinese were too new to the faith to join the Society, though Longobardo disagreed.[92] Jesuits working in Beijing proved more open to ordaining Chinese, at least the socially elite, but their colleagues in Macao, and those imprisoned in Canton like António de Gouveia (1592–1677), held that the existence of Chinese priests would only debase the priesthood.[93] In 1654 Gregorio Lopez (Luo Wenzao 羅文藻, 1615–1691) became the first Chinese priest, a Dominican, and pointedly suffered no special limitations on his priesthood. Emmanuel de Siqueira (Zheng Manuo Weixin 鄭瑪諾維信, 1633–1673) became the first ordained Chinese Jesuit. Entering the novitiate of Sant'Andrea at Rome in 1651, he later taught humanities at the Collegio Romano.[94] After spending time in Bologna and Lisbon, he returned to the Far East. Up to the time of

---

[87] Serafim Leite, *História da companhia de Jesus no Brasil* (Rio de Janeiro, 1938–50), II.437.

[88] June 16, 1561, Coimbra, in Hieronymus Nadal, *Epistolae et Monumenta P. Hieronymi Nadal*, Monumenta historica Societatis Iesu 13, 15, 21, 27, 90 (Rome: Monumenta Historica Soc. Iesu, 1900-), I.492–93.

[89] Paul A. Rule, "Jesuit Sources," in *Essays on the Sources for Chinese History*, ed. Donald Daniel Leslie (Canberra: Australian National University Press, 1973), 184.

[90] Li Yan and Du Shiran, *Chinese Mathematics: A Concise History*, trans. John N. Crossley and Anthony W.-C. Lun (Oxford: Clarendon Press, 1987), 204–5.

[91] Alden, 259.

[92] Dunne, *Generation*, 164.

[93] Alden, 265.

[94] Francis A. Rouleau, "The First Chinese Priest of the Society of Jesus, Emmanuel de Siqueira, 1633–1673," *Archivum Historicum Societatis Iesu* 28 (1959), 6, 13–15.

the suppression, no consensus ever emerged, nor did natives ever make up more than a small minority of the clergy in China.[95]

Organization is an art. Perhaps like other historians of Catholicism, I was first drawn to my subject in part because of a fascination with, and the desire to understand better, the often overwhelming and sometimes arcane institutional complexity of the Church, to keep archdeacons and coadjutors straight in my mind. Its graceful, streamlined organization makes the Society of Jesus stand out even in a line-up with the church's other constituent bodies. The more time I spent with the Jesuit structure, the more curious I became, not only as to how this institution functioned but also as to how it failed to function. How did the global Society fare in an imperfectly globalized world? We turn now to the fruit of those inquiries.

---

[95] See Charles R. Boxer, "European Missionaries and Chinese Clergy, 1654–1810" in *The Age of Partnership*, ed. Blair B. Kling and M. N. Pearson (Honolulu: University Press of Hawaii, 1979), 97–121.

3 Decentralizing the Society of Jesus

When I began researching this project, one expert on the Jesuits recommended that I read the Society's Constitutions, which he called the "Jesuit bible." Although he drew this metaphor to impress upon me the Constitutions' importance, we can strengthen the comparison by emphasizing rather the complex relationship between Christians and their Bibles, which they have interpreted and then followed, adapted, or ignored in accordance with circumstance and tradition.

Jesuit ambition was global, but it ran ahead of the globalizing possibilities of the early-modern world. Many months and many miles separated missionaries from authority in Rome. Friction from the realities of communications and transportation slowed and sometimes broke – and sometimes even promoted – the global network they were building. Disagreements regarding how best to pursue the all-important mission separated Jesuits from other religious orders, and from each other.

The Difficulties of Distance

In the pre-modern world, information was less likely than other commodities to travel great distances intact. Thus Chinese silk reached the Mediterranean by at least 150 B.C., while Pliny's *Natural History* (A.D. 70) still described blue-eyed Chinese harvesting silk from trees.[1] Even in the early-modern period, information remained in short supply. For news on the New World, the Roman Curia depended largely on the Spanish ambassador or on the cardinal in the consistory who cared for imperial interests. In response to the king's request for special permission to send religious to the Indies in 1554, Julius III forwarded the matter to

---

[1] David Christian, "Silk Roads or Steppe Roads? The Silk Roads in World History," *Journal of World History* 11 (2000), 16–17, 24.

various Spanish bishops, helplessly excusing himself as "not having sure knowledge" of the situation.[2]

This coincidence of globally expanding possibilities with enduring traditional obstacles is characteristic of early-modern communication.[3] With neither steamships nor a Suez Canal to speed their journeys, the voyage from Western Europe to east Asia lasted not weeks, but months or years. Over two years after his arrival in China, Jesuit missionary Johannes Terrenz Schreck (1576–1630) wrote to William of Bavaria, calling the duke's response to "my American writings" the first reply he had received from Europe.[4] Although during a stay in Macao Schreck also complained of receiving no letters from Europe, the two-year postal delay would soon seem not unusual to him.[5] Delay made the route between Lisbon and Beijing, via Goa, last two years, with surprising consistency: two years one way, almost two years back – sometimes even longer.[6] The Jesuit chosen to be the first vice-provincial for China died in 1623, two years after his appointment, but still well before news of it could reach him in Hangzhou 杭州.[7] When Schall wrote a letter to General Francesco Piccolomini (1649–51) on March 15, 1655, that general had already been dead for 45 months, and his successor dead for 3 years.[8] It would have been even more out of date by the time it reached Rome.

Although data for postal speeds become more plentiful in the eighteenth century, the speeds themselves hardly improved. The letter written by Johann Siebert on October 29, 1742, in Cochinchina reached the Countess Fugger in Augsburg at the end of January 1745.[9] Another eighteenth-century author finds a time lag of some 446 days between Patute, in the Vice-royalty of New Granada, and Graz, in the Duchy of Styria, impressively swift.[10]

---

[2] Pietro de Leturia, "Perchè la nascente Chiesa ispano-americana non fu rappresentata a Trento," in *Il Concilio di Trento I* (Trent: 1942), 35–43.

[3] Brandon Marriott, "The Rebirth of Hope in a Time of Upheaval: An Analysis of Early-Modern Millennial Movements Across the Abrahamic Tradition," *World History Bulletin* 23 (2007): 26–30,

[4] Schreck, Hangzhou, to William of Bavaria, September 4, 1622, BStB CLM 27323, fol. 10r.

[5] Schreck, Hangzhou, to Johannes Faber, August 26, 1621, in Hartmut Walravens, *China Illustrata: Das europäische Chinaverständnis im Spiegel des 16. bis 18. Jahrhunderts* (Weinheim: VCH, 1987), 25; Schreck, Suzhou in Xiading, to Johannes Faber, April 22, 1622, in ibid., 30.

[6] This is in the 1690s. H. Josson and Léopold Willaert, eds., *Correspondance de Ferdinand Verbiest de la compagnie de Jésus (1623–1688), directeur de l'observatoire de Pékin* (Brussels: Palais des académies, 1938), xvii–xviii.

[7] Dunne, *Generation*, 171.

[8] Schall von Bell, Beijing, to Piccolomini, March 15, 1655, ARSI JapSin 142, 45.

[9] Jaksch, 19.

[10] WB Nr. 391.

A fortunate correspondent would only have the delay to regret. In other cases, letters, especially those sent from Europe to Goa to be circulated throughout east Asia, would arrive at their destination in unreadable tatters. Sometimes they did not arrive at all.[11] Five years after Trigault's visit, Duke William had received no news from China, and did not even know if the Jesuit, his companions, and the gifts and equipment donated by the duke had arrived safely. The best information to reach the duke seems to have been a small book on news from China, sent by an assistant in Rome.[12] Of the "thirteen or fourteen" letters a Jesuit in Leuven had written to the missionary Petrus Thomas Van Hamme (1651–1727) in Mexico, only one ever arrived. Van Hamme did not doubt that his correspondent had been writing more frequently, but recognized the difficulty of any mail reaching him.[13] To express his hope that his letter written in Beijing would reach Portugal, Antoine Thomas realistically selected the verb *nanciscantur* ["is received"], with its highly conjectural connotations.[14]

What information did manage to get through was often simply wrong. As the contemporary Castilian proverb lamented, "from long journeys, long lies."[15] While by the end of the Seven Years' War a humbled Spain had actually lost control of Havana and Manila to the English, her loyal missionaries in Sonora celebrated news of a victorious Spain's capture of London.[16] Sometimes Jesuits would compensate for delays by consciously adjusting the truth. Mattheiu de Tournai described King Henry III's 1574 visit to the Avignon Jesuit college in glowing terms: "He has come with the Queen Mother [Catherine de'Medici] to our college and has demonstrated very much good will to us." The next month a correction reached Rome stating that the reported royal visit had not occurred, and what had been reported as fact was merely a hope.[17] This rhetorical

---

[11] P. Leão Henriques, Lisbon, to General, July 30, 1566, in Serafim Leite, ed., *Monumenta Brasiliae*, Monumenta historica Societatis Iesu, 79, Monumenta Missionum Societatis Iesu, 10 (Rome: "Monumenta Historica Societatis Iesu," 1956–), I.57–58. See also P. Leão Henriques, Lisbon, to General Borja, June 26, 1566, in *Monumenta Brasiliae* IV.348.

[12] Guilielmus, Munich, to Nonius Mascarenhas [Assistant in Rome], September 9, 1621, ARSI FG 722/17.

[13] "Postquam Europam deserui, misi ad R^{am} V^{am} 13 vel 14 epistolas, et unicam a R^a V^a accepi Mexici: non dubito, quin plures scripserit R^a V^a ... " Van Hamme, Nanjing, to Franciscus van Callenberghe, May 5, 1691, BRB 16.691–16.693, fol. 19r.

[14] Antonio Thomas, Beijing, to Duchess of Aveiro, September 15, 1688, RAH Jesuitas 16, no. 14b, fol. 2v.

[15] Gregorio García, *Origen de los indios del Nuevo Mundo*, ed. Andrés González de Barcia (Madrid, 1729), fol. 48v.

[16] Hausberger, *Jesuiten*, 81–2.

[17] A. Lynn Martin, *The Jesuit Mind: the Mentality of an Elite in Early Modern France* (Ithaca: Cornell University Press, 1988), 4.

approach recalls the classical Latin authors who wrote letters in tenses
that reflected the expected time of arrival. When reality coincided with
predictions, this was an effective method, but it made surprises especially
disastrous for the information network.

Another recurring problem was the interception of letters by various
authorities. When Jean-François Gerbillon, after the Nerchinsk negotia-
tions, sent a letter to Louis XIV's confessor François d'Aix de la Chaise
in Paris through the Russians, his intermediaries made a copy, which
eventually worked its way via Berlin to Leibniz.[18] Urging his correspondent to route letters via Canton, Van Hamme reported that mail, especially anything bound for Mexico, was subject to interception by the
Portuguese in Macao and Beijing.[19] Other routes were no safer, and
Van Hamme worried about correspondence being seized and opened in
London, and complained that even the Emperor of China interfered with
the mail.[20]

The Jesuits made use of several strategies to address these postal chal-
lenges. Codes and ciphers were sometimes used, especially with sensitive information, such as news of Trigault's suicide.[21] More routine were
alternate routing strategies. The Diestel and Grueber 1656 overland trip
to China had among its objectives an experiment with sending letters
via the caravans.[22] Jakob Dimer (1626–58) mentioned sending letters
from India to Germany in an English Protestant's ship.[23] Vital documents
would be sent in multiple copies with multiple captains traveling on multiple routes.[24] In Beijing, Van Hamme made four copies of one letter,
to be sent out on French, Portuguese, English, and Philippine boats.[25]
Even communications within the European continent proved difficult,

[18] Donald Lach, *The Preface to Leibniz "Novissima Sinica,"* (Honolulu: University of Hawaii, 1957), 15–16.
[19] Van Hamme, ["Metropoli Prov Hiiquam"], to Franciscus van Callenberghe and P. Conrad Janning, July 8, 1696, BRB 16.691–16.693, fol. 33r.
[20] Petrus Thomas Van Hamme, Beijing, to Conrad Janning, November 27, 1702, BRB 16.691/16.693, fol. 54r; Van Hamme, [China] to P. Proc., January 13, 1713, AGN AHH leg. 323, exp. 7, unfol.
[21] ARSI JapSin 161, II, fol. 116–7.
[22] C. Wessels, "New Documents Relating to the Journey of Fr. John Grueber," *Archivum Historicum Societatis Iesu* 9 (1940): 283.
[23] Jakob Dimer, extract from a letter to Germany, 1658, BHStA G. R. 1256 Nr. 5, [fol. 2r].
[24] Sabine Sauer, *Gottes streitbare Diener für Amerika: Missionsresien im Spiegel der ersten Briefe niederländischer Jesuiten (1616–1618)* (Pfaffenweiler: Centaurus-Verlagsgesellschaft, 1992), 84. Lamalle notes that in Portuguese *secunda via* still means *copia duplicata.* See Lamalle, "L'archivio," 99–100.
[25] Petrus Thomas Van Hamme, Beijing, to Conrad Janning, October 15, 1702. BRB 16.691/16.693, fol. 52r.

and Castner once found that the most secure route for letters between
Lisbon and Ingolstadt ran through England.[26]

Yet despite the claim that "it was not long before the Jesuits had worked
out an intelligence system unequalled by any state in Europe at the time,
with the possible exception of Venice," the early-modern Jesuits never
saw accurate and current distribution of news.[27] If their system was in
principle superior to those of the European states, the greater distances
involved negated any advantage. Pithily foregrounding the breakdown of
distant information exchange, one provincial in Castile chose a telling
metaphor to describe the lot of two Jesuits imprisoned by the Inquisition: "We know no more about the imprisoned fathers than if they were
in the Indies."[28] Still, attempts were made. Despite the two-year time
lag, Schreck tried to micromanage affairs in Germany, specifying, for
example, who should network with whom during breakfast.[29]

Distance did not just retard communication – it made travel deadly.
The dangers associated with a journey heightened the geographical distance between mission stations and with it the overall decentralization of
the Society. Trigault described at length the difficulties faced by missionaries, though he insisted there was no lack of willing volunteers.[30] Missionaries still complained about uncomfortable ship quarters in 1707, but
they should have considered themselves fortunate.[31] The Atlantic passage was relatively safe. From 1601 to 1650 only 1.7% (65 of 3,846) of
ships headed for the New World were lost.[32] The Cape route was another
matter. Of the thirty-four ships sailing from Lisbon or Goa in 1620–23,
eight were wrecked, two captured, and nine forced to return to home
port.[33] A major danger was piracy. Between 1623 and 1636 the Dutch
West Indies Company captured 547 maritime prizes, and Francis Drake
himself attacked the Cape route in 1586.[34] In 1690 Philippe Couplet

[26] Castner, Lisbon, to P. Josef Odermett, November 29, 1705, SBB PK Ms. Lat. 640, fol.
61v.
[27] Donald Lach and Edwin J. van Kley, *Asia in the Making of Europe* (Chicago: University
of Chicago, 1965–), I.315.
[28] William V. Bangert, *A History of the Society of Jesus* (St. Louis: Institute of Jesuit Sources,
1972), 111.
[29] Schreck, Suzhou in Xiading, to Johannes Faber, April 22, 1622, in Walravens, 33.
[30] RAH Jesuitas 91, no. 28, fol. 2v.
[31] "Breve Relación de las cosas sucedidas en la nueva Persecución de la China, sacada de la
compuesta en Macao por los P. P Misioneros Dominicos deterrado de aquellas Misiones
por Fr Pedro Muniz Domico," RBM II/1761, fol. 210.
[32] I base my calculations on Pierre and Huguette Chaunu, *Séville et l'Atlantique* (Paris: A.
Colin, 1955–6), VI, parte 2, 864, 906, 961–75.
[33] John Horace Parry, "Transport and Trade Routes," *Cambridge Economic History of Europe*
(Cambridge: Cambridge University Press, 1966–), II.195.
[34] Huonder, *Deutsche Jesuitenmissionäre*, 34; Vitorino Magalhães Godinho, *L'économie de
l'empire portugais aux XVe et XVIe siècles* (Paris: SEVPEN, 1969), 668.

(1623–1693) estimated that of the more than six hundred Jesuits who had been dispatched to China, only one hundred arrived. Soon after, Couplet himself died at Goa, en route to China.[35] No wonder that the 1631 journey of twenty-eight Dominicans from Spain to the Far East, during which six missionaries died, was described by a fellow Dominican in Manila as "prosperous."[36] The circumstances were so unpleasant that one official asked the Jesuit Georg Brandt about a colleague, "Father, tell me honestly, what did he ever do in his province to be condemned to go the Indies as punishment?"[37]

The Breakdown of Obedience

Although the first Jesuits saw themselves more as a missionary mendicant order than as tools of the Counter Reformation, historians have long regarded them as an elite "military" force controlled by an armchair general perched near, or on, the throne of St. Peter.[38] This impression has a long history. In the early eighteenth century José de la Puente y Peña, the Marquis de Villa Puente (died 1739), a prominent patron of the missions, referred to the Jesuits as soldiers.[39] Alden has shown the widespread and long-standing use of military imagery in ecclesiastical language.[40] The term *generalis*, with the intended meaning of "comprehensive," as in "general congregation," picked up a military connotation and encouraged the "shock troops" metaphor. The Society's historiography confirms what its constitutional organization leads one to expect, that at the very ends of the earth the "shock troops" of the Counter Reformation were a simple extension of the will of Rome – of their general, and by extension under the fourth vow, of the pope.

A cursory glance at the sources makes clear that this understanding has some grounding in fact. The awesome powers the Constitutions allocate to the general clearly suggest this. Ignatius himself esteemed most highly "the purity and perfection of obedience together with the true resignation of our wills and the abnegation of our understanding," and the Constitutions directed that Jesuits "should permit themselves to be

[35] Anton Huonder, "Eine Todesfahrt," *Die Katholische Missionen* (1918–19), 77.
[36] Letter of Fray Juan Garcia, OP, 1632, in Emma Helen Blair and James Alexander Robertson, *The Philippine Islands, 1493–1803* (Cleveland: A. H. Clark, 1903–9), 14.274.
[37] WB Nr. 27.
[38] See Rainer A. Müller, "Schul- und Bildungsorganisation im 16. Jahrhundert: Die Canisianische Kolegienpolitik," in *Petrus Canisius SJ (1521–1597) Humanist und Europäer*, ed. Rainer Berndt (Berlin: Akademie Verlag, 2000), 260–1.
[39] Marquis de Villa Puente, Mexico, to Jozé Pires [provincial of Japan], March 24, 1725, BA/JA/49-V-28. fols. 208v.
[40] Alden, 10.

moved and directed under divine providence by their Superiors just as if they were a corpse, which allows itself to be moved and handled in any way."[41] The Constitutions allowed that a Jesuit did not have to obey orders to sin, though this has, at least since the time of historian Jules Michelet (1798–1874), been mistranslated to suggest an obedience that includes even a willingness to sin.[42] In one sentence, a missionary uses the same Latin verb, *evocare*, to describe a missionary first *called* to the mission by order of the Jesuit general, and, second, *called* from this life to a better one by God.[43] This gives some sense of the authority of the general.

Numerous colourful anecdotes supplement these official documents in showing the emphasis on obedience. The austere Jesuit Alonzo Rodriguez declined soup prepared especially for him while he suffered from an illness. Ordered to consume "the whole dish [*escudella*]," the obedient, and literal-minded, priest consumed the soup and began to gnaw the wooden soup bowl itself.[44]

Examples of disobedience, however, can match these in number, if not in dramatic flair. When Grueber, returning to Europe, reached Agra, he needed a companion, Heinrich Roth (1620–68), who was unable to desert his post without his provincial superiors' permission, the *expressa superiorum licentia*. Roth's immediate superior advised him to go anyway.[45] In 1644 Schall disobeyed his superiors' orders to flee Beijing before the advancing Manchu.[46] The Franciscan Antonio Caballero de Santa María told of a Jesuit who disobeyed orders to remove him from China, and even sent a memorial to the general declaring his refusal to

---

[41] Ignatius of Loyola, "On Perfect Obedience," Rome, March 26, 1553 (accessed April 9, 2004), http://www.georgetown.edu/centers/woodstock/ignatius/letter25.htm; *Constitutions*, 245–49 [part VI, ch. 1, sec. 1, par. 547–550]. See Joseph de Guibert, *La spiritualité de la Compagnie de Jésus; esquisse historique*, ed. Edmond Lamalle, Bibliotheca Instituti Historici S.I. 4 (Rome: Institutum Historicum S. I., 1953), 163.

[42] *Constitutions*, VI.v. For example, Monod, "in his introduction to Böhmer's essay on the Jesuits ("Les jesuites," Paris, 1910, p. 13, 14) recalls how Michelet mistranslated the words of the Constitutions, p. VI, c. 5, 'obligationem ad peccatum,' and made it appear that they require obedience even to the commission of sin, as if the text were *obligatio ad peccandum*, where the obvious meaning and purpose of the text is precisely to show that the transgression of the rules is not in itself sinful." J. H. Pollen, "The Society of Jesus," *The Catholic Encyclopedia* (September 15, 2003). http://www.newadvent.org/cathen/ (Accessed May 7, 2004).

[43] Petrus Thomas Van Hamme, Beijing, to Conrad Janning, October 15, 1702. BRB 16691/16693, fol. 52r.

[44] Walter Walsh, *The Jesuits in Great Britain: An Historical Inquiry into Their Political Influence* (London: G. Routledge & Sons, 1903), 299.

[45] Wessels, "New Documents," 296.

[46] Dunne, *Generation*, 320–1.

battle against the rival friars.[47] Disobedience was born of necessity. The criticism against one provincial of Aquitaine that "on many occasions he does not know [the Constitutions], and it seems that he has never seen them, even though he has them in his room" could apply to many Jesuits.[48]

Jesuit disobedience reached the highest levels of the hierarchy, outraging even the papacy, to which the Society's ranking members theoretically owed a special obedience. As Astráin once pointed out, timely pontifical deaths frequently saved the Jesuits from the necessity to disobey.[49] Sometimes they were not as fortunate, as during the tumultuous pontificate of Innocent X (1644–55). An inquiry from Bishop Palafox prompted the pope to reaffirm that even the Jesuits had to obey those Tridentine decrees empowering the episcopacy.[50] When the papacy decided that the only Jesuit lands to enjoy tax exemption would be the colleges, the Mexican Jesuits rejected the decision on the usual ground: It lacked the approval of Castile's Council of the Indies.[51] Incensed, Innocent railed against the "regular clerics of the said Society, repeatedly using many sources as a pretext to allege that Our letters are not justified." The Jesuits' appeal to state against church rang hollow when King Philip IV of Spain (r. 1621–65) agreed with the pope.[52]

The forty-three painfully explicit, specific, and technically redundant stipulations that a decree of Innocent X applied to "the Society too" ["*etiam Societas*"][53] were necessary to bring to heel a China Vice-province that did not suffer direction from Rome lightly. This was not merely the paranoia of the curial chancellery. Clear though not unqualified, the bull reached China only to be sidestepped, and the situation worsened. On October 11, 1704, Pope Clement XI (1700–21) wrote General Michelangelo Tamburini (1706–30), demanding that the general allow no more

[47] J. S. Cummins, "Two Missionary Methods in China: Mendicants and Jesuits," *Archivo Ibero-Americano* 38 (1978): 54.
[48] ARSI Gall. 88, fol. 112–112v, quoted in Martin, *Jesuit*, 106.
[49] Lewy, 148, 150.
[50] Juan de Palafox y Mendoza, *Obras del ilustrissimo, excelentissimo y venerable siervo de Dios, don Juan Palafox y Mendoza* (Madrid: Imprenta de Gabriel Ramirez, 1762), XII.301.
[51] Ibid., XII.295. Charles E. Simmons, "Palafox and His Critics: Reappraising a Controversy," *The Hispanic American Historical Review* 46 (1966): 402.
[52] Palafox, *Obras*, XII.312–3.
[53] Whether the words "etiam Societatis Iesu" is an empty formula has been debated, as by Alexandre Brou, *Les Jésuites de la légende* (Paris: Victor Retaux, 1906–7), II.55 and Camille de Rochemonteix, *Les Jésuites et la Nouvelle-France au xvne siècle d'après beaucoup de documents inédits* (Paris: Letouzey et Ané, 1895–1896), I.xliii. "Etiam Societatis Iesu" appears in Clement X's bull "Illius qui caritas" of December 23, 1673. See Rafael Moya, "Hacia una participación fructosa de los religiosos en las misiones de Propaganda," in *Sacrae Congregationis de Propaganda Fide Memoria rerum* (Rome: Herder, 1971–6), vol. I/1.462.

perverse (*sinistras*) distortions of the pope's will, and threatening him with excommunication. On November 20, Tamburini responded by asserting on behalf of the Society a blind obedience [*obedientiam caecam*] to the pope. Desperate to be believed, the general delivered the memorial in person, accompanied by the upper Jesuit leadership. Tamburini promised that papal pronouncements of 1704 and 1710 would be obeyed, and he rejected in advance any Jesuit who might cleverly misinterpret this declaration of obedience. When the general begged the pope to believe his promise of the Vice-province's loyalty, probably neither man would have given much credence to historians' idea of a Society exemplary in its obedience to Rome.[54]

Several historians now recognize the extent and nature of Jesuit disobedience. Some trace this back to the Society's founder. As John Bossy remarked of Ignatius, "few religious superiors can have told members of their order so firmly to forget the rules and do what they thought best."[55] In 1549 Ignatius offered Nicolás Bobadilla (1511–90) a choice of three missions, "that you do as you please," because he knew ordering his subordinate to do something was pointless.[56] Speaking of a "psychological tendency . . . towards liberty" among the rank-and-file Jesuits, A. Lynn Martin has argued that Jesuit training actually "produced men who would be less inclined toward blind obedience."[57]

There are two further explanations for Jesuit disobedience and a more decentralized Society, one constitutional and one geographical.

First, the perceived authority of the general advanced the development of a constitutionalist movement. A Jesuit's letter to a superior, if marked "*soli*" on the envelope, would be opened only by the addressee, thus allowing a subordinate to go directly to the top, for in theory the general was immediately superior to all Jesuits. Rome had been selected for the Jesuit headquarters more for expediency than for ecclesiastical reasons, and unlike the Dominican masters-general, the Jesuit superior generals

---

[54] J. B. Goetstouwers, ed., *Synopsis historiae Societatis Jesu* (Leuven: Typis ad Sancti Alphonsi, 1950), 282. See also Jonathan I. Israel, *Race, Class, and Politics in Colonial Mexico, 1610–1670* (Oxford: Oxford University Press, 1975), 242; Cummins, *Question*, 82.

[55] John Bossy, "Postscript" in H. Outram Evennett, *The Spirit of the Counter-Reformation* (Cambridge: Cambrige University Press, 1968), 130. See also the instructions to Oliver Manare in Guibert, *La spiritualité*, 89, and Ignatius of Loyola, *Monumenta Ignatiana, ex autographis vel ex antiquioribus exemplis collecta, series prima: Sancti Ignatii de Loyola Societatis Jesu fundatoris epistolae et instructiones*, Monumenta Historica Societatis Jesu 40 (Rome: [Institum historicum S. I.], 1964–68), XI.542.

[56] Jean Lacouture, *Jesuits: A Multibiography*, trans. by Jeremy Leggatt (Washington, D.C.: Counterpoint, 1995), 86.

[57] A. Lynn Martin, "The Jesuit Mystique," *The Sixteenth Century Journal* 4.1 (1973): 33–35.

rarely left Italy.[58] Thus Rome was overwhelmingly dependent on the support, information, and goodwill of provincial officials around the world,
and although the general appointed the provincials, he necessarily relied
on the recommendations of the candidate's peers, mostly non-Romans.[59]
Generals Laínez and Francis Borgia (1565–72) in particular were absent
from Rome for long periods of time and so could not be overly concerned
with the careful selection of missionaries from the applicants.[60]

The superior general's centralized authority was most directly challenged in a series of constitutional crises.[61] The origins of these disputes
date back to the tenure of Spain's first provincial, Antonio de Araoz
(1515–73), the nephew of Ignatius' sister-in-law Magdalena de Araoz.
The would-be reformer called for a broad limitation of the general's
power and length of office, for the Spanish provincial to be elected by
the Spanish province, and for the creation of the office of a deputy (or
vicar-) general, resident in Spain, who would enjoy the powers of the
general in matters pertaining to the Spanish province.[62]

These sentiments survived Araoz's death to simmer under the tenures
of Mercurian (1573–80) and Aquaviva, the Society's first non-Spanish
generals. Philip II, said to want for Spain "much religion and few religious" – few members of religious orders, that is – lent his support to the
Spanish opposition against Rome, and the Spanish Dominicans' and the
Inquisition's hostility toward the Jesuits' special privileges encouraged
the revolt.[63] Although Pope Sixtus V (1585–90) generally supported the
Jesuits against Philip, he offered a concession in sending José de Acosta,
just back from the New World, to Spain to command the Spanish Jesuits
to obey even those royal decrees unconfirmed and unauthorized by Rome.
The conflict climaxed with the Fifth General Congregation (1593–94),
called by Pope Clement VIII (1592–1605) without consulting, much less
soliciting the approval of, General Aquaviva. The real motive force behind
this move was Philip, who secretly exercised his will in Rome through
the machinations of his agent Acosta, whose mission to Spain proved to

---

[58] Cummins, *Question*, 126; Alden, 9; *Constitutions*, 291 [part VIII, ch. 1, sec. 7, par. 668];
Lacouture, 64.

[59] Alden, 9.

[60] Josef Wicki, "Liste der Jesuiten-Indienfahrer, 1541–1758," in *Portugiesische Forschungen der Görresgesellschaft*, Aufsätze zur portugiesischen Kulturgeschichte 7 (Münster:
Aschendorffsche Verlagsbuchhandlung, 1967), 253.

[61] Lewy gives a generally better-balanced account than most historians, such as Pastor
who follows Astráin closely. Pastor, XXI.157; Antonio Astráin, *Historia de la Compañia
de Jesús en la Asistencia de España* (Madrid: 1909–25), III.372–77.

[62] Lewy, 146; Astráin, 103; Heinrich Boehmer, *The Jesuits: An Historical Study*, trans. Paul
Zeller Strodach (Philadelphia: Castle Press, 1928), 92.

[63] Roger Bigelow Merriman, *The Rise of the Spanish Empire in the Old World and in the New*
(New York: Cooper Square Publishers, 1962), IV.63.

be all too conciliatory.[64] Spanish dissidents used the Congregation, the first assembled during the lifetime of a sitting general, to decentralize the Society by shifting certain powers from the superior general to the provincial congregations. General Aquaviva succeeded in overriding their will; he was generally exonerated, with his authority left intact. It was not, however, a total victory for the independence of the Society, and the Congregation agreed to a papal proposal that future General Congregations meet every six years.[65]

The crisis outlived the Congregation. Spanish Jesuit Hernando de Mendoza's manoeuvrings nearly forced Aquaviva to move to Spain under papal orders (1604), an event which could have initiated a "Babylonian Captivity" of the Society somewhat akin to the Avignon papacy. Mendoza's failure earned him a punitive promotion to the Bishopric of Cuzco in Peru.[66] Memorials calling for curtailing the general's authority arrived at the Fifth General Congregation from beyond Iberia.[67] The Jesuit historian Juan de Mariana's (1536–1624) *Discurso de las enfermedades de la Compañía* [*Discourse on the Maladies of the Company*] (1625) made clear the continuing alienation felt in Spain.[68]

The great champions of the old Society in this dispute were the Germans, including Emperor Rudolf II (r. 1576–1612) and Duke William of Bavaria, who both wrote letters insisting that the Jesuits ensured Catholicism's survival.[69] When the Eighth General Congregation (1645–46) met to choose a new general, Innocent X asked it to consider a series of decentralizing proposals, including three-year term limits for all superiors and the election of provincials by provincial congregations rather than their appointment by the general. Faced with opposition from the Congregation, Innocent announced the implementation of term limits for all officials, save for the father-general.[70]

Geographical distance also made direct control by Rome problematic. The Constitutions themselves made concessions to distance. The rule requiring the general's consent for the dismissal of coadjutors includes an

[64] Lewy, 148–9.
[65] Padberg, "Congregations," 15–18; Lewy, 149.
[66] Lewy, 151.
[67] "Varii libelli supplices Summo Pontifici Clement VIII oblati a pluribus Societatis Jesu provinciis, pro reformatione obtinenda in eadem Societate," Liberius Candidus [Henri de Saint Ignace], *Tuba magna mirum clangens sonum ad Sanctissimum D. N. Papam Clementem XI* (Argentinae: 1713), 400–29.
[68] Juan de Mariana, *Discurso de las enfermedades de la Compañía: Con una disertacion sobre el autor y la legitimad de la obra y un apendice de varios testimonios de Jesuitas Españolas que concuerdan con Mariana* (Madrid: Imprenta de D. Gabriel Ramirez, 1768), 127.
[69] For example, William's letter of March 29, 1589 (Munich) in Francesco Sacchini, *Historiæ Soc. Jesu pars quinta, tomus prior* (Rome: 1661), 424. See Astráin, 476–7.
[70] Padberg, "Congregations," 22–4.

exception for "some very remote regions (such as the Indies)." Elsewhere the Constitutions allow that "in some very remote regions, such as the Indies, the general may leave to the discretion of the provincial to decide whether or not certain subjects should be admitted to profession without awaiting approval from here [in Rome] (since it would not arrive for several years)."[71]

Even with these compromises the Constitutions did not adequately recognize the decentralizing nature of distance. Acknowledging the importance of information delivered in person, it called for oral reports every three years, or every four years in the case of the Indies.[72] In India itself, even with this extra year, the stipulation went unfulfilled. A Jesuit provincial in Melaka wrote the general in 1565 about these oral reports, admitting that "this has never happened, and I do not think for now that it could be done, because the men who can inform are so necessary here that I do not think they can be sent."[73] Other orders took advantage of how great an obstacle distance was for the Jesuits. The Dominican China missionary Juan Baptista de Morales (1597–1664) explicitly made the connection between the Jesuits' work in distant China and their disobedience to Rome and loyalty to secular, and even infidel, rulers. When he arrived in China at Xiamen with Innocent X's decree against the Society, he personally witnessed the insubordination when the first Jesuit he met insisted that the pope was misinformed.[74] Earlier, Morales himself had sought papal approval for an extension of his own powers on the grounds of the distance between China and Rome.[75]

The generals in Rome depended on the procurators to connect them to the farthest missions. Even Ignatius seems to have recognized the situation when, in November 1547, he allowed Nicolò Lancillotto and the other Jesuits to select a procurator from India.[76] The following decade, when André Fernandes travelled from India to Europe as procurator, only the express command of Ignatius kept him from turning back after reaching Portugal. The missionary himself saw no point in visiting Rome.[77] Despairing of being able to use missionary letters to get a clear picture of the Indies, Ignatius in 1552 decided to recall Francis Xavier to Rome

[71] *Constitutions* 143–44 [part II, ch. 1, sec. 2, par. 208], 235 [part V, ch. 2, sec. 1, par. 517].

[72] Ibid., 294–95 [part VIII, ch. 2, sec. 1, par. 679].

[73] ARSI Goa 11, fol. 255r.

[74] Juan Baptista de Morales, China, [to Ignoli], November[?] 25, 1650, APF SOCG 193, fol. 358v. Ibid.

[75] Juan Baptista de Morales, Mexico, [to Ignoli], March 6, 1647, APF SOCG vol. 145, fol. 311v.

[76] DI 1.191.

[77] Ignatius to Jacobo Mirón, January 17, 1554, in *Monumenta Ignatiana*, VI, 204.

for a report.[78] The general informed Xavier, astonishingly, that the missionary could manage the Indies' business just as easily from Portugal.[79] The disruption this would have caused in the field, just to keep Rome up-to-date, would have been extraordinary. Only Xavier's death saved him from having to decide whether to make the trip. The connection between Rome and the Indies was so tenuous that the only solution to the lack of information was a deeply disruptive recall of the principal missionary.

The arrival of procurators from around the world was coordinated so that their stays in Rome might coincide. Aquaviva wanted the India procurator to leave a year early, so that he might recuperate from the ocean journey in Portugal and avoid crossing Spain in the summer heat. The India province also considered sending a replacement procurator, in case the first fell ill. One general suggested that an alternate procurator travel to Europe on another ship, to increase the odds that at least one would arrive. Still, Brazil refused to send a procurator in 1601 because the last one they had sent had not yet returned.[80] Further complicating the situation, European procurators arrived every three years while those from overseas came every four years. In an attempt to ease this confusion, the required minimum period between visits from an overseas procurator was lengthened from four to six years.[81]

Far from its centre, the Society did not look centralized at all. Throughout the seventeenth century, each college could acquire land without recourse to Rome. Even when General Gonzalez required provincial approval for land purchases in the Portuguese Assistancy – a sign of weak centralization – this never appears to have been solicited. Similarly, one general congregation's campaign against beards could not force Jesuits in China to shave. In the foreign missions even the Constitutions could go unheeded. Although the Constitutions required the provincials to report to the general monthly, Rome would receive reports from the more distant provinces sent only annually.[82] Similarly, the specification of three years as the normal term for a provincial was often ignored.[83] The first three vice-provincials of China (Dias, Furtado, and Aleni) enjoyed offices ranging from eight to fifteen years. The first vice-provincial to have the

[78] Xavier to Ignatius, January 29, 1552, in Francis Xavier, *Epistolae S. Francisci Xaverii aliaque eius scripta*, Georg Schurhammer and Josef Wicki, eds. (Rome: Monumenta Historica Soc. Iesu, 1944–45), II.287–88. See DI 3.3–4.
[79] Lacouture, 134.
[80] Leite, *Monumenta Brasiliae*, II.501–4.
[81] J. Wicke, "Die ersten offiziellen mündlichen Berichterstattungen in Europa aus den überseeischen Missionsgebieten der Gesellschaft Jesu (ca. 1553–1577)," *Neue Zeitschrift für Missionswissenschaft* 14 (1958), 261–62.
[82] Alden, 242, 287, 383.
[83] *Constitutions*, 316 [part IX, ch. 3, sec. 14, par. 757].

recommended three-year term was Álvaro Semedo, whose 1654–57 stewardship followed an earlier appointment to the same post, from 1645 to 1650.[84] Provincials at the ends of the earth held more power vis-à-vis Rome than Ignatius had envisioned.

This disparity between the reality and the aspiration to centralization was widespread in expansive early-modern bureaucracies. The royal administration of the Spanish colonies was also in principle centralized. No significant decision could be made without authorization from the Council of the Indies. Nonetheless, authorization, or even a simple refusal, could take years to arrive from Madrid, and lengthening delays created new circumstances that could excuse not following orders exactly.[85] As we have seen, the Jesuits shared with Spanish administrators both the circumstances as well as the solution of *obedézcase pero no se cumpla* – obedience without compliance. They could write Rome for further clarification of a directive, possibly sincerely, possibly as a diversionary tactic.

The Jesuit missions also departed from a centralized model through their facility for adapting to local circumstances. Most famously, in the controversy over Chinese rites the Jesuits argued, often against Rome, that local ceremonies honouring Confucius and family ancestors were not incompatible with the acceptance of Christianity. Practicality was favoured even in the few theoretical, and thus naturally centralizing, works that the Jesuits did pen. As Acosta advised in *De procuranda Indorum salute* (*On Attending to the Salvation of the Indians*, 1588), for example, "let us not prefer the idle ponderings of some amateurs to the experience and truth which actions teach."[86]

The Breakdown of Unity

National feeling proved to be the greatest obstacle to the Society's unity. This attitude was closer to the late-medieval proto-nationalism of Ernst Kantorowicz – a sense of *patria* as *corpus mysticum*, like the *corpus mysticum* of the church – than to the modern nationalism of Paul Tillich, where secular criticism has "dissolved the identity of religious consecration and group self-affirmation, and the consecrating religion is pushed

---

[84] See Dehergne, *Répertoire*, 318.
[85] Parry, *Spanish*, 276–77.
[86] José de Acosta, *De Procuranda Indorum Salute*, Collecion España misionera (Madrid: [s.n.], 1952), 48, 213. See also Anthony Pagden, *The Fall of Natural Man: The American Indian and the Origins of Comparative Ethnology* (Cambridge: Cambridge University Press, 1986), 198; Polzer, *Rules*, 46. Hausberger points out (*Für Gott*, 18) that Polzer does not mention *De Procuranda*.

aside and the empty space filled by the national idea as a matter of ultimate concern."[87] The nationalist sentiment of the early-modern Jesuits had not pushed religion aside. In Bossy's taxonomy of nationalism in the context of the Counter Reformation, this nationalist sentiment would be called "naïve," analogous to, but distinct from, an ecclesiastical or religious patriotism.[88]

Throughout its existence the Society of Jesus had to cope with such issues. Indeed, nationalistic tendencies fuelled the rites controversy, and thus led directly and indirectly to the Jesuits' suppression. Sometimes the Society was viewed as having special allegiance to one nationality or another. Paul IV (1555–59) was not the only pope to regard the Jesuits as members of a Spanish fifth column, yet the first Jesuits in Portugal were called the "Roman Fathers."[89] Farther afield the situation varied. During the early days of the mission, the Chinese referred to Jesuits as "Italians."[90] Those missionaries themselves, including Matteo Ricci, avoided the question of national divisions by presenting themselves as simply "European" – a cue Chinese sources quickly took up, referring to Ricci as *Ouluobaren* 歐羅巴人, "the European."[91] As today the people who most exclusively identify themselves as British live in Northern Ireland, so too in the early-modern world the true "Europeans" might be found in China.

The most salient feature of the Jesuits' naïve nationalisms was their divisiveness. Although traditional historians of the Society might consider it "absurd to suppose the existence of an order like that of the Jesuits divided for reasons of nationality,"[92] that was exactly the case. The minutes of the March–June 1539 Jesuit meeting in Rome exclaim "we were divided!" (*scindebamur*) followed by the explanation, "we were Frenchmen, Spaniards, Savoyards, Cantabrians...."[93] When Pius IV

[87] Ernst H. Kantorowicz, *The King's Two Bodies* (Princeton: Princeton University Press, 1957), 231–49; Paul Tillich, *Christianity and the Encounter of the World Religions*, Bampto lectures in America 14 (New York: Columbia University Press, 1964), 15.
[88] John Bossy, "Catholicity," 287–9, 294.
[89] Boehmer, *The Jesuits*, 105–6; Alden, 21, 26.
[90] Matteo Ricci, *Fonti Ricciane: documenti originali concernenti Matteo Ricci e la storia delle prime relazioni tra l'Europa e la Cia 1579–1615*, ed. Pasquale d'Elia (Rome: La Libreria dello Stato, 1942–49), I.cxli–cxlii.
[91] Chen Minsun, "Ferdinand Verbiest and the Geographical Works by Jesuits in Chinese 1584–1674," in *Ferdinand Verbiest (1623–1688): Jesuit Missionary, Scientist, Engineer and Diplomat*, ed. John W. Witek (St. Augustin: Institut Monumenta Serica, 1994), 128. See Cummins, "Two," 86–7.
[92] "Sería absurdo suponer la existencia de una Orden como la de los jesuítas dividida por razones de nacionalidad." Vincente D. Sierra, *Los Jesuitas Germanos en la conquista espiritual de Hispano-America*. Institucion Cultural Argentino-Germana 15 (Buenos Aires: n.p., 1944), 87.
[93] Lacouture, 68.

(1559–65) sent students of the Seminario Romano to attend classes at the Jesuits' Collegio Romano, one auxiliary bishop fumed, "It is intolerable to entrust the education of Roman youths to Germans and Spaniards, that is, to heretics and *marrani* [Jewish converts]."[94]

Such outbursts were met with exhortations against national loyalty, such as Castner's eloquent plea against a nationalized Society.[95] The hope that the Jesuits could prevail over national identity had been fostered from the beginning. To this end Ignatius had given a Frenchman charge of the Roman College, and assigned the Paris College to a Spaniard, and the Perugian College to a Fleming.[96] In 1569 General Borgia ordered his visitor, and the future father general, Everard Mercurian to "eliminate this humour" of national feeling that was incompatible with the "union of charity" in the Society.[97] Generals Aquaviva and Vitelleschi both urged that national loyalty be "drowned to death in the sweat sea of our holy Society" and that "the horrifying word 'foreigner'" be uttered no more.[98] Struggling against nationalistic rivalries within Sicily, Portugal, the Netherlands, and the New World, Nickel recalled that while Spain and France were waging war, the Palermo College saw a Fleming, a Lombard, a Castilian, a Frenchman, a Portuguese, a Piedmontese, and a Valtelline working together in perfect collegiality.[99] As Jorge Serrão, provincial of Portugal (1570–74), explained to Mercurian, the unity among nations was "*importantíssima*," and "there is no Italians nor Spaniards nor Portuguese, but perfection and the Company of Jesus."[100]

Each nationality had strong connotations, though the direction and strength of sentiment varied. Valignano, in effect, turned nationalities into verbs when he directed Jesuits in Asia to avoid "portugalizing" their converts. In order to bridge cultural divides the missionaries should rather "sinicize" themselves.[101] A common Jesuit locution in the Americas was to refer to the non-Indian population as "priests and Spaniards," incongruously partnering an occupation with a nationality.[102] This usage also

[94] Sacchini, *pars secunda*, liber octavus, no 22, pp. 303–4.
[95] "Brevis relatio circa adventum Patrum aliquot Gallorum in Chinam et gravissimas inde ortas dissensiones cum maxima infamia Societatis et praesenti adhuc totius Missionis periculo," Rome, March 1705, BNC FG 1247 no 5. fols. 1r-20v.
[96] Astráin 6.45–46. See Cummins, *Question*, 63.
[97] Martin, *Jesuit*, 115.
[98] Cummins, *Question*, 64.
[99] Astráin, 6.46.
[100] Francisco Rodrigues, *História da companhia de Jesus na assistência de Portugal* (Porto: 1931–50), 2.1, 333.
[101] Lach and Van Kley, *Asia*, I.800.
[102] Neumann, Sisoguíchic, to Gabriel del Castillo, December 30, 1696, AGI Guad. 156 fol. 29v; Eymer, "Declaración ante el Cap. Juan Francisco de Hessáin," Parral, December 9,

appeared in casualty reports.[103] In one instance a list of people specified both "priests" and "Spanish," suggesting that priesthood transcended nationality.[104]

Sometimes these preferences were founded on more reasoned concerns. Kino preferred northern European Jesuits for his missions in Mexico "because these climates are somewhat cold."[105] The Franciscan bishop of Beijing Bernardino della Chiesa (1644–1721) argued against the participation of German Jesuits in the China mission on the ground that their command of Italian would be insufficient, forcing Kilian Stumpf (1655–1720) to point out that he lived in Beijing with Italians who could translate for him.[106] In 1660 the Jesuit Jacinto Pérez requested central European missionaries for Chile for reasons of language and climate, "because on the one hand they have more phlegm than the Spaniards, and are thus more affectionate, and on the other, their languages are close to the Indians'."[107]

German Jesuits generally had a positive reputation. Both Adam Gilg's (1653–1709) letter requesting a foreign posting as well as the *Instrucción para los que tienen deseos de ir á las misiones de Indias* [*Instructions for Those Who Desire to Go to the Missions of the Indies*] cite Francis Xavier's praise of Germans as missionaries.[108] The Spanish mission procurator Juan Basquez, who escorted Johann Alberich (1586–1618) and Stumpf to the missions, was impressed by the Germans on the journey and wanted more of them.[109] By the end of the seventeenth century the creole Jesuits in Chile showed a greater love and respect for Bohemians and Belgians – far greater than for Spaniards.[110] On the other hand, several Germans betrayed a strong condescension toward other nations. Grueber remarked that the Portuguese in the olden days "proved things with few words

1699, AGI Guad. 156 fol. 916r; Haller, Satevó, to Gen. [Juan Fernández de Retana], December 6, 1696, AGI Guad. 156 fol. 1038v.

[103] "Certificación de los padres José Neumann, Francsico de Celada y Francisco María Pícolo," Sisoguíchic, January 4, 1693, AGI Guad. 156 fol. 1072r.

[104] "Certificación del P. Visit. Venceslao Eymer, P. Rect. Domingo de Lizarralde, P. Francisco de Celada, P. Luis Mancuso, P. José Neumann y P. Miguel de Ortega," Coyáchic, November 14, 1699, AGI Guad. 156 fol. 1034r.

[105] Eusebius Francisco Kino, *Crónica de la Pimería Alta: Favores Celestiales* (Hermosillo: Gobierno del Estado de Sonora, 1985), I.ii.1, 2, 6.

[106] Stumpf to B. della Chiesa, August 28, 1710, BNN (Cast. I) XI B-69, fol. 86v.

[107] Sierra, *Jesuitas*, 89.

[108] "Cuaderno de Instucciones para los misioneros de las provincias de Alemania," discussed in Pablo Hernández, *Organización social de la doctrinas guaraníes de la Compañía de Jesús* (Barcelona: G. Gili, 1913), I.347–9; Gilg, Český Krumlov, to Oliva, December 27, 1679, ARSI FG 756 Nr. 173. The Francis Xavier quotation is from Francis Xavier to Ignatius, January 29, 1552, *Epistolae Xaverii*, II.290. See also Ibid., II.349.

[109'] Huonder, *Deutsche Jesuitenmissionäre*, 14.

[110] WB Nr. 29.

but many deeds," while the "degenerate" contemporaries "roar like lions when they speak, but their deeds and actions are more timid than those of scared rabbits."[111]

Even the Germans were not universally loved. The Protestant Reformation's birth in Germany made their allegiance suspect and their preference for foreign missions over domestic unseemly.[112] In Mexico, missionary Joseph Ochs (1725–73) wrote in his diary (1755), "I was very much vexed to find that in their dictionaries the word *germania* means about the same as *gerigenza*, that is, rogue, gypsy, a vulgar language."[113] As late as 1750, António Gomes, the vice-provincial of China, would moan, "It is unbelievable that here the Germans govern; and if not for religious patience, I would be able to curse those who sent so many here; but as for those who are already here, there is no remedy but patience; but in the future they should be remain in Europe."[114] Subsequent history might have a silver lining in Gomes's eyes. At the time of Suppression, the German Jesuits deported to Europe were separated from their Spanish counterparts and interned individually in Spanish cloisters, to be sprung only by the enduring efforts of Empress Maria Theresa (1717–80).[115]

Franz Xavier Amrhyn's (1655–1731) guide for German missionaries, the *Documenta pro candidatis ad missiones Indicas* [*Documents for Candidates to the Indies Missions*], shows that national feeling was deeply engrained, even among those trying to uproot it. The missionary should encourage ill will neither between creoles and those born in Europe, nor between different nationalities. He should praise the Spanish and Portuguese way of life, customs, and character, and if this proves absolutely impossible, he should at least refrain from criticizing it. As he continues, Amrhyn betrays his own prejudices. The missionary should try, as much as possible, to protect the Indians from Spaniards and the Portuguese. The missionary should be friendly without singling out any close friends and without confiding his secrets, as "German sincerity goes poorly with the Iberian mentality." Elsewhere he mentions Spanish pride and untrustworthiness and implies their lack of education.[116]

---

[111] Bosmans, 63, quoted in Joseph Sebes, "Philippine Jesuits in the Middle Kingdom in the Seventeenth Century," *Philippine Studies* 26 (1978): 192–208.

[112] Cummins, *Question*, 66.

[113] Theodore Edward Treutlein, "Non-Spanish Jesuits in Spain's American Colonies," in *Greater America: Essays in Honor of H. E. Bolton* (Berkeley: University of California Press, 1945), 228.

[114] Rodrigues, 3.2, 136.

[115] Jaksch, 39; J. B. Mundwiler, "Deutsche Jesuiten in spanischen Gefängnissen im 18. Jahrhundert," *Zeitschrift für katholische Theologie* XXVI (1902), 623–4.

[116] Franz Xavier Amrhyn, "Documenta pro Candidatis ad Missiones Indicas," in Johannes Beckmann, ed., "Missionsaszetische Anweisungen aus dem 17. Jahrhundert," *Zeitschrift für Aszese und Mystik* 13 (1938), 208–9, 211.

There were indeed examples of interactions independent of national loyalty, as when Grueber spent legs of his travel on voyages with both English (Surat to Macao in March 1658) and Dutch merchants (Smyrna to Sicily in the winter of 1663–64).[117] Perhaps a Portuguese Jesuit would have been less ready to voyage with his nation's enemies. Valignano, who had a Neapolitan's aversion to the Spanish, who were ruling Naples, particularly sought to achieve a balance of nationalities in the Asian missions, mainly by bringing in Italians as a counterweight to the Iberians.[118]

Trigault's own distaste for national rivalry manifested itself in the broad range of the secular and ecclesiastical princes he visited. His fundraising efforts in Italy and Germany especially aroused grave concern at the courts of Spain and Portugal. What if sensitive information should reach the ears of princes not subject to His Most Catholic Majesty? During his first trip to Madrid, Trigault received a stern warning from a royal official threatening to prevent his return to China. This possibility would continue to dog his mission in Europe. Trigault himself remarked, "It seemed that I would be kept in Europe by several influential fathers from Portugal."[119] His preface to the Ricci diaries makes his position clear. Recounting the story of Ricci and his Italian compatriots meeting the king of Portugal before embarking in 1577, Trigault unexpectedly analyzed the king's comment, "How can I show enough gratitude to the [Jesuit] General, who gives us so much help for the Indies?" by focusing on the king's knowledge that "the Society is composed of groups of various nations under the standard of Jesus."[120]

Instead of emphasizing specific nationalities, Trigault thought more generally in terms of Europe. Indeed, he referred to his interviews with princes across the continent as his "*europea negotia.*" In part Trigault succeeded in uniting Europe because he presents himself not as a native of the Spanish Netherlands, but rather as a missionary of an international order returning from a tenure in a non-European land. In a letter, he proudly recalls being received by the duke of Parma "as if I were an ambassador from the king of China."[121] Trigault attempted to work around national loyalties by creating a world polarized between China and Europe.

Of course, Trigault held no illusions about Europe's unity. He left Cologne under heavy escort for fear of the Dutch, "whom I consider

[117] Wessels, "New Documents," 284, 297.

[118] Lach and Van Kley, *Asia*, I.800.

[119] Nicolas Trigault, "Litterae R. P. Nicolai Trigault ad PP. et FF. in China constitutos," in Lamalle, "Propaganda," 93.

[120] Nicolas Trigault, "Ad lectorem," in *De Christiana Expeditione apvd Sinas svspecta ab Societate Jesv ex P. Matthai Ricij eiusdem Societatis com[m]entarijs* (Augsburg: Christoph. Mangium, 1615), p. ii. Trigault wrote this preface January 14, 1615, well before he collided with Lisbon.

[121] Trigault, "Litterae," 92, 96.

treacherous." He did, however, condemn the lines dividing Europe into nation-states as a hindrance to his missionary work. Thus, when despairing of the wars between Savoy and Spain, and between the Archduke Ferdinand and Venice, he exclaimed, "May God pacify these disorders that so disturb the Church!" The Venetians underscored his point by capturing and imprisoning a Jesuit returning north from the seventh Jesuit General Congregation in Rome.[122]

Sometimes national differences found their resolution in an overarching Catholic unity. António Vieira ended a 1642 sermon calling for peace in Iberia so that the Portuguese would be free to bathe their swords "in the blood of heretics in Europe and the blood of the Muslims in Africa, the blood of the heathen in Asia and in America, conquering and subjugating all the regions of the earth under one sole empire so that they may come under the aegis of one crown and gloriously be placed beneath the feet of St. Peter."[123]

The bitterest conflicts, however, did not come from national loyalties. The controversies and animosities among Catholics ensnared the great names of the Catholic Reformation. Teresa de Ávila, Luis de León, Juan de la Cruz, Juan de Palafox y Mendoza, and even Ignatius himself all came to loggerheads with the Inquisition. In 1559 that institution arrested the primate of Spain, Archbishop Carranza of Toledo, despite Trent's approval of his *Commentaries*.[124] Indeed, the principal churchman at the finale of Trent was Cardinal Giovanni Morone, who, just three years before his appointment as papal legate to the Council in 1562, had been imprisoned in the papal Castel Sant'Angelo.[125]

Often such conflicts flared up between religious orders. The Jesuits attracted a heaping share of venomous hatred, and insults hurled against them achieved an impressive comprehensiveness. One author denounced them as "assassins, ferocious wild boars, thieves, traitors, serpents, vipers... filthy billy goats [and] repugnant hogs."[126] Even when subtle, these lost little of their sting. Bishop François Pallu used an encryption system that gave the Society the codename "Bernice," a name they

[122] Ibid., 112, 118, 119.
[123] Phelan, 120.
[124] T. M. Parker, "The Papacy, Catholic Reform, and the Christian Missions," in *The Counter Reformation and Price Revolution, 1559–1610*, volume 8 of *The New Cambridge Modern History*, ed. R. B. Wernham (Cambridge: Cambridge University Press, 1968), 62.
[125] John W. O'Malley, *The Fourth Vow in Its Ignatian Context: A Historical Study*, Studies of the Spirituality of Jesuits 15.1 (St. Louis: American Assistancy Seminar on Jesuit Spirituality, 1983), 19–20.
[126] Brou, 1.41–2.

shared with Herod's mistress.[127] Frequently grumbling about the Jesuits, the Domincan Juan Baptista de Morales (1597–1664) associated them with worldly things and bemoaned the division they had caused within the church. He pointed out the case of Juan del Espino in Spain, who had been thrown into an Inquisition prison because of his attacks on the Jesuits.[128] In fact, Baptista expected the greater struggle in China to be against the Jesuits rather than against the non-believers.[129]

This animosity ran in both directions. A 1675 Jesuit dispatch from Manila to Mexico gave a typical description of the Society's attitude toward the other orders. When the Dominicans came to China, their only work was to write against the Society. In the 1660s, when the Franciscan bishops and apostolic vicars arrived, they immediately began to oppose the Jesuits. The anonymous author repeated that neither their persons nor authorities had been approved by Lisbon, and so the Jesuits ignored this support from pope and Propaganda.[130] The Jesuits could also battle secular clergy, especially in the New World, where Kino wrote of the difficulties he had with the bishop in Guadalajara.[131]

The Jesuits' tactics went beyond name-calling. Jesuit intrigues led to the Franciscan Martín Ignacio de Loyola's immediate ejection from China. The friar, who was Ignatius's nephew, claimed that the Jesuits had deceived the Chinese authorities into entrapping him. The incident was not unique, and friars who managed to arrive in Beijing in particular did not last long. In 1634 Manuel Dias had Antonio Caballero de Santa María's own converts truss him up and remove him from the city. Three years later mandarin converts working for the Jesuits impersonated the authorities and "arrested" a pair of friars.[132] The China Jesuits clearly took to heart General Vitelleschi's order (1616) to "avoid giving hospitality to friars, on account of the possible danger involved."[133] The armed attack in 1623 of the Jesuits' lay allies against the Dominican priory in Macao prompted the defending friars to display a consecrated host in a monstrance from a high window. The order that came down to the

[127] Maggs Bros., *Bibliotheca Asiatica Part II: The Catholic Missions in India, China, Japan, Siam, and the Far East, in a Series of Autograph Letters of the Seventeenth Century* (London: Maggs Bros., 1924), 79, cited in Cummins, *Question*, 219.

[128] Letter from Juan Baptista de Morales, Mexico, [to Ingoli], March 6, 1647, APF SOCG vol. 145, fol. 311rv.

[129] Letter from Juan Baptista de Morales, Mexico, [to Ingoli], November[?] 21, 1646, APF SOCG vol. 145, fol. 300r.

[130] Anonymous, to Emmanuel de Villaboa, May 15, 1675, ARSI JapSin 163, fol. 9r.

[131] Kino, Villa de Sinaloa, to P. Prov. Bernardo Pardo, June 27, 1682, AHH México, leg. 278 exp. 5, unfol. "1r-1v."

[132] Cummins, "Two," 53.

[133] Dunne, *Generation*, 239.

attackers captures the tension between respect for a shared religion and hostility toward an enemy: "Genuflect and fire!"[134]

At times animosity between Catholic groups even overwhelmed confessional divisions. An archbishop of Dublin denounced the Jesuits as more dangerous than Luther and "worse than the Jews."[135] In the heat of the Rites Controversy the Portuguese, pro-Jesuit representative in Rome "in a tigerish rage had bawled at the pontiff" that he would rather recall his missionaries than accept the papal position – even if that meant leaving China to the Dutch Protestants.[136] In a letter to the vicar general of the Beijing diocese Carlo di Orazio da Castorano (1673–1755), Stumpf defined "our enemies" as Jansenists, Lutherans, and Calvinists – "any who join with sectarians against us." This in itself was an attempt to bridge the antagonism with the vicar general, who had amended his personal copy of Stumpf's *Informatio pro Veritate* [*Information on Behalf of the Truth*] with the words *lege Falsita* ["read as 'falsehood'"].[137]

This ill will was so ingrained that even ceasefires could spark shock and outrage. A temporary alliance in Mexico between Jesuits and Dominicans infuriated Palafox, who saw in this fraternal love only hypocrisy and opportunism.[138] The Jesuit province in Castile backed the bishop and strongly denounced the alliance.[139] Thus their hatred for other orders could even provoke controversy within the Jesuits themselves.

The perfectly unified Society remains a misconception corollary to the myth of the perfectly centralized Society. The Jesuits saw some of this animosity even within their own ranks.[140] Schall's animosity for Martini compelled him to connive at his expulsion from China, or at least do nothing to stop it.[141] After arriving in China, Diestel was said to have collected twenty-four different reasons why Schall himself should be incinerated.[142] The unified front appearing in most historical accounts of the China missions derives in part from the practice of burning all written opinions dissenting from the Jesuit party line. China remains perhaps the worst

---

[134] Domingo Fernández Navarrete, *Controversias antiguas, y modernas de la mission de la gran China* [partially printed in Madrid, 1679], 473–4, 609, cited in Cummins, *Question*, 169.

[135] *Historia Ordinis Jesuitici* (1593), quoted in Alden, 23.

[136] Arxo to the Duchess of Aveiro, September 4, 11, and 12, 1709 [property of C. R. Boxer], cited in Cummins, *Question*, 233.

[137] Stumpf to B. della Chiesa, October 21, 1717, BNN (Cast. I) XI B-69, 514; published in *Informatio* BAV Racc Gen Or. III 246 int 8, fol. 49v.

[138] Palafox, "Carta al Padre Horacio Caroche," *Obras*, xi.185.

[139] In Genaro García, *Don Juan de Palafox y Mendoza, obispo de Puebla y Osma, visitador y virrey de la Nueva Espana* (Mexico: Libreria de Bouret, 1918), 304.

[140] See Martin, *Jesuit*, 116.

[141] Dunne, *Generation* 332.

[142] ARSI JapSin 162, fol. 59.

case, but examples elsewhere abound.[143] The case of the Jesuit physician Johann Verdier (1649–ca. 1707) belies the notion that in New Spain the *patronato* afforded protection against any internal division.[144] In a passage excised from the letter collection *Neue Welt-Bott* (1726), the other Jesuits in Mexico call for his deportation to Bohemia, that they might "express their respect for him at a distance."[145] All this invidious cat-fighting explains Giovanni Battista Atanasio's weary remark to Polanco, "One can truly say that the Society has never suffered as much from others, whether heretics or not, as from its own sons."[146] Unfortunately the Society's policy of destroying records that reveal these disputes has limited the surviving evidence.

Clearly the Jesuits were divided, though historians may never know to what extent. John O'Malley has argued that the Society's model of the church was not basically institutional or hierarchical.[147] Alden, too, has enumerated the problems with the idea of a highly centralized Society: Why did China and Japan quarrel so much? Why was the Society divided by nationality? If the generals had the authority to send Jesuits wherever they were needed, why did China (and Mexico) have to send procurators to Europe to recruit?[148] Looking at the evidence, we see both the tendency toward centralization and the centrifugal forces opposing it. This was understood by contemporaries. Franz Xavier Amrhyn urged Jesuit missionaries to follow the Society's regulations so that a transcontinental unity could be achieved.[149] Something like this unity was achieved, but it was never perfect.

[143] Cummins, "Two," 58–60; Martin, *Jesuit*, 113.
[144] John M. Headley, "Campanella, America, and World Evangelization," in *America in European Consciousness, 1493–1750*, ed. Karen Ordahl Kupperman (Chapel Hill: University of North Carolina, 1995), 246.
[145] Eymer, Papigóchic, to P. Johann Walt, January 8, 1696, SUA Praha. Jes. III-419/3, fol. 224r-224v. This passage is omitted from the "Brief P. Wenceslai Eymer, der Gesellschaft Jesu Missionarii, aus der Böhmischen Provintz. An R. P. Joannem Walt, deß Profess-Hauses zu Klein-Prag in Böhmen Probsten," in WB Nr. 55. On the *Welt-Bott* see Claudia von Collani, "*Der Neue Welt-Bott*: A Preliminary Survey," *Sino-Western Cultural Relations Journal* 25 (2003), 16–43; Bernhard Duhr, *Deutsche Auslandsehnsucht im achtzehnten Jahrhundert aus der überseeischen Missionsarbeit deutscher Jesuiten* (Stuttgart: Ausland und Heimat Verlags-Aktiengesellschaft, 1928), 45–49; [Mary] Angela Blankenburg, "German Missionary Writers in Paraguay," *Mid-America* 29 (1947): 45–50.
[146] Giovanni Battista Atanasio, Andansa, to Polanco, December 4, 1572, ARSI Gall. 84, fol. 331r.
[147] O'Malley, "Mission," 9.
[148] Alden, 653.
[149] Amrhyn, "Documenta," in Beckmann, 207.

4   Imagining Global Mission

"I firmly assert that the highest art, which imitates reality itself, both expresses martyrdom in the martyrs, tears in the weeping, sorrow in the suffering, glory and joy in the risen, and fixes them in our hearts. This is indeed the substance of art."

– Jesuit art theorist Antonio Possevino (1603)[1]

As the previous chapter suggested, the Society of Jesus struggled to overcome the obstacles that their global and globalizing intentions created. The next trilogy of chapters pursues the ideal of global mission from its visual representation, to its internalization, and finally to its manifestation in the form of aspiration to missionary work.

Realizing the Global World

We can safely view the articulation of this global network at a remove of centuries. Such developments also impressed observant people of the time, and their responses give us a sense of their worldviews. Christian thinkers raided their traditions for the necessary metaphors, ideas, and justifications for comprehending the New World and the new age issued in by early-modern European expansion.

Writers signalled the importance of the discovery of America by locating it in the course of sacred history. In the dedication to his *Historia general de las Indias* [*General History of the Indies*] (1552), Francisco López de Gómara called it "the greatest thing after the creation of the world (excepting the incarnation and death of its creator)."[2] Gonzalo Fernández de Oviedo's praise for the circumnavigation of the globe exceeded this,

---

[1] Antonio Possevino, *Biblioteca Selecta* (Venice: Salacatius, 1603), II.545, quoted in J. P. Donnelly, "Art and the Early Jesuits: The Historical Context," in *Jesuit Art in North American Collections Milwaukee Haggerty Art Museum* (Milwaukee: Marquette University, 1991), 11–12.

[2] Francisco López de Gómara, *Historia general de las Indias* (Lima: Comision Nacional del V Centenario del Descubrimiento de America Encuentro de Dos Mundos, 1993), 1r.

for he ranked it the "greatest and most original event" after Creation.[3] How real were the new discoveries to the old world? Were they merely cartographical innovations?

Ideas of salvation played the key role in placing ultimate limits on the rapidly expanding cosmos. Medieval philosophers had hotly debated the possibility of a plurality of worlds, the *pluralitas mundium*. Thomas Aquinas, for example, allowed their existence within the *potentia dei absoluta* but not the *potentia dei ordinata* – that is, the dictates of His covenant prevented God from creating multiple worlds.[4] The discovery of America, the New World, stoked the debate, prompting López de Gómara to insist "that the world is one, and not many: as some philosophers think."[5] In his *Comentarios reales* [*Royal Commentaries*], "El Inca" Garcilaso de la Vega invited the proponents of multiple-worlds theory "to remain in their heretical imaginations until in hell they are disabused of them," but in the principal argument a plurality of worlds simply contradicted the divine plan for salvation.[6] What recourse had the inhabitants of an alternate world that knew not Christ's passion?

The early-modern globe saw what we view as modern and premodern beliefs coexisting without discomfiture. This era witnessed the transition in navigation from plane to spherical trigonometry, along with a heightened attention to spheres generally.[7] At the same time, however, Kino could still recommend travelling from Europe to China via the West Indies and the Philippines, and the return trip around the Cape of Good Hope, because the Primum Mobile, Ptolemy's crystalline sphere on which the stars are attached, rotates around the earth daily from east to west.[8] Sometimes the theological problems posed by the new world were quite practical: Must a cleric crossing what would become the International

---

[3] David A. Brading, *The First America: The Spanish Monarchy, Creole Patriots, and the Liberal State, 1492–1867* (Cambridge: Cambridge University Press, 1991), 34; Peter Burke, "America and the Rewriting of World History," in *America in European Consciousness, 1493–1750*, ed. Karen Ordahl Kupperman (Chapel Hill: University of North Carolina, 1995), 40. Richard Nixon used the same benchmark for a similar type of event when he praised the Apollo moon landing by declaring that "This is the greatest week in the history of the world since the Creation, because as a result of what happened in this week, the world is bigger, infinitely."

[4] Amos S. Funkenstein, *Theology and the Scientific Imagination from the Middle Ages to the Seventeenth Century* (Princeton: Princeton University Press, 1986), 140–5.

[5] López de Gómara, 1r.

[6] Garcilaso de la Vega, *Los comentarios reales de los Incas* (Lima: Gil, 1941–46), I.6.

[7] Francis M. Rogers, "Celestial Navigation: From Local Systems to a Global Conception," in *First Images of America: The Impact of the New World on the Old*, ed. Fredi Chiapelli (Berkeley: University of California Press, 1976), 688–91. Rogers also mentions that transcontinental airplanes are currently passing from the use of plane to spherical navigation.

[8] Bolton, *Rim*, 58.

Date Line read the breviary for the "lost" day? In fact, he is not so obliged, though the most fastidious, such as the Dominican Domingo Navarrete (1618–86), did so anyway.[9]

This time of fundamental changes for the globe saw fundamental changes in global mission. The early-modern world became decentred, and Jerusalem became deemphasized, a process that freed the missions from its centripetal pull. In our period only China would exhibit something like medieval Jerusalem's attractive power. Although disputed, Jerusalem's geographical centrality had long been acknowledged, as by the monk and pilgrim Bernard the Wise around A.D. 870.[10] This idea was understood to have a scientific basis. A column was erected on the spot where contact with the True Cross had affected a resurrection, and at noon on the summer solstice this column cast no shadow, thus establishing the location as being on the tropic of cancer. When Urban II called the first Crusade, he specifically cited Jerusalem's geographical centrality.[11]

Even a stylized world map from as late as 1535 can keep Jerusalem in her traditional home at the centre.[12] This map shows the endurance of the traditional world-view well after the discovery of America. Jerusalem remains at the midpoint between three symmetrical continents. America appears off in the lower left, balanced if at all by the only other part of the world outside the three continents – England, Denmark, and Sweden, the heretics' lands – perhaps suggesting a correspondence between the believers lost and the believers to be gained.

In contrast, an early example of Jerusalem's new position came with the 1459 world map of Fra Mauro (of Murano near Venice), which was commissioned by the king of Portugal.[13] Mauro's gigantic Asia edged Jerusalem off-centre to the west. Even such a slight caused concern, and the monk found himself obliged to offer an explanation: "Jerusalem is

[9] Navarette, *Controversias Antiguas*, 71; "Ratifiacion de verdades y retractacion de engaños, dirigida al entendimiento del Lector, no a la voluntad," BN Ms. 7522 p. 70, cited in Cummins, *Question*, 212.

[10] John Block Friedman, *The Monstrous Races in Medieval Art and Thought* (Cambridge, Mass.: Harvard University Press, 1981), 219–20.

[11] Alfred W. Crosby, *The Measure of Reality: Quantification and Western Society, 1250–1600* (Cambridge: Cambridge University Press, 1997), 25. Jerusalem is actually over eight degrees north latitude.

[12] "Jerusalem, die Mitte der Welt" ["Jerusalem, the Middle of the World, 1535], Archiv Geist und Leben (Munich), reproduced in Norbert Lohfink, "Zum Zion: Das Heilige Land und die Erkenntnis des Willens Gottes," in *Ignatius von Loyola und die Gesellschaft Jesu 1491–1556*, ed. Andreas Falkner and Paul Imhof (Würzburg: Echter, 1990), 73.

[13] Fra Mauro, world map (1459), <http://en.wikipedia.org/wiki/Image:FraMauroMap.jpg>, accessed May 1, 2004.

indeed the center of the inhabited world latitudinally, though longitudinally it is somewhat to the west, but since the western portion of the world
is more thickly populated by reason of Europe, therefore Jerusalem is also
the center longitudinally if we regard not empty space but the density of
population."[14] This explanation values people – and thus souls – over
space, even when it vastly overestimates Europe's population relative to
Asia's. Mauro does not make the modern argument that the longitudinal
center is arbitrary but simply allows the size of Asia to move it. In the
seventeenth century Jerusalem's centrality still had not disappeared. In
Peru, the Augustinian friar Antonio de la Calancha argued that Christ
had died on the cross facing west, foreseeing the future conversion of
the Americas.[15] Jerusalem was even considered again in 1884, when the
longitude that Greenwich straddles won the honour of being the prime
meridian.

Enveloping the world in their net, latitude and longitude did much to
unify space in a uniform way. Roger Bacon (ca. 1220–1292) had proposed them, and Nicholas of Cusa had employed them in his cartography.[16] Returning from Constantinople, Jacopo Angelo was shipwrecked
off the Neapolitan coastline, but managed to save a copy of Ptolemy's *Geographica*, which his 1406 Latin translation introduced to Western Europe.
Even if Ptolemy's book had not encouraged Columbus, it would still be
valuable for its system of mapping out the world, and for its lists, however speculative, of latitude and longitude for places in Asia, Africa, and
Europe.[17]

The accuracy of latitude and longitude mattered greatly for navigation, but rather less for global politics. Like the Portuguese in Brazil, the
Spanish in the East Indies spilled over the longitudes defined by the 1494
Treaty of Tordesillas, and improved knowledge of Asia later forced further modification to the boundary. For Alfred Crosby, the Tordesillas line

[14] G[erald] R[oe] Crone, *Maps and Their Makers: An Introduction to the History of Cartography*, 5th ed. (Hamden, Conn.: Archon Books, 1978), 53.
[15] "Antonio de la Calancha: Un Agustino del siglo XVII en el Nuevo Mundo," *Bulletin Hispanique* 84 (1982), 84, cited in Sabine MacCormack, "Limits of Understanding: Perceptions of Greco-Roman and Amerindian Paganism in Early Modern Europe," in *America in European Consciousness, 1493–1750*, ed. Karen Ordahl Kupperman (Chapel Hill: University of North Carolina, 1995), 96.
[16] P. D. A. Harvey, "Local and Regional Cartography in Medieval Europe," in *Cartography in Prehistoric, Ancient, and Medieval Europe and the Mediterranean*, ed. J. B. Harley and David Woodward, vol. 1 of *The History of Cartography* (Chicago: University of Chicago Press, 1987), 497; Crosby, 101. One example is a manuscript from a 1490 atlas by Henricus Martellus Germanus, the other a copper engraving dated Eichstätt 1491.
[17] Samuel Y. Edgerton, *The Renaissance Rediscovery of Linear Perspective* (New York: Basic Books, 1975), 97–9; Crosby, 97.

suggests the "Renaissance Europeans' confidence in the homogeneity of the world's surface even in lands and seas that neither they nor, as far as they knew, any other human had ever seen. They saw themselves not only as powerful enough to split the world like an apple, but as being able to do so in a way that was precise in theory and before long could be precise in fact."[18] How, then, were these new ideas and this new confidence portrayed?

Visual Expressions of Global Mission

It was a match made in heaven. Like the Society of Jesus itself, the Baroque style developed in sixteenth-century Rome before spreading – worldwide – in the course of the next two centuries. In the whole history of humanity, no time and no place has witnessed a mode of artistic expression better suited for the visual articulation of global mission. Naturalistic treatments of the exotic and the religious reached deep into viewers' hearts, and grand illusionistic ceilings drew them up into infinite panoramas that could both encompass and transcend the world. This chapter's treatment of the art of global mission attempts to function itself like a Baroque ceiling, making an argument by overwhelming the viewer – in this case, with examples. The power, prominence, and diversity of visual expressions of global mission demonstrate its centrality to early-modern Jesuit culture.

The question of the existence of a "Jesuit style" has long concerned art historians. A conservative approach is to speak at least of a new "formula for religious art," essentially its use as an instructional medium.[19] Bailey, however, has discovered in the missionary works what he calls the first truly global style in the arts, one immediate, approachable, inclusive, flexible, and inviting emotional surrender.[20] Correspondingly, Francis Haskell points out that the Jesuits "were above all missionaries," and this calling "gave a logical force to the ceilings of their churches that is lacking in most others."[21] We look first not at high art, but at the most natural visual medium for representation of the distances involved in mission work, cartography.

---

[18] Crosby, 106.

[19] Here in reference to Nadal's *Evangelicae historiae imagines, adnotationes et meditationes* (Antwerp, 1593–4), Thomas Buser, "Jerome Nadal and Early Jesuit Art in Rome," *Art Bulletin* LVIII (1976), 424. See Gauvin A. Bailey, *Between Renaissance and Baroque: Jesuit Art in Rome, 1565–1610* (Toronto: University of Toronto Press, 2003).

[20] Bailey, *Art on the Jesuit Missions*, 3.

[21] Francis Haskell, *Patrons and Painters: A Study in the Relations between Italian Art and Society in the Age of the Baroque* (New York: Knopf, 1963), 93.

Mapping the Mission

Expressing distance in a way that best facilitates comprehension, a map is supremely suited for expressing ideals of global mission. It is no coincidence that the early-modern world's great missionaries were also great mapmakers. Maps served an immediate and practical purpose for missionaries, for they located sources of water, natural terrain, and routes between mission stations. Such missionary maps sent on to Mexico City, and thence to Rome, also provided a graphic demonstration of their project's progress.[22]

In his eulogy for Kino, his companion Capitan Juan Mateo Manje (ca. 1670–1727) lists the Jesuit's glories as "discovering lands, converting souls."[23] Kino himself understood his roles as missionary and as royal cosmographer as complementary aspects of a single enterprise, and it was not wholly inappropriate that Manje lists exploration before mission.[24] Both purposes dovetail in Kino's depiction of the martyrdom of Francisco Javier Saeta (1664–95), centred dramatically on his 1696 map of the Pimería Alta.[25] The martyr towers over the Rio de S. Ignazio, with each knee resting on a church, with his feet gripping a bend in the river. The pose gives the illusion of depth, and literally writes martyrdom onto the landscape.

A second map, of Baja California, Kino sent on to Maria Guadalupe de Lencastre (1630–1715), the Duchess of Aveiro, along with a revealing explanation. "Your Excellency must pardon its small size," he pleads. "Perhaps through the help and intercession of the Holy Virgin María de Guadalupe His Divine Majesty will show me such grace that in time I may be able to send other and better and larger maps."[26] His hopes for the Virgin of Guadalupe's intervention with God on behalf of the missions parallels perfectly a request he makes of the Duchess, whose Christian name is María Guadalupe, to intervene with the king of Spain:

I beg also that . . . in Madrid you may arrange according to your pious and most prudent judgment for the promotion and conversion of the largest island of the world, filled with so many souls . . . and the natives of such good qualities that in no other part of the world can the many royal funds and the holy zeal of Europe

---

[22] Ernest J. Burrus, *La obra cartográfica de la Provincia Mexicana de la Compañia de Jesús (1567–1967)* (Madrid: Ediciones Jose Porrua Turanzas, 1967), 2*.

[23] "Elogio del Padre Kino por el Capitan Manje," reproduced in Burrus, *La obra*, I.193–4.

[24] See Kino, "Informe," Dolores, May 4, 1701, AHH México, leg. 278 exp. 39, unfol. 4v.

[25] Eusebius Kino, Map of the Pimería Alta (1696) (detail), reproduced in Bolton, *Rim of Christendom* (New York: 1936), opposite p. 290.

[26] Kino, San Lucas [Sinaloa], to the Duquesa de Aveiro, August 12, 1683, published in Burrus, *Kino escribe*, 213–7.

be better employed than now in this vast California . . . for I perceived that they had good souls.[27]

Perhaps the map most precious to Kino was not one he had made himself, but one he had brought from Bavaria. During his time there, the Jesuit Adam Aigenler (ca. 1633–73), Kino's mathematics professor, designed a *muy curioso* world map. The university at Ingolstadt had published Aigenler's map, which sparked Kino's desire to missionize abroad. The map sported a dedication to Ignatius and Francis Xavier with the epigraph, "the greatest service on behalf of the whole world." Kino's decision to take a world map with him to America shows its importance to him, and probably the map continued to inspire his mission work. Certainly, he did not bring it for navigational purposes, although he later noted with satisfaction that his professor had accurately depicted California as a peninsula, not an island – a fact Kino confirmed personally in his explorations of what we now call Baja California.[28] Aigenler himself later departed for the China mission.

When published far from their depicted locations, even local maps fostered the global ideal. The undistinguished cartographical history of Mexico's printing press encouraged the flow of maps abroad, and Rome was not the only European destination for Mexican maps. Although those that reached Madrid were typically guarded by the Casa de Contratación as state secrets, many Mexican maps found their way to wide publication in Germany. Indeed, Germany was the principal market for maps made by Jesuit missionaries in Mexico, before the Bourbon times drew France closer into the Spanish cultural sphere.[29]

The greatest impact on the progress of the missions, however, came from Jesuit world maps in China. Chinese visitors to the Jesuit mission in Beijing could admire an oval world map, probably a copy of Ortelius's 1564 rendering. Trigault recorded with relish the missionaries' earlier victory in breaking up the Sino-centric map and universe. The Chinese, he wrote, "believe that heaven is round, but the earth is flat, in the middle of which they suppose their kingdom is located" and that "their kingdom is limited by the same borders as this universe." To avoid offending this conviction, Ricci had taken care to make a world

---

[27] Kino, San Lucas [Sinaloa], to the Duquesa de Aveiro, August 12, 1683, published ibid., 213–17.

[28] Ernest J. Burrus, *Kino and the Cartography of Northwestern New Spain* (Tucson: Arizona Pioneers' Historical Society, 1965), 85 (index) and Plate II; Ernest J. Burrus, *La obra cartográfica de la Provincia Mexicana de la Compañia de Jesús (1567–1967)* (Madrid: Ediciones Jose Porrua Turanzas, 1967), 17, 155–6. The Latin epigraph reads, "*de universo terrarum orbe optime meritis.*"

[29] Burrus, *Obra*, 3*.

map with China in the centre. This worked, for as Trigault chortled, soon among the Chinese "most acknowledge that error of theirs and [were] amused."[30] He could take comfort in this alleged shift in world view because he had an analogous project in front of him – to break up the Eurocentrism of his audience and show the reality of China and the need for the salvation of Chinese souls.

Consider the pains Trigault takes to describe the latitude and longitude of China:

For towards the south China begins beyond the nineteenth degree of latitude, in an island they themselves call Hainam, which means the southern sea, and runs towards the north to the forty-second degree of latitude, to that northern wall by which the Chinese divide and protect their empire from the Tartars. In length, having begun at the one hundred twelfth [sic] degree of longitude at the Fortunate Islands, in a province which they themselves call Yunan, it ends at the one hundred thirty-second degree of longitude at the sea of the rising sun.[31]

At first glance, Trigault seems to be merely demonstrating the incredible size of China. Indeed, he often makes reference to "the great magnitude of this kingdom."[32] By placing China on a grid of crisscrossing lines of latitude and longitude, however, Trigault has quite literally mapped China onto the Europeans' world. By citing these coordinates, Trigault not only showed the distance of China from Europe but also made that distance comprehensible to Europeans. The forty-second degree of latitude which Trigault mentions also runs across Rome. Similarly, when Manuel Dias the Younger (1574–1659) and Longobardo designed a terrestrial globe in 1623, they prominently featured these all-important lines of latitude and longitude at every ten degrees. This graticule, no less than the painted ships sailing the oceans, reinforced the inscription, "Westerners traveled far and wide."[33] Chinese audiences could appreciate the underlying implications.

---

[30] Trigault, ed., *De Christiana Expeditione*, 5.

[31] Trigault probably makes an error, writing "centesimo duedecimo" for "centesimo secundo." Ibid., 6.

[32] Ibid., 9. This is by no means an isolated example in Trigault's writings. In another undated (c. 1624?) letter, he gives a similarly involved description of China's longitude and latitude ("Chinesis regni latitudo mathematica incipit a sinensis regni insula cui nomen Haynam in 19 gradu ab aequatore . . ."). In the previous paragraph he describes his journey between Europe and China in a manner similar to that used in his preface to *De Christiana Expeditione*, discussed above. Trigault, "Iter P. Nicolai Trigautii ex China in Europam et Chinemsium status," in Chretien Dehaisnes, *Vie du Pere Nicolas Trigault de la Compagnie de Jesus* (Paris: P. Lethielleux, 1864), 286–7.

[33] Helen M. Wallis and E. D. Grinstead, "A Chinese Terrestrial Globe A.D. 1623," *British Museum Quarterly* 25 (1962), 83. This might serve as an example of what Andrea Bacianini calls the *esotico accettabile*, an "exotic" that is "acceptable" because it is linked to the familiar.

Before departing, Trigault pursued another project which, though never implemented, distinctly reveals the missionary's own understanding of the new world. In late 1616 Trigault wrote, but failed to deliver, a letter to Pope Paul V (r. 1605–21), arguing that this exhilarating time for global missionary work necessitated the creation of an atlas, a *Theatrum orbis ecclesiastici* [*Theatre of the Ecclesiastical World*], that would show the state of conversions in each region of the world.[34] Although he did not provide details, the tentative title suggests that Trigault has in mind the *Theatrum orbis terrarum* [*Theatre of the World's Lands*] as a model. This pioneering geographic encyclopaedia by Ortelius had proved to be a tremendous scholarly – and commercial – success after its first publication in 1570. Although the *Theatrum* was never created, the same principle was realized in the world map of Jesuit Heinrich Scherer (1628–1704), a professor of geography at Munich.[35] Each corner features an allegory of representatives from one of the four continents hearing the gospel from a prominent Jesuit, either Ignatius, Francis Xavier, Patriarch of Ethiopia Andrés de Oviedo (1517–77), or Brazil missionary José de Anchieta (1534–97). Scherer peppered his world with radiant "IHS" monograms of the name of Jesus, a symbol of the Society since Ignatius had adopted it for his seal as general in 1541.[36] Each monogram represents a Jesuit mission, and the total effect suggests purpose, progress, and unfaltering growth.

Iconography of the Mission

If maps were the uniquely appropriate visual medium for expressing global mission, the most breathtaking visual expression came in the finer arts. Here, a more widely ranging artistic vocabulary nurtured greater creativity in representing the New World and the new world mission. Medieval representations of the earth dealt only with three continents. Typically, a circle (sometimes a square) would be divided up, with half assigned to Asia, and a quarter each to Europe and Africa. This division into three occurred after the Flood, and each of Noah's sons had become

[34] Lamalle, "La Propaganda," 64.
[35] Heinrich Scherer, "World Map," from the *Atlas Marianus* (Munich, 1702), reproduced in *Jesuit Art in North American Collections, Milwaukee Haggerty Art Museum* (Milwaukee: Marquette University, 1991), 68.
[36] Many interpretations of "IHS" have accumulated over the centuries, including "Iesus Hominum [Hierosolymae] Salvator" (Jesus the Saviour of Men [or of Jerusalem]), "In Hoc Signo" (in this sign [you shall conquer]), "In Hac Salus" (in this, salvation), "Iesus Habemus Socium" (we have a friend in Jesus). For Ignatius the primary, if not sole, association would have been with the first two and last letters of the name of Jesus in Latin or Greek.

the father of a continent, Sem, Ham, and Japhet of Asia, Africa, and
Europe, respectively. Similarly, the number of the kings at the Nativity
had been fixed at three since the third century, when each was meant
to represent a continent – hence one was represented as a Moor in late
medieval and baroque art – and so the entire earth was represented at the
birth of Christ.[37]

The discovery of America made all these obsolete, and a new idiom
was needed. By the 1570s the four continents had made their debut in
German and Dutch art. Personified into human form, they appeared
again in Cesare Ripa's *Iconologia* (1593), in which Europe's association
with Christianity allowed her the privilege of having the tokens of ruler-
ship as her attributes.[38] The number four has connotations of catholicity, as the world's directions, and winds, also numbered four.[39] Presumably, Ripa was cataloguing previous traditions rather than inventing a
new one. The attributes of the continents were never fixed, although
a crown, weapons, a church, or even a cross – despite the crucifixion
occurring in Asia – continued to stress Europe's pre-eminence, following Ripa. The others received exotic trappings and representative racial
characteristics.[40]

The four continents were frequently depicted also in secular works, still
with religious imagery, as in the Steineren Zimmer of the ducal palace
in Munich (1611–17). Images of the continents were ubiquitous, and
they even turned up outside monumental works. The Green Room of
the Prince-Bishop's Residenz in Würzburg still houses a baroque mirror
featuring the personification of the four continents, in which Europe car-
ries the cross. The four continents most typically surrounded globes or
adorned the frontispieces of books with geographical themes.[41]

One of the foremost connotations of this new world was religious, and
specifically missionary. Allegorical representations of the four continents
in connection with the world mission became popular in Bavaria, whether
in altars, in ceiling frescos, or on pulpits. The four continents could

---

[37] Hannelore Sachs, Ernst Badstübner, and Helga Neumann, *Christliche Ikonographie in
Stichworten*, 7th ed. (Munich: Koehler & Amelang, 1998), 168; Jutta Seibert, ed., *Lexikon
christlicher Kunst: Themen, Gestalten, Symbole* (Freiburg: Herder, 1980), 85.

[38] Cesare Ripa, *Iconologia; overo descrittione di diverse imagini cavate dall'antichita, e di propria
inventione [by] Cesare Ripa* (Hildesheim, New York: G. Olms, 1970), 333.

[39] John Baptist Knipping, *Iconography of the Counter Reformation in the Netherlands: Heaven
on Earth* (Nieuwkoop: De Graff, 1974), II.360–5.

[40] E. Kreutzer, "Erdteile," in *Lexikon der christlichen Ikonographie*, ed. Engelbert
Kirschbaum (Rome: Herder, 1968), I.663–4.

[41] Knipping, 361. For other examples of the Four Continents from non-Jesuit sources see
Georg Schreiber, *Deutschland und Spanien: volkskundliche und kulturkundliche Beziehun-
gen, zusammenhange abendlandischer und ibero-amerikanischer Sakralkultur* (Dusseldorf:
L. Schwann, 1936), 314.

represent the earth's peoples waiting for the Gospel, as is depicted on a chalice showing the Ship of the Church with the continents inhabited by pagans. The ceiling painting of the Benedictine monastery in Oberaltaich depicts the continents as animals pulling along Benedict's triumphal car, while four further scenes depict Benedictine missionaries working in the far reaches of the world.[42]

The allegorical figures of the four continents were used especially by the Jesuits. They were often portrayed as worshipfully paying homage, as in Matthäus Gunther's ceiling fresco for the Stiftkirche in Neustift bei Brixen. In the cupola of the Jesuit church in Mannheim can also be seen representations of the continents, probably free imitations after the work of Andrea Pozzo (1642–1709) in the Sant'Ignazio, discussed later in this chapter.[43] Another example is Giovanni Battista Tiepolo's fresco (1750–53) in the episcopal residence at Würzburg.[44] Cornelis Bloemaert's engravings for Bartoli's Jesuit *Historia*, which Joannes de Miele (Jan Miele; 1599–1664) cut in copper, depict the continents paying homage to Ignatius.[45] In Flanders the four continents appear in the support of pulpits, as they do in Antwerp's Church of Our Lady; indeed, a preacher's pulpit is an especially appropriate place for images with connotations of the propagation of Christianity.

While previously the world represented as a flat disk had served as an attribute of world conquerors, such as Alexander the Great, Constantine, and by extension Christ, after Columbus globes, orbs, and spheres came to represent the world and thus to play a role in expressing missionary zeal.[46] In Peter Paul Rubens' (1577–1640) *Triumph of the Faith* (1625/8) the church perches on a globe as if on a throne, in obvious demonstration of her authority.[47] Ripa had suggested representing Faith more aggressively, laying her right hand on a book while pressing down on a globe with her left foot.[48] The Jesuits also employed globes as symbols. One seventeenth-century German Jesuit's work shows God the Father holding

---

[42] Bauerreiß, VII.282; Kreutzer, I.663–4.

[43] Joseph Braun, *Die Kirchenbauten der Deutschen Jesuiten: Ein Beitrag zur Kultur- und Kunstgeschichte des 17. und 18. Jahrhunderts* (Freiburg im Breisgau: Herder, 1908), II.324; Emile Mâle, *L'art religieux de la fin du xvie siécle du XVIIe siecle et du XVIIIe siecle; etude sur l'iconographie apres le Concile de Trente, Italie-France-Espagne-Flandres*, 2nd ed. (Paris: A. Colin, 1951), 401; Schreiber, *Deutschland und Spanien*, 314.

[44] Seibert, 102.

[45] Knipping, illustration no. 112; Sachs, et al., 121; Daniello Bartoli, *Dell'historia della Compagnia de Giesu* (Rome: 1653), reproduced in Geoffroy de Grandmaison, *Saint Ignace de Loyola* (Paris: Laurens, 1930), 47.

[46] Sachs, et al., 121.

[47] Madrid, Prado; Sachs, et al., 237.

[48] Knipping, 349–50.

an orb in one hand, while pointing to a dove with the other.[49] Adriaen Lommelin (1640–75) took his inspiration directly from Abraham van Diepenbeeck (and, like Pozzo, indirectly from Luke's gospel) to depict the Church clenching a globe-earth above a blazing fire on an altar.[50] The text accompanying Lommelin's portrait of Francis Xavier explicitly compares the missionary to another world conqueror, Alexander the Great.

On the other side, a Protestant pamphlet from the early seventeenth century uses the globe to show Catholic missions in a negative light. Adam and Eve sit at the base of a tree, whose branches are all bent over to form a stage for the farce occurring above. A peasant, a knight, and a scholar literally bear the weight of the world on their shoulders. A globe presses down the three early-modern Atlases. Their plight is made far worse, however, by the Catholic monk desperately trying to dominate the slippery globe, in part by using the peasant's neck as a foothold to secure some purchase on the sphere. The others fare little better, as the monk balances himself by wresting away the knight's mace and bringing a flaming brand down on the academic's headdress.[51]

The fire motif was just as widespread. Lucas Vorsterman engraved a frontispiece for Jesuit Heribert Rosweyden's *Kerckelijke Historie* [*Church History*] in which the allegorical Church uses a torch to ignite lamps, which angels then pass on to East Indians and Africans.[52] In fact, fire is a variation of the divine light, which in an evangelical context was one of the most popular themes in German baroque frescoes, as for example, in that by Johann Hiebel in Klattau (1716–17).[53] Not every outstanding example of this missionary light in Jesuit art appears on a ceiling, and few could reach so widespread an audience as the frontispiece of Martini's popular

[49] Bayer. Staatsgemäldesammlung., Inv Nr. 10212. Beatrix Ettelt, ed., *Die Jesuiten in Ingolstadt, 1549–1773: Austellung in Ingolstadt 12. Oktober 1991 bis 12. Januar 1992* (Ingolstadt: Stadtsarchiv Ingolstadt, 1991), 11.

[50] Knipping, 349–50, plate 332. At least on one occasion Jesuits employed an actual globe to express their ideals. Working as missionaries in Szechwan 四川 when the rebel Zhang Xianzhong 張献忠 (ca. 1605–47) invaded the province in 1644, the Jesuits Gabriel de Magalhaens and Louis Buglio responded to his favour (which included official status and copies of "his own" poems) by making a sphere representing the heavens to give him. The implications of rule suggested by this gift are ironic, given that Zhang's kingdom would endure only three years until Manchu conquest. James B. Parsons, "Overtones of Religion and Superstition in the Rebellion of Chang Hsien-chung," *Sinologica* 4 (1956), 175.

[51] Reproduced in Jürgen Döring, "Weltkugel und Landkarte als Motive," in *Mittel und Motive der karikatur in fünf Jahrhunderten: Bild als Waffe*, ed. Gerhard Langemeyer, et al. (Munich: Prestel, 1985), 221.

[52] Knipping, 368; Max Rooses, *L'œuvre de P. P. Rubens; histoire et description de ses tableaux et dessins* (Anvers: J. Maes, 1886–1892), V.112.

[53] Hans Tintelnot, *Die barocke Freskomalerei in Deutschland: Ihre Entwicklung und europäische Wirkung* (Munich: F. Bruckman, 1951), 265. See illustrations nos. 19, 32, 52, 66, 72.

Novus atlas sinensis [*New Chinese Atlas*].[54] In the upper left corner, a sun illuminates the "IHS" monogram. The sun emits rays in all directions, but the most prominent beam aims down to the right, striking a mirror. A cross stands on top of this round dish-like mirror, the brim of which reads "*speculum sine macula*" ["mirror without blemish"]. The mirror is held by the personified church, a woman with the papal triple tiara perched above her long hair. She says, in words running above the ray of light, "ite angeli veloces ad gentem convulsam et dilaceratam isaiae xviii" ["Go, ye swift messengers, to a nation scattered and peeled, Isaiah 18"]. The reflection of the light from the mirror shines down to the lower left, where it ignites the torch held by a little angel. On a cloud underneath the sun stand more angels, holding a cross or a book, or presenting to the church a beaker of blood and a cup of flesh. Other angels, either bodiless or drastically foreshortened, appear to support the cloud upon which the church sits. Announcing, "clausa recludo" ("I open the closed places"), a man releases a door in the wall, revealing a world to another group of angels, who refer to a map of China on a globe, using a compass and a sighting rod. Connecting the Jesuits' patron to this new world, the door features the book's title, *The New Chinese Atlas by Martino Martini, S. J.*, and its dedication to Leopold I.

The most direct way to represent mission is, of course, to depict a missionary. The cult of Francis Xavier grew especially rapidly in Bavaria, and found expression in visual art, as well as in other devotions and confraternities. Francis Xavier was popularly known as a patron for those suffering from disease, and in southern Bavaria many a "Xaverl" was borne away from the baptismal font.[55] In the St. Peter's Church of Ghent a canvas by Nicolaes Roose shows Francis Xavier presenting Christianity simultaneously not only to the Chinese, but also to the American Indians.[56] At least by the eighteenth century portraits of Valignano and Ricci in Mandarin dress hung in the library of the Jesuit college at Ingolstadt.[57]

The sort of specific knowledge contained in atlases could also be pictorially organized around the figure of a tree, as in the genealogy of Saint Agatha or in the "family tree" of Mary designed by the Jesuits for Chinese audiences.[58] A parallel Protestant usage shows a hierarchy of

---

[54] Martino Martini, *Novus atlas sinensis* (Amsterdam: Bleau, 1665), BAV Barberini X I 46.
[55] Bauerreiß, VII.282, 310.
[56] Knipping, 368.
[57] Treffer, 1. See M. C. Osswald, "Die Entstehung einer Ikonographie des Franz Xaver im Kontext seiner kultischen Verehrung in den Jahren von 1552 bis 1640," in *Franz Xaver, Patron der Missionen*, ed. R. Haub and J. Oswald (Regensburg, 2002), 60–80.
[58] "Albero genealogico di S. Agata," incisione, sec. XVII, fondo benedettino, MDC; 聖母瑪利亞宗系像 BNC Mss. 72.B.299 進呈書像.

heresies, with Simon Magus at the trunk and a pope under the canopy with Muhammad.[59] The artistic representation of global mission most striking for its detail is Athanasius Kircher's (1602–80) "Horoscopium Catholicum Societatis Iesu," from his *Ars magna lucis et umbrae* [*The Great Art of Light and Shadow*] (1646).[60] The image draws on both the oil tree as an ancient symbol of wisdom as well as on the medieval tradition of the wood of life, *lignum vitae*, which dated back at least to Bonaventura and had clear associations with the crucifixion. The tree further suggests the great extent and tremendous growth of the Society, and gives the impression that this expansion is an effortless occurrence, as natural and expected as the growth of a tree.[61] A large banner cites a phrase from Psalms 51:10 (52:10), "sicut oliva fructifera in domo Dei" [as a fruit-ful olive tree in the house of God], but the more effectively deployed text is, "From East to West prayseworthy is the name of our Lord" from Psalms 112:3 (113:3). The repetition of this text in thirty-four differ-ent languages vividly reinforces its meaning. More impressively still, the entire image served Kircher in Rome as a universal clock, for "when a stylus was placed in each Province, and the device positioned vertically so that the Roman time was given correctly, the clock allowed the time in all the different Jesuit provinces to be read."[62] Like businessmen might rely on the clocks behind the hotel reception desks to time calls to Tokyo, London, or Paris, Jesuits in the garden at the Sant'Andrea al Quirinale novitiate in Rome could use sundials set to show the local time around the world for prayers, remembrance, and visualizing global mission.[63]

As we shall see in Chapter 6, the figure of the missionary and the figure of the martyr were close cousins. In these years, Jesuit representa-tions of martyrdom were unusual for coupling the geographically dis-tant with the chronologically recent – that is, for the featuring of exotic

---

[59] Reproduced in *Ignatius von Loyola und die Gesellschaft Jesu 1491–1556*, ed. Andreas Falkner and Paul Imhof (Würzburg: Echter, 1990), 100.

[60] "Horoscopium Catholicum Societ. Iesu" (1648), from Athanasius Kircher, *Ars Magnae Lucis et Umbae*, reproduced in Thomas M. Lucas, *Landmarking: City, Church, and Jesuit Urban Strategy* (Chicago: Loyola Press, 1997), 154.

[61] Jürgen Stillig, *Jesuiten, Ketzer, und Konvertiten in Niedersachsen: Untersuchungen zum Religions- und Bildungswesen im Hochstift Hildesheim in der Frühen Neuzeit* (Hildesheim: Bernward, 1993), 47.

[62] Michael John Gorman, "The Angel and the Compass: Athanasius Kircher's Geographi-cal Project," in *Athanasius Kircher: The Last Man Who Knew Everything*, ed. Paula Findlen (London: Routledge, 2004), 248–50.

[63] Peter Davidson, "The Jesuit Garden," in *The Jesuits II: Cultures, Sciences, and the Arts, 1540–1773*, ed. John W. O'Malley, Gauvin Alexander Bailey, Steven J. Harris, and T. Frank Kennedy (Toronto: University of Toronto Press, 2006), 93. I am grateful to Meredith Beck Sayre for this reference.

and contemporary examples and settings.[64] Thus, the walls of the recreation room of the Sant'Andrea novitiate depicted martyrdoms around the world, described by Louis Richeôme in his *La peinture spirituelle* [*Spiritual Painting*] of 1611. Here, Richeôme explained, novices "every day after supper... have a little time for honest recreation in which to reflect on what you listened to during the meal, whether histories, which are depicted on the paintings in the tableaux placed on the walls in great numbers, or on some other matter of edification, or honest pleasure." These images of Jesuit martyrs were selected to "push you softly toward your duty."[65] The cycle may have been expanded to include new martyrs as word of their deaths reached Rome, so that the recreation room functioned as what Bailey has called "a sort of trophy case for Jesuit martyrs."[66] The global range of the Society's edifying deaths made the recreation room itself global. Richeôme marvelled that "in an instant" a novice could travel from Asia to America, "without leaving the harbour of this room."[67] The ultimate effect on the novices is easy to imagine. Rodolfo Acquaviva (1550–1583) had probably seen the first of these martyrdom images when he was training at Sant'Andrea. A large representation of his own murder in Goa would soon hang from the same walls.

More influential were the late sixteenth-century Jesuit-sponsored ambulatory frescos of Santo Stefano Rotondo, focussing on the early church's martyrdoms. No description can surpass that by Charles Dickens, who saw in these edifying deaths "such a panorama of horror and butchery" that "no man could imagine in his sleep, though he were to eat a whole pig raw, for supper."[68] These images found new life – and new, global mobility – when they were reproduced as a series of engravings. Copies were sent "far and wide, even to the Indies, that the infamy of this most disastrous persecution [in England], the phrenzied rage of the heretics, the unconquerable firmness of the Catholics, may be known everywhere."[69] Through these prints, the frescos could trumpet dying for

---

[64] Bailey, *Between*, 66; Brad Gregory, *Salvation at Stake: Christian Martyrdom in Early Modern Europe* (Cambridge, Mass.: Harvard University Press, 1999), 303–307; Mâle, *L'art religieux*, 118–20; Brockey, 227–28. For an argument against martyrdom representations as characteristically Jesuit, see Alexandra Herz, "Imitators of Christ: The Martyr-Cycles of Late Sixteenth-Century Rome Seen in Context," *Storia dell'arte* 62 (1988): 53–70. For a discussion of the exotic in Jesuit art see Bailey, *Between*, 39, 108, 179, 269.

[65] Louis Richeôme, *La peinture spirituelle, ou, l'art d'admirer, aimer et louer Dieu en toutes ses oeuvres, et tirer de toutes profit saluterre* (Lyon: 1611), 153, 237, cited in Bailey, *Between*, 61, 67.

[66] Bailey, *Between*, 44.

[67] Richeôme, *La peinture spirituelle*, 191, 211, cited in Bailey, *Between*, 67.

[68] Charles Dickens, *Pictures from Italy* (London: Penguin Classics, 1998), 136.

[69] "Annals [of the English College in Rome] for AD 1582," in Henry Foley, ed., *Records of the English Province of the Society of Jesus* (London: Burns and Oates, 1880), VI.83.

the faith not only to those Jesuits studying at Rome's German-Hungarian College, but also to those actively working in the field, either among heretics or pagans.[70] The series' finale, "All Saints," vividly invokes contemporary missions by identifying martyrs who died in lands overtaken by Protestantism and suggests that missions were less exotic than universal. This bridges the centuries between the ancient and early-modern martyrdoms. Other Jesuit churches in Rome featured similar images, but the trend was not limited to Italy. Work began in the St. Michael's Church in Munich for a monument to three Japanese martyrs, Paul Miki, John Gato, and James Kisai, soon after their beatification in 1627.[71]

Even the varied motifs outlined above do not exhaust the iconographic strategies for representing global mission. The very inclusion of exotic peoples shows the church's expansion, as on the cover of Cornelius Hazart's *Catholisches Christenthum* [*Catholic Christendom*], which features a Mughal, an American Indian, and a Chinese before a personified Church wearing the papal tiara and cupids bearing a shield with the IHS motif. The Jesuit church in Landshut combined a variety of traditions, including Ignatius sending Francis Xavier out to the missions, the martyrdoms in Japan, and a mission ship bearing the IHS on its sail.[72] In the 1663 *Crônica da Companhia de Jesus no Brasil* [*Chronicle of the Society of Jesus in Brazil*] by Simão Vasconcellos, a frontispiece also portrays the Society as a ship, emphasizing the activities of the Jesuits overseas. Letters on one sail proudly boast, "Unus Non Sufficit Orbis" – one world is not enough.[73] One world, however, would have to suffice the Jesuits. It is clear from all the examples presented here that they intended to win it.

Because of Jesuit prominence in education, the various iconographies of global mission worked in concert to find visual expression in *Thesenblätter*, illustrated single-sheet records of theses that were defended by one or more students before a professor. These often also contained dedications, whether to living patrons or to saints. Although the genre has a long history, their publication became common during the course of the sixteenth century. One *Thesenblatt* engraved by Bartholomäus Kilian

---

[70] Kirstin Noreen, "*Ecclesiae militantis triumphi*: Jesuit Iconography and the Counter-Reformation," *Sixteenth Century Journal* 29 (1998): 682.

[71] Bailey, *Between*, describes martyrdom images, for example, in S. Tommaso di Canterbury (161–63), in S. Vitale (178–80), and in the St. Andrew Chapel in the Gesù (235–37). See Oskar Münsterberg, "Bayern und Asien im XVI., XVII. und XVIII. Jahrhundert: Ein Beitrag zur Geschichte des ostasiatischen Kunstgewerbes in seinen Beziehungen zu Europa," *Zeitschrift der Münchener Altertumsvereins* N. F. 6 (1894): 16.

[72] Schreiber, *Deutschland und Spanien*, 314.

[73] Bangert, 92. The church is portrayed as a ship in a 1657 Thesenblatt listed in *Jesuiten in Ingolstadt*, Kat. Nr. 197.

shows Francis Xavier being taken up into heaven, while on an oversized map a European points to Lisbon, and an Asian indicates India, thus showing the extent of the Jesuit's earthly travels.[74] This *Thesenblatt* was dedicated to Maximilian II Emanuel, presumably to attract the elector's attention to the student, his Jesuit teacher, and the Jesuit order, for they undoubtedly thought the idea of mission would appeal to him.

The *Thesenblatt* plate "Die Weltmission der Gesellschaft Jesu" ["The World Mission of the Society of Jesus"], engraved by Kilian after a painting of Johann Christoph Storer, was recycled for use by defendants from at least three universities: Dillingen in 1664, Freiburg in 1672, and Prague in 1705.[75] A group of saints stands on a cloudbank around Christ to represent the Jesuits' various tasks, as a 1672 dedication text explains. Peter and Paul represent the defence of the papacy, St. Catherine (patron of scholars) represents the struggle against heresy, and the martyr Ignatius Theophorus represents the confession of faith. The Society's great task, the mission, is represented throughout the work, and many of the usual motifs appear here. A putto holds up in front of Christ's cross a shield that repeats from Luke's gospel, "Ignem veni mittere in terram" ["I am come to send fire on the earth"], and indeed, rays of light shoot from the wound in Christ's side downwards to Ignatius's heart, whence the saint redirects this fire into the hearts of various Jesuits: Francis Xavier, Canisius, Aloysius Gonzaga, Andreas Bobola, and Andrés de Oviedo. Gaspar Barzaeus rests his hand on a globe, indicating his own mission area of Ormuz. The fire from Ignatius also illuminates the shimmering, immaterial IHS monogram, held aloft by two putti. An American Indian, an Indian from Goa, and an African prince represent the world's peoples. A centrally featured world map shows all the Jesuit mission areas on a heart-shaped cartographical projection under the motto, "Dei et proximi Amor" ["Love of God and Neighbour"]. Another motto identifies the heart-shaped world with the "Cor Viri desideriorum/S[ancti] Ignatij De Loyola" ["Heart of the Desires of the Man St. Ignatius of Loyola"].

Painting the Mission

Much of these visual expressions of mission occurred in the context of the princely patronage of artists. Most striking is Rubens' work for Bavarian

---

[74] Sibylle Appuhn-Radtke, *Das Thesenblatt im Hochbarock: Studien zu einer graphischen Gattung am Beispiel der Werke Bartholomaus Kilians* (Weissenhorn: A. H. Konrad, 1988), 11–18, 262 (n. 65).
[75] Ibid., 256 (n. 63).

nobles. In particular, he undertook several commissions for Wolfgang Wilhelm, the duke of Neuburg.[76] In 1613 the duke had converted to Catholicism, a move that had won him the promise of salvation, the hand of Maximilian's sister Magdalena, and alliances with Bavaria and Spain. He immediately gave Our Lady's Church to the Jesuits and commissioned three paintings for it from the Rubens workshop. The duke also used art to strengthen ties to Munich. In 1621 he requested an alabaster relief for an altarpiece featuring St. Michael, known as *archangelus Bavaricus*, the Bavarian archangel.[77]

For the greatest painted celebration of the global mission the Jesuits turned to one of their own. Born in Trent, Andrea Pozzo joined the Society as a lay brother at the age of twenty-two. The extraordinary perspective of his work in Jesuit churches at Turin and Mondovì led General Oliva, who had personally seen his paintings, to call Pozzo to Rome. Arriving only after Oliva's death, Pozzo found himself without a patron, and so accepted lowly duties doing decorations for festivals and *teatra sacra* until a stage set he had constructed out of rags thrilled Rome.[78] Just as fame came to Pozzo, the Duke of Savoy, his former employer, recalled the artist to decorate a gallery. Pozzo begged Charles de Noyelle, the new general, to force him to stay in Rome, but the Society could ill afford to offend so powerful a duke. Pozzo then went secretly around the general to the pope, who agreed to forbid him to leave. Despite the pope's admission of this intervention, the enraged duke blamed the Jesuits, and the Jesuits blamed Pozzo for the ruinous consequences for the Society's work in Savoy.[79]

With the church of Sant'Ignazio mired in financial difficulties, the rector of the Collegio Romano was eager for any kind of dome, or at least something temporary to fill the overhead space.[80] Unfortunately, neighbouring Dominicans of Santa Maria sopra Minerva opposed any dome, which would block light to their library. Desperation and necessity begat invention, and Pozzo conceived of a flat canvas with the perspective of a dome. In 1688 he stripped off the stuccowork ("more suitable for a kitchen than for a church," Pozzo grumbled) and began work on the

---

[76] Konrad Renger, "Ruben's Bavarian Altarpieces and Counter Reformation Propaganda," *Rubens dall'Italia all'Europa* (Vicenza: Neri Pozza, 1992), 21. See also Michael Jaffé, "Rubens before 1620, with Particular Reference to Aspects of His Commissions for the Company of Jesus," in *Rubens dall'Italia all'Europa* (Vicenza: Neri Pozza, 1992), 13–20.

[77] Ibid., 22–25, 28.

[78] Haskell, 88; Lina Montalto, "Andrea Pozzo nella chiesa di Sant'Ignazio al Collegio Romano," *Studi romani* 6 (1958), 668.

[79] Haskell, 89.

[80] Ibid., 89. Financial records are at ARSI FG 1239, 1345, 1346.

vault. Accounts vary, but he probably was painting the ceiling in the early 1690s.[81]

Continuing on the nave's real architecture, foreshortened columns surge seamlessly into an infinity of space rendered with an endless perspective. The four continents are all illuminated by the universal truth of Christianity, shining from deep space high above. Each of the great vault's abutments supports one of the four continents.[82] Fire or light features in each continent's representation. A small flame appears on the boss to the left of the Europe grouping, an angel bearing a flaming brand assists America in her assault on the giants of Idolatry, two cherubs at Asia's right shoulder bear a brazier, and another angel lunges over the African crocodile's tail to drive a torch towards a giant's head. Such fires complement the light shining down from above. The origin of these centripetal rays of flickering light is Ignatius himself, floating on a mass of cloud and angels, surrounded by clouds bearing other Jesuits at a respectable distance. One ray of light strikes a mirror emblazoned with the Jesuit monogram. Another, which must be centripetal on theological if not on visual grounds, extends to the Trinity, where the Holy Spirit's dove wings partially eclipse a new burst of light. Only the viewer standing on the gold disc at the nave's centre sees the four continents in proper perspective. Only in this Jesuit church in Rome does the proper ordering of the world become clear, for only here does the illusion of being at the centre work.[83]

Prince Anton Florian of Liechtenstein (1656–1721), sent to Rome in 1689 as Emperor Leopold I's ambassador, saw the ceiling and immediately requested an explication of the symbolism. Pozzo obliged, and also gave the prince a copy of the first volume of his *Perspectiva pictorum et architectorum [Perspectives of Painters and Architects]* in 1694.[84] Pozzo remembered finding his inspiration in the Gospel of Luke: "I am come to send fire on the earth; and what will I if it be already kindled?" He applied the words to Ignatius, whom he described as "a great instrument in this great work; having himself being most zealous in propagating the Catholic Religion, the Light of the Gospel through all the world." The figure of Jesus is depicted in the middle of the vault, and he "sends a ray

---

[81] Bernhard Kerber, *Andrea Pozzo*, Beitrage zur Kunstgeschichte 6 (Berlin: de Gruyter, 1971), 54, 69–70; Haskell, 90. See P. Wilberg-Vignau, *Andrea Pozzos Deckenfresko in S. Ignazio: mit einem Anhang: Archivalische Quellen zu den Werken Pozzos* (Munich: Uni-Druck, 1970).

[82] Andrea Pozzo, vault fresco of S. Ignacio, Rome, reproduced in *Church St. Ignatius of Loyola, Rome* (Rome: Chiesa di Sant'ignazio, 1991).

[83] A viewer standing on the same spot in late antiquity would find himself in the Temple of Isis, a reminder of imperial Rome's own centrality in the ancient world.

[84] Montalto, 673; Richard Bösel, "Pozzo, Andrea," *Dictionary of Art*, ed. Jane Turner (New York: Grove, 1996), XXV.414.

of light to Ignatius's heart, which then comes from that, transmitted to the various beasts arranged from the four Parts of the World, depicted by me with their emblems [*Geroglifici*] in the four imposts of the vault." Invested with this light, each part of the world "throws back the greatly deformed monsters of Idolatry, or of Heresy, or of other vices, which earlier had ruled them." The four continents, now made fertile by this divine light, send up into heaven a harvest of souls, who "either passed from Idolatry to the Faith, or from a faith dead for the perversity of its customs were returned to Grace" through the work of men like Francis Xavier. The name of Jesus is illuminated to show that "every thought, every affection, and every work of Ignatius tended towards nothing other than *ad Majorem Dei Gloriam*" ["for the greater glory of God"]. Pozzo speaks of the two most effective ways to convert the world, depicted on opposite sides of the vault – divine love, and the fear of punishment. Fire represents both.[85]

The missionary motif runs through much of Pozzo's work.[86] He also executed the painting *Preaching of St. Francis Xavier* (1672 Novi Liguri, Collegiata), a cycle of frescos in San Francesco Saverio, the Jesuit church in Mondovì (1676), *St. Francis Xavier Baptising Queen Neachile* (1690; Sansepolcro, S. Francesco Saverio), and, to the left of the high altar in the Sant'Ignazio, *Sending St. Francis Xavier to the Indies* (1700).[87] He was clearly aware of his role in proclaiming Catholicism. Furthermore, the Jesuits' global network allowed Pozzo a worldwide influence. His popular *Perspectives* was translated into Chinese soon after its publication (Rome, 1693–1700), and the Jesuits' most famous painter in China, Giuseppe Castiglione (1688–1766), claimed to have studied under him.[88]

Because of Pozzo's work in the Sant'Ignazio, the visual representations of God's sending out divine light, illustrating "I am come to send fire on the earth," became very popular, especially in Germany. So too was the portrayal of apostles, saints, and angels spreading Christianity from a central figure – a personified faith, or the church, or the Virgin

---

[85] Pozzo, reprinted in Hans Tietze, "Andrea Pozzo und die Fürsten von Liechtenstein," *Jahrbuch für Landeskunde von Niederösterreich*, new series 13–14 (1914–15), 434–46.

[86] I disagree with Schadt (at 153, 157), who considers "*Verherrlichung*" more central than mission to the fresco. The artist's own explanation explicitly highlights the mission. Hermann Schadt, "Andrea Pozzos Langhausfresko in Sant' Ignzaio Rom. Zur Thementradition der barocken Heiligenglorie," *Das Münster* XXIV (1971), 153–60.

[87] Bösel, 413; Montalto, 671.

[88] Bösel, 416. See Elisabetta Corsi, "Late Baroque Painting in China Prior to the Arrival of Matteo Ripa Giovanni Gherardini and the Perspective Painting Called *Xianfa*," in *La missione cattolica in Cina tra i secoli XVIII–XIX: Matteo Ripe e il Collegio dei Cinesi*, ed. Michele Fatica and Francesco D'Arelli (Naples: Istituto Universitario Orientale, 1999), 102–22, esp. 109–11.

Mary – to the four continents.[89] After completing the Ignazio fresco Pozzo may have spread these ideas personally as he travelled north across the Alps to renovate the Jesuit church in Vienna.

An early example drawing more generally on missionary motifs is Hans Georg Asam's fresco ceiling in Tegernsee (1690), which depicts a Herculean St. Christopher bearing both the Christ child and a globe.[90] These themes flourished fully in Germany only during the next century. Mostly active in Bohemia, Moravia, and Silesia, Felix Anton Scheffler (1701–60) designed a representative composition, probably for a side chapel in the first bay of the north aisle of the Jesuit church in Brno. The surviving preliminary drawing shows angels drawing light from Ignatius's heart to the personified four continents:[91] An elephant and feathered headdress denote America; a horse and a turban, Asia; a crocodile and a spear, Africa; a bull, church, and imperial crown, Europe.[92] The lay Jesuit Christoph Thomas Scheffler (1699–1756), brother to Felix Anton and student of Asam, painted the ceiling frescos of the former Jesuit church in Dillingen in 1750–51. Their main theme focuses on the Virgin Mary as the Queen of Heaven and Earth; four frescos in the first and last sections of the nave support the ceiling's message by depicting Jesuit mission activity in faraway locales.[93] Franz Gregor Eckstein executed a similar ceiling fresco for the castle chapel at Krawarn (Kravaře), featuring Ignatius, the Jesuit monogram, and Africa.[94] For the 1746 fresco of the vision of the wounded Ignatius at Pamplona, in the northern nave of the St. Barbara Cathedral in Kutná Hora, the Jesuit artist Karel Kovář anticipates the global nature of the Society in a moment from the pre-Jesuit life of its founder by including an elephant, a horse, a camel, and a lion, along with racially distinct human representatives of the four quarters of the earth.[95]

[89] Tintelnot, 265.

[90] Ibid., 40.

[91] "Allegory of the World Mission of the Jesuits," reproduced in Thomas DaCosta Kaufmann, *Central European Drawings, 1680–1880: A Selection from American Collections* (Princeton: Princeton University Press, 1989), 67. See ibid., 66; idem, "East and West: Jesuit Art and Artists in Central Europe, and Central European Art in the Americas," in *The Jesuits: Cultures, Sciences, and the Arts, 1540–1773*, ed. John W. O'Malley, Gauvin Alexander Bailey, Steven J. Harris, and T. Frank Kennedy (Toronto: University of Toronto Press, 1999), 276–77.

[92] Gertrud Schiller, *Ikonographie der christlichen Kunst* (Gutersloh: G. Mohn, 1966), IV.108. See Ernst Dubowy, "Felix Anton Scheffler: ein Beitrag zur Kunstgeschichte des 18. Jahrhunderts," *Jahrbuch des Vereins für christliche Kunst in München* 6 (1925/6), 89–281.

[93] *Die Jesuiten in Bayern, 1549–1773: Ausstellung des Bayerisches Hauptstaatsarchiv und der Oberdeutschen Provinz der Gesellschaft Jesu*, Ausstellungskataloge der Staatlichen Archive Bayerns 29 (Weissenhorn: A. H. Konrad, 1991), 85–86, reproduced as colorplate 81.

[94] Detail in Tintelnot, no. 66.

[95] Karel Kovář, *Vision of the Wounded Ignatius* (1746), Barbara Cathedral, Kutná Hora, reproduced in Blanka Altová and Jan Kulich, *St. Barbara Cathedral* (Libice nad Cidlinou: Gloriet, 2003).

Finally, we turn to one comprehensive fresco that stands out as the most extraordinary celebration of global evangelization and also seamlessly represents a marvelously modern understanding of globalization. Its content, setting, and back-story are all global. According to tradition, when threatened by the Turks, the Holy House of the Virgin Mary was evacuated from Nazareth aerially by angels. After three years at Tersatto in Dalmatia, it ended up (again through angelic airlift) in Loreto, Italy. Recreations of the House multiplied across Europe. As a *vera effigies*, a true external likeness, each derivative copy acquired the internal sacredness of the original. Inspired by a visit – not to the original, but to the recently constructed Mikulov Loreto house in Moravia – Baroness Benigna Katharina von Lobkowicz (1594–1653) began constructing a new Loreto house at Prague (1626), under Capuchin custodianship. Physically and thematically next to the Prague Loreto is the Church of the Nativity of Our Lord (ca. 1722–27). In the church's second vaulting bay appears a fresco by the Bavarian Johann Adam Schöpfl (1702–72). The subject is traditional, the adoration of the magi, and the traditional global expression of the magi appears as usual. Here, however, the magi are simply in the first row of a large crowd of global representatives, who, in order to complement the magi's gold, frankincense, and myrrh, bring towering bundles of goods. These packages are wrapped, undifferentiated, and therefore more universal – like the widgets native to modern economic theories. Here is the religious understanding of the two sides of the merchant-missionary symbiosis, commercial globalization as homage to Christ, for the greater glory of God.

As we have seen, images of global mission developed that incorporated elements of both the mission and the globe. The variety of media in which expressions of global mission appear and the creative ways in which the idea is depicted suggest its new importance. The universal mission of the medieval church has taken on an unparalleled specificity, reflecting in part the increased opportunities for the expansion of Christianity. Thus the appearance of four continents in frescoes gives global mission a particularism altogether lacking in earlier times, without compromising its universalism. Clearly global mission had arrived, but how was distance understood by the authors and audiences of these works? The following chapter analyzes other expressions of global mission to appreciate more fully the connotation distance held for these missionaries.

5   Space, Time, and Truth in the Jesuit Psychology

Understandings of distance are not uniform. A modern alternative approach to distance comes with topology, the study of the nonquantitative properties of geometric spaces. The iconic topological schematic is the tube map of the London Underground, revealing which lines connect to which, without specifying how many kilometres separate you from Stockwell station. In late-medieval Europe distance could be understood in a similarly fluid way, and the schema of the London Underground finds distant cousins in the programs of medieval sacred art, with their relative scales, curious metrics, and iconographical wormholes.[1] The fifteenth century came to know a "finite, spatially referenced spherical earth, a *tabula rasa* on which the achievements of exploration could be cumulatively inscribed," where measured distance became more geographical than iconographical.[2] Wolfgang Schivelbusch has described the mental annihilation of space brought about in the nineteenth century as railways overtook stagecoaches, travelling at three times the speed; here we witness a yet more significant revolution.[3] Instead of lands moving three times closer, we see lands previously existing in conjecture and legend being drawn onto the map itself.

In addition, the still-developing global map warped understandings of geography, most strikingly in the idea that New Spain was close to China, a misconception residual of the miscalculations of Columbus, who had underestimated the distance between Japan and the Canary Islands by two-thirds. In 1565 Pedro Meléndez, to whom the Spanish crown

---

[1] See David Woodward, "Maps and the Rationalization of Space," in *Circa 1492: Art in the Age of Exploration*, ed. Jay A. Levenson (Washington, D.C.: National Gallery of Art; New Haven: Yale University Press, 1991), 83.

[2] Woodward, 85. See Mary W. Helms, "Essay on Objects: Interpretations of Distance Made Tangible," in *Implicit Understandings: Observing, Reporting, and Reflecting on the Encounters between Europeans and Other Peoples in the Early Modern Era*, ed. Stuart B. Schwartz (Cambridge: Cambridge University Press, 1994), 355.

[3] Wolfgang Schivelbusch, *The Railway Journey: The Industrialization of Time and Space in the 19th Century* (Berkeley: University of California Press, 1986), 36.

had assigned the conquest of Florida, wrote the Jesuit general asking for missionaries for this land "very near Tartary, China, Melaka."[4] So, too, a missionary in Newfoundland warned Rome that English progress in Virginia and New England would bring heresy to China, being "so near...and of such easy journey and passage."[5] In one letter home, a Jesuit in Mexico discussed the evangelization of Japan as following immediately from the conversion of California.[6] Even at an ocean's remove, China shaped the thoughts and actions of the administrators and explorers of the Americas. This sense of geographical closeness approximates the annihilation of space often associated with contemporary globalization, but equally remarkable is the peculiar relationship between space, time, and truth that was distinctive to early-modern Catholicism.

The Fullness of Space and the End of Time

As agents of global religion, missionaries often had to discover the globe as they went along. If evangelization served explorers as a justification for their explorations, exploration also served missionaries as a practical necessity, for the most distant souls had to be reached before they were converted. Thus was born a missionary cognitive map that both unified the world and helped fill in its details. Longitude and latitude caught every potential mission station in their net. Two distant viewers could observe the same comet to remind themselves of their inhabiting a single world. Through the missionaries' efforts, every corner of the world was becoming better known, and indeed, the most distant corners often became the best known. From 1708 to 1718 French Jesuits completed a mapping of China under the patronage of the Kangxi 康熙 emperor, the first systematic trigonometric survey of a state.[7] In Europe itself, mapping also went hand in hand with religious expansion. After the Cromwellian conquest, William Petty directed the mapping project necessary for the

[4] Sierra, *Jesuitas*, 48.
[5] Letter of Simon Stock, London, to Propaganda, Rome, May 31,1625, in Luca Codignola, *The Coldest Harbour of the Land: Simon Stock and Lord Baltimore's Colony in Newfoundland, 1621–1649* (Montreal: McGill-Queen's University Press, 1988), 84.
[6] Gilg, Pópulo, to Jakob Willy, January 21, 1701, ARSI Ang. fol. 254v.
[7] James A. Millward, "'Coming onto the Map': Western Regions' Geography and Cartographic Nomenclature in the Making of Chinese Empire in Xinjiang," *Late Imperial China* 20.2 (1999): 61–98, at 72; Theodore N. Foss, "A Western Interpretation of China: Jesuit Cartography," in *East Meets West: The Jesuits in China, 1582–1773*, ed. Charles Ronan and Bonnie Oh (Chicago: Loyola University Press, 1988), 209–51, at 228.

Protestant confiscation of Catholic estates, and made Ireland thereby the best-surveyed European land.[8]

A map usually requires names. Most places already had names, and depending on their estimation of local culture, missionaries outside of Europe sometimes gave new names, as in Mexico, and sometimes kept the originals, as in China. Understanding how missionaries named places gives insight into how they understood their surroundings – a field of study known as environmental psychology.

Occasionally names would be chosen by lot. Each member of the party might have an equal chance of having the discovery named after his name-saint, and thus indirectly after himself.[9] The place names scattered across Baja California can serve us as examples. The Laguna de San Salvador took its name from Salvador, an Indian boy from Yécora traveling with Father Goñi, and the mountain San Eusebio was named after St. Eusebius through the luck of Eusebius Kino.[10] Other places acquired names through resonance of symbols, as with the four mountains named after the four evangelists. A third practice was perhaps the most useful for propagandistic purposes, for what ruler could neglect missions in a place bearing his or her name? Thus Kino advocated, and sometimes used, the "renowned name of the New Philippines of the Western Indies" to describe Sonora and California, as he writes in 1704, "with the same and even more propriety than that with which, on account of the Catholic zeal of Philip III [sic, really II], the conquered islands of the Eastern Indies in Asia were called the Philippines."[11] Four years later Kino began calling the same area the "New Kingdom of New Navarre,"[12] perhaps as an indication of his loyalty to the embattled Bourbon king Philip V.

Besides these naming strategies there remained another approach, one often applied with systematic regularity: The discovery would be named after the saint whose feast fell on that, or on the following, day. Thus when Kino travelled through the area near the Gila River, he quite consciously renamed places with dates from the sacred calendar: "The first village, that of El Tusónimo, we named La Encarnación, as we arrived there to say Mass on the First Sunday of Advent; and because many other Indians came to see us from the village of El Coatóydag, four leagues farther on,

[8] Nicholas Canny, "Early Modern Ireland c.1500–1700," in *The Oxford Illustrated History of Ireland*, ed. R. F. Foster (New York: Oxford University Press, 1989), 146–47.
[9] For the strength of this kind of name-association see Howard Hibbard, "*Ut picturae sermones*: The First Painted Decorations of the Gesù," in *Baroque Art: The Jesuit Contribution*, ed. Rudolf Wittkower and Irma B. Jaffe (New York: Fordham University Press, 1972), 33–34.
[10] Bolton, *Rim*, 149.
[11] Eusebius Kino, May 1704 dedication, *Crónica*.
[12] Kino, November 21, 1708 letter, *Crónica*.

we named the latter San Andrés, as the following day was the feast of that holy Apostle."[13] This practice was not restricted to priests. For the first island he landed on in the Philippine archipelago, Magellan chose the name "St. Lazarus," after a key figure in that day's gospel.[14] On September 28, 1542, the vigil of St. Michael Archangel, Cabrillo entered a choice harbour which he named San Miguel, a name it held for sixty years until Vizcaino changed it to San Diego.[15] The existence of date-names not associated with saints, such as the Puerto del Año Nuevo (the Port of the New Year) on the Pacific coast of Baja California, discovered on December 30, 1684,[16] suggests the primary referents of these names were not the individuals, but the holy days themselves.

This phenomenon appears most conspicuous where these date-places come quickly one after the other. A modern historian can date the passage of explorers with a map and a church calendar. Following Kino's 1695–96 map, we can trace his path across the St. Thomas River, Nochebuena (Christmas Eve), Natividad (Christmas), S. Estevan (St. Stephen), Los S. S. Martyr. Innocentes (Holy Innocents), and S. Thom. Cant. (Thomas Becket), corresponding to feasts on December 21, 24, 25, 26, 28, and 29.[17] This would be analogous to an American exploring the moon in January and February and naming a series of craters in order, after Martin Luther King, Jr., Robert E. Lee, Abraham Lincoln, and George Washington, corresponding to their "feast days" on the 15th and 19th of January and the 12th and 22nd of February, respectively – though a missionary felt his sacred calendar more intensely than most Americans feel their holiday calendar.

Regardless of these explorers' intentions, sprinkling the landscape with dates bound time to space in an immediate, local way. The dates of the cyclical, annual sacred calendar, but not the years, were thereby embedded in the landscape. When later explorers would revisit a site, or pore over maps, they would have reminders of the time of the discoverers. The mapped cycle would correspond to their present cycle. On one feast of St. Bruno, Kino named the Campo de los Sandías after the watermelons

[13] November 29, 1694, Bolton, *Rim*, 284.
[14] Catherine Lugar, "The History of the Manila Galleon Trade," in *Archaeological Report: The Recovery of the Manila Galleon Nuestra Señora de la Concepción*, ed. William M. Mathers, Henry S. Parker III, and Katherine A. Copus (Sutton, Vermont: Pacific Sea Resources, 1990), 42.
[15] Engelhardt, 25.
[16] Bolton, *Rim*, 189.
[17] Kino, San Lucas – San Bruno, to P. Paul Zingnis, with Diary of the Trip to California, September 29 to December 15, 1683, BHStA Jes. 607/127. See Peter Stitz, "Deutsche Jesuiten als Geographen in Niederkalifornien und Nordmexiko im 17. und 18. Jahrhundert," (M. S. thesis, Jena, 1930), 10–11.

on the beach at the foot of a hill, but the date drew him up its crest, from where he could see California, and remember naming San Bruno, exactly seventeen years before.[18]

Concerns about time had long been central to the mission, for eschatology had long been involved with the missionary expansion of the church beyond the borders of the known world. The most vivid medieval example was the identification of the threatening Turks and Tartars with Gog and Magog, the satanic powers that Revelations tied to the beginning of the end of the world. Already around the seventh century this understanding appeared in the *Revelations* of Pseudo-Methodius ("*St. Methodius of Patara*") and the *Cosmography* of Aethicus Ister, and its acceptance by Roger Bacon, Albertus Magnus, Vincent of Beauvais, and Marco Polo assured it a life into the fourteenth century.[19] The warlike nature of these peoples confirmed this identification in Christian scholars' minds, although other possible candidates coexisted. In 1237–38, on the way to a mission in "Great Hungary" (southern Russia?), the Dominican Julianus met with Mongolian ambassadors who called their homeland "Gotta," which the missionary identified with the biblical river Gozan, and concluded that the Mongols were in fact the Ishmaelites.[20] The medieval missionaries, like their early-modern counterparts, made sense of a newly discovered people by placing them in the soteriological process – in the Middle Ages as antagonists, and in early-modern times as objects of conversion.[21] The missionaries of both eras understood a strange, new geography in terms of old, familiar revelation.

Among the great variety of nuances in the early-modern missionary eschatology, one observation stands out: The increased tempo in missionary expansion demonstrated that the end of the world was near. In *De extremo Dei iudicio et Indorum uocatione* [*On the Last Judgement of God*

---

[18] Bolton, *Rim*, 436–37.

[19] E. R. Jones, "The Image of the Barbarian in Medieval Europe," in *Facing Each Other: The World's Perception of Europe and Europe's Perception of the World*, ed. Anthony Pagden (Aldertshot: Ashgate Variorum, 2000), 45; Andrew Runni Anderson, *Alexander's Gate, Gog and Magog, and the Inclosed Nations*, Monographs of the Medieval Academy of America, no. 5 (Cambridge, Mass.: The Medieval Academy of America, 1932), 46–47; Folkert Reichert, "Chinas Beitrag zum Weltbild der Europäer. Zur Rezeption der Fernostkenntnisse im 13. und 14. Jahrhundert," in *Das geographische Weltbild um 1300*, ed. Peter Moraw (Berlin: Duncker & Humblot, 1989), 52–53.

[20] "Epistula de vita Tartarorum," in Heinrich Dörrie, *Drei Texte zur Geschichte der Ungarn und Mongolen: Die Missionreisen des fr. Julianus O. P. ins Uralgebiet (1234/5) und nach Rubland (1237) und Bericht der Erzbiscofs Peter uber die Tartaren*, Nachrichten der Akademie der Wissenschaften in Göttingen I, Philologisch-Historische Klasse 6 (Göttingen: Vandenhoeck & Ruprecht, 1956), 167. The river Gozan is from I Chronicles 5:26.

[21] Jones, 45; Anderson, 44–48, 52–53; Ernst Sackur, *Sibyllinische Texte und Forschungen: Pseudomethodius Adso und die tiburtinische Sibylle* (Halle: M. Niemeyer, 1898), 74–75.

and the Vocation of the Indians] (Antwerp, 1567) the Flemish theologian Joannes Fredericus Lumnius reads the conversion of the Indians as a sign of imminent last days.[22] Typically everything, explicitly or implicitly, is attributed to divine providence. Thus in the Domincan Gaspar da Cruz's exposition, God retains agency: "God ordained the discoveries made by the Spaniards in the New World, and that done by the Portuguese in the navigation of India. *By these means*, God *through his servants* has converted many peoples newly to the faith."[23] God holds the initiative, and missionaries are his instruments. Less often is any human agency emphasized, but the Franciscan Gerónimo de Mendieta does write of the importance of the Spanish kings' obligations and actions.[24]

Early thought understood the end to be fixed in time, and the speed of the prerequisite universal conversion kept pace with this timetable. Columbus calculated the end of time by adding seven thousand years to Pierre d'Ailly's date of creation to yield 1656. Because the world would be converted by that time, Columbus thought, his explorations, with their missionary underpinnings, would almost certainly go well.[25] This same idea that the end would hasten conversion recurs in the writings of the Franciscan Toribio de Benavente Motolinía (died 1568), who justified to Charles V the use of force by referring to the necessity of universal conversion before the end, adding the proverb, "better good through force than bad through free will."[26]

At times, the converse relationship appears dominant. Rather than the certainty of the end accelerating conversion, the observable fact of increasing conversions was taken to accelerate the end. Thus Juan de

---

[22] Joannes Fredericus Lumnius, *De extremo Dei iudicio et Indorum vocatione libri duo* (Antwerp: Tilenium Brechtanum, 1567); Johannes Beckmann, "Utopien als missionarische Stoßkraft," in *Vermittlung zwischenkirchlicher Gemeinschaft: 50 Jahre Missionsgesellschaft Immensee*, ed. Jakob Baumgartner (Schöneck-Beckenried: Neue Zeitschrift fur Missionswissenschaft, 1971), 383.

[23] My emphasis. *South China in the Sixteenth Century, Being the Narratives of Galiote Pereira, Fr. Gaspar da Cruz, O. P., Fr. Martin de Rada OESA*, trans. Charles R. Boxer (London: Printed for the Hakluyt Society, 1953), 51, [prologue].

[24] Gerónimo de Mendieta, *Historia eclesiástica indiana, obra escrita á fines del siglo XVI por fray Gerónimo de Mendieta, de la Orden de San Francisco; la púbica por primera vez Joaquín García Icazbalceta* (México: Antigua librería [Impr. por F. Diaz de Leon y S. White], 1870), 18, 25.

[25] J. Specker, "Missionarische Motive im Entdeckungszeitalter," in *Mission, Präsenz, Verkündigungs, Bekehrung?*, ed. Horst Rzepkowski, Studia Instituti Missiologici Societatis Verbi Divini 13 (St. Augustin: Steyler, 1974), 89; Phelan, 21. See Christopher Columbus, *The Libro de las profecías of Christopher Columbus*, trans. Delno C. West and August Kling (Gainesville: University of Florida Press, 1991), 11. See also Rosario Romeo, "Le scoperte americane nella coscienza italiana del cinquecento," *Revista Storica Italiana* 65 (1953), 244.

[26] Pedro Borges Morán, "El sentido trascendente del descubrimiento y conversión de Indias," *Missionalia Hispanica* 13 (1956): 173–4.

Ávila (1502–69), the reformer of the secular clergy in Spain, could write a memorial to the Council of Trent pointing to the missionaries' lust for souls and the Spaniards' lust for gold as quickening the imminent arrival of both Christ and Antichrist.[27] Similarly, Esteban de Salazar (1532–96) delivered a sermon enjoining his audience not to doubt they were arriving at the "desert." He made his point by bringing up the missionary progress already made and predicting its completion before too many centuries pass.[28]

Still other thinkers took the discovery of the Indians as likely to retard the end of the world. The Spanish Carmelite Tomás de Jesús (1564–1627) advocated this view, as Acosta had done earlier.[29] The Mexican historian of his own Dominican Order, Dávila Padilla (1562–1604) expanded on this idea, explaining the dearth of miracles in New Spain as an indication that God was slowing down the eschatological clock, allowing time for the preaching of the gospel in every corner of the world.[30]

The intricate connection between time and space thus endured. Contemporaries understood what we call the "early-modern" missions as the final stage in the course of the world and the spreading of the faith. Bidding farewell to the first twelve friars to undertake the conversion of the Aztecs, the Franciscan Minister General described their mission as beginning the last evangelization before the end of the world. That twelve friars were chosen was no accident, but a deliberate recreation of Christ's having chosen twelve disciples – appropriate because the Franciscans were completing the proselytizing work begun by the first twelve.[31] The geographical space created for the church by the first disciples would now be magnified by their successors. The eschatological link between time and space became explicit in Motolinía, who identified the west with the end of the world: "Since in the beginning the Church flourished in the East, which is the beginning of the Earth, it must now in the end of the ages flourish in the West, which is the end of the Earth."[32]

---

[27] Juan de Ávila, *Dos memoriales inéditos del Juan de Avila para el Concilio de Trento*, Miscelanea Comillas 3 (Comillas, Santander: Universidad Pontificia, 1945), 85.

[28] *Veynte sermons*, fol. 145v, quoted in Borges Morán, "El sentido," 174.

[29] Tomás de Jesús, *Stimulus missionum* (Rome, 1610), 6, quoted in Borges Morán, "El sentido," 176.

[30] Agustín Dávila Padilla, *Historia de la fundación y discurso de la provincia de Santiago de México, de la Orden de Predicadores*, 3rd ed., Colección de grandes cronicas mexicanas 1 (Mexico: Editorial Academia Literaria, 1955 [1596]), 323.

[31] Mendieta, *Historia*, ii.44–8, cited in Phelan, 23. See Phelan, 52; Boxer, *Church Militant*, 113.

[32] Motolinía, *Historia de los Indios de la Nueva España* (Barcelona, 1914), 56, 160–61, cited in E. E. Sylvest, *Motifs of Franciscan Mission Theory in Sixteenth Century New Spain* (Washington, D.C.: Academy of American Franciscan History, 1975), 123–24.

Compared to the mendicants, the Jesuits eschatological expectations may appear dampened.[33] Why? N. S. Davidson asserts that the old attitude was common in early sixteenth-century Mexico, late sixteenth-century frontier areas, and by the seventeenth century was most pervasive in the Portuguese territories.[34] Adriano Prosperi characterizes the old Franciscan missionary outlook with "peregrinatio" and "ire ad infideles" as expressions of a personal religious inquietude in the face of apostolically vast distances. He contrasts this to the later Jesuit emphasis on a stable, mission-in-residence dedicated to the long-term transformation of an entire society.[35] Had the Spanish world become more domesticated by the time the Jesuits arrived in force? Given prophecy's tendency to protect itself against falsification, perhaps the end's having not yet come took the wind out of the eschatological sails. Perhaps the discovery that the Christian converts were not as converted as they should be marked a shift from "clock-oriented" to "task-oriented" time, from the emphasis on quantities of converts to a more realistic approach.[36] Perhaps the Franciscan-to-Jesuit changeover involved a shift of emphasis from time to space.

The Jesuits, however, attempted to combine the old dynamism with the new stability. Nadal describes a missionary "journey" as itself as "the most ample 'place,'" one which "reaches as far as the globe itself... the most glorious and longed-for 'house' for these theologians." The Jesuits' goal is "to procure the salvation and perfection of all women and men. They understand that they are to that end bound by the Fourth Vow to the supreme pontiff: that they might go on these universal missions for the good of souls by his command, which by divine decree extends throughout the whole church."[37]

In contrast to the old monastic vow of *stabilitas loci* (stability of place), which bound the monk to a particular monastery, Nadal translates a placeless movement (John O'Malley calls it an "apostolic mobility") into a

---

[33] Hausberger's verdict is even stronger (*Für Gott*, 15–16).

[34] N. S. Davidson, *The Counter-Reformation* (Oxford: Basil Blackwell, 1987), 60.

[35] Prosperi, "L'Europa cristiana," 210, 217.

[36] Helen Couclelis, "Aristotelian Spatial Dynamics in the Age of Geographic Information Systems," in *Spatial and Temporal Reasoning in Geographic Information Systems*, ed. Max J. Egenhofer and Reginal G. Golledge (New York: Oxford University Press, 1998), 114.

[37] O'Malley's translation, from John W. O'Malley, *To Travel to Any Part of the World: Jerónimo Nadal and the Jesuit Vocation*, Studies in the Spirituality of Jesuits 16.2 (St. Louis: American Assistancy Seminar on Jesuit Spirituality, 1984), 8, 10. See Nadal, V.773–7, V.442–4, and IV.178–80. O'Malley points out that this is a vow to God, not to the pope. However, this was a common contemporary expression used, among others by Nadal himself. John W. O'Malley, *The First Jesuits* (Cambridge, Mass.: Harvard University Press, 1993), 7.

kind of place.[38] Perhaps Nadal hoped through this translation to bring the appearance of stability to this new Jesuit rootlessness. Ignatius himself had understood the failure of his proposed mission to Jerusalem as heralding a shift from the *stabilitas* of the holy city to the *mobilitas* of a moving apostolate.[39] Still, as Prosperi points out, apocalypticism could underlie all missionary work, even if not always explicitly.[40]

From without, the Society appeared to be continuing the mendicants' program. Writing during the revolt of the Low Countries, Lumnius described the Jesuits as angels sent *"missi"* by God to the newly discovered lands of Isaiah in preparation for the millennium and Last Judgment.[41] When Ferdinand von Fürstenberg (see Chapter 8) established a foundation for the preaching of the gospel "until the end of the earth," he could be referring to spatial or temporal limits.[42]

Aspects of apocalypticism also appear in the Jesuits' own writings. Trigault recognized the discovery of the New World as providential in its timing, for the age of the evangelization had been "brought to us" by God.[43] Vieira interpreted Portugal as the Fifth Monarchy of Danielian prophecy, and expected the imminent conversion of the Jews.[44] As we shall see in the next chapter, the global struggles against the devil, with their predetermined apocalyptic outcome, endured in the Jesuit understanding. These battles cannot be understood without an eschatological backdrop.

The clearest description among the Jesuits came from José de Acosta. For him the prophetic story became one "natural y moral," and the preaching of the Word to all the peoples of the world was a sign of the impending end.[45] Still, the end could not arrive until China was converted, a difficult task that ruled out an apocalypse in the near future.[46] Like Tomás de Jesús, Acosta argued that the discovery of new lands had

[38] O'Malley, *To Travel*, 5.
[39] Edward Farrugia, "Im Banne des Orients: Werdegang und Zukunftsorientierung des hl. Ignatius von Loyola," in *Ignatius von Loyola und die Gesellschaft Jesu 1491–1556*, ed. Andreas Falkner and Paul Imhof (Würzburg: Echter, 1990), 398. For similar ideas in Suárez's *De Religione Societatis Jesu*, see Paul V. Murphy, " 'God's Porters': The Jesuit Vocation According to Francisco Suárez," *Archivum Historicum Societatis Iesu* 70 (2001): 3–28.
[40] Prosperi, "L'Europa," 204.
[41] Ibid., 202; idem, "America e Apocalisse," *Critica storica* XIII (1976): 1–67.
[42] RAH Jesuitas 16, no. 13.
[43] RAH Jesuitas 91, no. 28, fol. 8v.
[44] Phelan, 120–1; Boxer, *Church Militant*, 115–8.
[45] Prosperi, "L'Europa," 203–4.
[46] José de Acosta, *De temporibus novissimis libri quatuor* (Rome: Ex Typographia Iacobi Tornerij, 1590), 28–29, 32–34.

delayed the arrival of the end.[47] The *Tercero catecismo* [*Third Catechism*] (1585) of Lima, of which Acosta was almost certainly the principal author, described the world as having become old and giving off signs of death, and "when the entire universe has had preached the Gospel, then will come the end."[48]

Thus eschatology continued to bind time and space even in the Jesuit understanding. The Catholic Church had some claims to universality since antiquity, and in the early-modern period it acquired the opportunity to become global as well. As the church filled up space, time ran out. Thus Joseph Needham, drawing on Paul Tillich, rightly describes time in the Christian view as "directed and meaningful, witnessing an age-long battle between God and evil powers . . . in which, since the good will triumph, the temporal world is ontologically good."[49] Nevertheless, Needham's conclusion that "time predominates over space" does not follow, for, as we have seen, either could be taken as a "directed and meaningful" measure of the eschatological battle. This connection between space and time is more explicit with these Catholic missionaries than are the analogous space-and-time continua ascribed to the Aztecs and the Chinese Mohists.[50] The prevailing European intellectual attitude towards time itself likely supported placing it in such tight correlation to space. The idea of physical motion (locomotion) bound Aristotle's time to space, an idea which would endure until Newton, who defined an "absolute, true and mathematical time" flowing "without regard to any thing external."[51]

Indeed, sometimes ecclesiastical time and space were related by describing the church's locomotion through the world – not necessarily with an explicit eschatological aspect. In his *Historia* the Franciscan Bernardino de Sahagún (ca. 1500–90) recounted the expansion of

---

[47] Idem, *De Natura Nova Orbis libri duo*, 41–42.

[48] *Tercero Cathecismo y exposición de la doctrina christiana por sermones, para que los curas y otros ministros prediquen y enseñen a los indios y a otras personas* [Lima: 1585], in *Doctrina christiana y catecismo para instruccion de los indios*, Corpus Hispanorum de Pace XXVI-2 (Madrid: Consejo Superior de Investigaciones científicas, 1985), fol. 205rv [pp. 757–58]. See León Lopetegui, *El padre José de Acosta, S. I., y las misiones* (Madrid: Consejo Superior de Investigaciones Científicas, Instituto Gonzalo Fernández de Oviedo, 1942), 523–24.

[49] Joseph Needham, "Time and Eastern Man," in *The Grand Titration: Science and Society in East and West* (Toronto: University of Toronto Press, 1969), 290; Tillich, 23, 30.

[50] See Carrasco; Needham, "Time," 222.

[51] Aristotle, *Aristotle's Physics, Books III and IV*, trans. Edward Hussey (New York: Oxford University Press, 1983), 208a.27–35, 218b, 21–219a,10; Isaac Newton, *The Mathematical Principles of Natural Philosophy*, ed. Andrew Motte and Florian Cajori and Florian Cajori (Chicago: Encyclopaedia Britannica, 1955), I.9. See Ernest Nagel, *The Structure of Science: Problems in the Logic of Scientific Explanation* (London: Routledge & Kegan Paul, 1961), 179, and Couclelis, 113.

the church from Palestine, to Asia (Minor?), Africa, Germany, and to
Europe. He noted how the church had since declined then in each of
these areas. In his time the church had moved on to the Americas,
but he feared it would not last long, that America would be merely
a road to China. There lay his great hope, as he expected Christianity to endure for some time among that "very clever people, of great
orderliness and great knowledge."[52] A modification of this idea appeared
in a Jesuit's writing. In his short work on Francis Xavier, the Munich
provost Anton Crammer described the great missionary's plan, or perhaps ascribed one to him: Not content to evangelize the Orient, Xavier
also intended missions to the "midnight lands of the world" (Crammer
is playing on *oriens*, the rising sun). Xavier would use China itself as a
springboard to Tartary and Muscovy, then on to reclaim the Swedish and
Dutch kingdoms, thence to Germany and Italy, where he would return to
Ignatius.[53]

The most dramatic expressions of the space and time of global mission
appeared as prophecy, and the most articulate prophet of the missions
was not a Jesuit but a Dominican; we focus on the Italian philosopher
Tommaso Campanella (1568–1639) here because his writings illuminate
some of the Jesuits' less systematic texts – although no direct influence
is certain. Campanella attempted much practical work for the mission,
from urging Queen Henrietta Maria (ca. 1639) to convince her husband
Charles I (r. 1625–49) to permit Catholicism in England, to working
towards the foundation of a missionary college in Calabria, the proposed
scope of which he later expanded to include all of Europe.[54] His ideas
quickened interest even in Protestant circles, and may have inspired Leibniz.[55] Certainly his works reached Paul V, Gregory XV (1621–23), and
Urban VIII (1623–44), and they made an impression on both the Spanish
Carmelite Tomás de Jesus (1564–1627) and on Francesco Ingoli (1578–
1649), the first secretary of the Congregation for the Propagation of the
Faith.[56] Campanella's greatest contribution was theoretical, born from
a conflict between two ideas, one of which lay at the heart of what he

[52] Bernardino de Sahagún, *Historia General de las cosas de Nueva España*, ed. Angel María
Garibay (Mexico: Porrua, 1956), III.355, 357.
[53] Quoted in Schreiber, *Deutschland und Spanien*, 313.
[54] Tommaso Campanella (ca. 1639), *Lettere*, ed. Vincenzo Spampanato (Bari: G. Latera,
1927), 403; idem, February 14, 1630, *Lettere*, 227–30.
[55] Franz Rudolf Merkel, *G. W. von Leibniz und die Chinamission: Eine Untersuchung über die
Anfänge der protestantischen Missionsbewegung*, Missionswissenchaftliche Forschungen 1
(Leipzig: Hinrichs, 1920), 25.
[56] Josef Metzler, "Wegbereiter und Vorläufer der Kongregation: Vorschläge und erste
Fründungsversuche einer römischen Missionszentrale," in *Sacrae Congregationis de Propaganda Fide Memoria rerum* (Rome: Herder, 1971–76), I/1.74–5.

considered his most important composition and motivated the entire corpus of his writings.[57]

The first of the incongruous ideas was a concern for humanity and a belief in its global unity. At one level, this idea derived from an Old Testament understanding of ethnology. Adam was the sole origin of all peoples. The Americans thus descended from him, and a son of Noah established colonies in China.[58] With his characteristically provocative tone, Campanella had asked in the early work *Atheismus triumphantus* (1605–7) how a benevolent God could have abandoned for so long the Tartars, Japanese, and Chinese, as well as the inhabitants of the two polar regions.[59] *Quod reminiscetur* [*That Shall Remember*] (ca. 1606) repeated the idea that all men were brothers, and repeated the same question.[60] This concern endured, and reappeared in the *Theologia* (1614–24): So many peoples reside in the newly discovered worlds, yet so few had had the opportunity to reach salvation through an effectively European Christ.[61]

Such a concern for these soteriologically disadvantaged peoples ran up against the second idea, Campanella's urgent eschatological vision. At earlier stages in his thought, this eschatology found justification in stars, in politics, and in history – but the discovery of the Indies breathed new life into it.[62] Echoing papal language, Campanella writes of the unification of Christendom into one flock with one shepherd, "And the Christians will triumph, and Christ will come to judge, and thus the end."[63]

The result was a burning need for global mission. The late hour had created an urgency for the political and religious unity of mankind. In the *Articuli prophetales* [*Prophetic Points of Time*] (1607–9) Campanella envisioned a clearly directed movement of the church through Spain, into Peru, crossing the Pacific to Japan, then tracing the Asian littorals into the Red Sea, and finally returning to its origin, so that the Jews might

---

[57] Campanella also wrote on the missions in *Discorsi universali del governo ecclesiastico* (1593). See Giovanni di Napoli, "Ecumenismo e missionarismo in Tommaso Campanella," *Euntes docete* 22 (1969): 266–7, 293.

[58] Giuliano Gliozzi, *Adamo e il Nuovo Mondo* (Florence: La nuova Italia, 1977), 362.

[59] Campanella, *Atheismus Triumphatus seu Reductio ad religionem per scientiarum veritates... contra Antichristianismum Achitophellisticum* (Rome: 1631) 9–10.

[60] Campanella, *Quod reminiscentur et convertentur ad dominum universi fines terrae* (Ps. 21), ed. Romano Amerio (Padua: Ex officina libraria Cedam, 1939), 37 [fol. 25v]. Thomas à Jesu's *De procuranda Salute Omnium Gentium* probably influenced Campanella in writing *Quod reminiscetur*. See Kowalsky and Metzler, 12, and André-Jean Marquis, "Le traité missionaire 'Quod Reminiscentur' de Tommaso Campanella," *Neue Zeitschrift für Missionswissenschaft* (Supplementa) 17 (1971): 349.

[61] Campanella, *Teologia*, ed. Romano Amerio (Milan: Società editrice "Vita e pensiero," 1936–80), XVIII, 30; XXVII, 16, 48, 50, 52, 110.

[62] Headley, 263. Borges Morán, "El sentido," 173, disagrees.

[63] Quoted in Romeo, 375.

know the truth.[64] Earlier he had hoped to shift the Holy City from Rome[65] to Jerusalem to speed the arrival of the millennial kingdom, heaven on earth. From the new global capital the pope and the Spanish king would rule the world. Key to his objective of world conversion was a federation of European states that would secure peace as a prelude to a new, unified world mission. This evolved in his thought to become a general assembly at Rome of all peoples' rulers, Christians, Jews, Muslims, and pagans, to participate in a disputation over the true faith.[66] (A similar idea would later appear in Emeric Crucé's 1623 recommendation for a Venice-based Society of Nations, which would even include the Turks and Chinese.)[67] Thus the new lands, including an entire new hemisphere, which had had to await God for 1,495 years, now witnessed the time when all people would be united, one flock and one pastor.[68]

The Truth and Authority of Distance

This space-time continuum has a third component at a meta-religious level. As space filled and time ran out, the truth of Christianity, including the truth of this same time-space continuum, became ever more evident.

Sometimes the very expansion of Christianity served as a marketing strategy for new converts. In Mexico, the Jesuit Andrés Pérez de Ribas (1576–1655) used world maps to impress Indians, and he stressed the existence of peoples – powerful, rich, and cultured – who had adopted Christianity.[69] Kino also used a world map to demonstrate his authority. He remembered Bac, the village he had renamed San Xavier, now in modern Arizona:

I spoke to them the Word of God, and on the map of the world I showed them the lands, the rivers, and the seas over which we fathers had come from afar to bring

[64] Campanella, *Articuli prophetales*, ed. Germana Ernst (Florence: La nuova Italia, 1977), 144.
[65] Rome would first be conquered by the Turks. Ibid., 232.
[66] Campanella, *Teologia*, XXVII.128; idem, *Articuli Prophetales*, 144, 384–85; idem, *Atheisums Triuphatus*, 108; idem, *Quod reminiscetur*, 30. He had previously suggested a federation of European states under papal presidency. See Napoli, 288, and Metzler, "Wegbereiter," 75.
[67] Emeric Crucé, *Le Nouveau Cynée: ou, discours des occasions et moyens d'établir une paix générale et la liberté du commerce par tout le monde* (Paris: EDHIS, Éditions d'histoire sociale, 1976 [1623]), 61–2.
[68] Campanella, *Quod reminiscetur*, fol 8v-9r [p. 14].
[69] Andrés Pérez de Ribas, *Libro Séptimo*, 139rv, cited in Charles W. Polzer, "The Evolution of the Jesuit Mission System in Colonial New Spain, 1600–1767," (Ph.D. diss., University of Arizona, 1972), 106; Pérez de Ribas, *Historia de los triumphos de nuestra Santa Fe entre gentes de las más bárbaras y fieras del nuevo obre* (Madrid: Alo[n]so de Paredes, 1645), 69.

them the saving knowledge of our Holy Faith ... I told them also how in ancient times the Spaniards were not Christians, how Santiago came to teach them the Faith, and how the first fourteen years he was able to baptize only a few, because of which the Holy Apostle was discouraged, but that the Holy Virgin appeared to him and consoled him, promising that the Spaniards would convert the rest of the people of the world. And I showed them on the map of the world how the Spaniards and the Faith had come by sea to Vera Cruz and had gone into Puebla and to Mexico, Guadalaxara, Sinaloa, Sonora, and now to ... Dolores del Cosari, in the land of the Pimas.[70]

The underlying message occasionally was spoken outright. In Sahagún's *Libros de los coloquios* [*Books of the Dialogues*] or *Pláticas* [*Conversations*], the first twelve Franciscans stressed Christianity as a world religion, and the Indians were asked, who has ever heard of your idols?[71]

In a similar way, Ricci presented world maps to Chinese scholars and officials. Giving them access (through the map) to the world symbolized his being able to give them access (through Catholicism) to the wider world. The Taichang 泰昌 emperor (r. August to September 1620) himself issued edicts requesting copies. Ricci effectively "wrote on the map that the Christian religion was the greatest on earth."[72] On some copies he added the Jesuit monogram. Trigault referred to Ricci's map as "bait," marvelling how it "undoubtedly drew many Chinese into the net of the church."[73]

Chinese readings of Ricci's map mistook common-noun phrases for names of countries, suggesting that the work overwhelmed rather than efficiently conveyed geographical information – which may well have been the Jesuits' intention. For example, one crude reproduction of Ricci's world map, the Fangyu Shenglüe 方輿勝略 (1609–10), mistook a phrase in the description of Switzerland, understanding "thirteen cantons" 十三郡 to be a proper place name. "The region produces precious stones and timber" from the description of the Nile Valley yielded a non-existent land called "石鳥木," "Stone Bird Tree."[74]

Two comprehensive lists of reasons to believe Christianity argued that the religion's worldwide expansion offered clear proof of its truth: the *Third Catechism* of Lima and Zumárraga's *Doctrina cristiana* [*Christian Doctrine*]. The Catechism's seventh argument reads, "With this very faith

[70] Kino, *Crónica*, 122.
[71] Ursula Lamb, "Religious Conflicts in the Conquest of Mexico," *Journal of the History of Ideas* 17 (1956): 530.
[72] Kenneth Ch'en, "Matteo Ricci's Contribution to and Influence on Geographical Knowledge in China," *Journal of the American Oriental Society* 59 (1939), 343–46.
[73] J. F. Baddeley, "Father Matteo Ricci's Chinese World Maps, 1584–1608," *The Geographical Journal* 50.4 (1917): 259–60; see also Ch'en, 358.
[74] For the general reception of Ricci's map in China see Ch'en, 346–59.

and word of God, they converted all the world, kings, and lords, and the wise, and the powerful, and everyone was subjected to the word of God, and to the faith of Jesus Christ." Therefore, the argument ran, Christianity was true.[75] Zumárraga's presentation is more nuanced. He began with the first apostles, arguing that because they were simple, illiterate men, their success in spreading the gospel testified to its truth.[76] Likewise, its continued existence, and its future continuation until the end of the world, indicated the work of God.[77] He further justified the divine favour of the global mission by arguing that Christ existed simultaneously in every consecrated host throughout the world, just as one person could be multiplied through multiple mirrors.[78]

These examples suggest how distance enhances the authority of Christianity; distance could similarly boost the personal authority of the missionaries. In China Jesuit missionaries frequently began their writings by pointing out how far they had travelled.[79] Trigault in particular used distance thus as evidence of his efforts. He listed the various places he had travelled through, carefully noting the distance – which he said gave him time to contemplate further the propagation of the faith.[80] Given the era's transportation incapability, any vastness of space corresponded to a vastness of time, often to permanency. Ricci thought to make use of this permanency to impress the Chinese emperor. In a memorial presented to the Wanli 萬曆 emperor in 1601, he explained that Jesuit missionaries leave Europe with the intent to work for the rest of their lives in their new country.[81] The idea of permanency to which Ricci drew the emperor's attention also appeared in more personal discourse. Expressing something like the sentiments of an Irish "American wake," Jesuit Ignaz Kögler (1680–1746) wrote his brother before leaving for the China mission: We probably will never see each other again on the earth, but

[75] *Tercero catecismo*, fol. 24v (p. 396).
[76] Juan de Zumárraga, *Doctrina breve muy provechosa de las cosas que pertenecen a la fe catholica y a nuestra cristiandad en estilo llano para común inteligencia* (México: 1543), ajjjr, quoted in Pedro Borges Morán, *Métodos Misionales en la Cristianización de América. Siglo XVI* (Madrid: 1960), 314.
[77] Zumárraga, *Doctrina breve*, ajjjr, quoted in Borges Morán, *Métodos*, 317.
[78] *Doctrina cristiana en lengua española y mexicana, por los religiosos de la Orden de Santo Domingo, obra impresa en México por Juan Pablos en 1548, y ahora editada en facsímil*, Colección de incunables americanos, siglo XVI, 1 (Madrid: Ediciones Cultura Hispánica, 1944), fols. 108r-v.
[79] For example, Martini introduces himself in his treatise on friendship 逑友篇, "九萬航洋。來友之道。" ARSI JapSin I,101, fol 2r.
[80] RAH Jesuitas 91, no. 28, fol. 2r.
[81] Chen, 124–33; Henri Bernard, *Le Père Matthieu Ricci et la société chinoise de son temps* (Tientsin: Hautes Études, 1937), II.8; *Tianxue chuhan* 天學初函, ed. Li Zhizao 李之藻 (Taibei: 1965, reprint of Hanzhou 1629 original), III. 1936.

after being separated for the sake of God, how sweet it will be to be reunited in blessed eternity.[82]

Jesuits thus used the authority of distance not just to impress potential converts. Canisius employed lists of place names to show the geographical extent of the Jesuits' labours.[83] He enhanced his own prestige by enumerating the many and varied places to which he must write: "to Barcelona, to the Spanish Court, to Louvain, ... to Trent, to India."[84] The idea of distance holds weight in a 1554 attempt to impress municipal authorities in Cologne, which then lacked a strong Jesuit presence. Canisius highlighted the Society's wide geographical range, reaching even exotic lands where natives feasted on human flesh. This range helped justify the aptness of the Society as an instrument of this Catholicism. The willingness of the Jesuits to fight ("not with sword but with the Word and Spirit of God") and to be martyred (as recently occurred in India) was made plain. A social range ("rich and poor, powerful and weak") complements the geographical range – although, as we have seen, the Constitutions themselves argue for a concentration of efforts on social elites.[85]

Early-modern Catholics and their potential converts used distance in other creative ways. In the Americas we can find two examples of people manipulating – indeed, diminishing – the sense of distance in order to heighten personal authority.

By 1642 Juan de Palafox y Mendoza was perhaps the most powerful man in Mexico. Not only bishop of Puebla and archbishop-elect of Mexico (an honour he declined), he also served as visitor-general and acting viceroy of New Spain. His influence was even felt in the Philippines, an administrative extension of Mexico. Through Domingo Navarrete's assistance, for example, Manila University adopted the statutes Palafox had devised for Mexico.[86]

---

[82] Ignatius Kögler, Rottenburg, July 15, 1715, BStB CLM 1403, fol. 62r. Administrative opposition also worked against returning to Europe: Indeed, Aquaviva at one point personally and repeatedly blocked the return of a missionary who had spent a decade in Peru. See Broggio, 23.

[83] For example, see Canisius, Ingolstadt, to Ignatius, February 1551, in Engelbert Maximilian Buxbaum, *Petrus Canisius und die Kirchliche Erneuerung des Herzogtums Bayern, 1549–1556* (Rome: Institutum Historicum S. I., 1973), 274–77. See also Otto Braunsberger, ed., *Beati Petri Canisii Epistulae et Acta* (Freiburgi Brisgoviae: S. Herder, 1896–1923), I.301–5.

[84] Braunsberger, I.189–92.

[85] Letter of Johann Rhetius, Rome, to Konstantin Lyskirchen, Cologne, July 10, 1554, Vii fol. 17, published in Joseph Hansen, ed., *Rheinische Akten zur Geschiche des Jesuitenordens, 1542–1582*, Publikationen der Gesellschaft für Rheinische Geschichtskunde 14 (Bonn: Hermann Behrendt, 1896), 247–50.

[86] The introduction to the English edition of his China history grievously misidentifies Palafox as a Jesuit who served as bishop of Osma before becoming a viceroy. Juan de Palafox y Mendoza, *History of the Conquest of China*, ed. H. S. Bhatia (New Delhi: Deep & Deep Publications, 1978), 5, 10. See Cummins, *Question*, 79.

Palafox's interests did not stop at Manila. In his writings, he frequently stresses the essential unity of society by describing it as a single body. This organic metaphor suggests a similar essential unity of the Catholic world in his understanding of ecclesiology.[87] In practice, his interests and ambitions embraced a wide part of this Catholic *organum*, for the bishop of Puebla adduced Mexico's proximity to China to justify extending his jurisdiction across the Pacific to the Middle Kingdom, although Beijing is in fact closer to Rome.[88] He strengthened this position by emphasizing the Spanish king's authority in the China missions. At any rate, the bishop declared, even if the converts were not subjects of Spain, the missionaries certainly were.[89] Palafox's efforts form only one part of the disputes over jurisdiction in China, which are discussed in Chapters 7 and 8.

As viceroy, Palafox had access to news from China as it passed from Manila through Mexico to Spain.[90] Receiving semiannual reports, Palafox formed a not entirely favourable opinion of a people he considered "effeminate," especially in comparison to the invading Manchu.[91] Palafox's interest in China prompted him to write a history of the Manchu conquest, based mostly on reports from Manila.[92] For the Jesuits in China he harboured a special animosity. Indeed, Palafox found the Jesuits' behaviour odious on a worldwide scale.[93] Because of his wide geographical perspective, Palafox could naturally speak of the controversies in the Philippines and New Spain in a single breath.[94]

Before crossing the Atlantic, Palafox had also travelled through the Holy Roman Empire. Named "Chaplain and Superior Almoner," in 1629 he joined the Infanta Maria Anna's (1606–46) entourage for her trip to Vienna to marry Archduke Ferdinand, her cousin. Palafox took a circuitous route home to Madrid, passing through the Palatinate,

[87] Israel, 202–3.
[88] Juan de Palafox y Mendoza to Innocent X, January 8, 1649, in *Obras*, XI.114. As the crow flies Beijing is 12,473 kilometres from Mexico City, but only 8,138 kilometres from Rome.
[89] Letter [to the king of Spain], August 15, 1646, APF SOCG 193, fol. 35r, 38v.
[90] Walravens, 181.
[91] Palafox y Mendoza, "Historia de las Guerras Civiles de la China, y de la Conquista de Aquel Dilatado Imperio por el tartaro," *Obras*, X.275, 373. See Cummins, *Question*, 80.
[92] Juan de Palafox y Mendoza, "Histoire de la conquête de la Chine par les Tartares," *Recueil de voyages au nord* (Amsterdam, [1731]), VI.119–462, in *The Making of the Modern World*, Thomson Gale (2006), Simon Fraser University (2 August 2006) http://galenet.galegroup.com.proxy.lib.sfu.ca/servlet/MOME?af=RN&ae=U107642310 &srchtp=a&ste=14. The *Recueil* also includes relations of Verbiest's voyage to China, and of the Franciscan Luis Hennepin's to Mexico.
[93] Palafox y Mendoza, *Obras*, XI.213; idem, *Carta del Illmo. y venerable siervo de Dios Don Juan de Palafox, obispo de Puebla, al santisimo papa Inocencio X, sobre los asuntos que tuvo con los jesuitas* (Mexico: V. G. Torres, 1841), 7.
[94] Letter [to the king of Spain], August 15, 1646, APF SOCG 193, fols. 38v.

Flanders, and France.[95] Until his death he treasured a crucifix, recovered from an abandoned German chapel, where Protestants had broken off its arms.[96] Palafox never forgot what he saw in Germany, and he incorporated his experiences into his later attacks. When condemning his Jesuit antagonists, he was quick to denounce the Society's acquisition of German lands and churches recovered from Protestants who had seized them from other Catholic orders.[97] Thus his particular regional interests in his own Mexico, in China (in his mind, no less his own), and in Germany allowed him to present a truly global world of evidence in his letters to king and pope to support his case against the Society. In Germany they improperly kept confiscated property for themselves; in China they monopolized the mission.

The bishop did not limit his efforts to appeals to Europe. When Navarrete and his fellow Dominicans arrived in Mexico (August 13, 1646) en route to promulgate the pope's decree in China, Palafox was able to lend them the library he had collected on the controversy over the compatibility of Chinese rituals with Christianity.[98] These works included a treatise written by Diego Morales, the Jesuit rector in Manila, in defence of the Jesuits' strategy – precisely what the papal decree was to outlaw. By reading the treatise, the Dominicans could anticipate the Jesuits' objections waiting for them across the Pacific.[99] In fact, when Palafox saw the decree, he could predict with perfect foresight how the Jesuits would object: Because the papal decree had not been submitted to Madrid, the Jesuits in China would reject it as an infringement on the king's *patronato* authority. The bishop immediately attempted to prepare for this by writing Philip IV, asking for his intervention to prevent the false teaching of Christianity from occurring under Spanish authority.[100]

---

[95] "Capellán y Limosnero Mayor." See Israel, 200; García, *Don Juan de Palafox y Mendoza*,45; Brading, 228. The Castilian Council of State had refused the suggestion that a Capuchin be appointed, because of the close ties between that order and the duke of Bavaria. See Dieter Albrecht, *Die auswärtige Politik Maximilians von Bayern 1618–1635* (Göttingen: Vandenhoeck & Ruprecht, 1962), 22. See García, 53.

[96] Palafox y Mendoza, *Vida Interior*, in *Obras*, I.51–52.

[97] Idem, *Obras*, XI.310–11. See idem, *Carta al Innocent X*, 137–39, 144–49, 163–78.

[98] Cummins, *Question*, 81.

[99] Letter of Padre fr. Domingo Navarrete al R. P. Visitador de la Compañia Luis de Gama a Macao, B. Cas., 1074, fol. 127r; Navarrete, "Libro de controversias de China," BL Add Ms 16933, fol. 260r. See also Domingo Navarrete to R. P. Visitador de la Compañia Luis de Gama a Macao, fol. 127r.; letter from Juan Baptista de Morales, Mexico, [to Ingoli], November[?] 21, 1646, APF SOCG vol. 145, fol. 297v; Letter from Juan Baptista de Morales, Mexico, [to Ignoli], March 6, 1647, APF SOCG vol. 145, fol. 311v.

[100] Navarrete, 332, 339, 468–9, 616, 615. See Cummins, 80.

Palafox supported another extraordinary person who bridged, in her own way, the Pacific's vastness. Distance and salvation dovetail in the life (and accounts of the life) of Catarina de San Juan, called *La China Poblana* ("The Pueblan Chinese"), a Bengali princess brought to Mexico in 1619 as a slave. Before her 1688 death in Puebla, a series of visions prompted her prophecies, which one of her confessors, the Jesuit Alonso Ramos, had published after her death. Though in life she enjoyed the support of Palafox, the Mexican Inquisition soon condemned her "unedifying and contradictory" pronouncements.[101]

The Ramos narrative of Catarina's life specifies that some of the "many people from the Orient" who passed through Puebla informed her that her mother had been baptized, and that her father had died greatly desiring the same.[102] In fact, although Catarina lived "so very retired from the world," still God would carry her "many leagues" away that she might travel in spirit to see the Jesuit missions. These raptures also gave her visions of infinite souls perishing in hell, which she observed with a severe soteriology: "If so many souls are lost, it is because they want to be lost." A second account of her life frequently depicts her as "not having anything in her mouth" except phrases like "a beast," "an ass," "a Chinese bitch," and "a demon that deserves to be in hell for its sins" – all in reference to herself. Her use of "Chinese" parallel to "bitch" suggests a derogatory meaning, one in keeping with the term's connotations in Mexico more generally. Nevertheless, she (or rather, her biographer) twisted all this around to stress the austerity of the life and to honour the humility of the spirit of a "Chinese bitch baptized standing up." Inverted through the Christian tradition of self-debasement, these negative implications all become pious, and distance regains its positive connotation, in a round-about way.[103]

The most intricate use of distance took advantage of implications about the missionary's own religiosity. Distance could show a love of God, a love of one's fellow, and a lack of self-love. Continuing a medieval tradition, Francis Xavier preceded the signature on his letter to Ignatius of April 9,

---

[101] Nicolás León, *Catarina de San Juan y la China Poblana*, 5th edition (Puebla: Ediciones Altiplano, 1971), 106–7. For biographical details, see especially Nicolás León, 11, and Alonso Ramos, *Prodigios de la omnipotencia y milagros de la gracia en la vida de la venerable sierva de Dios Catharina de S. Joan...* (Puebla: Imprenta plantiniana de D. Fernandez de Leon, 1689), fols. 5r, 78v-79r. For how a contemporary German audience could read the life of Catarina, see Ulrike Strasser, "A Case of Empire Envy? German Jesuits meet an Asian mystic in Spanish America," *Journal of Global History* 2 (2007): 23–40.

[102] Ramos, fol. 20v-21r.

[103] José del Castillo Graxeda, *Compendio de la vida y virtudes de la venerable Catarina de San Juan*, Bibliotheca Angelopolitana 3 (Puebla: Gobierno del Estado de Puebla, Secretaria de Cultura, 1987), 111–12, 119–20, 149, 173, 176–7.

1552, with "Your least son and farthest exile,"[104] thus drawing a new parallel between the superlative of distance and the superlative of self-abasement, which had appeared in Christian letters at least since St. Patrick in the fifth century. Distance also served as a context to highlight the strength of love. The first sentence in a letter by Gilg to Jakob Willy, visitor of the Bohemian province, stressed distance twice: the "so great distance" that Gilg's own prayers must be borne back to Jakob, and the distance the visitor's "most familiar love" must travel to "these here very ends of the earth."[105] Although a modern postcard mailed from far away may indicate friendliness for the effort distance entails, prayers involve the same amount of effort regardless of the location of the recipient. It is thus distance per se that indicated love for Gilg. The Jesuit visitor Antonio Leal understood distance in this way even when dealing with physical objects, and he made this connection explicit when he wrote to Kino, "the cross and the shells came with your Reverence's letter . . . and I greatly rejoice at seeing them, because of the distance whence they sent them, which is an indication of friendliness."[106]

Such an attitude makes somewhat more comprehensible the principle – not always accepted by all Jesuits – that a distant soul is an attractive soul. Bolton relates the story that an heiress of the Borgia family contacted the Jesuits about making a gift to found three new missions. Asked for her geographical preference, she instructed the Jesuits to establish them "in the most outlandish place in the world." The Jesuits used their atlases to determine an answer: "The most outlandish place in all the world is California." The result was three new missions in Baja California, which the Jesuits considered the missionary field most remote from civilization.[107] Other writers explicitly correlate distance with attraction. In *De Christiana Expeditione* [*On the Christian Expedition*], Trigault's edition of Ricci's papers, the salvation of distant souls is all the more important because of the distance involved. What was probably the most controversial section, on Chinese religious customs and rituals, begins with a request that the reader recognize in these chapters "an opportunity to sympathize with this people and to pray to God for their salvation." The next sentence outlines this opportunity: Despite being obscured in pagan darkness for millennia, the Chinese "through their own innate genius and through the goodness of God" realized their own deficiency. There

[104] Francis Xavier, *Epistolae*, II.376.
[105] Gilg, Pópulo, to P. Jakob Willy [visitator and viceprovincial of Bohemia], January 21, 1701, ARSI Ang. 35, fol. 549r–549v.
[106] Bolton, *Rim*, 431.
[107] Bolton offers neither a source nor the original word he translates as "outlandish." Ibid., 594.

is, moreover, a proportional relationship between their cultural distance and salvation, for "the more deeply enveloped [the Chinese] are in the shadows of ignorance, the more vehemently [the Europeans] should pray to God for the salvation for these peoples."[108]

Even a Chinese convert can use physical distance, in tandem with cultural distance, to underscore the necessity of the Chinese mission. An officer in Fujian named Qiu 丘 wrote the Jesuit missionaries to stress the distance between China and the West ("tens of thousands of *li* 里") and maintain that the only common ground between the two is the Catholic religion.[109] Thus he accentuates the difference between the two peoples. Instead of inferring from this that the Catholic faith is inappropriate for China, Qiu emphasized its importance as the only possible link between the two worlds. Conspicuously, this Catholicism appears independent of culture, and thus no more European than Chinese.

Indeed, one way to better understand the Jesuits' rhetorical deployment of the idea of distance more generally is by investigating such Chinese responses to it. The late Ming anti-Jesuit polemicist Wei Jun 魏濬, writing in the "*Li Shuo Huangtang Huoshi*" 利說荒唐惑世 ["The Ricci Teachings Are Absurd and Deceitful"] worked backward to prove that Ricci was not a world traveler. He first denounced Ricci's world map ("like the trick of a painter who draws ghosts in his pictures") on the grounds that China is located off-centre, an idea manifestly ludicrous since in China at midnight one "can see the pole star in the *zifen* 子分." That empirical evidence contradicts Ricci's geography "really shows how dogmatic his ideas are!" [110]

The assumption that distance implies authoritative knowledge is never challenged. On the contrary, it is the linchpin of Wei Jun's argument. Because Ricci is so ignorant, he must not have come from a distant place:

---

[108] Trigault, ed., *De Christiana Expeditione*, 92.

[109] "…萬里之遙。所得同者。獨此聖教至公之理。" In the 閩中將樂縣丘先生致諸位神父書, ARSI JapSin I, (38/42), 40/3, fol. 2v.

[110] "試于夜分仰觀。北極樞星乃在子分。則中國當居正中。" *Zifen* 子分 usually refers to the period from 11 P.M. to 1 A.M., and here perhaps refers to the sky directly overhead. The north star is in roughly the same position twenty-four hours a day, so the reference to midnight is obscure. Wei Jun 魏濬, "Li Shuo Huangtang Huoshi" 利說荒唐惑世, in Changzhi Xu 徐昌治, ed., *Po Xie Ji* 破邪集 (水戶市 弘道館 安政乙卯, 1855), 3/37. My translations draw on parts of Wei-hua Chang, "A Commentary of the Four Chapters on Portugal, Spain, Holland, and Italy in the History of the Ming Dynasty," *Yenching Journal of Chinese Studies*, Monograph no. 7 (1934), 161–62, and were polished by Desmund Cheung. For a discussion of the importance of the pole stars in Chinese astronomy, see Joseph Needham, *Science and Civilisation in China* (Cambridge: Cambridge University Press, 1954), vol. II, 229–262. He includes on page 243 a diagram showing the *zi* 子 portion of the celestial equator.

"Those who trust him say that the people in his country are fond of traveling afar, but such an error as this would certainly not be made by a widely-traveled man." Despite the famous and long-standing presumption that the Middle Kingdom is self-sufficient in knowledge, the idea that distance suggested the ability to teach knowledge with authority has classical roots. Noting that Mencius had travelled a thousand *li* to reach his court, King Hui 惠 of Liang 梁 assumed the scholar had brought some valuable teachings for his kingdom.[111] Distance also brought authority in part because it makes confirmation difficult, as Wei Jun explains: "The map of the world which he made contains elements of the fabulous and mysterious, and is a downright attempt to deceive people on things which they personally can not go to verify for themselves."[112]

In the "*Xiedu Shiju*" 邪毒實據 ["Substantive Proof of Evil Poison"], the critical late-Ming author Su Jiyu 蘇及寓 explained how the Jesuits used distance to imply their impartiality as well as their authority: "When these barbarians [the Jesuit missionaries] say falsely that they come from a great distance of 90,000 *li*, it is because they want us to believe that they have no ulterior motives behind them, so as to prevent us from worrying about their aggressive purposes." Su rejected this totally, arguing from unnamed evidence that the Jesuits had already overrun more than thirty countries. "When they arrive in a country," Su warns, "they will certainly ruin that country." He admitted that the distance of these conquests makes it difficult to prove, but he somehow knew of an example closer to home, the Philippines – "whose kings they killed and whose people they robbed. It required only a few of them to subdue an entire country. Are not these facts obvious proofs of their aggressive nature?"[113]

Another Chinese anti-Jesuit pamphlet sought to block Jesuit recourse to this strategy by denying the distance involved. First, it directly questions the Jesuits' claim to have come over great distance: "You are said to have come over 90,000 *li*, but who knows if this is not a lie?" Then it points out the hole in the Jesuits' story: If they came alone, from so far, so long ago, how can they continue to offer these "strange objects" as gifts? Were the Jesuits strong enough, it asks rhetorically, to have carried all these things themselves? Finally it presents another explanation of the Jesuits' background: "I have also come to know your origin: You were born in

---

[111] Mencius, 1.2. ("王曰,「叟,不遠千里而來,亦將有以利吾國乎?」").

[112] "直欺人以其目之所不能見。足之所不能至。無可按驗耳。...信之者乃謂其國人好遠游。斯非游遠者耶。" Wei Jun 魏濬, 3/37–8.

[113] "—此夷詐言九萬里。夫詐遠者。令人信其無異志。...到—國,必壞—國。" Su Jiyu 蘇及寓, "*Xiedu Shiju*" 邪毒實據, in Changzhi Xu 徐昌治, ed., *Po Xie Ji* 破邪集 (水戶市:弘道館,安政乙卯, 1855), 3/33. See also Chang Wei-hua, 162–3.

a little country near Xiangshan, you are clever and crafty, and you covet the sacred treasures of China."[114]

This last point, that the Jesuits' home was not at all distant from China, received official sanction. The Official History of the Ming Dynasty 明史 conflated Spain and the Philippines into a single country, located in the Indian Ocean, and Portugal 佛郎機 was located near Melaka. The gazetteer *Da Qing Yitong Zhi* 大清一統志 [*Great Qing Unified Annals*] (completed 1820) also placed Portugal near Melaka.[115] Both works noted that the Portuguese were Buddhist before their conversion to Catholicism, an idea perhaps echoed by the first character of the Chinese name for Portugal, *fo* 佛, which also means "Buddha."[116] Was this an attempt to show that Portugal's religion was only slightly more (or less?) prestigious than Buddhism, which centuries earlier had lost its attraction for most educated Chinese?

An alternative Jesuit approach in China was to minimize cultural distance by stressing the common origin of the Europeans and Chinese, and the common basis of their religions. In the explanation published in 1663, the convert Li Zubai 李祖白, a student of Schall, appealed to the fact that all mankind originated in Judea to prove the familial relation between the Chinese and the Europeans – and to describe Catholicism as a resurgence of ancient Chinese religion. This strategy backfired as the Jesuits' Chinese opponents hastened to reassert distance between the two cultures. Yang Guangxian 楊光先 (1597–1669) wrote an outraged rebuttal, condemning the idea that "inhabitants of the myriad countries both in the East and the West were descendents of the heretics (i.e., the Jews), that one of them had become [the ancient] Emperor Fu-hsi [of China] in the Middle Kingdom, and that both the Six Classics and the Four Books [of China] are only commentaries on the heretic [Jewish] scripture!"[117]

---

[114] "汝謂九萬里來。[誰知其非說謊乎] 汝既孤身至此。去家已遠歷年已久。何緣與汝文者猶有本國異物贈之豈汝脅力甚大。當日所[?]之物。[...]吾亦閱汝之根底矣。生於近香山之小國。聰明奸宄。意在覬覦中原神器。" 闢邪集, ARSI JapSin II, 77, fols. 13v-14r. Either 1643 (Chongzhen 崇禎 16) or 1703 (Kangxi 康熙 42).

[115] Zhang Tingyu 張廷玉, *Ming Shi* 明史 (Beijing: 中華書局: 新華書店北京發行所發行, 1974), XIII.8361–82, XIII.8411–38; Muzhang'a 穆彰阿, *Da Qing Yitong Zhi* 大清一統志 (Taibei: 藝文印書館, 196-?), vol. 154 (卷 424). See Ch'en, 354, 356.

[116] Zhang, XIII.8411–38; Muzhang'a, vol. 154 (卷 424). See Ch'en, 356.

[117] Yang Kuang-hsien's memorial of September 15, 1664, and Letter to censur Xu Zhijian, April 21, 1664, cited in John T. Young, "An early Confucian attack on Christianity: Yang Kuang-Hsien and his Pu-te-i," *Journal of the Chinese University of Hong Kong* 3 (1975): 173–4; Jacques Gernet, *Chine et christianisme: action et reaction* (Paris: Gallimard, 1982), 176; Lo-shu Fu, ed. *A Documentary Chronicle of Sino-Western Relations, 1644–1820*, Monographs and papers (Association for Asian Studies), no. 22 (Tucson: University of Arizona Press, 1966), I.35, II.447; Väth, 297.

The weight of distance and history in both the Chinese and Christian cultures thus set off sparks when the two traditions collided. Less balanced power relations and less cross-cultural interest led to a different story in Mexico, one less accessible to historians. (There one early Franciscan, unschooled in native languages, taught the concept of hell by burning alive Indians' dogs and cats.)[118] Such dialogues, and pantomimes, rightfully command historians' attention, and this chapter has used them primarily to better understand the missionaries. The ending of time and the filling of space coloured the Jesuit mentality. Notions of distance tended to be limited to discussions, or more often displays, of authority, such as we have seen here in the Chinese and American contexts. In the Jesuit missionaries' own motivations, however, distance played a role that was minimal and sometimes even antagonistic. The missionary stimulus is the subject of the next chapter.

---

[118] Ricard, *Spiritual Conquest*, 104.

6   The Missionary Motivation

> "Do you remember that passage in which [Rousseau] asks the reader
> what he would do if he could become wealthy by killing an old Chinese
> mandarin, without leaving Paris, just by an act of will?"
> "Yes."
> "Well then?"
> "Oh, I'm on my thirty-third mandarin."
>
> – Honoré de Balzac, *Père Goriot* (1835)

Originating with Denis Diderot, popularized and misattributed to Henri
Rousseau by François-Auguste-René Chateaubriand, this tale of a perfect
crime, which robs a Chinese mandarin of life and fortune by the magic of
hypothesis, throws the ideas of morality and distance into tension. Would
you sacrifice a man on the other side of the globe in order to acquire
his wealth? With the early-modern expansion of Europe, thousands of
prospective missionaries faced a parallel question: Would you sacrifice
yourself to secure the salvation of someone on the other side of the globe?
Both questions weigh the value of a distant soul against that of a near life.
In his 1809 *Génie du Christianisme* [*Genius of Christianity*], Chateaubriand
uses his own response to demonstrate the reality of the conscience.[1]
This chapter examines the response of the early-modern Catholic missionaries to demonstrate the reality of a new global perspective in
Christianity.

   This fundamental question in the description of this global religion is
one of motivation. Why did so many Jesuits, along with religious of other
orders, experience the desire to win the souls of those far away? Outside
of religion, the more natural instinct, perhaps, is to undervalue people at
a distance, to sense that one of "us" is worth more than one of "them."
As late as the 1930s the *Times* of London could print the headline "Small
Earthquake in Chile: Not Many Killed."[2] Even today newsroom walls

[1] See Carlo Ginzburg, "Killing a Chinese Mandarin: The Moral Implications of Distance,"
New Left Review 208 (1994): 107–19.
[2] Mordecai Richler, *The Best of Modern Humor* (New York: Alfred A. Knopf, 1983), xvi.

114

might display variations of a facetious journalistic rule of thumb for use in calculating the value of a story: "1 American = 10 Europeans = 100 Chinese = 1000 Africans." Neither instance lacks a black humour, and both reveal a human reality. The Jesuit mentality of valuing the far over the near is unusual. Joseph Needham described it as "a mobilization of oecumenical idealism something like that which the League of Nations or the United Nations have now and then been able to command in our own time."[3] What drove it?

Recruitment of Missionaries

The prime agents behind recruitment efforts were the procurators. The American provinces regularly sent provincial procurators to Europe. Thus was Trigault's tour through Europe predated by the travels of Diego de Torres Bollo, from the Paraguay Province, through Germany, Italy, Poland, and Flanders in search of recruits – who in fact would initially be prevented from going overseas by the Council of the Indies. China also sent a steady stream of procurators, including Couplet and Alexander Ciceri, who went to Germany.[4]

The early writings that attracted missionaries were general descriptions, not materials designed specifically for recruiting purposes. For example, during his travels in Europe, Trigault used a single book as his chief propaganda tool – the diaries of Matteo Ricci, the founder of the Jesuit mission in China. Recovered from among his personal effects after his death, Ricci's journals were taken to Europe by Trigault, who hoped to translate them from Italian into Latin during the voyage. The sailors' distracting noise prevented the translation until Trigault arrived in Rome, but the work was published soon afterwards as the *De Christiana Expeditione*. He prefaced Ricci's writings, one of the earliest substantial accounts of China available to Europe, with his own one-book introduction providing the necessary sinological background. Similarly, Roth, having returned to Europe from China, wrote a letter to a Jesuit in the Upper German Province that circulated and excited missionary desire.[5]

---

[3] Needham, *Science and Civilisation in China*, vol. IV, 2.170.
[4] Borges Morán, *El envió*, 90, 105–6, 149–74; Lázaro de Aspurz, 177–80; Huonder, *Deutsche Jesuitenmissionäre*, 209. For the importance of the procurators in recruitment, see Christoph Nebgen, " . . . dahin zillet mein verlangen und begierd. Epistolae Indipetarum der Deutschen Assistenz SJ als Quellengattung," in *Sendung – Eroberung – Begegnung: Franz Xaver, die Gesellschaft Jesu und die katholische Weltkirche im Zeitalter des Barock*, ed. Johannes Meier (Wiesbaden: Harrassowitz, 2005), 90–2.
[5] Hermann Hoffmann, "Philipp Jeningens Missionssehnsucht," *Theologische Quartalschrift* 30 (1930): 353.

Although such general accounts of the mission undoubtedly quick-ened enthusiasm, texts written specifically to recruit new missionaries later appeared. As vice-provincial of the China missions (1676–80), Ver-biest extended a request to all Jesuit centres throughout Europe for mis-sionaries, especially those competent in theology, philosophy, mathemat-ics, and astronomy. Jesuits in Beijing printed Verbiest's original call, and within four years French and Latin copies appeared in Europe.[6] That appeal struck a responsive chord in Upper Germany, where according to Kino,

many men ... are most desirous of going to China, and they are undoubtedly more apt candidates because they are thoroughly versed, especially in mathe-matics and various branches of science; above all, they are richly endowed with religious virtues demanded by Father Berbiest [sic]. I am convinced that in no other Province ... are there so many Jesuits as in the Upper German Province who devote so much attention to mathematics and this particularly in order to go some day to the Chinese missions. ... I could easily name thirty or more. ... As they see at every turn in the libraries and elsewhere in the Province the pictures repre-senting Adam Schall and Martin Martini, they believe that they are unmistakably called to follow them by volunteering for China.[7]

Kino himself was soon in a position to entice other Germans to Mex-ico. Writing to Paul Zingnis in Germany, Kino reported that his spiritual charges were building a guest house for anyone who might come from his "beloved province of Upper Germany."[8] In a letter to the provost of Pöllau, Andreas Mancker suggested that the similarity between the Cal-ifornian and German climates would make Germans particularly suited for that mission.[9] In 1691 demand was sufficient for General González to pass around a circular asking all the houses of the Bohemian Province for missionaries.[10]

---

[6] Verbiest, Beijing, to the Fathers of the Company in Europe, August 15, 1678, ARSI JapSin 145 20–39v, and BRB Ms 16.691–3, published in Josson and Willaert, eds., 230–53. See John W. Witek, *Controversial Ideas in China and in Europe: A Biography of Jean-Francois Foucquet, S. J. (1665–1741)*, Bibliotheca Instituti Historici S. I. vol. 43 (Rome: Institutum Historicum S. I., 1982), 21.

[7] Kino, Cádiz, December 14, 1680, in Burrus, ed., *Kino escribe*, 63. See also ibid., 120–22, 133–35.

[8] Kino, San Lucas – San Bruno, to P. Paul Zingnis, with Diary of the Trip to Califor-nia, September 29 to December 15, 1683, BHStA Jes. 607 Mappe Eusebius Kinus II 607/127.

[9] Andreas Mancker, "Schreiben eines österreichischen Jesuitenmissionärs an den Probst zu Pöllau betreffs seiner Reise nach Mexico und seiner Erfahrung daselbt," ed. Josef von Zahn, *Steiermärkische Geschichtsblätter* 1 (1880): 37.

[10] María del Carmen Anzures y Bolaños, "El Florilegio Medicinal de Johannes Steinhöfer: una contribución a la entobotánica mexicana," *Ibero-Americana Pragensia* 21 (1987): 104.

The Aspiration to Missionary Work

To get a better feel for the texture of the desire these efforts nourished, we first turn to poetry, perhaps the medium most successful in capturing the urgency of the enthusiasm for mission. In its ranks the Society of Jesus numbered several poets with global ambitions. Jakob Balde (1604–68), for example, long desired to become a missionary. In 1640 he composed a secular poem on the hundredth anniversary of the Society, an over-the-top expression of esteem for missionary activity, and he would later express missionary enthusiasm even in theatre works, such as *Alexis Madurensis* [*Alexis the Mandarin*].[11]

The great Jesuit poet of the mission, however, was Friedrich Spee von Langenfeld (1591–1635). Even before enrolling in the Jesuit college in Cologne, Spee was already pining for the foreign missions. In November 1617, while teaching poetry at Worms, he wrote a letter to the Jesuit general, asking that the wish he had held "almost from the cradle" be fulfilled. His parents had tried to get him to forget this idea, he wrote, but "those distant lands had wounded my heart" – a leitmotif that also appears in his masterwork, the *Trutz-nachtigall* [*Rival Nightingale*]. Indeed, Spee cited a missionary vocation as his main motive for joining the Society. He claimed to have no gifts to recommend him for the mission, except for his desire and his piety. General Vitelleschi's response was typical. He refused, "in part because others from closer lands are available, in part because in Germany a great field of work stands open to the Society."[12] As we shall see in the following chapter, this sentiment was widespread even among German Jesuits.

By 1620 Spee had already composed several cantos for catechumens, and in 1623 he also wrote a song for Easter entitled, "Die ganze Welt, H[err] Jesus Christus" ["The Whole World, Lord Jesus Christ"].[13] His most affecting invocation of mission was the "Poëtisch gesang von dem H. Francisco Xauièr der geselschafft IESV, als er in Jappon schiffen

---

[11] Bernhard Duhr, *Geschichte der Jesuiten in den Länder Deutscher Zunge* (Freiburg im Breisgau: Herder, 1907–28), 2:2.601, 609. On the importance of theatre for recruitment of missionaries see Nebgen, 88.

[12] Emmy Rosenfeld, *Friedrich Spee von Langenfeld: Eine Stimme in der Wüste*, Quellen und Forschungen zur Sprach- und Kulturgeschichte der germanischen Völker 2 (126) (Berlin: Walter de Gruyter & Co., 1958), 22–23; Karl-Jürgen Miesen, *Friedrich Spee: Pater, Dichter, Hexen-Anwalt* (Düsseldorf: Droste, 1987), 69, 73–75; Paul-Werner Scheele, "'In Spe spes': Friedrich Spees frühe Dichtungen als Hoffnungsimpulse," in *Friedrich von Spee: Priester, Poet, Prophet*, ed. Michael Sievernich (Frankfurt am Main: Josef Knecht, 1986), 67–70.

[13] R. Gerlich and T. van Oorschot, "Spee von Langenfeld, Friedrich," in *Diccionario histórico de la Compañia de Jesús: biográfico-temático* (Rome: Institutum Historicum, 2001); Rosenfeld, 22; Scheele, 67–70.

wolte" ["Poetical Song about St. Francis Xavier of the Society of Jesus, When He Wanted to Embark for Japan"], one of about fifty learned songs, many with classical allusions in form or substance, published in the *Trutz-nachtigall* fifteen years after his death.[14] The song begins by evoking the difficulties and dangers facing the missionary: "Alle waren ihm entgegen . . . Wind, vnd Wetter; Meer, vnd Wällen. . . . " ["Everything was against him . . . wind, and weather, sea, and waves. . . . "]. The poem's speaker calls on the hearer to speak no more about the disconcerting weather, which would never bother a hero or a knight: "Schweiget, schweiget von gewitter, / Ach von winden schweiget stil: / Nie noch warer Held, noch Ritter / Achtet solcher kinderspil" ["Be silent, be silent about the storm / oh, be silent and calm about the winds: / Neither a true hero nor a knight / heeds such child's games"]. After four verses of building up the contrast between the immense dangers and the missionary's resolve, the poem explains the solution. The missionary is driven by a desire for souls, for he is one "who only thinks of finding souls, beautiful souls without measure." A line in the final, sixth stanza repeats the key word, "Seelen, seelen muß ich haben" ["Souls, souls I must have"].[15]

Global mission reappears in Spee's *Güldenes Tugend-Buch* [*Golden Book of Virtues*], a devotional manual exploring the three divine virtues of faith, hope, and love. Spee developed it in the course of his ministry of weekly spiritual exercises to Cologne's Ursuline order, sometimes informally called the female branch of the Jesuits. The earliest extant copy dates from 1640.[16] The sixteenth chapter deals with love, specifically with the love of one's neighbour. The speaker reminds his spiritual daughter that the desire to win souls is a "righteous, proper" [*rechtschaffene eigentliche*] love of neighbour. "So tell me, my child," he prompts her, "if you had the opportunity, would you not have the desire and passion to travel to the most distant Indies of this world to bring thousands and thousands of unbelieving peoples back to Christian belief and baptism?" The expected answer is given, in the affirmative.[17]

---

[14] This work would later be dear to the Romantics, especially Friedrich Schlegel and Clemens Brentano. Spee's working draft, now called the "Straßburger Autograph" (Strasbourg Universitätsbibliothek, Ms 2328. [L. germ. 353], and an additional 1634 manuscript (Stadtbibliothek Trier, Sign. Hs 1118/2283 8°) also survive.
[15] Friedrich Spee, *Trutz-Nachtigal*, ed. Theo G. M. van Oorschot, Friedrich Spee Sämtliche Schriften I (Bern: Francke, 1985), 94. Dimler suggests that ocean symbolizes obstacles to Francis Xavier's desire for souls. G. Richard Dimler, *Friedrich Spee's Trutznachtigall*, German Studies in America 13 (Bern: Herbert Lang, 1973), 31.
[16] BNF All. 134.
[17] Friedrich Spee von Langenfeld, *Güldenes Tugend-Buch*, ed. Theo G. M. van Oorschot, Friedrich Spee Sämtliche Schriften II (Munich: Kösel, 1968), 364.

Spee progressively took Vitelleschi's original response to heart. Already in the early 1620s, as a young professor of logic at Paderborn, Spee spent his free time "missionizing" the neighbouring nobility, enjoying particular success among the earthy Westphalian *Landjunkers'* wives. From the fall of 1628 he worked as a missionary among Lutherans in Peine, "not without a healthy fear," for the archbishop of Cologne, Ferdinand of Bavaria (1612–50), had only recently ordered its recatholicization, despite pressure from the Brunswick dukes. He was both too successful a missionary and not quite successful enough, for on April 29, 1629, an anti-Catholic fanatic wounded him near Woltorf. After recovering from his injuries, the erstwhile missionary retired to Paderborn to teach moral theology.[18]

Salvation and the "Lutheran" Jesuits

How typical was Spee in his hunger for "souls, souls" and for mission? The question of why a man would want to become a Jesuit missionary presupposes the question of why he would want to become a Jesuit at all. Certainly many bright students were inspired to join through the overtures of their Jesuit instructors – and the Jesuits had themselves educated many or most recruits[19] – but what was the inner motivation? Thomas V. Cohen has explored this fundamental question of motivation by studying sources from opposite ends of Europe: a 1561–62 survey asking Iberian Jesuits why they had joined the Society[20] and a collection of spiritual autobiographies from the Polish Province (1574–80).[21] He approaches his sources with care, for "the stated motive may have been a motto, a sort of shorthand, for an elaborate dialectic, only part of which ever surfaced into consciousness. Also the remembered, stated motive might indeed have been more a justification, to friends, colleagues, and onlookers, for the act of choice than it was the real thought and feeling of a recruit."[22]

Cohen's results present a Society of Jesus very different from the traditional one, our understanding of which depended so heavily on historians'

---

[18] Theo G. M. van Oorschot, "Friedrich Spees Rolle und Schicksal bei der Rekatholisierung von Peine in den Jahren 1628–1629," in *Friedrich Spee im Licht der Wissenschaften*, ed. Anton Arens (Mainz: Gesellschaft für Mittelrheinische Kirchengeschichte, 1984), 21–22, 26, 28–33; Miesen, 111; Dimler, 12.

[19] Cohen, "Why," 251.

[20] This source is a thirty-question survey administered in the Jesuit provinces of Portugal, Castile, Andalucia, and Aragon in 1561–2; designed by Jerome Nadal as a pre-visitation measure, it includes the question, "With what motives or inclinations he entered the Company and who received him, and where?" Cohen, "Why," 239, citing "Responsa ad Interrogationes P. Nadal," ARSI FG 77.1–77.4.

[21] Joseph Warszawski, *Unicus Universae Societatis Iesu Vocationum Liber Autobiographicus Poloniae Provinciae Proprius (1574–1580)*, (Rome: n.p., 1966).

[22] Cohen, "Why," 240.

suspicions and assumptions. Mission, even taken broadly to include heretics with the infidels, is all but non-existent. Of the 695 Iberians who responded, only ten (1.4%) mentioned any desire to evangelize the Indies, while letters from the Indies had motivated nine (1.3%). Four (0.6%) sought martyrdom. What of the shock troops of the Counter Reformation? Only two respondents had admitted entering the Society to oppose heresy (0.3%). The Polish autobiographies confirm these findings. Only one writer mentioned the Indies, and the opportunity to teach heretics attracted a single Jesuit. When describing their motivation these Jesuits made scant use of words like "Germany" or "India," "heretics" or "infidels."[23]

How, then, did these men explain their decision to become Jesuits? Salvation dominates their answers. Sixty-four Jesuits of the Polish province cited a fear of the dangers of the world or a desire to save their own souls. An Iberian respondent recalled "seeing myself so lost and entwined in vices that thinking of death made my hair fall out and so it seemed to me there was no penance or mortification I would not undertake to satisfy our Lord, and so I spoke to a father of the company and got them to receive me in Simancas." Cohen describes these answers as "curiously negative": "They describe less what one would do inside the Order than what one would refrain from."[24] This is an intense, almost selfish, concern for the salvation of the soul. The "worldly asceticism" Max Weber ascribed to the Jesuits here seems more ascetic than worldly.[25]

The temptation to call these concerns "medieval" comes from a misunderstanding of the Jesuits as an "enlightened" or "rational" phenomenon.[26] It would be fairer, and no less striking, to describe these Jesuits as "Lutheran," in the sense that they participate in the same religious conflicts as the young Martin Luther. Luther became the Augustinian hermit Brother Martin in response to a vow to Saint Anne for saving him from an electrical storm, while Eusebius Kino became the Jesuit Eusebius Franciscus Kino to fulfill a vow to St. Francis Xavier for saving him from a desperate illness.[27] The two men walked different paths and found different interests along the way, but the fundamental motive force for each remained an intense concern with personal salvation, which

---

[23] Ibid., 241, 248–50.
[24] Ibid., 241, 250.
[25] Max Weber, *The Protestant Ethic and the Spirit of Capitalism*, trans. Talcott Parsons (London: Routledge, 1992), 95–96; idem, *Sociology*, 120.
[26] Weckmann offers compelling reasons why the Jesuits were "medieval." Weckmann, 130.
[27] Burrus, *Kino and the Cartography*, 3; Peter Stitz, "Kalifornische Briefe des P. Eusebio Francsico Kino (=Chini) nach der oberdeutschen Provinz, 1683–5," *Archivum Historicum Societatis Iesu* 3 (1934): 112.

then blossomed into a concern for the salvation for others. Nor is Kino an exception. Philipp Jeningen wrote the general in 1671 to report that Francis Xavier's intercession to rescue him from death had led to an oath to do everything he could to be sent to the missions. In a follow-up letter the next year, Jeningen offered to collect money for the China mission in Germany and then bring it to Rome. Perhaps he could leave for the missions from there. Jeningen mentioned his desire to postpone acting as a priest until he reached China. The difficulties of the missionary life attracted Jesuit recruits as a way to mortify the flesh and the will.[28]

Of course, the strength of this general inclination varied from individual to individual, or within the lifespan of a single Jesuit. The following rough typology of possible Jesuit attitudes, illustrated in Chart 1, is based on how much they cared for their own souls and how much they cared for the souls of others.

The zone at the chart's lower left indicates a minimal concern for souls and is suggestive of the tradition that would be condemned as the Quietist heresy. It was espoused first by the Spanish mystic Juan Falconi (1596–1638), most famously in Rome by the Spanish priest Miguel de Molinos (1628–96), and most definitely in France by Jeanne-Marie de la Motte Guyon (1648–1717) and François Salignac de Fénelon (1651–1715). Fénelon's teaching that the quietest could attain a love of God so powerful as to make irrelevant, or even harmful, any thought to the salvation of one's self or one's neighbour, technically called the "caritas pura," was condemned by Pope Innocent XI (1676–89) in 1699.[29] In papal eyes, no soteriology could neglect a concern for the self. Jesuits populated this area very sparsely, if at all.

The lower right corner of the chart pairs a disinterest in personal salvation with a high interest in the salvation of others. Here we find the Jesuit stereotype, selfless in his concern for the spiritual well-being of others. Cohen's research, as well as this project, suggests that very few Jesuits were of this type. Although other Christians might appear in this corner, the popular image of Mahayana Buddhism's bodhisatvas may be the perfect representative. These selflessly postpone entry into *nirvana* until they have helped every sentient being become enlightened.[30]

The upper left corner couples the disinterest in the welfare of others with an intense interest in one's own salvation. This does correspond with Cohen's findings, but many Jesuits of this sort left the order. After

---

[28] Hoffmann, "Philipp," 361–64; Cohen, "Why," 241.

[29] Leszek Kolakowski, "Quietism," in the *Encyclopedia of Religion* (New York: Macmillan, 1987), XII.154–55.

[30] On the accuracy of a Boddhisatva "postponing" nirvana, see Paul Williams, *Mahayana Buddhism: The Doctrinal Foundations* (London: Routledge, 1989), 52–54.

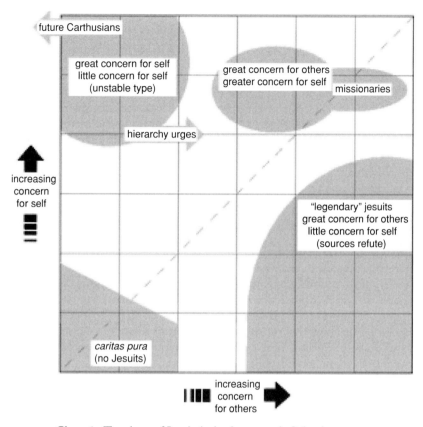

Chart 1. Typology of Jesuit Attitudes towards Salvation.

studying the statements of Jesuits seeking to abandon the Society, Martin reports that all "the testimonies reveal a tendency to withdrawal from the Society's apostolic labours, to embrace the perfection and salvation of one's own soul but to consider the perfection and salvation of the soul of a neighbour to be a distraction or an imposition."[31] Typically these discontents proposed switching to the Carthusians, famously "never reformed because never deformed," the only religious order Ignatius saw fit for an ex-Jesuit to join.[32] There was a strong tendency within the Society to encourage Jesuits in this "selfish" corner to adopt a concern with the souls

---

[31] Martin, *Jesuit*, 26.
[32] See Charles Van de Vorst, "La Compagnie de Jesús et le passage à l'ordre des Chartreuz (1540–1694)," *Archivum Historicum Societatis Iesu* 23 (1954): 3–34.

for others in addition to, rather than in place of, a concern for personal salvation. Ignatius was remembered declaring that "he wanted none in the Society just to save their own souls if, beyond this, they did not all make ready to save the souls of other people."[33]

The vast majority of Jesuits found themselves in the large upper right section, indicative of an intense concern for self and others. Most apparently found themselves on the upper half of the diagonal, for they explicitly expressed more concern for themselves than for others. Missionaries do not seem to have been the exception. In fact, they were never forced to choose, because to a great extent it was in the very act of labouring for the salvation of potential converts that the Jesuit missionary worked out his own salvation. As Martin explains, the missionaries' seeking "God in all things permitted an active apostolate; Jesuits could seek God and consequently their own salvation in the classroom, pulpit, confessional box, hospital, prison – in short, wherever another soul needed saving." The missionaries feared for their own salvation, because the salvation of the world was their own responsibility.[34] From the Sisoguíchic mission in northern Mexico, Neumann wrote to the general that the missionaries' goals were peace and the good of their souls.[35] Another Jesuit directly tied converts' salvation process to his own by understanding their souls as redeemed by the blood of his own redeemer.[36] Kino began an extraordinary passage routinely by describing the beneficiaries of missionary work as, first, Christ, and, second, the Indians themselves. Then, he goes on rather strangely to present as a lesser alternative to missionary work the immediate enjoyment of happiness in heaven with the angels.[37]

The motivation that most characterizes the missionary Jesuit, in the strict sense, was a stated need to celebrate or do "the work" of God. Writing to the general, Schall stressed that the desire to glorify God and save souls motivated him. He explicitly distinguished between divine motivation and human factors, which would instead encourage him to return to Germany.[38] Kögler mentioned that he became a missionary

[33] James Brodrick, *Origines et expansion des Jésuites* (Paris: SFELT, 1950), 96.
[34] Martin, *Jesuit*, 78; Dominique Deslandres, "The French Jesuits' Missionary World," in *The Jesuits: Cultures, Sciences, and the Arts, 1540–1773*, ed. John W. O'Malley, Gauvin Alexander Bailey, Steven J. Harris, and T. Frank Kennedy (Toronto: University of Toronto Press, 1999), 261.
[35] Neumann, Sisoguíchic, to Gen. Juan Fernández de Retana, January 4, 1692, AGI Patronato 236, R.1 (2) fol. 681r.
[36] Bartche, Warsaw, to Jesuit general, February 7, 1696, ARSI Pol. 79 fol. 204r.
[37] Kino, Cádiz, to the Duquesa de Aveiro, September 15, 1680, published in Burrus, *Kino escribe* 85–91.
[38] "Epistola P. Adami Schall ad P. Generalem Mutium Vitelleschi," [Rome], January 2, 1616, ARSI G. Sup. 18-II 293r, published in Huonder, *Deutsche Jesuitenmissionäre*, 207.

because he had no other purpose than to work for God.[39] Sometimes this "work" could take very physical form. Another asked that he at least be sent to serve "like a burro" to carry the missionaries' baggage.[40] There was a palpable sense that overseas missionary work was the only way to do God's work. In autumn 1687 the "Conqueror of the Turks" Prince Charles of Lorraine was in Innsbruck, and went to call on some Jesuit missionaries passing through from Bohemia. He asked whether they were going to the missions of their own free will or under the command of their superiors. The reply – that they had prayed for years for grace from God and a commission from their Company – impressed the prince. The Jesuits politely pointed out, "What we have requested of God is nothing in comparison to the dangers of the wars against the Turks." The prince, however, firmly declared, "No, no! We fight for God's cause [*Gottes Sache*], but also for our families, our house, and the Empire." The missionaries, the prince implied, worked for God's cause only.[41]

What did missionaries take "God's cause" to be? Often they understood their specific way of carrying out God's work as a discernable vocation. Indeed, hopeful men applying for a missionary position frequently cited a specific vocation, as did Martini in 1634.[42] Kino also ranked discernment of a mission vocation higher than the mission itself: "It is better to live in accordance with the will of God, empty of every disordered passion, than to convert the entire world in accordance with your own will."[43] General Vitelleschi's recruitment letter addresses itself to God, in the hope that He would set Jesuit hearts aflame to water infertile lands with their sweat and blood.[44] The ultimate source of missionaries' motivation was God.

The subtle relationship between these concepts appeared clearest in Franz Xavier Amrhyn's guidelines for future missionaries. He advised aspirants that to become a missionary without a God-given vocation would most certainly bring their own salvation into grave danger. On the other hand, a refused call could contradict God's plan for certain distant souls to be saved only by that specific would-be missionary. Refusal to accept a missionary vocation also endangered the aspirant's salvation.[45]

---

[39] Duhr, *Deutsche Auslandsehnsucht*, 21.
[40] November 16, 1716. Duhr, *Geschichte*, 4:2.509.
[41] Jaksch, 15.
[42] Martini to M. Vitellesco, August 11, 1634, ARSI FG 740, fol. 209r.
[43] "Kino, Hall, to P. Gen. Gian Paolo Oliva, January 31, 1672, ARSI FG 754 Nr. 99, published in Pietro Tacchi Venturi, ed., "Sei lettere inedite del P. Eusebio Chino al P. Gian Paolo Oliva Gen. d. C. d. G." *Studi Trentini di Scienze storiche* 11 (1930): 11–12.
[44] Miesen, 71.
[45] Amrhyn, "Documenta," 203–4.

A call from God was thus both the necessary and sufficient condition for missionary work. Called, a man must serve; not called, he must not serve. "God's work" found expression as missionary work, but remained a higher purpose than the mere salvation of souls. If the applicant simply desired to win Indians' souls, Amrhyn continued, he might find himself teaching Spaniards' children far from the "mission." If he became a missionary to save his own soul, he might find more obstacles to perfection abroad than in Europe. The principal reason must be, I want to go to the Indies because God wants it.[46]

A parallel motivation that recurs in the Jesuit missionaries' writings was the desire to win the red crown of martyrdom. This was a common theme in the *epistolae indipetarum* ("*indipetae*"), letters written to Rome by hopeful aspiring missionaries.[47] Georg Gerstlacher described the impression a representation of a martyrdom made on him as a young boy.[48] Stressing how longstanding his desire was, Johann Steinhöffer claimed to have hoped since he was twelve years old to save lost souls and become a martyr.[49] Aspiring missionary Michael Durst complained, "If I stay in Germany, then I can't give my life for the friends and enemies of Christ."[50] Accordingly, if the famous persecution in Japan was a local setback, missionaries in Mexico perceived it as a devastating disaster for them, for how could they now compete with the Japanese province for recruits? The authors of the letters in *Auß America* had to work overtime to emphasize that New Spain offered equally attractive opportunities for martyrdom.[51] This was no easy task, for death at the hands of the uncivilized Indians of northern New Spain, who killed without allowing missionaries to choose death of their own will, conformed neither to the theology of martyrdom, nor to the literary tradition of martyrologies rooted in the persecutions of ancient Rome.[52]

---

[46] Ibid., 204–5. See also Giovanni Pizzorusso, "Le choix indifferent: mentalités et attentes des Jésuites aspirants missionnaires dans l'Amérique française au XVIIe siècle," *Mélanges de l'Ecole Française de Rome Italie et Méditerranée* 109 (1997), 881–94, at 888.

[47] Grulich, 39–40. See Pizzorusso, 890; Gregory, 250–314. For a discussion of *indipetae* from Naples, see Jennifer D. Selwyn, *A Paradise Inhabited by Devils: The Jesuits' Civilizing Mission in Early Modern Naples* (Ashgate: Aldershot/Hants England, 2004), 98–105. For *indipetae* of China-bound Jesuits, see Brockey, 225–33.

[48] ARSI FG 754, fol. 474, quoted in Nebgen, 89.

[49] Steinhöffer, Brünn [Brno], to P. Prov. Tirso González, July 5, 1691, ARSI FG 756 Nr. 312.

[50] January 3, 1615. Duhr, *Geschichte*, 2:2.595.

[51] See Sauer, 37–38, 82.

[52] See Antonio Rubial García, *La santidad controvertida: hagiografía y conciencia criolla alrededor de los venerables no canonizados de Nueva España*, Mexico: UNAM, 1999, 155–60.

Even early on this tendency was so disruptive that in March 1567, General Borgia, writing to the provincial of Andalusia, demanded that future American missionaries be not only "eager to die, but counselled to safeguard their lives, to better use them in the service of the Lord our God."[53] Still, the Jesuit leadership sent mixed messages. As mentioned in Chapter 4, the walls of the novitiate at Sant'Andrea al Quirinale in Rome depicted martyrdoms around the world, and the St. Michael's Church in Munich had an oil painting representing three Japanese martyrs.[54] The idea was not to live a missionary's life but to die a martyr's death.[55] A final example shows how controversial the hopes of martyrdom could be. In 1638 a Spanish Jesuit at Macao claimed to have already died and been resurrected so that he might go to Japan and die, again, as a martyr. He declared he could not deviate from his mission, even if his innards were pulled out through his mouth, even if he had to travel to Japan flying on the Jesuit martyr's cloak he had with him. Though he would be thrice expelled from the Society, this father Cypriano won the approval of the ranking Jesuit, the visitor Manuel Dias the Elder (1549–1639), and of the Macanese people, who applauded his sermons with riots.[56]

The Jesuits were unique in their great enthusiasm for the mission. The Society as a whole rarely wanted for volunteers, as recruits offered themselves spontaneously, or at the prompting of the propagandistic literature, to their provincials or the general. Other orders had to recruit more actively, and that recruitment literature offers an excellent perspective on what the recruiters (whose job it was to know) expected likely motivations to be.[57] In 1574 Mendieta suggested Franciscan recruiters stress the need for missionaries, the possibility of living in accordance with the Franciscan rule, and the spiritual benefits coming from the papacy. These papal favours included a plenary indulgence identical to the one given crusaders, a papal benediction, the privilege to travel as if doing so out of obedience to the Holy See (though technically the travel was voluntary), suffrage (that is, works for the sake of souls in purgatory),

[53] Felix Zubillaga, *La Florida: la mision jesuitica (1566–1572) y la colonizacion española* (Bibliotheca Instituti Historici S. I., v. 1. Rome: Institutum Historicum S. I., [1941]).

[54] Louis Richeôme describes them in his 1611 *La peinture spirituelle*. See Mâle, 120–21; Bangert, 110.

[55] In 1671 Rome sent out a directive ordering missionaries travelling to China to avoid exhausting themselves with onboard preaching: The passengers' spiritual and physical well-being was the responsibility of the ship's royal chaplain. The Jesuit leadership hoped to improve the odds of the missionaries' actually reaching their destination. December 18, 1671. Duhr, *Geschichte*, 2:2.354.

[56] Boxer, "Macao," 85–86.

[57] Borges Morán, *El envío*, 127, 149.

five private masses for each priest, and three hundred Our Fathers and Hail Marys for each lay brother. A missionary who died en route would still win these blessings. In being mentioned in the masses, he would be considered already a member of the overseas province he was joining.[58] Indeed, Franciscan and Dominican missionaries enjoyed many such spiritual benefits. In 1522 Adrian VI promised them the same rewards as the apostles had merited and gave them the pontifical benediction.[59] Pope Pius V (1566–72) extended to the Dominican missionaries a plenary indulgence, once in life and again at the time of death. He also offered a plenary indulgence on the day they took to the sea and on the day they disembarked.[60]

Did less heroic spiritual privileges also attract Jesuits? As we might expect, little could be more attractive to missionaries who were intent on their own salvation. Addressing General Borgia on behalf of the Florida expedition in 1566, the Jesuit martyr Pedro Martínez (1533–66) had written, "It now remains to conclude the letter with the matter most precious in my eyes, and so I left it for the end; and it is to humbly beg His Holiness, through you, to give us those favours which the priest Doctor Avellaneda requested writing to Rome, and which you will see are appropriate for us."[61] Martínez specifically asked for a pontifical benediction and a plenary indulgence for those who die on the job.[62] Similarly, the Jesuit Pedro Menéndez de Avilés asked Pius V in 1570 for "the most extensive indulgences and pardons there are" for Jesuits in Florida.[63] In fact, the early Jesuit missionaries did enjoy many such privileges. Pius V fulfilled every spiritual request of the Jesuits traveling to Florida.[64] On September 8, 1573, Gregory XIII extended a plenary indulgence to all Jesuits dying on voyages to or from America, granted for ten years, and he extended the duration for a further decade in 1579.[65] Contrary to earlier historians'

---

[58] "Avisos para nuestro Rmo. P. General Comisario de las Indias," undated, in Joaquin García Icazbalceta, ed., *Nueva colección de documentos para la historia de Mexico* (Mexico: Andrade y Morales, sucesores, 1886–92), 160–1.

[59] Balthasar de Tobar, *Compendio bulario indico*, ed. Manuel Gutierrez de Arce, Escuela de Estudios Hispano-Americanos (Consejo Superior de Investigaciones Cientificas) Publicaciones 82 (Seville: [Escuela de Estudios Hispano-Americanos], 1954), I.172.

[60] *Unigeniti Dei Filii*, Rome, August 22, 1571, in Tobar, I.384 (extract); *Semel in vita et in mortis Articulo*, Rome, February 18, 1568, in ibid., I.366.

[61] Pedro Martínez, Hispali, to Borgia, March 1, 1566, in Félix Zubillaga, *Monumenta Antiquae Floridae (1566–1572)* (Rome: Apud "Monumenta Historica Soc. Iesu," 1946), 40.

[62] Pedro Martínez to Borgia, Sanlúcar, June 1, 1566, in Zubillaga, *Monumenta*, 71.

[63] "Algunas indulgencias y perdones, los más amplios que obiere lugar." October 14, 1570, in Zubillaga, *Monumenta*, 451.

[64] Tobar, I.390–1.

[65] Borges Morán, *El envío*, 197.

assertions, these benefits were not restricted to the sixteenth century.[66] In 1685 or 1686 Van Hamme received a papal benediction before his voyage to Mexico.[67] Even as late as 1728 Benedict XIII (1724–30) offered a plenary indulgence to the Jesuits, on the condition that they devoutly pray for the success of the global mission.[68] To some extent all these spiritual perquisites made up for the great physical risks, for though perils might endanger the body, eternal salvation became ever more assured.

What of the truly worldly motivating factors, such as opportunities for wealth? The English Dominican Thomas Gage "alleged that *his* recruiting master had been Bacchus, for he had been recruited with copious drafts of sherry."[69] Less spiritual honours, such as the title of "universal preacher," began to become common in missionary recruitment just before the suppression of the Society, though this was never a major factor and not a factor at all in the seventeenth century.[70] Certainly, it remains hard to separate missionary zeal and zeal for gold. Columbus and his patrons showed enthusiasm for converting Indians, and a generation later Cortés claimed his only goal was to bring them to the holy faith.[71] Apparently many became missionaries because they found their current situations unbearable. Franz Xavier Amrhyn cautions applicants motivated by a dislike of their superior or by the failure to become a professor. If you cannot tolerate your unbearable German superiors, Amrhyn asks, how can you hope to cope with the Indians, or to endure the Spaniards' pride?[72]

A motivation that most historians neglect, but which appears quite probable in prosopographical analysis, comes from considerations of family. Johannes Maria Ratkay's (1647–83) uncle Nikola Ratkaj was a Jesuit missionary in India and Tibet.[73] Trigault's brother Elie Philippe

[66] Ibid., 199, had not found any similar *gracias* from 1601–1901, except mentioned by P. Manuel Mingo de la Concepción, recruiter of the Colegio de Tarija. Borges Morán suggests (197) that sixteenth-century benefits were more numerous than we can prove. The indices of the Jesuit archive in Rome indicate the existence of such documents, especially from the eighteenth century.

[67] Luis González Rodríguez, "Un cronista flamenco de la Tarahumara en 1688: Petrus Thomas van Hamme," *Estudios de historia novohispana* 3 (1970): 135.

[68] "Indulgencias / Condedidas pelo santissimo padre / Benedicto XIII / AOS RELIGIOSOS DA COMPANHIA DE JESU...," BL Add MS 21003, fol. 17r.

[69] Cummins, *Question*, 74.

[70] Borges Morán, *El envío*, 200–1.

[71] *Colección de documentos inéditos relativos al descubrimiento, conquista y organización de las antiguas posesiones españolas de ultramar*. 2. ser. (Madrid: Real Academia de la Historia. Madrid, Est.tip. "Sucesores de Rivadeneyra," 1885–1932), Tomo 38, 181; idem, Tomo 26, 21.

[72] Amrhyn, "Documenta," 211.

[73] George J. Prpic, "Rev. Juan M. Ratkay S. I., First Croatian Missionary in America (1647–1683)," *Radovi Hrvatskoga povijesnog instituta u Rimu* 3–4 (1971): 182.

(1575–1618), and nephews Michel (1602–67) and Nicolas (1611–66), also left for the China missions (1618, 1629, and 1643, respectively). Joseph Neumann's younger brother Johann Baptist Neumann (1659–1704) was chosen in 1690 for the Paraguay missions.[74] Kino explained how the presence of his relative Martini attracted him to the China mission.[75] Presumably family connections quickened zeal for the missions in all these cases; perhaps they also improved one's chances for getting an assignment.

Another possible motivation for leaving Europe was an urge to see the wider world. A wanderlust spread across early-modern Europe, as an English preacher suggested in his sermon against those ever "curious to know the places, cittys, rivers and geography of China, whilst ignorant of their owne Country."[76] As we have seen in Chapter 4, this interest in the exotic featured prominently in the visual arts. One Dutch painting shows a Madonna with child surrounded by representatives from every major ethnic group.[77] In his illustrations from the life of Christ, Maarten de Vos added a Chinese man to the crowd beneath Pilate's lithostroton.[78] Both these examples show the soteriological objective of global mission – to bring the exotic into direct, personal participation with Christ's passion. Naturally, the missions enjoyed no immunity from exotic cravings, and Gregory XIV finally had to condemn missionary-sightseers.[79] Some of the German missionaries took pride in being so far away.[80] Drawn to the exotic, both the painter and the missionary can be called orientalists, but this is a sacred orientalism, and the oriental never eclipsed the sacred. The preface of Maurile de Saint-Michel's *Voyage des isles camercanes* (1652) needed forty-two pages of biblical citations to convince the reader to continue reading. The mere exoticism of it, the Discalced Carmelite author

---

[74] Hugo Stroni, *Catálogo de los Jesuitas de la Provincia del Paraguay (Cuenca del Río de la Plata) 1585–1767*, Subsidia ad Historiam S.I. 9 (Rome: Institutum Historicum S.I., 1980), 199.

[75] Kino, *Crónica*, III.ii.13; idem, *Kino's Historical Memoir of Pimería Alta. A Contemporary Account of the Beginnings of California, Sonora, and Arizona, by Father Eusebio Francisco Kino, S. J., Pioneer Missionary Explorer, Cartographer, and Ranchman. 1683–1711*, ed. Herbert Eugene Bolton, Spain and the West 3–4, Semicentennial Publications of the University of California (Cleveland: The Arthur H. Clark company, 1919), II.77–78.

[76] Johann Grueber, *Als Kundschafter des Papstes nach China 1656–1664: Die erste Durchquerung Tibets*, ed. Franz Braumann (Stuttgart: K. Thienemann, 1985), 14; Cummins, *Question*, 252.

[77] Knipping, 260, 367.

[78] J. C. Visscher after Maarten de Vos, from the series "Theatrum Passionis et Mortis Domini et Servatoris Nostri Iesu Christi," described in ibid., 370.

[79] Cummins, *Question*, 5.

[80] Letter of Adam Gilg to an anonymous Jesuit, June 26, 1687, BStB CLM Nr. 26472, fols. 114r–114v.

thought, would not suffice.[81] One traveler had reached Seville, known then as the "new Babylonia," and was already en route to Peru when a divine inspiration moved him to scuttle his plans and flee to Lisbon to become a Jesuit. When it threatened personal salvation, the exotic could dampen missionary zeal. Two Jesuit missionaries feared the Antilles for their nude women; as one explained, "My own vice is obviously lust, and my adolescence was slippery."[82] Thus, sometimes religious enthusiasm even worked against an oriental wanderlust.

The Devil's Cold War

The desire for salvation and the global perspective dovetailed in missionary concerns about the Devil's efforts worldwide, and it is in the concept of satanic interference that much of the old Franciscan millenarianism endured in the Jesuit mission writings. The Jesuit missionaries did consider themselves participants in an epic race, less against the clock than against the Devil.

The question of the Jesuits' belief in active diabolism has captured the attention of scholars, with perhaps the most forceful position taken up by Peter A. Goddard in his study of demonology in New France. He contrasts on the one hand a belief in a "diabolic conspiracy" and the "real presence of the Devil" (as described by historians who "have taken the *Relations* at face value"), with a demonology "characterized by doubt and caution," that is, "a version of the diabolical that features the illusory, the fraudulent, and the error ridden."[83]

These two opposite positions are both correct. Jesuits did, and do, believe in the reality of the Devil, and doubt and caution are not incompatible with active diabolism. Indeed, the more dangerous the diabolic conspiracy, the more necessary both doubt and caution become, in particular instances. Then as now the Devil does not operate in ways that lend themselves to public, scientific inquiry. Goddard's Devil shies away from the Jesuits, and appears as "more fox than sheepdog or puppet master."[84] This is true to form, for the Devil is the master of illusion and trickery. Like a fox, he exists and is no less a threat for his wily methods.

---

[81] Luca Codignola, "The Holy See and the Conversion of the Indians in French and British North America, 1486–1760," in *America in European Consciousness, 1493–1750*, ed. Karen Ordahl Kupperman (Chapel Hill: University of North Carolina, 1995), 197.

[82] Bernardus Laynac to general, April 4, 1664, ARSI FG vol. 757, doc. 114, fol. 159r.

[83] Peter A. Goddard, "The Devil in New France: Jesuit Demonology, 1611–1650," *Canadian Historical Review* 78 (1997): 42, 51.

[84] Ibid., 54.

If active diabolism means the natives' "conviction of diabolical anti-truth," then extreme scepticism is warranted. Indeed, most Jesuit letters make no reference to the Devil whatsoever. Regardless, those references that are made impress for their intensity, and when taken globally they paint the picture presented here. Much of the discrepancy in interpretation comes from each historian's expectations: A diabolism "distinctly less prominent than we might expect"[85] is a weak diabolism, and one more prominent than expected, a strong diabolism. A comparative study across time and space, even a rudimentary counting of the word "devil" and its synonyms, might move in the direction of providing a more objective yardstick. Except for the impulse to contour the Jesuits' religion more closely to modern Catholics', there is no reason to dismiss the idea of an "Empire of Satan" as rhetorical fancy, without dismissing as well the belief in God. References in Jesuits' writings to demons must not be rejected, without any other evidence, as mere literary flourishes or as simple metaphors for the presence of evil in the world. Walter Stephens' characterization of pre-twelfth century demonology treatises as "short on theory and [with] no apparent need for complicated explanations" describes just as well the letters of Jesuit missionaries, although the same could not be said of early-modern treatises.[86] The fifteenth- and sixteenth-century height of European obsession with demonic reality was still too recent, and the modern sensibility would come only in the eighteenth century, and even then bring comfort only to the most liberal theologians.

To early-modern Jesuits, the Devil was intensely real, enough to appear in the form of Saint Paul, make noises, flip objects over, or even attack people physically.[87] Thus Canisius complained that the Devil's annoyance at one particular priest's presence in Bavaria prompted diabolical interference with his studies.[88] Satan's great ambition, however, was to thwart the missionaries. Stressing the special relation Satan has to the missions, Stumpf collapses sacred history to set up a parallel in which the fallen angels are like the non-believers kept from the faith. Addressing his treatise to the angels, he asks,

What caused the rebellion among you in heaven? Had the Lord made those fellow citizens of yours evil? You will say, because of the ambition of Lucifer. I will say that from the very same cause the evils and losses of the Mission are born. Satan, who because of his own ambition dragged his tail destroying a third of the stars,

---

[85] Ibid., 51, 52.
[86] Walter Stephens, *Demon Lovers: Witchcraft, Sex, and the Crisis of Belief* (Chicago: University of Chicago Press, 2002), 26–7.
[87] Martin, *Jesuit Mind*, 81.
[88] Braunsberger, ed., II.56–8.

excited dissension in the missions to snatch the reward of Redemption from three parts of all the world's men, partners in his own damnation.[89]

In the Jesuit Paul Ragueneau's version of Catherine de St-Augustin's autobiography (1671), the wilds of New France itself became the kingdom of Satan, and the saint understood the torment her war with Satan brought her as a kind of penance for others' sins.[90]

The Devil would move against the missionary at the very outset by perverting the vocation. Franz Xavier Amrhyn cautioned applicants not to send too many *indipetae* requests to Rome, lest they allow Satan to encourage the thought that the missionary position was obtained through ambition and incessant cajoling, rather than through the will of God.[91] The Devil encouraged the delusions that a missionary would be better off elsewhere or that missionary work required no special academic preparation. Even as late as 1770 the recruiter for the Colegio de Misiones de Tarija in Bolivia found the Devil robbing him of potential overseas missionaries – by convincing them they could more effectively find salvation in Spain.[92]

Diabolic interference increased in the missions themselves, and manifested itself in every facet of missionary life. Deprived of contact with God, pagans had received nothing but news of the Devil.[93] Sometimes blanket statements attribute every impediment to Satan, as when the Devil stirred up troubles in China in 1628.[94] More often missionaries blamed quite specific hindrances on the Devil, or on his demonic servants such as the Great Fifth Dalai Lama, Ngag-dbang-rgya-mtsho (1617–82), whom Grueber called the Devil's godfather.[95] The manifestation of an evil spirit preceded many Indian rebellions, and when Indians failed to understand the language in which the gospel reached them, Manje explained it as the work of the demon "Caos."[96] In the Mariana Islands

---

[89] StAK Jesuiten 732, p. 2.

[90] Paul Ragueneau, *La vie de la Mère Catherine de Saint-Augustin, religieuse hospitalière de la Miséricorde de Québec en la Nouvelle-France* (Paris: Florentin Lambert, 1671), 64, cited in Anya Mali, "Strange Encounters: Missionary Activity and Mystical Thought in Seventeenth Century New France," *History of European Ideas* 22 (1996): 84.

[91] Amrhyn, "Documenta," 205.

[92] Ibid., 212–13; Borges Morán, *El envío*, 163.

[93] Romeo, 336.

[94] "Triumphos, Coronas, Tropheos," RAH Cortes 566, no. 27, fol. 489r.

[95] Adelhelm Jann, *Die katholischen Missionen in Indien, China, und Japan: Ihre Organisation und das portugiesische Patronat vom 15. bis ins 18. Jahrhundert* (Paderborn: F. Schöningh, 1915), 384.

[96] Eymer, "Declaración ante el Cap. Juan Francisco de Hessáin," Parral, December 7, 1699, AGI Guad. 156 fol. 1083v-1097v, at 1085v; Cap. J. M. Manje, "Relacion itineraria

the Devil stirred up a tempest against the peace of the mission, choosing a Chinese man as his instrument to spread a "*diabolico rumor*" against the efficacy and healthiness of baptism. Any setback could be attributed to the Devil, because he was the master of using various instruments to do his work.[97]

The Devil enjoyed a reach as global as the Jesuits'. Missionaries identified him as the object of pagan tribes' worship, and Francisco López de Gómara's 1552 *Historia general de las Indias* [*General History of the Indies*] related how the Devil appeared to his native worshipers in the Caribbean.[98] Jesuit writers attributed native resistance to the Devil's ability to inflame passions (such as the failure of the first missionaries in the Marianas), or they described troubles as a "rebellion of the Devil" [*Aufstands des Teufels*] which could only be overcome through God's "counter-invasion" [*Eingreifen*], as with the rebellion of the Tepehuanes in Mexico.[99] In 1638 an Italian Jesuit in Macao cast out a devil working to subvert conversion efforts in China, and the same devil admitted to also having instigated wars in England.[100] On a world stage, a ritual such as this exorcism dramatically locates the local in a global religious and historical context. This global range could depreciate victories, and the French witch hunter Pierre de Lancre recognized that his job had become more difficult with the mass immigration of refugee demons fleeing missionaries in Japan and America.[101] The breadth of the diabolical warfare's geographical range was matched by chronological depth. In the 1620s one Jesuit accused Satan of having interfered centuries earlier with the Nestorian mission, which the Jesuit considered part of "our holy faith."[102]

The demons' extraordinary ability to exert Satan's will anywhere in the world, in the Jesuits' understanding, recalls the attribute of the superpowers of the Cold War of the last century – especially in its bipolar stage before 1960 – which indeed serves in many respects as an excellent

---

del nuevo descubrimiento que hizieron los R Padres Eusbio Kino y Adamo Gil, 1699," BN Ms. 3165 f. 182–225, at fols. 197v-198r.

[97] "Relacion de las Empresas y sucessos espirituales y temporales de las Islas Marianas . . . " 1676–86, ARSI Phil. 13 [141r-194v] at fols. 145v-146v.

[98] López de Gómara, chapter xxvii, fol. 11v.

[99] ARSI Phil. 13, fol. 146r; WB Nr. 25.

[100] Juan Cortés Ossorio, *Reparos historiales apologeticos dirigidos al excelentissimo Señor Conde de Villavmbrosa . . .* (Pamplona: 1677), fol. 44v. UCSD Man.

[101] Pierre de Lancre, *Tableau de l'inconstance des mauvais Anges et Demons, où il est amplement traicté des Sorciers et de la Sorcelerie* [Paris: n.p., 1612], ed. Nicole Jacques-Chaquin (Paris, 1982), 80.

[102] "Triumphos, Coronas, Tropheos," RAH Cortes 566, no. 27, fol. 491r.

explanatory metaphor. Both struggles were fought globally, but indirectly, and missionaries struggled for the souls of pagans just as Kennedy hoped to win the "hearts and minds" of the Third World. Eisenhower's image of Southeast Asia as a series of dominos matches, in substance if not in choice of metaphor, Canisius's missionary concerns for Eastern Europe and beyond.[103] The parallel between the two conflicts helps us understand the intensity with which the Jesuits fought, for apocalyptic endgames cast sombre shadows over both. The missionary "cold war," in fact, was necessarily apocalyptic, and perhaps even more intensely fought, as the stakes were far greater. The victor, however, was known in advance, for the Fourth Lateran Council in 1215 had taught the defeat of Satan and his forces at the end of time.

In broad scope we have seen a movement from a medieval universalism to a Franciscan global apocalypticism. This change came when the realistic chance to work in foreign missions made global impulses a reality, and the realistic chance that the world would end gave them an urgency. Among the Jesuits the explicit pressures of literally running out of time disappeared, but the struggle with the Devil made the task no less urgent. Perhaps some of the edge had been lost by the eighteenth century, when the global mission becomes a decorous subject for ceilings.

In terms of missionary motivation two conclusions must be drawn. First, relatively few Jesuits – especially in the earliest times – had any real interest in the mission as such. Second, Jesuits' missionary interest is best understood in the selfish, negative, medieval sense. Mission is a part of this fundamental soteriology driving the Catholic reformation. The typical Jesuit's concern for distant souls derived from his concern for the soul least distant, his own. Of course, this cannot be simply unravelled, for the self and the others had their salvations greatly mixed up in each other. There was, moreover, an undeniable, human diversity to these Jesuits' motivations and goals. In working out their salvation, they thought or acted globally, but we also see that these salvific priorities could be intensely personal and local. Some sought salvation in martyrdom. Some saw an impending end of time that made matters of salvation particularly pressing. Others preserved their lives to build a missionary enterprise that would endure for centuries to bring salvation to as many as possible. It is difficult to evaluate the depth and breadth of the enthusiasm for martyrdom and the belief in an immanent end; expressions of both are more intense than frequent. It is difficult to sum up all these Jesuits in a single formula. It is easy, however, to point to the common concern of

---

[103] Canisius, Piotrcovia [Pieterkow = Piotrków], to Laynez, November 27, 1558, Braunsberger, ed., II.335.

all – salvation. How this salvific imperative for mission became realized in practice is the subject of the next chapter, which outlines the institutional parameters for mission negotiated among the Society of Jesus, the Iberian empires, and the Holy Roman Empire, and tracks the actual movement of missionaries between Germany, Mexico, and China.

7   The Jesuit Missionary Network

"To the missionaries of the Society of Jesus, both to those triumphant in Heaven as to those fighting in the four parts of the earth against the forces of hell."
— Joseph Stöcklein, dedication of the *Welt-bott* (1726)

How did the motivations described in the previous chapter translate into reality? In the early-modern period thousands of Jesuits served abroad as missionaries. Restricting our survey, we have basic information on the fifty-three Jesuit missionaries who travelled between Germany, Mexico, and China in the seventeenth century. Most joined the Society before they turned nineteen, and the youngest, Daniel Januske (1661–1724), was fifteen.[1] Once admitted, they would wait on average another thirteen or fourteen years before being selected as a missionary. Of our fifty-three, at least eleven taught as professors. Ten died en route, but those who reached their stations would typically enjoy a tenure there of almost two decades. The most enduring, Joseph Neumann, arrived in Mexico in 1680 and died in 1732, fifty-two years later, at the age of eighty-four. He was already twenty-five when he joined the Society but had to wait only five years before being sent abroad. The single most impressive facet of these men's collective biography, however, is their global movements.

From Germany to China and Mexico

In the sixteenth century, the struggles against Protestantism within the Holy Roman Empire made Germany a net importer of missionaries. Canisius considered the entry of twenty Italians into the Society as momentous as gaining a single German.[2] In 1562, the Jesuit general declared

---

[1] ARSI 1681 Boh. 20.85v; 1685 Boh. 22.47r; 1690 Boh. 23.145r; ARSI Boh. 20.85v, 22.47r, 23.145r.
[2] Canisius, August 31, 1551, in Braunsberger, ed., I.380.

that no German Jesuit could go into the foreign missions because each one was needed in Germany. This was also true for Bohemia, where the utraquist church's continuing independence, since the Compact of Iglau in 1436, invited caution, and so only two Bohemians were sent abroad before 1678. German missionaries from other religious orders had gone abroad with greater frequency. The Bavarian Franciscan province worked in Cairo, and had sent many missionaries to the Near East, while other Bavarian Franciscans worked in Eastern Europe and East Asia.[3]

The 1562 prohibition was eventually forgotten, or expired, for the first German Jesuit to serve as a missionary overseas appears to have been Peter de Gouveia from Edister, who was made coadjutor of the village of San Bernabé in Brazil sometime before 1598. Eleven years later the Hamburger Johann Hermes was also sent to Brazil.[4] A single letter places Anton Welser in Mexico in 1611, when he was rector in Regensburg. If the letter is correct, he would have been the first German Jesuit in New Spain.[5] Most missionaries sent abroad in this period, however, worked in Ottoman-held southeastern Europe. By 1668 this tendency would develop into a movement (spearheaded by Paul Tafferner, who had been confessor to the imperial ambassador to Constantinople) to send German Jesuit missionaries to minister to the Germans, Hungarians, and Slavs enslaved by the Turks.[6]

Among the Jesuits, the desire to go abroad was great even in the earliest stage. Reports from the Indies appeared during the sixteenth century in Dillingen, Ingolstadt, Munich, and Augsburg in Latin and in German. Canisius himself requested permission to go to the Indies, and he circulated around the province letters from the missions while praising their usefulness. In 1561 he offered General Laínez four missionaries from his own province: "May the Lord desire to take these our province's offerings, which will not be the last to protect the Company of Jesus in the missions of the Indies."[7] The general refused this offer of missionaries and repeated that there were not enough to suffice for Germany.[8]

In 1603 Diego de Torres Bollo won permission to include twenty Italians in his expedition, which in Germany caused a new flourishing of *indipetae* request letters, as did Trigault's tour in the next decade.

[3] Grulich, 18; Bauerreiß, VII.279–80.
[4] Sierra, *Jesuitas*, 67–68; Huonder, *Deutsche Jesuitenmissionäre*, 11.
[5] "Ex literis P. Antonii Welser," México, February 18, 1611, BHStA Jes. 594, fol. 1r; published in Alegre II.562. See Duhr, *Geschichte*, 2:1.234 n.1.
[6] Hausberger, *Jesuiten*, 36; Huonder, *Deutsche Jesuitenmissionäre*, 31–32.
[7] Canisius to Salmeron, December 13, 1561, in Braunsberger, ed., III.329. See also Braunsberger, ed., I.119, 147, 263, 269, 293, 304; II.69, 206, 259, 263, 269, 281, 680.
[8] Huonder, *Deutsche Jesuitenmissonäre*, 10–11.

Thirty-one requests came from the Upper German province before the end of 1615. In that year and the next a total of forty-nine letters to the general came from the Ingolstadt college alone.[9] On January 23, 1616, news reached Germany that Vitelleschi, motivated by the procurators' difficulty in finding sufficient recruits from Spain, had decided to allow the first contingents of German missionaries: three from Austria for the Asian missions and four from the Upper Germany province – from the college at Ingolstadt – for those in America.[10] Ingolstadt went wild. One Johann Irling wrote a letter to Vitelleschi, reporting that "almost nobody thinks about studying anymore, the usual works stand paralyzed." Indeed, the masters "ought to resign themselves to silence until the inflamed spirit falls calm by itself."[11]

Those hoping for missionary assignments took no chances, applying ten or more times.[12] Twenty-one applications over the course of thirty-two years seem the record, held by Philipp Jeningen. Sometimes hopefuls contacted missionaries directly, although it is uncertain what effect this could have. "As a famous mathematician you show China the stars," one Jesuit wrote to Amrhyn, and asked, "bring me to you, we are both ready to pour out our blood."[13] Most *indipetae* letters came from Ingolstadt, where the scholastics of the Upper German province studied philosophy and theology, or from Altötting, where they completed the third probation after their studies were completed.[14] Trigault recorded both the fervour and the aptitude of Ingolstadt's aspiring missionaries: "Everyone there is burning with longing for our mission, and if I found anyone of a suitable nature and ability, I believe he would be found there, and I think some should be nominated from there." Unable to respond individually to all these requests, the general wrote his appreciation to their rectors, expressing his sorrow that all their wishes could not be fulfilled.[15]

The contents of these letters suggest how competitive the selection was and what traits the applicants thought would appeal the most to the general. If they were not shrewdly writing what they thought would get them an assignment, they had read other missionaries' writings, and could draw

[9] Sierra, *Jesuitas*, 68–69; Huonder, *Deutsche Jesuitenmissionäre*, 13.
[10] Sierra, *Jesuitas*, 69.
[11] Duhr, *Geschichte*, 2:2.596; Huonder, *Deutsche Jesuitenmissionäre*, 12–3; Treffer, "Iter," 3.
[12] Huonder, *Deutsche Jesuitenmissionäre*, 11–12; Sierra, *Jesuitas*, 71.
[13] Hermann-Ludwig Högner, *Philosophie und Medizin in Ingolstadt: Professoren der philosophischen Fakultät von 1641 bis 1720*. (Ph.D. diss. Erlangen, 1976), 8.
[14] Hoffmann, "Philipp," 260, 350–51.
[15] Nicolas Trigault, "Litterae R. P. Nicolai Trigault ad PP. et FF. in China constitutos," in Lamalle, "La propaganda," 107. See Duhr, *Geschichte*, 2:2.601, 609.

on that set of words and ideas. Some men mentioned that a missionary already in the field had requested their company, or merely that a previous missionary had shared a first name with the applicant. Philosophical, artistic, astronomical, and, most often, mathematical talents were highlighted. Georg Balde emphasized his youth, which he said would make learning Arabic, "Indian," or Japanese much easier.[16] Some announced they were making pilgrimages, others that they had in various difficult situations taken vows to become missionaries. Some wrote that they entered the Society only in hopes of working in the missions. In his application for a mission post in China, Leonard Piertz, who taught mathematics and physics at Würzburg, stressed that he was training strenuously by hiking.[17] Kino wrote, "I can say that from the moment I heard that Fathers Beatus Amrhyn and [Kino's teacher] Adam Aigenler were appointed to China... desires arose in me of obtaining a similar mission such that I could scarcely be satisfied until the matter had [been] commended to God and... to my most reverend Father."[18] Michael Staudacher enclosed a copy of his oath, written out in his own blood.[19] This mode of application is clearly nonutilitarian but intentionally symbolic: Staudacher wrote in blood not because he had run out of ink but to express his sincerity, his intensity, and the sacrifices he would be willing to make. In these Jesuits' letters we see little of the real or pretended modesty of Christopher of the Holy Trinity, whose application to Propaganda highlighted his humility by stressing his own incompetence.[20]

In total, the Roman archive of the Society of Jesus preserves today 1,539 *indipetae* written by 727 Jesuits from the German, Bohemian, and Austrian Assistancies between 1614 and 1728. These represent 11.0% of the letters and 11.8% of the *indipetae*-writing Jesuits contained in the archive, from all Jesuits worldwide. Christmas, Ephiphany, and the feast day of St. Ignatius proved popular days to write *indipetae*, but well surpassing these three combined is the number of letters dated December 3, the feast day of Francis Xavier. Many Jesuits wrote on January 1 – given the personal nature of their motivations, described in the

---

[16] Grulich, 39–40; Duhr, *Geschichte*, 2:2.601.
[17] Grulich, 39–40; Huonder, *Deutsche Jesuitenmissionäre*, 11–12; Leonard Piertz to General, Würzburg, October 11, 1692, ARSI Rhen. Sup. 42, fol. 92, published in Bernward H. Willeke, "Würzburg und die Chinamission im 17. und 18. Jahrhundert." *Reformation und Gegenreformation*. Festschrift für Theobald Freudenberger. *Würzburger Diözesangeschichtsblätter* 35/36 (1974): 427.
[18] Bolton, *Rim*, 36.
[19] Huonder, *Deutsche Jesuitenmissionäre*, 11–2. See Nebgen, 82–83.
[20] Christopher of the Holy Trinity, Paris, to Ingoli, January 10, 1642, APF SOCG 141, fol. 23r.

previous chapter, this represents perhaps an early example of New Year's resolutions.

After leaving Germany for the Spanish Netherlands, Trigault found more recruits closer to home. In Antwerp Trigault visited his family and convinced his brother, a nephew, and a cousin to go back to China with him.[21] The intense competition for the missionary vocations makes the choice of three of Trigault's own kinsmen intriguing. During Trigault's tour of Europe, the general selected the first four Jesuits from the Ingolstadt college for the foreign missions. On February 8, 1616, Andreas Agricola left for Paraguay, and Kaspar Rueß, Ferdinand Raiman (or Reinmann), and Michael Durst started off for Peru. The following year Johann Alberich was selected for the China mission.[22] Rueß wrote in a thank-you letter of January 31, 1616,

> I don't even know where to begin. I am so full of jubilation and outside myself with joy. Your Paternity truly made me happy with such cheerful news. I also don't know what on this earth I would rather have. Yes, I will go, I will fly, to wherever the good God, wherever holy obedience calls me. The bloody murderer's hand does not frighten me; neither the tides of the unencompassed ocean, nor the wild, horrifying customs of the barbarians can make me waver for a minute from what is before me.

Continuing, Rueß promises to pray daily for the general, mentions his superior's help in outfitting the expedition, and puts in a good word for another Jesuit's request.[23]

Still, the old feelings endured. When he heard of the first missionaries' departure, Jakob Rehm, rector of the Ingolstadt college, was said to have exclaimed, "But why do they travel to the distant parts of the world? The time is near, when we in Germany ourselves will have an Indies, where the number of all the workers now in the province will not suffice."[24] In conversation with Kaspar Lechner, Rehm said that despite their praiseworthy zeal,

---

[21] Dunne, *Generation*, 176.

[22] E. Goercke, "Die ersten deutschen Überseemissionare der Jesuiten stellte das Ingolstädter Kolleg der Societät Jesu," *Ingolstädter Heimatblätter* 49 (1986): 33. See also Duhr, *Geschichte*, 2:2.477.

[23] "Ich weiss gar nicht, wo ich anfangen soll. Ich bin so voll des Jubels und außer mir von Freude. Wahrhaft beseligt hat mich Ew. Paternität durch die so frohe Botschaft. Ich weiß auch nicht, was ich auf Erden Lieberes hätte vernehmen können. Ja ich gehe, ich fliege, wohin der gut Gott, wohin der heilige Gehorsam mich ruft. Nicht schrecken mich die blutige Mörderhand, nicht vermögen weder die Fluthen des unermeßlichen Oceans noch die wilden, grausamen Sitten der Barbaren mich einen Augenblick in meinem Vorhaben wankend zu machen..." Rueß to General, January 31, 1616, reprinted in Huonder, *Deutsche Jesuitenmissionäre*, 13. See Duhr, *Geschichte*, 2:2.477.

[24] Franz Hattler, *Der ehrwürdige Pater Jakob Rem aus der Gesellschaft Jesu und seine Marienconferenz* (Regensburg: Manz, 1881), 184.

Still I can not approve these things, though they are well-intentioned, because we are robbing our province of labour. In twenty years the Catholic religion in Germany will experience such a growth and will affect so many conversions from every social class that, with the lack of secular clergy, our own will not suffice to bring all the wandering sheep into Christ's flock.[25]

The idea of this "German Indies" suggests a basic unity in the Jesuit concepts of their missionary work among Protestants and non-Christians, to which we will return in Chapter 10.

This unity of missionary work complicated the choice of assignment location, itself often a decision carrying spiritual overtones. The Constitutions instructed the aspiring missionary of his duty "without interposing himself in favor of going or remaining in one place rather than another, to leave the disposition of himself completely and very freely to the superiors who in the place of Christ our Lord directs him in the path of his greater service and praise."[26] Franz Xavier Amrhyn advised the missionary to avoid longing for a mission station other than the one chosen for him.[27] Many letters express exactly this attitude, an impressive indifference to destination. Wanting only to follow the will of "Jesus my Saviour," Jérôme Queyrot declared, "I do not ask to be sent into the Indies, I do not imagine Constantinople, I do not long for Canada."[28] No lack of available knowledge forces this mind-set, which reinforces the centrality of personal salvation. If they pursued others' souls to save themselves, those souls could belong to Turks or to Chinese. As Christopher d'Authier de Sisgau (1609–67) explained, "If one's own salvation could be won by the salvation of the rest of the world, it mattered little where one was, as long as the harvest of souls was abundant."[29]

Many could not help themselves. One worthy Jesuit expressed a preference for the Canadian cold.[30] In Kino's case, the provincial left the decision in the recruits' hands. Kino and fellow Tyrolean Antonio Kerschpamer were to choose who would go to Mexico, and who to the Philippines. Kino desperately hoped to reach the Philippines, the springboard into China, but he offered the decision to his companion, for either he did not want to assert his will over God's or he did not want to appear selfish. When Kerschpamer refused this gesture, they had to resolve their

---

[25] Huonder, *Deutsche Jesuitenmissionäre*, 14.
[26] *Constitutions*, 274–75 [part VII, ch. 2, sec. 1, par. 622].
[27] Amrhyn, "Documenta," 206.
[28] ARSI FG 752, fasc. 20, fol. 4r.
[29] Quoted in Deslandres, "French," 266. See Pizzorusso, 884–86.
[30] Philippus Garzeau to the general, March 19, 1665, ARSI FG 757 doc. 128, fol. 178r.

"devout quarrel" by drawing lots. Kino's fate was Mexico, and only fever-ish prayer restored serenity to his soul.[31]

In the seventeenth century, the situation changed as the provinces grew.[32] By 1650 the number of Jesuits in the Upper German province reached 627, in the Upper Rhenish 288, in the Lower Rhenish 493, in Austria 800, and in Bohemia 611, for a total of 2,819 "German" Jesuits. Around 1670 the German Assistancy had 6,601 members, more than the Spanish (2,040) and Italian (2,937) Assistancies combined.[33] Given the successes of the efforts against Protestantism, Germany could afford to be more generous with her missionaries. Between 1600 and 1670, a total of more than thirty missionaries from the German Assistancy went to the Asian and American missions.[34] This would increase rapidly in the century's last third. All told, from 1610 to 1730, some 760 Jesuits from the three core German provinces went abroad as missionaries, and contributions from the Austrian and Bohemian Provinces push the total number into the thousands. This chapter's next two sections follow the trails of these German missionaries into Mexico and China.

Patronage and Regulation in Mexico

As we have seen in Chapter 2, the royal authority to assign missions to Jesuits derived from the crown's responsibilities of church patronage.[35] Largely limited to issuing bulls naming the bishops,[36] the papacy recog-nized its impotence and delegated its responsibility to the Castilian crown. The crown, in turn, sub-delegated this responsibility by transferring the Indians' obligatory monetary and service tribute over to Spaniards known as *encomenderos*, who would then pay the salaries, or expenses, of priests who ministered to the Indians.

The privilege of royal *patronato* allowed the crown to select the mis-sionaries, as well as the route by which they arrived at their stations. Sometimes a royally appointed bishop took up his new diocese without

[31] Kino to Aveiro, November 16, 1680, printed in Burrus, *Kino escribe*, 111.
[32] This same transition between importer and exporter of missionaries would be made later by the United States, an ecclesiastical colony of Ireland before its 1908 independence from Propaganda. See Neill, *History*, 457.
[33] Huonder, *Deutsche Jesuitenmissionäre*, 15; Felix Alfred Plattner, *Deutsche Meister des Barock in Südamerika im 17. und 18. Jahrhundert* (Freiburg: Herder, 1960), 17.
[34] Duhr, *Geschichte*, 2:2.599–60, 605–6; Huonder, *Deutsche Jesuitenmissionäre*, 9–15.
[35] In fact, in 1572 Philip II suggested America should be a patriarchy. The Patriarch would be named by the king and reside in Madrid. A "royal vicarate" – weaker than a patri-archy – was also proposed. Hubert Jedin, "Weltmission und Kolonialismus," *Saeculum* 9 (1958): 396; Beckmann, "Glaubensverbreitung," 256.
[36] Beckmann, "Glaubensverbreitung," 260.

bothering to wait for the authorizing papal bulls. Sometimes an entire diocese would be created without the knowledge of Rome. Spanish America's governors, *audiencia* presidents, and viceroys were instructed to keep an eye on all religious bodies in their districts, and to make visitations, so as to better prepare triennial reports for the crown.[37] Unlike the Jesuit general's representatives, royal officers were to have access to provincial meetings, and they retained the right to confirm the top religious officials in their office. Royal officials were to support those religious working in the Indians' *conversiones* and *doctrinas*.[38]

The Jesuit province in Mexico faced a perennial difficulty in finding missionaries. The lack of creoles interested in joining the Society exacerbated the situation, as the provincial procurator Tomás Domínguez attested in 1634.[39] A possible explanation came from the south, from the Vice-royalty of New Granada. The president of the Audiencia of Santa Fe reported that creoles saw few opportunities for advancement, because every position was filled by the general, who favoured the educated and the gray-haired. Furthermore, the Society's operating outside the system of *misiones* and *doctrinas* prevented its members from obtaining benefices. Thus the Jesuits tended to resist the trend toward increased creole participation in the religious life. In 1646 the Society accepted only five, a limit raised to ten in 1655.[40]

Spain could not or would not supply enough missionaries to compensate. In the 1580s the frequency of religious returning to Spain from Mexico, coupled with the assurances of the creoles, convinced the Madrid authorities that Mexico City was overflowing with religious, easily enough to sustain the rest of New Spain. In truth, there was a definite tendency for missionaries to stay close to centres of power, population, and comfort, so the overabundance in the capital corresponded not to an abundance but to an enduring lack of missionaries in the far reaches of the colony.

---

[37] *Recopilación de leyes de los Reynos de las Indias: Prólogo por Ramón Menéndez y Pidal, estudio preliminar de Juan Manzano Manzanos* (Madrid: Ediciones Cultura Hispánica, 1973), I.XIV.1, "Que los Vireyes y Presidentes informen cada tres años sobre el estado de las Religiones, para dar licencia á los Visitadores," August 17, 1636 and "Que se dé el auxílio á los Prelados y Visitadores que fueren á reformar sus Religiones," January 10, 1561, ibid., 42–43 (I.115); Parker, 56.

[38] "Que si los Capítulos se hicieren fuera de donde está el Virey, escriba á los Religiosos, encargándoles la observancia de su Regla; y si estuviere donde se hicieren, se halle presente," August 25, 1620 and "Que las Audiencias, que se declara, no dén auxílio á las Religiones sin comunicar al Virey," February 13, 1627. *Recopilación*, 60, 64 (I.120, I.121); "Que los Religiosos sean honorados y favorecidos de los Ministros Reales," July 19, 1566 and January 27, 1572. Ibid., 65 (I.121).

[39] Alegre, II.660.

[40] José Jouanen, *Historia de la Compañía de Jesús en la antigua Provincia de Quito, 1570–1774* (Quito: Editorial Ecuatoriana, 1941–3), I.230; Borges Morán, *El envío*, 40.

The general sentiment was that distant missions were the responsibility of those missionaries arriving from Spain for that specific work. The Jesuits were the major exception to this tendency, for their superiors in Mexico could generally direct them to where they were needed, and they did not leave Spain with specific destinations already determined.[41]

In the 1590s, as the Mexican Province was still praising the generosity of the Spanish provinces in sending missionaries, the Philippine Jesuits were already pointing out that "the Provinces of Castile abound with subjects, many of whom have a vocation for the Indies, and these, if they would send them to us, would do great things and would suffice to populate this vice-province."[42] The Mexican praise came to conform to the Philippine complaint in the course of the seventeenth century.

In 1631, the eleventh provincial congregation of New Spain wrote the general to complain that the ability to choose missionaries for America rested wholly with the European provincials – that is, the Spanish, as foreigners never had this ability – rather than with the mission procurators. In fact, the complaint continued, the missionaries dispatched by peninsular officials too often proved of little use. This suggests that it was not the general in Rome but the peninsular provincials who made the actual decisions, and no evidence indicates that Rome took the congregation's recommendation to heart.[43] For their part, the Spanish provinces protested their inability to provide the necessary Jesuits, and Rome generally accepted this position, despite the general's setting of quotas. Vicar-General Florián de Montmorency, for example, wrote the provincial of Mexico in 1649 to affirm that "there is no room for doubt that the Spanish Provinces, if they receive no help from the other provinces, will be unable to supply by themselves the necessary personnel for the Indies."[44]

Two years later the Mexican procurator Diego de Monroe asked the general to order the Spanish provincials not to resist allocating to America some of those most virtuous Jesuits best suited for missionary work.[45] Sympathizing with such requests from the New World that expeditions coming from Spain not consist solely of young, inexperienced Jesuits, General Oliva suggested that it would be possible if the Spanish crown would only allow foreign missionaries.[46] A decade later found the Mexican Province repeating its protests that the Spanish provinces hindered

[41] Ibid., 41–43.
[42] Antonio Astráin, *Historia de la Compañia de Jesús en la Asistencia de España* (Madrid: 1909–25), IV.486; Borges Morán, *El envío*, 338.
[43] Alegre, II.417–8, II.655.
[44] Lázaro de Aspurz, 205.
[45] Letter from Nickel to Didace de Monroy, 1655, in Alegre, III.383–5.
[46] On August 30, 1661. Jouanen, I.231–2.

the passage of capable Jesuits and always sent those least appropriate for missionary work. The province requested that the Spanish send not all potential missionaries but "several good subjects," and that they not hinder the enlistment of those who wanted to go. In fact, Spanish superiors did put pressure on subjects not to request a mission assignment.[47]

Eventually General Oliva designed a plan (1672) whereby every six years each of the four Spanish provinces would recruit and train thirty-three missionaries (and the Sardinian province eighteen), for which the American provinces would foot the bill – 600 pesos per person. The Mexican Province would receive twenty-four of these one-hundred-fifty missionaries. This system specified that the Spanish provinces increase their recruitment by the necessary amounts, and that the missionaries they send be educated and devout. It is doubtful that this strategy was ever successfully executed.[48] Looking back the next year, Sebastián Izquierdo, the Assistant for the Spanish Province in Rome, commented that since 1647 "the procurators that have come from all the Indies' provinces to bring back missionaries (as because of their poverty the Spanish provinces are without subjects and each day are getting worse) had hardly been able to assemble half the number the Council allowed them, and many of these were novices received to be taken away."[49] An alternative answer was necessary.

The natural solution, to recruit non-Spanish Jesuits, was long resisted at the highest level. Already in the 1510s the crown attempted to regulate even nonmissionary immigration to the colonies, insisting on purity of ideology and blood. The 1680 *Recopilación de las leyes de los reinos de Indias* [*Compilation of the Laws of the Realms of the Indies*] specified the death penalty for foreign traders. Thus enterprising Germans arrived in chains, as pirates, and were surrendered to the Inquisition. A number of other Germans turned up in trials for heresy, for inquisitors often regarded "German" and "Lutheran" as synonyms.[50]

From 1552 all religious traveling to America needed express licence from the crown.[51] Without the approval of the Council of the Indies, no

---

[47] Alegre, III.395–6, III.388–96.
[48] AGN Jes. I-11 exp. 96, fol. 336r–339v. See Lázaro de Aspurz 174; Hausburger, *Jesuiten*, 54.
[49] Borges Morán, *El envió*, 250. Borges Morán on page 301 calls him "Procurador General."
[50] Vincente Riva Palacio, ed., *México a través de los siglos* (Mexico: Ballescá y comp.a, 1887), IV.500, 507, 570; Hartmut Fröschle, *Die Deutschen in Lateinamerika: Schiksal und Leistung* (Tübingen-Basel: Erdmann, 1979), 478, 508; Victor Wolfgang van Hagen, *Der Ruf der Neuen Welt: Deutsche bauen Amerika* (Munich: Droemer Knaur, 1970), 86.
[51] Borges Morán, *El envió*, 328.

regular could enter America.[52] The preference that missionaries be Spanish went back even further to a May 1519 *cédula* ordering Seville's Casa de Contratación to allow passage to twenty Franciscans "being as the said friars are natives of my Castilian realms."[53] Officials also looked for religious zeal, exemplary life, and the recommendation of the superior.[54] Provincials of Central European provinces wrote out letters of recommendation for their recruits, to attest to their worthiness, their birthplaces, and the length of their memberships in the Society.[55]

In 1574 Philip II, and in 1603 his successor Philip III, prohibited the religious orders from sending recruiters to Spain. Instead, provincials were to send annual reports of the number of religious in their provinces, via viceroys, *audiencias*, or governors, to the Council of the Indies, which would use the information to determine how many new religious needed to be sent. Petitions for missionaries from civil or ecclesiastical authorities could also be forwarded through these channels to the Council. Having approved the request, the Council would then place an "order" with the local religious orders' representatives.[56]

The Jesuits circumvented this decision by using the procurator and vice-procurator sent by each province for the General Congregation to press the crown and the general for each new missionary expedition. Not every procurator worked for an expedition, but every expedition was achieved in this way.[57] Throughout the century papal intervention would be applied to help recruiters. Innocent XII's (1691–1700) papal brief *Adeo nobis cordi est* (April 26, 1695) recommended the Paraguay missionary Ignacio Frias to Charles II of Spain (r. 1665–1700) and asked

---

[52] "Que á los Comisarios que llevaren Religiosos no se entreguen los despachos hasta que hayan dado la nómina," July 10, 1612, *Recopilación*, I.xiv.5 (I.104).

[53] Lázaro de Aspurz, 321.

[54] "Que no pase á las Indias Religioso que no esé en obediencia de su Prelado, y llevare licencia," October 28, 1535; "Que no pasen á las Indias Religiosos que no sean quales conviene," February 17, 1531, *Recopilación*, I.xiv.13 & 15 (I.107).

[55] For examples, see AGI CC 5550, unnumbered bundle (Prague, January 30, 1692); AGI CC 5550, bundle labeled "289–305" (Vienna, February 31, 1686; Prague, January 21, 1686).

[56] "Que los Provinciales tengan hecha lista de sus Provincias, conforme á este ley" D. Felipe II en la Ordenanza 16 del Patronazgo," *Recopilación*, I.XIV.2 (I.103). Reaffirmed in the Recopilación of 1681, the Recopilación also drew from *real cédulas* of 1631 and 1646 to specify that the (often voluminous) auxiliary documentation from ecclesiastical and civil authorities should accompany solicitations for the organization of missionary expeditions. See Borges Morán, *El envió*, 109–13; *Recopilación*, I.102–3 (libro I, tit. 14, ley 1) May 15, 1631, March 10, 1646 and I.103 (ley 4) March 8, 1603. See *Recopilación*, I.XIV.3 and 4 (I. f. 60rv).

[57] Ibid., 100, 105, 106. In addition, at the end of the century the province of New Granada proposed establishing, at its own expense, a college in Salamanca for young missionary hopefuls. See Broggio, 25.

the king to authorize the Jesuit to assemble an expedition, composed half of Spaniards and half of Italian subjects of the Spanish or of the Austrian Habsburgs.[58] Foreign Jesuits always needed the licence of the general, who gave aspirants' names to the procurators as they arrived in Rome. The final approval of the nominees by the general usually took some time, perhaps even years.[59]

German missionaries took a fairly uniform route to the New World. First they travelled overland to Genoa, or sometimes to Amsterdam. Riding horses was a luxury introduced during Francis Borgia's generalship (1565–72), and previously Jesuits had traveled on foot, begging.[60] Civil and ecclesiastical authorities eagerly extended generous hospitality to the travelling Jesuits. From Genoa the future missionaries would cross the Mediterranean, sailing to Spain. Kino's ship, the *Capitana*, spent four days trying to enter the Cádiz harbour. It faced the twin obstacles of stormy weather and strict immigration laws, which a raging epidemic had further tightened. Finally, port officials boarded the vessel, inspected her cargo, allowed her shrewd Captain Columbus to entertain them in high style, and then permitted entry into Cádiz. It was too late. The missionaries had missed their transatlantic connection and would spend a year-long layover in Spain.[61]

Until Cádiz became the authorized port of departure in 1720, Spanish missionaries would wait in Seville. After a week-long quarantine period, they would meet their procurator.[62] Armed with the Council's *despacho*, they applied to the Casa de Contratación, which would disburse money for the journey as well as for food, clothing, books, vestments, and the tools of their trade, as well as pocket money for the intermediate stations. These naturalization documents survive.[63] Lists of Jesuits going to the Spanish colonies might flag the presence of any foreign Jesuits with crosses marked next to their names.[64] Sometimes the royal *cédula* authorizing the travel and funding for foreign missionaries would explicitly explain why no suitable Spaniards were available.[65]

---

[58] Anton Huonder, *Deutsche Jesuitenmissionär*, 24.
[59] Borges Morán, *El envió*, 323.
[60] Scaduto, 327.
[61] Eusebius Kino, Diary of Travel from Genoa to Sevilla, June 12 to July 27, 1678, BHStA Jes. 607/125.
[62] Grulich, 31; Huonder, *Deutsche Jesuitenmissionäre* 33; Treutlein, "Jesuit Travel," 109, 111–13; Borges Morán, *El envió*, 89; Hausberger, *Jesuiten*, 48.
[63] "Que á los Religiosos que por órden de el Rey pasaren á las Indias, se les socorra como se ordena," July 10, 1607, *Recopilación* ley 6 (I.104–5). See for example AGI 12–2-2/8.
[64] See for example AGI CC 5550, bundle 12, fol. 7r-9v "Nómina de 41 jesuitas" at 7r.
[65] See for example royal *cédula*, April 24, 1671, AGI Mex. 2731, carpeta "Religion de la Compania de Jhs," 209r-212r, at 210v-211r.

In Seville, missionaries in transit originally slept on the second floor of the Colegio de San Hermenegildo (now the Esceula de Bellas Artes) but their presence caused such excitement among the college's residents that from 1689 the Nuesta Señora de Guadalupe served as a new hospice. Seville would eventually have several houses set aside for them, where they could study the relevant languages and learn various pioneering skills. Sometimes natives from the mission lands were in residence. Similar houses developed in other way-stations, such as Mexico City, Mozambique, and Goa.[66] Before leaving, missionaries would present themselves before a board of inspectors who would record name, nationality, and a physical description.[67] One eighteenth-century Jesuit remarked that "no butcher eyes a calf as these men eyed us."[68]

The voyage from Spain to Mexico was far safer than that to India. Leaving Spain at the beginning of July, the expedition would reach the Caribbean in August, and Veracruz in September. Each year two or three galleon fleets would leave for America: one via Puerto Rico, Santo Domingo, and Havana to Veracruz, and the others for Cartagena and either Buenos Aires or Montevideo.[69] The late sixteenth century saw 150 to 200 ships leave per year (in 1600, the mean was 169), with a total tonnage ranging from 30,000 to 40,000 tons. The typical fleet would enjoy a two-galleon escort. The seventeenth-century slump got underway in the late 1620s, and by the 1660s the fleets had shrunk to some 30 ships total, per year.[70] This recovered somewhat in the last third of the century.

En route, sailing through the calm Golfo de las Damas (the "Ladies' Gulf"), Jesuits could escape their cabin (sharing a ten-foot by nine-foot room with twelve other Jesuits was not uncommon) to watch sailors enjoying shark baiting and cock fighting. As Veracruz treacherously combined a shallow port with a sudden north wind, many passengers died when their ship went aground at their destination port. After a very uncomfortable week there, Jesuits proceeded on horses or mules, through dust and

---

[66] Augustín Galán García, "La organización misional jesuita y su hospicio de Indias en Sevilla (1566–1717): Notas para su estudio," *Archivo Hispalense* 220 (1989): 105–6, 113; Jaksch, 17.

[67] See for example AGI CC 5550, bundle 12, fol. [f.10′r-10′v] "Ante el Senor Dⁿ Franº Lorenzo de San Milian," Cadiz, June 20, 1687, at 10′r.

[68] P. Joseph Och in "Nachrichten, von seinen Reisen nach dem spanischen Nord-Amerika . . . 1757–1767 . . . " in Christoph Gottlieb von Murr, ed., *Nachrichten von verschiedenen Ländern des spanischen Amerika* (Halle, 1809), quoted in Treutlein, "Jesuit Travel," 112. See Ibid., 111; Hausberger, *Jesuiten*, 48–9, 143; Borges Morán, *El envío*, 386, 471–3; Grulich, 34.

[69] Grulich, 32.

[70] I base this evaluation on Chaunu and Chaunu, *Séville*, VI(1).168.

mosquitoes to Puebla de los Angeles and then to Mexico City. Missionaries destined for the Philippines would stay at a hospice in San Borgia, near the capital, and then to Acapulco, where they would embark on the hundred-day voyage to Manila.[71]

The recruitment of foreign missionaries led to new problems. The royal reluctance to bring foreign missionaries into Spanish territory must be seen in the context of a more general xenophobia. For example, late in the sixteenth century the General Inquisitor Cardinal Gaspar de Quiroga (1512–94), threatened with excommunication – under royal approbation – any Spanish provincial who permitted a Spanish Jesuit to leave the country. In another instance, Dionisio Vásquez and Enrique Enríquez, who were among those Spaniards working to decentralize the Society, pointed out the danger of infection by heresy risked by six Jesuits destined for Transylvania.[72]

Subjects of territories belonging to the Spanish crown enjoyed a privileged status. Subjects of collateral or allied dynasties, especially the Austrian line of the House of Habsburg, were less frequently accepted. After 1616, missionary candidates were divided into three categories: "citizens of these realms" (subjects of the crowns of Castile, Navarre, and Aragon, including Sardinia), "reliable foreigners" (subjects of the king of Spain, that is, Portugal during the union, Naples, Sicily, Milan, Flanders, and Franche-Comté, subjects of the House of Austria, subjects of those princes allied to Spain, and by deference subjects of the papal states), and "suspicious foreigners" (the French, English, Dutch, and – after 1640 – Portuguese).[73]

In 1574 the Sicilian Vicente Lanochi became the first Jesuit to go to Mexico who was considered more "foreign" than the few Flemings who preceded him. Between 1574 and 1595, fourteen Italians were allowed to go. In 1603, however, the Council blocked passage of an expedition of thirteen Italians on grounds of their nationality, until Diego de Torres Bollo used his influence to secure dispensations.[74]

Francisco de Figueroa was the Jesuits' chief lobbyist for a more liberal policy toward foreign Jesuits. A Spaniard, from 1592 to 1600 he served as a confessor and preacher in Mexico until he was ordered back to Europe to bring current mission news to Philip III and General Aquaviva. From 1603 to 1623 he was mission procurator for America in

---

[71] Treutlein, "Jesuit," 119–21; Grulich, 34.

[72] Hausberger, *Jesuiten*, 35; Borges Morán, *El envío*, 35–57; Bangert, 110–12; Astráin, III.352–69.

[73] Lázaro de Aspurz, 185, 223–31. See Hausberger, *Jesuiten*, 36; Huonder, *Deutsche Jesuitenmissionäre*, 18.

[74] See Sierra, *Jesuitas*, 68.

Spain.[75] His efforts led to the crown allowing twenty-eight Italian, German, and Dutch Jesuits to cross the Atlantic (1615–18). The 1620 German edition of *Auß America* was written to support Figueroa's work against the crown's growing mistrust. The editor therefore excluded a particularly detailed ethnographical description that betrayed the Spaniards' distrust of foreigners. The edition pessimistically anticipated an increasingly illiberal policy.[76]

Auß America's predictions were correct. In the middle of the seventeenth century the rise of new sea powers and Spain's defeat at the hands of France intensified the xenophobic atmosphere.[77] During the Thirty Years' War, the Council's discovery of foreign Jesuits offering falsified names to royal officials led to the cancellation of the 1628 expedition of nine Italians and Belgians.[78] In the 1640s some seven dozen foreign Jesuits had been gathered in Seville to embark for the missions. The Germans among them, however, had arrived dressed in secular garb, which they had worn through Protestant lands, among Protestant soldiers, and on the Protestant ships that had brought them to Cádiz. As the Chile procurator Jacinto Pérez noted in his memorial, this was "how those who live in heretical lands always travel to help Catholics, by mixing among them." Intended to avoid trouble, this strategic subterfuge alarmed Seville's royal officials, who took the Jesuits to be an expeditionary force for some enemy's conquest of the New World. They immediately prohibited further passage. According to the Río de la Plata provincial procurator Juan Pastor, the royal ministers informed the king, who then ordered the Germans' expulsion. Then in 1650 a royal *cédula* commissioned an investigation as to which Jesuits on the Río de la Plata were foreigners. A dispute between Bernardino de Cárdenas, the bishop of Asunción, and the Jesuits in Paraguay, many of whom were non-Spanish, prompted Philip IV on June 1, 1654, to outlaw the sending of foreign missionaries to the colonies.[79]

This could not last. The continued need for missionaries forced a second royal *cédula* (December 10, 1664) to renew permission to subjects of the Spanish and Austrian Habsburgs. The non-Iberians among these, however, were limited to a quarter of the total number of missionaries

[75] Francisco Zambrano and José Gutierrez Casillas, *Diccionario Bio-Bibliográfico de la Compañía de Jesús en México* (Mexico: Editorial Jus, 1961–1977), VI.654–72, esp. 666–7.
[76] *Historie du Massacre* II/4; Letter of Martin Spillebeen, Mexico, May 19, 1617, quoted in Sauer, 43.
[77] Sierra, *Jesuitas*, 101, 105.
[78] Borges Morán, *El envió*, 300.
[79] Sierra, *Jesuitas*, 99–101; Lázaro de Aspurz, 201–16.

and were required to be chosen by the general of the order and to spend a
year in the Province of Toledo, where their behaviour and character could
be observed.[80] Twelve days earlier General Oliva had sent a memo to the
German and Belgian provinces announcing the impending decree and
requesting suitable candidates.[81] Only a single foreigner, from Milan,
was sent during this time. In the 1670s, Boranga, from the Austrian
Province, spent a year in Madrid waiting in vain for permission to pros-
elytize in the Mariana Islands.[82] Insisting on the need for foreign missionaries, Sebastián Izquierdo noted in a 1673 memorial that "European
Jesuits who go to the Indies, chosen and selected from their provinces,
are much more appropriate for the missions of the Indies than the Indians, since the Europeans who go to the Indies all have a special vocation
for them."[83] Melchor Antonio Portocarrero Lazo de la Vega, the Conde
de la Monclova, Viceroy of Peru, would repeat this sentiment in 1691.
The Jesuit position, as expressed by Izquierdo, was that the crown had
the obligation to help as many Indians as possible by sending to them as
many missionaries as possible, as quickly as possible and at royal expense.
Neither quotas nor quarantine periods were acceptable. The Jesuits, more
than the other orders, were reluctant to recognize the royal privileges that
the crown understood to accompany the royal *patronato*.[84] Fortunately, a
cédula of March 12, 1674, countermanded the period of observation and
raised the quota from a quarter to a third.[85] When not enough foreigners
could be gathered to fill the quota before the fleet departed, permission
was requested to carry over the remainder to the next departure. Though
approval had been secured for seventy-eight Jesuits, only forty-one were
sent.[86] This *cédula* inaugurated the period (1678–93) with the highest
number of annual *indipetae* requests from Central Europe, as shown in
Chart 2.[87]

For all their worries, the immigration authorities could not or would
not sort out German geography. In 1691 Anton Sepp von Reinegg wrote
that the Spanish officials did not distinguish between the various German
lands: "Being a Bavaria, Swabian, Swiss, Palatinate, etc., is just the same
as if they were Tyrolese, or even Viennese," for no one pays attention to

[80] AGI 122-3-2, quoted in Sierra, *Jesuitas*, 105; Royal *cédula*, April 24, 1671, AGI Mex.
2731, carpeta "Religion de la Compania de Jhs," 209r–212r, at 211r.
[81] Huonder, *Deutsche Jesuitenmissionäre*, 21.
[82] Lázaro de Aspurz, 228–29.
[83] Printed in Sierra, *Jesuitas*, 411–2.
[84] Borges Morán, *El envió*, 48–9, 67.
[85] Printed in Lázaro de Aspurz, 236–37. See also AGI CC 5550, bundle 12, fol. 7r-9v,
"Nómina de 41 jesuitas" at 7r; Sierra, *Jesuitas*, 106–7.
[86] AGI CC 5550, bundle 12, fol. 7r-9v "Nómina de 41 jesuitas" at 7r, 7v.
[87] For a detailed survey of these waves of applications, see Nebgen, 76–95.

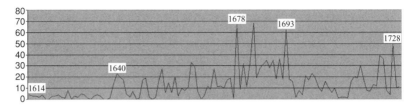

Chart 2. *Indipetae* from Central Europe preserved in ARSI

this in Spain. It suffices that "we are sent to the Indies from the Upper German province, and are not French, which is the only nation excluded and hated in Spain."[88] Still, even in the 1690s the papacy felt it necessary to send letters to Spain recommending Austrian missionaries.[89]

With the outbreak of the War of the Spanish Succession, all foreign missionaries, especially those subjects of Austria, Bohemia, and the other states of the Holy Roman Empire, were forbidden to travel to the colonies. The royal confessors desperately argued against this policy. In 1702 Juan Martínez de Ripalda, procurator for the Indies in Madrid, recommended eight German missionaries on the grounds that their superiors and rectors were Spanish, the Germans would be separated, and they were "subjects of great spirit and religion." Citing the law and the missionaries' unproven loyalty to the Spanish crown, the authorities denied his request.[90] A royal *cédula* of February 18, 1707, increased the quota to two-thirds while denying permission to subjects of the new Bourbon dynasty's enemies, that is, Austria, Aragon, Catalonia, and Valencia.[91] In 1711 four Bavarians and a Swiss were denied permission. After the war, an October 23, 1715 decree lifted the quota entirely, and the national restrictions partially. It continued to ban Neapolitans and Milanese, then subject to the Austrian Habsburgs, as well as those coming from the Austrian and Bohemian Provinces.[92] These restrictions would soon end, and Austrian missionaries resumed travel to the colonies in the 1720s.[93]

The early eighteenth century saw decreasing tolerance. Although the absolute number of German Jesuits increased during the first half of the

[88] Anton Sepp, *An Account of a Voyage from Spain to Paraquaria, Perform'd by the Reverend Fathers, Anthony Sepp and Anthony Behme* [translation of *Reissbeschreibung* (Nuremburg:1697)] (London: J. Walthoe [etc.] 1752), V.681.
[89] For example, see Huonder, *Deutsche Jesuitenmissionäre*, 24.
[90] Huonder, *Deutsche Jesuitenmissionäre*, 25; Duhr, *Geschichte*, 4:2a.504.
[91] Lázaro de Aspurz, 245–46.
[92] Sierra, *Jesuitas*, 112; Hausberger, *Jesuiten*, 39; Huonder, *Deutsche Jesuitenmissionäre*, 28.
[93] Lázaro de Aspurz, 248; Huonder, *Deutsche Jesuitenmissionäre*, 28.

century, in 1734 a *cédula* reestablished the quota at one quarter.[94] The reigning royal absolutism of the age felt little sympathy for an international Society of Jesus. In 1760 Charles III ended all traffic of foreign missionaries into the colonies and in 1767 suppressed the Society in Spanish territory.[95]

This was the end of an impressively international movement of missionaries. In the seventeenth century, the crown sent 3,814 Jesuits to the New World, about 1,000 Central Europeans, and 20,000–25,000 Spanish religious. Of this last figure, 16,000 were sent in a narrowly missionary capacity.[96] At the time of the expulsion of the Society, 277 (10.6%) of the Spanish colonies' 2,617 Jesuits were not Spanish.[97] Even at its zenith the German Jesuit presence in the capital remained quite modest. In 1696 only 2 of the 152 Jesuits in Mexico City were German, and they were both lay brothers. The newer missions in the north, however, held sizable German cohorts: four of the eleven Jesuits in the mission of San Francisco Xavier in Sonora (Gilg, Kappus, Kino, and Januske), two of the seven in the mission of San Joaquin and Anna in the Tarahumara (Neumann and Verdier), and three of the five in the recently established mission of Guadalupe (Haller, Eymer, and Hostinsky).[98] Once in the missions, Germans held a disproportionately high number of offices, despite official sanctions and unofficial prejudice against this.

Some of the Indians associated Spanish Jesuits with the colonial project while excusing the Central European Jesuits, and thus the latter could enjoy a greater popularity as missionaries. Furthermore, the Central Europeans remained more publicly critical of colonialism, as when Neumann blamed one Indian rebellion on the colonizers scouting out the missions for gold and slaves.[99] The Spanish Jesuits, however, could also be critical of colonialism,[100] and some Jesuits from Central Europe seemed to compensate for their foreign background by adopting an exaggerated pro-Spanish patriotism. Despite the prejudices they faced, German missionaries usually remained loyal to the Spanish crown. Kino, for instance, sided with the Bourbon Philip V against the Hapsburg claimant, and dedicated his *Favores celestiales* [*Celestial Favours*] to his king.[101]

---

[94] Duhr, *Geschichte*, 4:2a.505; Lázaro de Aspurz, 249, 252.
[95] Lázaro de Aspurz, 249, 252; Borges Morán, *El envió*, 251–60.
[96] Borges Morán, "Características," 621.
[97] Friedrich Schwager, *Die katholische Heidenmission der Gegenwart im Zusammenhang mit ihrer grossen Vergangenheit* (Steyl: Missionsdruckerei, 1907), 17.
[98] ARSI Mex. 8, fol. 331r–335v.
[99] Kalista, "Los misioneros," 157–58.
[100] Ibid., 160, admits this, but argues that it was not as frequent or as pronounced among the Czechs.
[101] Hausberger, *Jesuiten*, 32; Kino, *Crónica*.

Patronage and Regulation in China

The Catholic Church in China lay under the Portuguese royal *padroado*, although this did not cause quite as much difficulty for foreign missionaries as in Spanish America. Gregory XIII in *Ex pastorali officio* (January 28, 1585) gave the Society the exclusive right to evangelize Japan and China, under the *padroado* of Portugal. The crown, however, was not eager to extend this right to Jesuits of every nation. Previous policy had been far more open. During the reigns of John III (1521–57), of Sebastian (1557–78), and of Cardinal Henry (1578–80), almost half the missionaries working under Portuguese auspices in Asia were not Portuguese, and most foreign missionaries working in Brazil and India were Spanish. A sea change was signalled by a 1575 report from a fortress captain in the East Indies that Spanish missionaries were lobbying Philip II to invade China.[102] Such a move clearly threatened Portugal's influence in Asia. The mission procurator Alessandro Vallareggio informed General Mercurian of the upshot: Because Lisbon could not accept a Spanish missionary presence in India, China, and the Moluccas, the crown would permit only Italians, Portuguese, and Germans in Asia and exclude the Spanish, French, and English from missions in Brazil.[103] During most of the Philippine period (1580–1640) no Spanish missionaries sailed for Brazil, and very few for Asia. Hailing from lands not threatening Portugal's global position, Germans and Italians stepped in to fill the openings. Most German missionaries sailing from Lisbon went to China.[104]

In the first decade of the seventeenth century, about half a dozen ships left Portugal annually for Asia. They were only four times more likely to arrive safely than to be lost at sea.[105] The safer land route, to the Jesuits' frustration, remained blocked by the expanding Muscovite state. The typical Portuguese carracks, like their Spanish cousins, combined illegally high tonnages and illegally sparse armament. The Portuguese crown awarded captaincies more for sycophantism than seamanship, and often a captain would have "never seen any water other than that of the Tagus," as António Vieira snapped. Departures from Lisbon and Goa were frequently delayed to give the crown officials time to gather together enough money to pay the crew's wages.[106]

---

[102] Alden, 267–8.
[103] Leite, 2.439.
[104] Alden, 267–8.
[105] Charles Ralph Boxer, "The *Carreira da India*: Ships, Mens, Cargoes, Voyages," in *From Lisbon to Goa, 1500–1750: Studies in Portuguese Maritime Enterprise* (London: 1984), 33–4; Godinho, 672–5.
[106] Boxer, "*Carreira*," I.34–6, 45–6, 55; Chaunu and Chaunu, *Séville*, I.276–9.

Missionaries to China usually left Lisbon in March or April by way of the Carreira da India and reached India in about half a year, barring a hostile conspiracy of winds and waves. Like "human termitaries," ships to India would have hundreds of people on board. Sometimes a majority of these would lie sick with plague below deck.[107] In a strategy called the *volta do mar*, the ships sailed west until they came near Brazil, where they picked up winds and currents to slingshot them around the Cape of Good Hope, preferably in July. Ideally, the fleet could spend July and August at Mozambique. Monsoons, however, forced some one fleet in eight to call and winter there, or in Malindi or Socotra, in which case the trip's total duration could easily reach eighteen months. Most fleets that avoided this delay arrived after a voyage of five to six-and-a-half months, typically reaching India in early September.[108] Dimer speaks of his "very fortunate" five-month trip from Lisbon to Goa.[109] Delays could come from prolonged calls in port, navigation errors, contrary winds, or Dutch and English pirates. After 1576, the ships would proceed directly to eastern India without stopping in Goa, and 1706 saw direct service between Lisbon and Macao. The leg of the voyage between Goa and Macao normally lasted four or five months. From Macao missionaries might proceed on junks up the Beijiang River 北江, then along its tributary to Nanxiong 南雄. The Meiling 梅嶺 Ridge would be crossed by foot or sedan chair. In Jiangxi 江西 Province a ship could be used to travel the Gan 贛 River toward the cities of the north.[110]

In practice, for foreign missionaries the administrative obstacles proved almost as difficult as early-modern global travel. The seventeenth century began with the viceroy of Portugal blocking the passage of a group of Italian Jesuits to the Indies, stating that he would not let them go without approval from the king. General Aquaviva wrote Philip III to praise them, who "for the love of God and the salvation of souls have gone to Portugal from such distant lands."[111] He added a list of eleven reasons why they must not be denied passage, focusing on the inability of Spain and Portugal to supply enough missionaries, the lack of heresies in Italy to keep the Jesuits busy in domestic missions, and the great zeal with which they were leaving their home to serve God – and the king – in such distant

---

[107] Aldo Caterino, "Transoceanic Navigation in the Seventeenth Century: The Portuguese Route to the Indies," in *Martino Martini: A Humanist and Scientist in Seventeenth Century China*, ed. Franco Demarchi and Riccardo Scartezzini (Trento: Università degli Studi di Trento, 1996), 70; Huonder, "Todesfahrt," 77.

[108] Godinho, 666–7.

[109] Dimer [to German provincial?], 1658, BHStA G. R. 1256, Nr. 5, [fol. 2r].

[110] See Väth, 234–36; Grulich, 31–32; Alden, 628.

[111] 1600 or 1601, ARSI FG 1452/2.

lands. Royal and divine work were seen as running parallel.[112] The issue's resolution came much later, when a special tribunal in Madrid decided that Italians would only be accepted if they were Spanish subjects or from the Papal States.[113]

Late in 1617 Trigault arrived in Madrid, where Philip III offered to support financially the foundation of fifteen residences with three hundred missionaries. The company then pressed on to Portugal, as the *padroado* regulations required the expedition to depart from Lisbon. The authorities there, however, feared that Philip was seeking to open the door to Spanish commercial interests in the East. They therefore refused to grant Trigault and his recruits passage until he had rejected Philip's generous assistance. Also, a royal council in Madrid limited Trigault to bringing only ten non-Portuguese missionaries. Even the Portuguese Jesuits themselves, to Trigault's disappointment, objected that his expedition included too many Germans and Belgians.[114] This tension between the Portuguese and Spanish, enduring despite the union of the two crowns in 1580, suggests that the rivalry Trigault fought so constantly was indeed more nationalistic than dynastic.

The situation for foreign missionaries deteriorated under the Portuguese Restoration.[115] On February 20, 1649, King John IV (r. 1640–56) prohibited any non-Portuguese missionary from traveling overseas unless (1) he switched membership to a Portuguese province, (2) the port of departure was Portuguese, and (3) if for any reason he did not actually embark he must return to his native country.[116] The worst crisis was yet to come. Reports reached Lisbon that non-Portuguese Jesuits in India refused to accept the Restoration and continued to recognize the Spanish king as their own, and Grueber and Diestel's attempt to establish an overland route – fully independent of Portugal – contributed to this alarm. Luiz de Vasconcelos e Sousa, the Count of Castelo Melhor, rushed to denounce the two explorers' efforts as a threat to the crown's *padroado* privileges, and John's successor Alfonso VI (r. 1656–83) forbade any foreign missionary from sailing to Asia. Only Martino Martini, as the China vice-province's mission procurator, could calm the situation by stressing that the Portuguese visitor to East Asia had himself approved the Grueber-Diestel expedition. Martini neglected to mention that the

[112] ARSI FG 1452/3.
[113] Alden, 270.
[114] Dunne, *Generation*, 177–78; Lamalle, "Propaganda," 78; ARSI Goa 9I, fol. 31r.
[115] Alden, 268.
[116] F. Mateos, "Sobre misioneros extranjeros en Ultramar," *Missionalia Hispanica* 15 (1958): 245.

Jesuit General Nickel, who was German, had personally orchestrated the affai-.[117]

In his 1679 *Rationes praecipuae pro expeditione Japonica* [*Particular Ways for the Japanese Expedition*], Antoine Thomas also tried to lobby the general on behalf of non-Portuguese missionaries. German and Belgian missionaries in China and all of Asia had proved their loyalty to Portugal, he pointed out. Could the Portuguese crown not recognize this, and place its full confidence in them, especially in a matter not at all dangerous to its interests? At the turn of the century, non-Portuguese Jesuits in China still had to swear an oath of loyalty to the crown. Restrictions on, and prejudice against, non-Portuguese Jesuits continued during the reigns of Peter II (1683–1706) and John V (1706–50). In fact, in 1692 Manuel Correia, the Provincial of Brazil, asked that no Italian and German Jesuits be sent to Brazil, but rather that they all be directed to the East Indies.[118]

The continued rules against non-Portuguese Jesuits in China were steadily undermined by the papacy's efforts to erode the *padroado*. In *Onerosa pastoralis officii* (December 12, 1600), Clement VIII acknowledged the Portuguese failure to meet their responsibility and disputed therefore Portugal's right to route all missionaries through Lisbon.[119] In 1608 Paul V allowed Spanish mendicants to enter Asia on non-Portuguese ships, and in 1633 this privilege was extended to all religious – and in 1673 extended even to secular clergy.[120] Pope Innocent X insisted in 1648 that the Portuguese monopoly was obsolete and that even if every religious in Portugal were dispatched to the Indies, the demand would remain unsatisfied. In response, King John IV denied that the crown had ever blocked foreign missionaries, but merely had required them to obtained royal permission, to sail on Portuguese ships, and to remain subject to Portuguese oversight. He maintained his right to refuse missionaries who were potentially disloyal, including those subject to the Spanish crown during Portugal's war of independence.[121]

---

[117] Alden, 271.

[118] Anthony Thomas, *Rationes praecipuae pro expeditione Japonica* [1679?], written to General, printed in Sonkeikaku Library – Maeda Ikutoku Kai Foundation, eds., *Jesuit Missions in Japan: Original Letters and Reports 1663–1688* (Tokyo: Yushodo, 1975), I.28–29; Claudia von Collani, "P. Kilian Stumpf SJ – Nachfolger des hl. Kilian in China," *Würzburger Diözesangeschichtsblätter* 51 (1989): 552; Alden, 268; Leite 7,101–2.

[119] "Onerosa pastoralis officii cura," Bull. Roma. X [Romae 1867] 631, December 12, 1600, in Standaert, ed., 296–7.

[120] Paul V, "Sedis Apostolicae providentia," Bull. S. C. de Prop. Fide, June 11, 1608, in *Collectanea S. Congregationis de Propaganda Fide seu decreta instructiones rescripta pro apostolicis missionibus* (Rome: [Ex typographia polyglotta S. C. de Propaganda Fide], 1907), I.143; Urban VIII, "Ex debito pastoralis officii," Bull. S. C. de Prop. Fide I.81, February 22, 1633, in ibid., I.81.

[121] Boxer, *Portuguese*, 233–4.

In 1673 Clement X buttressed the papal argument by declaring that *padroado* rights do not exist *extra dominium temporale regni Portugalliae*, beyond where the crown enjoys actual control ("temporal dominion") – thus excluding independent kingdoms in Asia and Africa.[122] In response, Alfonso VI sourly suggested rerouting those missionaries coming to China in contradiction to his understood *padroado* privileges to areas more in need of them, such as Greenland.[123] The crown continued to pursue its prerogatives. Early in the eighteenth century, King John V forbade promulgation of any papal decree until a reply to his most recent entreaty had also been received.[124] Provoked by Bishop Ferdinand of Paderborn's financial contributions, John decided in 1705 to provide additional funds for his "own subjects" in China, apparently as a point of honour.[125]

All of the papacy's attacks directly threatened the Jesuits' domination of the missions. The Portuguese monopoly, however, had not been strictly enforceable even before the popes officially shattered it. The Spanish in Manila could slip with relative ease across the South China Sea to the mainland. Macao was off limits for them, as the Portuguese feared the mounting Spanish influence, and the Jesuits supported their patrons – and had their own investments in the silk trade to safeguard. The Jesuits were as loath to open up their spiritual monopoly in China as the Portuguese were to weaken their own political and economic foothold. The Jesuits justified their opposition to the papal decrees against the Portuguese position by appealing to their duty to conform to the Portuguese *padroado*.[126]

Who, then, were the missionaries in China? In the early 1620s, only ten of the twenty-eight Jesuit missionaries in China were Portuguese.[127] In comparison, the Japan province in 1620 (six years after the national ban on Christianity) had 106 Jesuits: 50% Portuguese, 19.8% other Europeans, 27.4% Japanese, and 2.8% Luso-Asian. The Chinese vice-province had twice the proportion of "foreigners" as did the Japanese – and this would increase over the century. Midcentury saw a China mission staffed by even fewer Portuguese. Taking the origins of visitors and

---

[122] Ibid. Clement X's 1673 Brief to the Archbishop of Goa is printed in Domingo Fernández Navarrete, *Tratados históricos, políticos, ethicos, y religiosos de la Monarchia de China* (Madrid: 1676–79), 515–18.

[123] "Instruttione data dal Principe di Portogallo al suo ambasciatore in Roma," February 5, 1674, BNC FG 1383 no. 22., fol. 1v.

[124] Van Hamme, "Imperio de China," to P. Proc., January 13, 1713, AGN AHH leg. 323, exp. 7, unfol.

[125] Castner, "Brevis animadversio circa ea, quae ad Fundationem Monasteriensem Spectant" [1705], BNC FG 1247, no. 5, 20r.

[126] ARSI JapSin 163, fol. 9r.

[127] Table 11.4, Alden, 275, based on ARSI JapSin 134, fol. 301r-447r.

vice-visitors as an index points to 1650–80 as a transition period, for earlier all but three visitors were Portuguese; after, only two were. Overall, eighteen of the forty-one visitors (44%) were Portuguese. Twenty-one German Jesuit missionaries worked in China before 1690. In 1700, there were 122 Catholic missionaries in China, of whom 67 (55%) were Jesuits. Of the 257 Jesuits arriving in the seventeenth century, only 111 (43%) were Portuguese.[128] In the seventeenth century, ten times as many Jesuits arrived in Spanish America as in China. The Jesuit missionaries in China, however, had origins that were far more diverse. In the end, the Jesuits proved more successful than the Portuguese at maintaining a monopoly.

Transpacific Transfers

The global circulation of missionaries was not as simple as a flow from Europe to the East and West Indies. As we have seen with Kino, not all foreign postings were equally desirable. Above all others, the China mission mesmerized generations of missionaries, abroad as well as in Europe.[129] Many missionaries now closely associated with the New World had in fact intended to use the Americas to reach China. Inspired by dreams of converts, by hope for martyrdoms, and by each other, Domingo de Betanzos, Martín de Valencia, Juan de Zumárraga, and even Bartolomé de las Casas were caught up in plans for a transpacifc mission. This attitude endured through the century. An English publication of *The Strange and marueilous Newes . . . of China* (1577) reported, "There hath been made within this citie of Mexico, generall prayers and supplications, beseeching the Almightie God to lighten this strange people with the knowledge of the holy fayth and woorde."[130] The Franciscan Bernardino de Sahagún spoke for many of his colleagues when he declared the primary significance of the missionary work in New Spain to be a stepping stone to China, where Christianity could take stronger roots.[131]

Administrative ties between the Philippines and Mexico magnified China's attractive force. In 1650 the Jesuits in Manila had written Manuel Dias the Younger (1574–1659), vice-provincial of China, offering to send missionaries. Two letters around the same time written by Christians in Zhangzhou 漳州 to Ignacio Zapata, provincial of the Philippines, requested missionaries, but this plan fell through, for unclear reasons.

[128] Alden, 250, 276; Standaert, ed., 307; Dehergne, 398–404.
[129] For more information, as well as for the background of movement across the Pacific, see Clossey, "Merchants," 41–58.
[130] Quoted in R. McLachlan, "A Sixteenth-Century Account of China," *Papers of Far Eastern History* Canberra 12 (1975): 78–9, 82.
[131] Sahagún, III.357.

In 1673 Philippine Jesuit Procurator Francisco Messina was in Macao, where he received promises that at least one maritime Chinese province would be reattached to the Philippines province (and thus placed ultimately under Mexican authority), a hope the Philippine Jesuits seemed to take seriously.[132]

In the end, however, relatively few missionaries crossed the Pacific to Asia, in part because of overlapping and repeated ecclesiastical and civil prohibitions, and the mendicant orders brought Mexican missionaries into China with greater frequency than the Jesuits. In the seventeenth century, only one Jesuit native to Mexico reached China: Didace Barreto was active in Hangzhou and Nanjing in the early 1640s, before he left the Society to join the Manchu armies.[133] Peter Van Hamme travelled west from Europe across the Pacific to his China posting, and he spent a year layover in the missions of northern Mexico. Looking back, he explained that God had called him to China because he was not worthy of becoming a martyr in Mexico, a variation on the idea that a martyrdom was easier to come by in Asia. More common was the aspiring martyrs' belief that they pursued what Brad Gregory has described as "an imitation of Christ that only spiritual arrogance could – mistakenly – make them think they merited."[134]

This chapter has shown how the Jesuit missionary network expanded to fit the opportunities laid out by global sea and land passages in the early-modern world. Although the movements of missionaries are traced out here, much research could be pursued looking at the implications of these movements and the political realities that encouraged them. For example, in the 1560s, early in the Society's history, recruits were surprisingly young. Only some 10% of applicants were in their thirties, and very few in their forties. The overall median age for applicants was nineteen. In Spain, only 9.8% were under seventeen, in Germany, 31.8%.[135] This apparently continued, at least among missionaries, in the next century. When the provincial congregation of New Granada asked General Oliva that he send "not just any young and inexperienced men, but those mature in virtue and advanced in learning and religion," the general replied (August 30, 1661), "If the Catholic king will allow it, as we do hope, that other Jesuits besides the Spanish be sent to the provinces of the Indies, it will not be difficult to respond to your province's wishes. This we vehemently

---

[132] Sebes, "Philippine Jesuits," 193–4, 197–8, 205.
[133] Louis Pfister, *Notices biographiques et bibliographiques sur les Jésuites de l'ancienne mission de Chine, 1552–1773* (Wiesbaden: Kraus, 1971), 295. Pfister suggests "Nova Hispania" is the Philippines, but I see no evidence to support this.
[134] Gregory, 285–7.
[135] Cohen, 251.

hope and will diligently seek."[136] Spain's antiforeigner policies, however, led to a trend of ever younger missionaries, for German missionaries tended to be older than average.[137] Presumably, Spain would have seen a good investment in recruiting these young Jesuits as missionaries, for assuming they worked until death, a younger Jesuit would be more worth the transportation costs. Such aspects of this network, including finances, are considered in the next chapter.

[136] Jouanen, I.232.
[137] Beckmann, "Missionsaszetische Anweisungen," 202; Duhr, *Geschichte*, 2:2.596.

8   The Jesuit Financial Network

The Economy of Jesuit Missions

Robert Scribner once wrote that the sacred was "always experienced from within the profane." The reverse is equally true, and the sacred and profane have been more mixed up than they are today. Only during the late eighteenth century was the economy perceived as a distinct entity, in many ways more fundamental than religion.[1] In the early-modern world, economics and religion can never be entirely separated. Sometimes the relationship was direct, and the "Christian" rebellion of Japan (1637), for example, had immediate economic consequences. Often it is more unexpected, as when in the 1630s a proposed canal between the Manzanares and the Tagus rivers was submitted to a committee of theologians, who piously rejected it: "If God had intended the rivers to be connected, He would have made them so."[2] Acosta's economic analysis included a religious factor modern economists would reject, for he pointed out that the lands with the greatest mineral wealth were also the most Christian.[3]

Despite common parlance, the Society of Jesus is, strictly speaking, a mendicant order. The Constitutions commend poverty to the point of denying the Society's missions the luxury of a stable financial foundation, and the Jesuits sometimes circumvented such restrictions by founding and funding a college to serve as a mission.[4] This is not how scholars know the Jesuits, and this is not how most contemporaries knew them. A saying in Portuguese Asia advised you to "guard your wife from the

---

[1] Robert Scribner, "Cosmic Order and Daily Life: Sacred and Secular in Pre-Industrial German Society," in *Popular Culture and Popular Movements in Reformation Germany* (London: Hambledon, 1988), 2. See Roland Robertson, "Economics and Religion," *Encyclopedia of Religion* (New York: Macmillan, 1987), V.1–11.
[2] Jan de Vries, *Economy of Europe in an Age of Crisis* (New York: Cambridge University Press, 1988), 169–170.
[3] Beckmann, "Utopien," 399.
[4] Castner, "Brevis animadversio circa ea, quae ad Fundationem Monasteriensem Spectant," [1705], BNC FG 1247, no. 5, fol. 20r.

friars, but watch your wallet with the Jesuits."[5] Jesuit financial endeavours were born of necessity. The inability of the Portuguese crown to honour its *padroado* duties pressured the China mission especially to seek alternate funding. Although royal authorities were not always derelict in their responsibilities, the very distance that made missions attractive served to complicate the financial support they needed.

This section describes the Jesuits' global efforts to sustain themselves in Germany, Mexico, and China. For clarity, comprehensiveness, and accuracy, the seventeenth-century China missions' accounts compare poorly with the disciplined columns of incomes and expenditures found, say, in late eighteenth-century records from the California missions.[6] Extant records do give a sense of the chief income sources for each mission region.

The economy of the Jesuits in Germany was the most straightforward of the three sites under study. Their financial support, essentially urban based, rested on donations and income from real estate, along with the interest paid on loans to princes, bishops, and communes. The tendency to take over (discretely, they hoped) houses won back from the Protestants brought the Jesuits additional wealth,[7] together with the rancour of the religious orders who had originally owned the houses.

The Mexican situation was somewhat more complicated. There the Jesuits' principal source of income was the king of Spain. Although seculars typically were responsible for paying their own fares to the New World, the responsibility for the orders' expenses fell to the crown.[8] Thus, when Mexican missionaries spoke of alms (*"limosnas"*), when not otherwise specified, these were royal (*"del Rey"*).[9] In 1572 Philip II complained, or boasted, that the *patronato* cost him 100,000 gold gulden annually.[10]

Costs mounted before the missionary even reached his mission. Starting June 18, 1581, the crown paid 1.5 *reales* per day (for up to one month) per religious for traveling expenses accrued while en route to Spain. The one-month limit was removed on May 8, 1595, and the Jesuits' request for 2.5 *reales* per day led in 1607 to a compromise of 2 *reales* daily. The royal treasury took into account the various necessities (provisions, clothing, fare, beds, transportation of baggage), and occasionally also paid for

[5] Cummins, *Question*, 27.
[6] For an example of the latter, see "Estado de la entrada y salida de Caudales en la Caxa del Fondo piadoso de las Misiones de Californias en todo el año proximo pasado de 1787," AGI Mex. 2731, carpeta "Nueva España", unfol.
[7] Müller, "Schul- und Bildungsorganisation," 274.
[8] Meier, 15; Jedin, "Weltmission," 395.
[9] For example, Hostinský, Santo Tomás, to the P. Proc. Gen. Antonio García, April 21, 1725, AHH México, leg. 321 exp. 50, fol. 1r.
[10] Jedin, "Weltmission," 395.

additional books or other useful items.[11] Once the missionaries arrived in Seville, the Casa de Contratación provided seven *reales* for each day of travel, computed at the rate of eight leagues a day. This remained constant throughout our period, despite inflation. Figures for the distances involved were provided by the postal service.[12] The Jesuits had to provide certification of the place and date of departure, although these data were irrelevant to their reimbursement, especially when errors were made in the calculation.[13] Some official of the Jesuit college would certify the presence of outbound Jesuits staying there, as well as the lengths of their stays.[14]

It was occasionally proposed that the American provinces would help pay for bringing missionaries over, and around 1670 the Casa altered its policy and directed the Jesuits to seek reimbursement from the royal treasuries of the territories for which they were bound.[15] In 1680 Ratkay reported that each missionary received from the king 300 thalers to cover initial outfitting, room, and board.[16] The food allowance for Jesuits travelling to the colonies was also a royal expense, but this responsibility also was passed from the Seville treasury to those of Veracruz and Mexico City.[17]

The crown awarded each mission a subsidy at its foundation, intended to pay for chalices, bells, and other basic accoutrements. Each missionary, in addition, received a generous annual salary, around 400 pesos at the end of the sixteenth century. Jesuits would receive bonuses for special services (35 pesos annually for running a school for Indian children) or for living in remote areas (50 pesos annually for missions among the Acaxees and Ximimíes). King Philip V (1700–46) paid 6,000 thalers per year for the California missions. The head of each *doctrina* drew a salary, technically an alms, from the crown.[18]

The Jesuits did not distinguish between missionary vocations in the strict sense and the other institutional positions, despite the objections of the crown. Because it was not known at the time of departure from Spain

---

[11] Borges Morán, *El envió*, 364, 390–1, 402–45. For an idea of the necessary equipment see N. Trigault, RAH Jesuitas 91, no. 28, fol. 3r.

[12] "Correo Mayor" at AGI CC 5550, bundle labelled "289–305" (Seville, May 15, 1687).

[13] For example, in the AGI CC 5550, bundle 12, fol. 28r-29r, the *viatico* in the final sum should be 213248. See Borges Morán, *El envió*, 365–6.

[14] For example, see the certification by vice rector P^e Pedro de Cuellar for Haller, Kall, and Verdier. Cadiz, May 17, 1687, AGI CC 5550, bundle 12, fol. 12r.

[15] Astráin, II.514–6; Zubillaga, *Monumenta Mexicana*, V.478, VI.453–4; Borges Morán, *El envió*, 449.

[16] WB Nr. 28.

[17] "Nómina de 41 jesuitas," AGI CC 5550, bundle 12, fol. 7r.

[18] WB Nr. 72; Tibesar, Borges, and Burrus, "Missions," IX.949; Polzer, *Rules*, 6.

whether a Jesuit was a missionary in the strict sense, all Jesuits were paid by the crown.[19] Of course, the crown did not pay for procurators coming from America to recruit and bring back missionaries.

These incomes allowed the Jesuits to accumulate wealth, primarily in the form of rural properties – *haciendas* – that produced food and cash crops as well as livestock, but also in investments in mills and urban real estate. They were able to build up this portfolio directly and indirectly by turning to their wealthy friends and lawyers, who were often Jesuit educated. More questionable business practices, such as illegally obtaining real property from the viceroy or paying off literate Indians who might contest transactions, also improved the Jesuits' worldly success. On the eve of suppression, the Mexican province had the resources to acquire the 54-ton *Laurentia*, an investment unparalleled in the Spanish Assistancy.[20]

Because the Jesuit missions were so far from commercial centres, the actual transport of goods was more problematic than any financial difficulties. Characteristically, Jesuit memorials from northern Mexico for new equipment would mention that the previous year's requests remained unfulfilled.[21] In 1718 Neumann made a point of placing orders via alternate routes to increase the odds that one would arrive.[22] Even when supplies came, many errors were made. Jiri Hostinksy, who had a two-year surplus of chocolate although and because he hated it, begged not to be sent any more.[23] Neumann, who wore size-fourteen shoes, complained that for two years he had received nothing bigger than size twelve.[24] Sometimes it was the royal *limosna* itself that never arrived, a quandary with which Neumann in particular was familiar.[25]

Other problems were purely financial. Less serious was the reassignment of extraordinary funds to other purposes. For example, the

---

[19] Polzer, *Rules*, 46–47, 447.

[20] Herman W. Konrad, *A Jesuit Hacienda in Colonial Mexico: Santa Lucía, 1576–1767* (Stanford: Stanford University Press, 1980); Francois Chevalier, *Land and Society in Colonial Mexico: The Great Hacienda* (Berkeley: University of California Press, 1963), 243–44; Joseph P. Sánchez, *Spanish Bluecoats: The Catalonian Volunteers in Northwestern New Spain, 1767–1810* (Albuquerque: University of New Mexico Press, 1990), 14.

[21] Neumann, Caríchic, to the P. Proc. Cristóbal de Laris, August 29, 1712, AGN Jes. I-14 exp. 80, fol. 612r. See also Neumann, Caríchic, to the P. Proc. Gen. Juan de Iturberroaga, August 3, 1711, AGN Jes. I-14 exp. 276, fol. 1438r, and Hostinský, Santo Tomás, to the P. Proc. Gen. Antonio García, March 8, 1718, AGN Jes. II-29 exp. 148, fol. 162r.

[22] Neumann, Caríchic, to the P. Proc. Gen. Antonio García, January 22, 1718, AGN Jes. II-29 exp. 144, fol. 158r.

[23] Hostinský, Santo Tomás, to the P. Proc. Gen. Antonio García, March 8, 1718, AGN Jes. II-29 exp. 148, fol. 162r.

[24] Neumann, Caríchic, to the P. Proc. Gen. Antonio García, January 22, 1718, AGN Jes. II-29 exp. 144, fol. 158r.

[25] Eymer, "Certificación," Papigóchic, January 20, 1703, AGN AHH, leg. 301 caja 1, fol., 312r.

expedition to California of Kino and Isidro de Antondo y Antillón could not be funded, because the crown had just ordered the viceroy to ship a large sum of money to Spain, and the previous expedition in 1683–85 had cost an impressive 225,000 pesos. Perhaps because of the War of the Spanish Succession, the eighteenth century began with serious deficiencies even in the royal *limosna*. By 1708, for several churches and for the partial subvention of Jesuits in northeast Mexico the king owed a total of 151,403 pesos in back pay, the equivalent of four years' worth of payments.[26]

The Jesuits had to turn to alternative sources of income. As the "cleverest of all the orders in finding rich benefactors," the Jesuits raised much money locally from merchants and secular clergy.[27] The Pious Fund, begun in 1696–97 for Lower California, became one of the most famous alms collections in Mexico. To support Kino, Juan María Salvatierra (1648–1717) and a professor of philosophy at the Jesuit Colegio Máximo named Juan de Ugarte went door to door collecting funds. Although the first round netted a single peso, the Pious Fund grew and continued to exist even into the twentieth century. Don Alonso Dávalos, the Conde de Miravalles, and Don Matheo Fernandez, the Marquis de Buena Vista, subscribed for 2,000 pesos, and the Confraternity of Dolores (College of Saint Peter and Paul in Mexico) subscribed for 8,000 pesos.[28] Juan Caballero y Ocio, a priest and Querétaro's great benefactor, donated 20,000 pesos, while the treasurer at Acapulco provided transportation across the gulf.[29] The Marquis de Villa Puente also gave at least 200,000 pesos to the California mission.[30]

The China mission had the most diverse sources of income, and the greatest need. In accordance with the Royal Patronage, the Portuguese crown held the primary responsibility for the mission finances. Indeed, the crown agreed to pay the missions' daily expenses and the costs of some of the foundations using funds from the income of the royal customs house in Melaka.[31] On November 12, 1603, Philip II ordered that funds

---

[26] Stitz, "Deutsche Jesuiten," 23; Eusebio Francisco Kino, *Cartas a la Procura de Misiones*, ed. Manuel Igancio Pérez Alonso (Mexico: Universidad Iberoamericana, 1987), 21 [19].

[27] Chevalier, 239–41.

[28] Peter Masten Dunne, *Black Robes in Lower California* (Berkeley: University of California, 1952), 41; Bolton, *Rim*, 343. 10,000 pesos rather than 2,000, according to Alegre, III.131.

[29] Miguel Venegas, "Empressas Apostólicas de los PP. Missioneros de la Compañía de Jesús de la Provincia de Nueva España Obradas en la Conquista de Californias, debida y Consagradas al Patrocino de María Santíssima, Conquistadora de Nueva Gentes en su Sagrada Imagen de Loreto. Historiadas por el Padre Miguel Venegas de la Misma Compañía de Jesús." N.p., 1739, BLB Bolton MS. 683, ii.iii.10–13; Alegre, III.131.

[30] Dunne, *Black Robes*, 107, 298.

[31] George B. Souza, *The Survival of Empire: Portuguese Trade and Society in China and the South China Sea, 1630–1754* (Cambridge: Cambridge University Press, 1986), 24.

be disbursed sufficient to support the missions in the Indies. However, the money only arrived at half the specified amount, and new attempts to restore the stipend failed.[32] Philip III raised the amount to 3,000 *pardãos* at Trigault's request, and just before losing the Portuguese crown Philip IV established an annual donation of 4,000 pieces-of-eight to the China Jesuits. The next year the Duke of Braganza, crowned John IV, either confirmed this donation or set up a new foundation, at the amount of 3,000 *serafini* per year.[33]

Additional travel funds were typically awarded by the crown on a case-by-case basis. Subsidies were only partial, usually not covering half the expenses – Valignano complained that the funds sufficed to pay only for the necessary clothing.[34] The crown only contributed funds for outward travel. Procurators on business trips to Europe received nothing, though they could recoup loses by bringing things with them from China to sell.[35]

The Jesuits' financial difficulties went beyond the crown's frequent delinquency – on occasion, money would flow in the opposite direction, from the Jesuits back to colonial officials. At times this occurred in Europe itself, as in 1641, when the Portuguese province gave King John IV over 2 million *réis*, though presumably this had no direct effect on the China Vice-province. Sometimes the income intended for the Society was merely redirected. In theory, customs collected at Diu were to support the China mission, but in 1656 the fortress captain commandeered for real or pretended military needs the six-*conto* inheritance left to the Society by a wealthy merchant. Three years later Diu borrowed 7.5 million *réis*, in part from the Jesuits, to pay its troops and to compete with Dutch bribes to a local native ruler. The loan probably remained outstanding. The eighteenth century saw this trend worsen. Even expenses properly belonging to the crown fell to the Society, as when the China Vice-province paid 200,000 *réis* for the 1726 embassy of Alexandre Metello de Sousa Menezes. In the following years the Jesuits gave the Estado da India a massive loan, at eight per cent interest, guaranteed by income from crown lands and some islands near Goa, to underwrite the reconquest of Mombasa.[36]

In addition, the Jesuits had to spend precious time working for the colonial administration and thus became more closely entwined with the

[32] Ricci, *Fonti Ricciane*, II.269; Fortunato Margiotti, *Il Cattolicismo nello Shansi dalle origini al 1738* (Rome: Edizioni 'Sinica Franciscana,' 1958), 378.
[33] Lamalle, "La propaganda," 66–8, 113; Margiotti, 378.
[34] Alden, 325, 636.
[35] Ibid., 539, 637. See "Rol da Matolotagem que se dá a cada hum dos Padres que vão pera o Reino por ordem do P.ᵉ Vizitador," in DI 10:429–31.
[36] Alden, 330–1, 333; Souza, 188–90.

management of empire than did their Spanish counterparts. At Diu, by 1635, they were placed in charge of the small copper or tutenag coins called *bazarucos*, a duty they also had at Damão, in response to rumours of fraud. Jesuits managed the royal revenues as well as the weapons and munitions stores at Bassein, Chaul, Damão, Onor, and Mozambique.[37]

The provision of royal income to the Asian missions faced insurmountable obstacles. The chaos of royal finances, the failure to budget, graft, haphazard reports, and the usual delays and hazards of sea travel led to payments "delayed, paid only partially, offered in depreciated currency, or entirely delinquent." The situation deteriorated during the Philippine period as Spain neglected Portuguese colonial defence, and it was compounded in the early seventeenth century by the growing Dutch presence. As one popular saying had it, royal payments arrived *tarde, mal, e nunca* ("either late, incomplete, and never"), and military and civil authorities had even less success than the church in getting their financial support.[38] The missions would need nonroyal sources of income.

The papacy occasionally paid additional funds. These originated in the papal Christmas dues collected in Spain, but were routed through Lisbon to Goa. Unfortunately for the China mission, all this money was specified for churches and seminaries in Japan, and China saw none of it.[39]

Early on, the primary internal means of economic support seems to have been investment in maritime trade. The Jesuits contracted arrangements with Portuguese shippers, and undertook part ownership of vessels. Later the Vice-province shared title to the não *S. Pedro e S. João*, which in the 1740s plied the routes between Portugal and East Asia. Probably the most risky investments Jesuits used was the sea loan (*respondência*), where the principal was not guaranteed if the goods were lost in shipping.[40]

This maritime trade mostly ran between Macao and Japan. Sometime after the 1560s, China restricted her nationals from trade with the "dwarf robbers" of Japan, where "dwarf" 倭 was a cutting Chinese pun on the word "Japanese." This gave the Portuguese and the Jesuits an opportunity, and the increased production of silver in Japan made this opportunity opportune.[41] Merchants operating out of Macao exchanged raw and manufactured silks and gold for silver. Before the founding of the China Vice-province, the Jesuits were doing quite well. Between 1555

---

[37] HAG MR 43 fol. 139, cited in Souza, 188–90; Alden, 342–43.

[38] Alden, 326–7; Boxer, *Portuguese*, 77.

[39] Alden, 372; Margiotti, 387.

[40] Souza, 34, 113–14, 188–90; "Receita do cabedal da v. prov.ᵃ da China . . . 18 de dezembro de 1661 ate o fim de junho de 1667" in ARSI FG 721/II/6: 2603–495 of 5160 – 387 (at 23r, 24r). See Alden, 563; Boxer, "Macao," 70–3.

[41] Boxer, *Portuguese*, 63; Subrahmanyam, *Portuguese*, 138.

and 1570 they took in 18,000–20,000 *cruzados* annually. This "ridiculous quantity" has been defended on the grounds that a captain could make 60,000 *cruzados* on a single voyage,[42] but in fact a captain could make enough on a single voyage to retire in fine style.[43] Figures show a 15-year total of 270,000 to 300,000 *cruzados*, an amount roughly equivalent to a captain's profits from five trips, thus roughly equal to five fortunes.

In 1578 Valignano secured an agreement with the Macao-to-Nagasaki silk-trade merchants that won for the Society 100 of the 96,000 kilograms (1,600 *piculs*) of silk sent annually. Because Mercurian had forbidden the Jesuits to participate in the silk trade, illegal under canon law, Valignano's deal needed – and received after the fact – approval from the Jesuit General Aquaviva, Pope Gregory XIII, and the royal officials in Goa and Macao.[44] A bewildering series of injunctions and approvals followed, including Sixtus V's (1585) ban and subsequent reversal (1587), along with a second ban (1597) and countermand (1606). The matter remained under debate as the trade continued at varying levels. From 1582 to 1620, mean net profits reached 0.96 *contos* per year, a high figure given that fourteen of thirty-eight expeditions failed to reach Nagasaki.[45] As with all Jesuit trade, the volume and duration of illicit transactions remains obscure. After it was founded, the China Vice-province continually demanded that its superiors in Macao grant it some portion of the silk trade profits, with little success. Their request to be allowed 10 or 20 *piculs* (160 to 320 kilograms) of silk was finally agreed to by the general in the 1630s.[46]

Around the same time Japanese imports of raw silk had reached a staggering 280,000 kilograms per year, perhaps four times the annual rate at the turn of the century. When in 1636 the Tokugawa Shogunate prohibited Japanese nationals and ships from trading or residing overseas, the Portuguese, and to a lesser extent the Chinese and Dutch, share of the trade improved markedly as Japanese merchants became desperate for alternative suppliers. The good fortune did not last, and economic hardship pressured some twenty thousand Japanese Christians to reject both

[42] Juan Ruiz-de-Medina, " 'El Trato de la seda' en Japon y los jesuitas," in *Ecclesiae Memoria: Miscellanea in onore del R. P. Josef Metzle O. M. I. Prefetto dell'Archivo Segreto Vaticano*, ed. Willi Henkel (Rome: Herder, 1991), 314–15.

[43] Boxer, *Portuguese*, 63.

[44] Souza, 37l; Margiotti, 369–71; Charles R. Boxer, *The Christian Century in Japan, 1549–1650* (Berkeley: University of California, 1951), 118.

[45] Ruiz-de-Medina, 314–15; Margiotti, 370, 372–77; Alden, 535, calculates based on Charles R. Boxer, *The Great Ship from Amacon, Annals of Macao and the Old Japan Trade, 1555–1640* (Lisbon: Centro de Estudos Históricos ultramarinos, 1959), 43–100.

[46] Margiotti, 374–5.

local authority and the Tokugawa Shogunate in the Shimabara Rebellion of 1637. Suppressing the uprising in the following year, Shogunate authorities blamed the rebellion on the Portuguese, who allegedly had hoped to invade Japan. All contact with the Portuguese was outlawed.[47] A special embassy from Macao in 1640 failed when sixty-one of its members were beheaded, with a lucky thirteen spared to explain to Macao how serious the Japanese were about the exclusion.[48] In 1662 the Manchu rulers responded to the forces gathering in Fujian and Taiwan under the Ming loyalist pirate Koxinga (Zheng Chenggong 鄭成功, 1624–62) by ordering the evacuation of the coastal areas, a measure that remained in effect for five years. The mid-1660s found the Beijing Jesuits without influence at the court, and thus unable to lobby for Macao.[49] These factors, and the loss of Melaka to the Dutch, ended the position and prosperity of Macao.

Some Jesuit trade activities were motivated not by profit but by a desire to please allies and Chinese officials. Thus Jesuits traveling from Goa to Japan would discreetly make investments in China, where rates of returns were very high.[50] Also, in the 1580s one Ming official in Canton flamboyantly insisted that he pay the Jesuits in silver for the gifts they pressed upon him, but later secretly tipped them off that the silver was actually an advance payment for more "gifts."[51]

The seventeenth century witnessed a gradual reallocation of investment funds from maritime trade and loans to real estate. In 1621 General Vitelleschi joined pope and king in approving the Jesuits' investment in houses in Macao.[52] The Vice-province earned income from the commercial and residential properties it held there, and by about 1730 it would also hold real estate in Beijing. The Jesuits also owned the tiny Ilha Verde island in Macao's harbour, which provided pineapples, figs, and peaches for the college and for profit. The Japanese province similarly concentrated its investments in Macao, as a safe alternative to the uncertainties of Japanese politics and Dutch interference with sea traffic. Macao also proved safer than Bombay, where in 1667 the English governor, Gervase Lucas, appropriated Jesuit properties on Bombay Island.[53]

[47] William Atwell, "Ming China and the Emerging World Economy, c.1470–1650," in *The Ming Dynasty, 1368–1644, Part 2*, Vol. 8, *The Cambridge History of China*, ed. Frederick W. Mote and Denis Twitchett (Cambridge: Cambridge University Press, 1998), 399, 410–11; Boxer, *Great Ship*, 146.
[48] Subrahmanyam, *Portuguese*, 172.
[49] Boxer, "Macao," 74.
[50] Alden, 549, 564; Margiotti, 386.
[51] Alden, 549–50.
[52] Margiotti, 382.
[53] Alden, 391, 397, 445.

As the seventeenth century concluded, the Jesuits in East Asia shifted their real-estate portfolio from urban Macao to rural northern India.[54] The Vice-province sent Wenzel Pantaleon Kirwitzer (ca. 1589–1626) to Goa with "some pieces" (Chinese slaves?) to sell for funds to acquire land in that city or in the north. Because of Mughal and Portuguese opposition, this attempt failed, but Manoel Coelho soon travelled to Melaka to inquire about purchasing real estate there. Coelho found "very fertile and abundant and cheap" land, as well as a cooperative local Jesuit superior. Chinese labour, Coelho reported, would have to be brought in to supplement the indolent local Malays. This new plan failed as Melaka attracted the interests of the Dutch and the Sumatrans. Returning its attention to India, the Vice-province purchased the incomes of Paspuly (1722) and Olnem (1729), in the northern province "Salsete do Norte" between Damão and Bassein.[55] In 1730 the College of Macao owned four villages in India: Arem, Mirem, Malvara, and the so-called "collarias of Tanna." The procurator sent all disposable income from these villages to Goa by means of letters of exchange, currency (*larins* and *pagodas*), or merchandise, all of which were converted into silver specie or bullion to be forwarded to China. These revenues covered most of the Vice-province's operating expenses, but were terminated with the Maratha invasions of the 1730s.[56]

Although specific regulations governed private gifts, the Jesuits also enjoyed a wide range of such donations either in money or in kind, in addition to being assigned the administration of legacies. Some of this stemmed from Europeans in Asia. The Jesuit Macao merchant Gaspar Viégas made modest gifts that funded Michele Ruggieri's and Ricci's initial efforts in China.[57] More substantially, the seed money for the Jesuits' silk trade came from Luís de Almeida (ca. 1525–1583), who had left Lisbon for a six-year career as a merchant in the Far East. In 1555 he became a Jesuit and donated to the Society all his assets, a fortune variously described as worth 2,500 to 5,000 *cruzados* of silver.[58]

Other funds came from Chinese, especially from the Jesuits' converts. The official Fan Wencheng 范文程 sent the mission thirty gold pieces

[54] Souza, 191–2.
[55] Alden, 385, 392, 545. The identification of these "pieces" as Chinese slaves is Alden's suggestion. See Manoel Coelho to Vitelleschi, December 12, 1621, in ARSI Goa 18, fol. 54v.
[56] Souza, 192; Alden, 386–7, 394.
[57] Noël Golvers, *François de Rougement, S. J., Missionary in Ch'ang-shu (Chiangnan): A Study of the Account Book (1674–1676) and the Elogium* (Leuven: Leuven University Press, 1999), 590; Alden, 349.
[58] Fr. Manuel Teixeira, *Luís de Almeida, S. J., Surgeon, Merchant, and Missionary in Japan* (1970–1976[?], np); Boxer, *Great Ship*, 5; Alden, 349; Ruiz-de-Medina, 313.

annually, to be spent on the church and on presents for Schall.[59] Further, socially prominent Chinese women donated between 800,000 and 4,800,000 *réis* to the Vice-province.[60] In 1636, twelve Portuguese in Macao, or the representatives of those deceased, contributed 2,000 *réis* apiece to found a college in Hangzhou 杭州. They requested that the Jesuit general in Rome be informed that they might enjoy the privileges customarily extended to such donors.[61] Single Portuguese men who lived in Asia were more likely to make donations than those living in Portugal; among the Chinese, benefactresses were more common than benefactors. In addition, the Jesuits earned interest from loans made to Chinese.[62]

Money might also come from farther afield. The English Catholic baronet William Godolphin (ca. 1640–1710) pledged 4,000,000 *réis* to the Vice-province, although his relatives in England refused to ever send the money. María Guadalupe de Lencastre's son, the Duke of Arcos, set up a 720,000-*réis* annuity for the Jesuits' China Vice-province in 1709. This reversed a family tradition of money flowing in the opposite direction, for in 1615–17 Alvaro de Lencastre found himself unable to repay the Lisbon Jesuit college of Santo Antão a loan of approximately 42 *contos*.[63] This avenue was so critical that Grueber and Roth argued for establishing a mission station on the Chinese border at Xining 西宁, to facilitate the transfer of funds from Europe to the Chinese Mission via Armenian or Indian merchants.[64] King Philip III (r. 1598–1621) offered the money for the foundation of fifteen residences to Trigault, who collected other donated monies in Naples.[65] On December 15, 1616, the Congregazione della Natività di Nostra Signora in the Jesuit professed house of that city founded the Monte della Madonna dei Poveri Vergognosi as a charitable institution that would loan money at low rates of interest. It pledged more than 2000 *ducati* from its profits for China and Japan, but the enterprise soon failed, and it is not certain that any money was ever sent.[66]

---

[59] Johann Adam Schall von Bell, *Lettres et Mémoires d'Adam Schall, S. J.: Relation Historique*, ed. Henri Bernard, trans. Paul Bornet (Tientsin: Hautes études, 1942), 145.

[60] "Rol dos fundadores da vice provincia de China" (1727), ARSI FG 722/17.

[61] "Treslado do contrato que fez a Companhia de JESUS com os doze fundadores do Collegio da Cidade de Hancheo na Vise Prov.ª da China," [December 27, 1636], ARSI FG 722/17.

[62] Alden, 360; Golvers, *Rougement*, 590–2.

[63] Alden, 355, 374, 555–9.

[64] "Secundo, possent, si opus esset, hinc ex Europa dirigi pecuniae usque in illam civitatem pro subsidio Missionum Sinicarum," published in Wessels, "New Documents," 288.

[65] Margiotti, 388. See "P. Joannes Antonius Lothedus donavit..." [1652] and "Inter memorias P Nicolas Trigautis..." [1655, describing foundations from 1616], ARSI FG 722/17.

[66] Margiotti, 388.

In the end, none of this sufficed. Debt overwhelmed the China Vice-province from its birth until the suppression of the Society. It was the principal debtor of the Japan Province, from which it also received direct grants of 500 *taeli* per year, every year from its foundation until 1632. After much legal wrangling, this fund may have begun to flow again at the instigation of Visitor Simão da Cunha in 1656.[67] When a special procurator for the Portuguese Assistancy was established at the Spanish court during the Philippine period, its cost was to be shared among the Portuguese provinces based on their ability to pay, and China and Japan were both so poor that neither was asked to give anything at all.[68]

Because of the extreme cost of maintaining a missionary in China, most of the collected income went towards personnel. A single mission-ary entailed annual costs of approximately 30,000 *réis*, in 1645, or 62,600 *réis*, in 1730, although the China Vice-province did not have to pay for incoming human capital. Indeed, when the rector of New St. Paul's Col-lege in Goa requested subventions from the Vice-province to pay for the training of missionaries, General Gonzalez blocked the move. Most interesting for our purpose here is the money expended elsewhere. The Lisbon-based mission procurator for the Indies spent almost a quarter of his income in support of the canonization of Francis Xavier.[69] Money came all the way from Asia to promote the beatification of Brazil's Forty Martyrs (1570) and José de Anchieta.[70]

Global Financial Connections

Beyond regional campaigns to raise money and transoceanic requests to royal patrons, the Jesuits developed a truly global financial network, one so strong that moneys would be exchanged between Germany and China, Germany and Mexico, and Mexico and China.

The German financial contributions to the Chinese mission have long been recognized but underestimated. K. S. Latourette remarked that "now and again some German prince assisted with financial contribu-tions, but no German state as such had much part in missions."[71] In fact, especially in light of the scantiness of papal and royal funds, the var-ious German contributions formed the largest and most stable external

[67] Alden, 553; Margiotti, 379–81.
[68] "Varias lembranças," BNL FG 4254, fol. 102v.
[69] Alden, 533, 641–43.
[70] "O dinheiro que deve vice provincia da China a prov.ª de Japam" (1659) in BA/JA/49-V-11, no. 76, fol. 508.
[71] Kenneth S. Latourette, *A History of Christian Missions in China* (New York: Macmillan, 1929), 42.

source of income. Trigault commented on the importance of establishing such alternate revenue, here referring specifically to the *montes pietatis* such as the one founded in Naples: "It often came into my mind that nothing could be more helpful than if monetary sodalities and monts could be established for the propagation of the faith."[72] Still, German funds faced the same problems as the Portuguese. A 1672 report noted next to the entries of Emperor Ferdinand III, the duke of Bavaria, and the count palatine of Neuburg that nothing had arrived.[73] Five years later the procurator Sebastião de Almeida again reported that the imperial 1,000 gulden had not been received from Ferdinand III, nor the 500 gulden from Bavaria, nor the 100 ducats from the count palatine of Neuburg.[74] Although the 1670s may have been a difficult decade for funds from Europe, these records suggest the enduring expectation of money from German sources.

The China mission's principal German patrons were the dukes of Bavaria. The "Romanization" of Bavaria, in which Munich increasingly embraced a Catholicism specifically Roman, has become a common trope in the historical scholarship of the duchy, but one could just as appropriately speak of a globalization of the *pietas bavarica*, the Bavarian piety.

Early in his rule Duke Albert V (1550–79) found he could be a tolerant man whenever the estates withheld his income, and he gave in to many of their religious demands, such as not fining utraquism. After the declared discovery of a conspiracy of radical nobility in 1564, he became more severe, and pushed through stricter religious policies, including restrictions on travel to Protestant lands. The duke promptly requested Jesuits from Canisius, four of whom conducted a domestic mission in rural Bavaria.[75] In 1570 the privy council formed as part of the blossoming professional bureaucracy and appropriated jurisdiction in all religious matters, largely from the episcopal hierarchy. Slowly Albert even overcame his muted aversion to the Jesuits, whom he, as an art patron, had considered philistine. By 1577 when his advisors dared to describe his son Ernest as too *jesuiterisch* ("jesuitical"), he leapt to their defence, declaring his hopes that "our son is 'Jesuit' enough, that is, god-fearing, honest, and learned, pious and zealous." His enthusiasm for the missions was more long-standing, and letters from the Indies forwarded to him by Canisius he had translated into German for his wife Anna.[76]

[72] Trigault, "Litterae," 92.
[73] "Rol dos Benifeitores da V Prov^a da China," Macao, November 8, 1677, ARSI FG 722/17.
[74] Margiotti, 393.
[75] O'Malley, *The First Jesuits*, 127.
[76] James Brodrick, *Saint Peter Canisius, S. J., 1521–1597* (London: Sheed and Ward, 1935), 139; Bauerreiß, VI.268; Braunsberger, ed., II.281, 292.

William V "the Pious" (1548–1626, r. 1579–1597) inherited his father Albert's belated affection for the Company, despite more than once avowing that his own will often ran against, and overcame, the Jesuits'.[77] He also continued the drive toward greater control of religious affairs. The Concordat of 1583 created ducal rights of presentation to ecclesiastical offices and of oversight of clerical property. William's debts, reaching totals he himself sheepishly called "somewhat strange," forced his abdication in 1597, when his son Maximilian (1573–1651, r. 1597–1651) became duke. The Bavarian estates assembled only twice during Maximilian's reign, for their continuing tax outlays gave him an effective independence. The ducal economy soon improved, and in the early seventeenth century the salt monopoly alone yielded the dukes 400,000 gulden annually.[78] It was William's religious enthusiasm and Maximilian's financial and administrative genius, and the resulting treasury, that would allow contributions to the China mission.

The two dukes' advisors further set the stage. Both had Jesuit confessors.[79] In addition, Johann Baptist Fickler (1533–1610), young Maximilian's tutor, was keenly interested in the Jesuits' work in Asia, a concern perhaps related to his duties as curator of the dukes' collections of curiosities. His enthusiasm was shared by Aegidius Albertinus (1560–1620), who served Maximilian as librarian and secretary and had close connections both to the Jesuits and to Spain. Albertinus quickened interest in Asia by translating Giovanni Botero's *Relazione* (1611), in addition to rendering several collections of Jesuit letters into German.[80]

On August 8, 1616, Trigault arrived at the Wittelsbach court in Munich, one stop on his whirlwind tour, the Bavarian part of which also included Augsburg, Dillingen, Neuburg an der Donau, Ingolstadt, and Würzburg. His stay was to become the highpoint of his recruitment drive, for "all these things which I have mentioned up to now are small if they are compared with the singular generosity of the Bavarian family." This generosity prompted him to give a detailed description of the court. After acknowledging the reigning duke, Maximilian, he singled out William V, "who, having abdicated now for a long time, makes times for himself and for God, so that you may consider him a man of the Society in all matters." His intent discussion of the other princes and their wives suggests Trigault's interest in and familiarity with them. The prince of Neuburg, for example, recently converted from the Lutheran heresy by the "great goodness of the German Church." Trigault saw this *magnus bonus* of the

---

[77] Bauerreiß, VI.266–7.

[78] F. L. Carsten, *Princes and Parliaments in Germany: From the Fifteenth to the Eighteenth Century* (Oxford: Clarendon Press, 1963), 389, 392, 394.

[79] Albrecht, *Die auswärtige Politik*, 20.

[80] Lach and Klay, *Asia*, II.ii.243–8.

German Church in its ability to effect a conversion. He happily recorded the care with which William received *De Christiana Expeditione*, who "had read our history from beginning to end so attentively that in his own hand he jotted down all of his questions in a commentary, from which he then drew out so pious and judicious a discussion that I could not be more amazed." Furthermore, William remained generally close to and candid with Trigault, who "could hardly . . . believe with how much trust in us both he and the other princes make known their intentions and affairs." Trigault's unspoken solicitation did not abate William's enthusiasm, "for he placed into my unsuspecting hands a document certifying an annual donation of five hundred gulden, and he paid out the stipulated amount by hand into a silk sack." At the time this foundation was created to last as long as William would last, after which its future was uncertain.[81]

Sensibly, Trigault cultivated his relationship with the Wittelsbachs. He mentions that William confirmed his donation "to me and my friend in a letter written by his own hand."[82] This close association continued for many years. In 1620 Trigault wrote William to ask him to have excerpts from the *De rei christiane statu apid Sinas* [*On the State of Christianity among the Chinese*], accompanying the letter, dispatched to Jesuits in Augsburg, Munich, Ingolstadt, and Dillingen. He further thanked William for the gifts, and requested that he work to persuade Maximilian to get the financial support secured for the future.[83] That same year the Jesuit Hieronymus Rodericus wrote an additional thank-you letter to William.[84] Mindful of the importance of stewardship, in 1624 Trigault ("spreading the faith of Christ in the most remote provinces") wrote a letter to Maximilian from China.[85] In 1628 Nonius Mascarenhas wrote William yet another thank-you letter, perhaps for some new generosity.[86]

---

[81] Trigault, "Litterae," 101–3. See also Heinz Dollinger, *Studien zur Finanzreform Maximilian I. von Bayern: Ein Beitrag zur Geschichte des Fruhabsolutismus*, Schriftenreihe der Historischen Kommission bei der Bayerischen Akademie der Wissenschaften 8 (Göttingen: Vandenhoeck u. Ruprecht, 1968), 443; Väth, 34–5; Hermann Schneller, "Bayerische Legate für die Jesuitenmissionen in China," *Zeitschrift für Missionswissenschaft und Religionswissenschaft* 4 (1914), 177–79; Georg Leidinger, "Herzog Wilhelm V. von Bayern und die Jesuitenmissionen in China," in *Forschungen zur Geschichte Bayerns* 12 (1904): 171–5.

[82] Trigault, "Litterae,"103.

[83] Idem to William, February 2, 1620, BStB CLM 27323 p. 2, 3.

[84] Macao, February 20, 1620. This was at BHStA Jesuitica 588.4–6, but apparently is now lost.

[85] Nicolas Trigault, "Ex litteris P. Nicolai Trigault, ad serenissimum Electorem Bavariae et alios Bavariae duces, datis 20 octob. 1624," in *Vie du Pere Nicolas Trigault de la Compagnie de Jesus*, ed. Chretien Dehaisnes (Paris: P. Lethielleux, 1864), 275.

[86] Mascarenhas, Rome, April 29, 1628, ARSI FG 722/17.

Maximilian's personal piety pushed him toward an alliance with the emperor who had bestowed the Palatine line's electoral dignity on him in 1623, just as his princely aversion to increased imperial power pushed him away. No such conflict qualified his relation with the church. The duke freely intervened in internal ecclesiastical affairs, taxing the clergy, supervising the financial administration, regulating rites and religious festivals, and eroding episcopal jurisdiction.[87]

Although he supported the Capuchins in their local missions, Maximilian enjoyed an especially close relation with the Jesuits, whom he esteemed for their judiciousness. He founded colleges for them in Burghausen, Mindelheim, and Amberg, and then financially supported and personally attended the colleges' theatrical productions. In moves suggestive of the Society's potential for decentralizing, Maximilian intervened, both openly and clandestinely, on behalf of his Jesuits with the general in Rome.[88] His particular interest in Jesuit missions found expression in the English College at Liège, and his enthusiasm extended to women of the Institute of Mary, who were disparaged as "Jesuitesses" by their many enemies. Maximilian greeted Mary Ward, who founded in 1609 the Institute of the Blessed Virgin Mary – the "English Ladies" – as she arrived from Rome on January 7, 1627, by declaring that just as Bavaria first received Christianity from English missionaries, so too would it be renewed by English women. His support went beyond mere encouragement, and in April 1627 the duke supported a house in Munich for ten of Mary Ward's sisters, at the cost of 2,000 gulden per year.[89]

Evidently Trigault's efforts through William to secure continued funding were also successful, for Maximilian confirmed this 500-gulden amount on March 16, 1626. Early in the next year the elector directed the president of the court treasury to request payment for 1627 and to ask whether the China Jesuits should get a more generous amount.[90] With French and Swedish troops, the 1649 plague, and the post-war economic depression wrecking havoc in Bavaria, by 1651 inflation and Austrian competition had reduced the annual net from the salt monopoly to 72,000 gulden. From the evacuation of the privy council to Salzburg in April 1632[91] all payments to China ceased.

---

[87] Carsten, 393.
[88] Dieter Albrecht, *Maximilian I. Von Bayern 1573–1651* (Munich: Oldenbourg, 1998), 322, 331; Bauerreiß, VII.75; Duhr, *Geschichte*, II.2; Robert Bireley, *Maximilian von Bayern, Adam Contzen S. J. und die Gegenreformation in Deutschland 1624–1635* (Gottingen: Vandenhoeck und Ruprecht, 1975).
[89] Albrecht, *Maximilian*, 320, 323.
[90] Decree of Duke-Elector Maximilian, March 16, 1626, BHStA Jes. 588, p. 7.
[91] Münsterberg, 20; Carsten, 408; Schneller, 181.

Inspired by Martino Martini's requesting payment of the outstanding sum, in 1654, Archduchess Maria Anna of Austria (1610–65), Maximilian's widow, issued a decree to renew the foundation set up by Trigault "for the *Patres* traveling to the unbelievers," the paperwork for which "seems to have been lost during the recent war troubles." Desiring a full accounting, she ordered her registry to immediately and industriously search out the amount of the previous payments and the record of which years it had been paid out.[92] A year and a day later, on August 11, 1655, the princess offered Martini 1,500 gulden as interim support. This extraordinary payment did not apply to the outstanding balance, and remained distinct from the actual payment for 1652–54, which was disbursed in 1654. On September 16, 1654 (or 1655), the new elector Ferdinand Maria (r. 1651–79) renewed the 500-gulden foundation, annually, conditional on the treasury's ability to bear the burden.[93]

The requested reports came to Ferdinand Maria at the end of 1655 and described an "account, which was fully paid out to the Jesuits in China from 1626 to 1655, inclusive, and which still remains outstanding."[94] This was accompanied by a testimonial from the court treasury's council against the claims (*praetensiones*) of the Jesuits in China: "Although the fathers probably deserve the assistance they claim for all the years that have flowed by, we see neither the obligation nor the possibility" to help. To send eleven thousand gulden into another land "and even into the new world" was irresponsible.[95] The exoticism of China that had worked in favour of the missions until the devastation of the Thirty Years' War forced the Wittelsbachs to make difficult decisions. Now China's distance became more a hindrance to Bavarian financial support of the missions, for Trigault's global religion had met the bottom line. In his reply on December 23, the elector agreed.

The annual payments resumed intermittently from 1659 to 1687, routed through Rome and Vienna. In 1671 Amrhyn and Aigenler received a part of this money, but in 1682 Elector Maximilian II Emanuel (r. 1679–1726) suspended the annual donation again.[96] In 1686 the councils, director, and president of the court treasury sent a resolution to the elector pointing out the legal possibility to stop making payments and the actual difficulty in continuing them. The resolution included evidence from the original foundation, as well as from the 1627 and 1654 recapitulations. On March 12, 1687 the elector gave notification to pay

---

[92] August 10, 1654, BHStA Jes. 588, p. 19.
[93] Schneller, 181–82; Huonder, *Deutsche Jesuitenmissionäre*, 54.
[94] "Conto," BHStA Jes. 588, p. 28–9.
[95] December[?]12, 1656, BHStA Jes. 588, p. 30–1.
[96] 1686, BHStA Jes. 16, 260. See Schneller, 184.

the 1686 amount, but left the balance for 1687 unpaid. On behalf of his colleges in China, the rector of the Munich College requested payment of this amount, and to this end he cited the previous dukes' great zeal for souls, Ferdinand Maria's heroism in protecting Christendom from the Turks, and Maximilian's founding of the English College at Liège, "through which England under the so lengthy and bloody persecution was still kept in part held for the Catholic religion."

Despite the rector's efforts, on January 15, 1689, a resolution of the privy council set March 28 as the date for the last mission payment, on account of "hard times and great war expenditures."[97] That year, when the fund had grown to 20,200 gulden, earning a 4 to 6 percent return, the Turks overran the land in which the foundation's principal had been invested. Maximilian Emanuel's enthusiasms for China were reduced to his large collection of "Indian" porcelain, a fashion he had adopted in imitation of Versailles.[98]

Mauritia Febronia neé de la Tour d'Auvergne de Bouillon (1651–1706), the widow of Ferdinand Maria's brother, Maximilian Philip (1638–1705), renewed Bavarian support for the missions with three foundations.[99] In 1703 she established a 200-gulden annual payment to support a Jesuit missionary in China, and allocated another 50,000 gulden to support several more missionaries in China in her 1705 Testament.[100] A 1706 codicil added 10,000 gulden for the construction of a small seminary.[101] Not all her mission patronage occurred far away, for the widow also willed 1,000 gulden for a mission station in Mindelheim in Swabia.[102] A technicality allowed the Imperial Court to refuse to recognize the codicil, but in 1717 the intervention of Francisco de Fonseca (1668–1738), the general procurator for the Indies, prompted Maximilian Emanuel to pay out 60,000 gulden, the original amount.[103] Thus a century of Bavarian financial support of the China mission came to an end. It would remain unmatched by the generosity of the papacy or of the Portuguese crown.

---

[97] January 15, 1689, BHStA Jes., p. 37–8.
[98] Alden, 373, 564; Claudius C. Müller, "400 Jahre Sammeln und Reisen der Wittelsbacher," in *Wittelsbach und Bayern: 400 Jahre Sammeln und Reisen – außereuropäische Kulturen*, Austellung of the Dresdener Bank and the Staatlichen Museums für Völkerkunde München (Munich: Hirmer Verlag, 1980), 16.
[99] BHStA Jes. 16, 260.
[100] "In nom de Pere, du Fils et du St Espirit," Turckheim, September 20, 1705, ARSI FG 722/17.
[101] Codicille, Turckheim, June 15, 1706, ARSI FG 722/17.
[102] Bauerreiß, VII.285.
[103] Antonio Franco, *Synopsis Annalium S. J. in Lusitania ab anno 1540 usque ad annum 1725* (Augustae Vindel.: Sumptibus Philippi, Martini, & Joannis Veith, Hæredum, 1726), 457.

Only briefly could the Habsburgs eclipse the Bavarian munificence. The first imperial assistance to the China missions came in the form of clocks and mathematical instruments given Trigault by Emperor Ferdinand II (r. 1620–37).[104] Ferdinand had familial ties to Bavaria, for he was the grandson of Duke Albert V, and in 1600 he married Maria Anna of Bavaria, another of Albert's grandchildren. Monetary funding began in 1654, when Emperor Ferdinand III (r. 1637–57), at the request of Martini, contributed 1,000 gulden per year, drawn from a tax on Bohemian salt and beer.[105] Already in March 1655 the imperial advisors wanted to postpone the 1,000-gulden payment, drawing sharp protest from the Austrian Jesuit Melchior Mayr.[106] In 1664 Ferdinand III's son Leopold I (r. 1658–1705) assured the Jesuit General Oliva that these payments would continue and that all Jesuits en route via land to China, or in China itself, were under imperial protection. Further, these funds would be directed to the German assistant rather than to Portugal, and the emperor promised to appeal to the pope to overrule Portugal's probable objections.[107] In the later part of the century a flare-up of the Turkish situation distracted Vienna. From 1668 until his death Leopold redirected half these funds to the Hungarian mission, but after 1708 the full amount continued regularly to China. The Austrian Jesuits' 1717 attempt to commandeer the China funds for local purposes failed. In addition to this major funding, Leopold I promised financial support to offset the publication costs of *China illustrata*.[108]

Imperial support was not always simple donations. Twenty-seven pounds of musk, which Martini had sent on the *La Concepción* to support the China Vice-province, were confiscated in Manila by royal authorities. Andres de Ledesma, the Jesuit provincial, petitioned the local *audiencia* for its return, but support also came from farther afield. At the request of Martini, then procurator for the China mission, Ferdinand III, who was Martini's sovereign, wrote Philip IV of Spain in 1654 to request fraternally and benevolently that the royal officials of Manila pay an alms to the China mission equal to the amount hoped to be gained from the sale of the confiscated musk.[109] A royal *cédula* in 1655 requested a report of the governor and *audiencia* of Manila. The matter seems to have been

---

[104] Klaus Maurice, "Propagatio fidei per scientias: Uhrengeschenke der Jesuiten an den chinesischen Hof," in *Die Welt als Uhr: Deutsche Uhren und Automaten, 1550–1650*, ed. Klaus Maurice und Otto Mayr (Munich: Deutscher Kunstverlag, 1980), 37.
[105] "De Caesarea Clementia," September 9, 1654, ARSI FG 722/17.
[106] March 30, 1655, ARSI FG 722/17.
[107] Leopold I to General Oliva, September 17, 1664. Leopold I, 123.
[108] Grueber to Kircher, March 17, 1670, Margiotti, 393; Huonder, *Deutsche Jesuitenmissionäre*, 47–8.
[109] Ferdinand III, Vienna, to Philip IV, November 17, 1654, AGI MP-DR, 5.

resolved by a second royal *cédula*, in 1662, ordering that the Jesuits be reimbursed.[110]

Even lesser German princes made contributions. In 1678 Ferdinand von Fürstenberg had just become prince-bishop of Münster when there came into his hands a copy of the letter from Verbiest to the Jesuits in Europe,[111] which heightened his interest in distant missions. In addition, when in 1680 the Jesuit Heinrich Isaac informed him of conditions of the missions to the North, Fürstenberg decided to support them through his own means.[112] In 1682 he established a special foundation for missions. His stated motivations were varied: "to honour god," "to promote the well-being of his soul and the souls of his family," "to rescue nonbelievers and straying believers in the homeland, to spread the light of the true gospel in the remote lands of the heathen and thus to snatch many damned souls away from eternal ruin," and "to draw down grace and mercy to the Christian homeland, so threatened by heresy." Linking foreign and domestic missions in this way, Fürstenberg also cited the speed and range of the Jesuits' global expansion.[113] His foundation suggested chronological as well as geographical breadth, for he listed the "apostles" St. Thomas and St. Francis Xavier as patrons and so connected the missions back to the Apostolic Age, either directly (Thomas) or indirectly through a kind of informal apostolic succession (Francis Xavier).[114]

The specifications of his endowment were complex. The foundation provided support for thirty-six missionaries in fifteen missions – eight in Asia, three in Hamburg, one in Hameln, and otherwise two missionaries per mission. The various mission stations divide naturally into four groups described in Table 4.[115]

As bishop, Fürstenberg was responsible for the missions of his diocese, and as apostolic vicar, for those in the North. Certainly these regions

---

[110] AGI Filip. 22, R10, N55; AGI Filip. 330, L6, fol 14v–15v.

[111] Born October 21, 1626; since 1661 Fürstbischof of Paderborn, since 1678 Fürstbischof of Münster; died June 26, 1683. Otto Mejer, *Die Propaganda, ihre Provinzen und ihr Recht. Mit besonderer Rücksicht auf Deutschland*, Zweiter Teil (Göttingen and Leipzig: Dieterischen Buchhandlung, 1853), 314; Otto Maas, "Die Stiftung Ferdinands von Fürstenbergs zum Besten der ostasiatischen Missionen," *Theologie und Glaube* 25 (1933): 701; Huonder, *Deutsche Jesuitenmissionäre*, 561. See "Litterae a R. P. Ferdinando Verbiest S. J. ex China datae ad Celsissimum Principem Paderbornensem et Monasteriensem Ferdinandum de Fürstenberg (datae ex Curia Pekinensi 9ª Octobris 1684) allatae post huius mortem, quibus gratias agit pro fundatione Missionum Chinensium," ed. Josson and Willaert, 469–74.

[112] Johannes Metzler, *Die Apostolischen Vikariate des Nordens* (Paderborn: Drucku Verlag der Bonifacius, 1919), 56.

[113] RAH Jesuitas 16, no. 13, fol. 1r. See Maas, 702.

[114] BStB CLM 26472, fol. 120r.

[115] Based on Maas, 703.

Table 4. *Ferdinand von Fürstenberg's mission stations*

I. Fürstenberg's dioceses
    Paderborn[†]
    Münster
II. Neighbouring areas (all within 200 kilometres of Paderborn or Münster)
    Emsland, at Meppen
    The Duchy of Westfalia-Engern, at Arnsberg[†]
    Nassau, at Siegen[†]
    the Weser region, at Hameln[†]
III. "The North" (all within 425 kilometres of Paderborn or Münster)
    Bremen and Verden
    Hamburg
    Lübeck
    Glückstadt in Schleswig-Holstein
    Friedrichstadt on the Eider River, in Schleswig-Holstein
    Fridericia in Jutland
IV. Asia
    China and Japan

[†] (to remain under the protection of the bishop of Paderborn)

would get indirect benefit from a stronger missionary presence in the neighbouring regions (like Emsland), just as the Bavarian dukes felt it necessary to extend their own spiritual authority beyond the geographical limits of their temporal authority. Presumably these neighbouring regions were included in the apostolic vicariate. Asia is a special case. For the missions "in the Kingdom of China and the adjacent islands" the foundation of 15,000 *daleri* capital provided 750 *daleri* annually for the support of six missionaries. An additional fund of 3,000 *daleri* yielded 150 *daleri* each year for expenses involved in converting the currencies, indicating another difficulty German benefactors had to overcome.[116]

The money came with certain stipulations. It could not be used for any other purpose, and the missionaries must send reports of the state of the mission. Fürstenberg named the future bishops of Paderborn and Münster protectors, in cooperation with the head of the family von Fürstenberg. This provision suggests that the foundation had both aristocratic and episcopal underpinnings. Other missionaries might be chosen only if no Jesuits were available. The bishop specifically instructed the missionaries to follow the exhortations of Francis Xavier for the salvation of souls. Fürstenberg wrote the pope on March 25, 1682, and the Jesuits' twelfth general congregation on April 15. The congregation decided that

[116] BStB CLM 26472, fol. 120r.

the stipulations of the foundation were compatible with its own regulations.[117] Unlike the Wittelsbachs, Fürstenberg was content to send the
money via Rome.[118]

After Fürstenberg's death, his foundation experienced a difficult history.[119] French Jesuits convinced his successor that the moneys never
arrived in China, and that missionaries should be sent via the ("shorter
and safer") French route rather than the Portuguese one, especially since
the Portuguese were xenophobic. Persuaded, the successor issued a new
foundation, declaring that he would fund four additional French missionaries, that all funds should be sent via the French, that the original eight
missionaries must not be Portuguese, and that four should be German
or Belgian.[120] The funds were restored in 1708 by the prince-bishop
Franz Arnold von Metternich through the intervention of Fonseca.[121]
With the 1773 suppression of the Society in Westphalia, secular priests
took over the European missions, while the China missions grinded
to a halt. Propaganda tried to appropriate the China mission funds
in vain.[122]

Other bishops followed suit with donations. The Jesuits' first princely
protégé in Germany, Duke Ernest of Bavaria, won both the Hildesheim
episcopacy (1573) and, with Spanish military assistance, the Cologne
archbishopric and its electoral dignity (r. 1583–1612) when the archbishop Gebhard Truchsess von Waldburg had tried to make the see
Protestant. Holding both bishoprics was in direct opposition to the letter
and spirit of the Tridentine decrees, but it was the beginning of a pattern rather than an exception. The episcopal mitres of Liège, Münster,
and Paderborn also fell under what might be called the Wittelsbachs'
horizontal (securing concurrent multiple bishoprics) and vertical (securing the coadjutorships and thus succession) "secundogeniture" of the
lower Rhine.[123] For most of the seventeenth century the family also held
benefices in Cologne, Liège, Münster, Hildesheim, Stablo-Malmedy,
Freising, Regensburg, and Berchtesgaden. In fact, for only six of those
hundred years did it not have simultaneous control of Cologne, Liège,

[117] Maas, 702; F. J. Micus, ed., *Denkmale des Landes Paderborn* (Paderborn: Junfer-
     mann'sche Buchhandlung und Buchdruckerei, 1844), 62–63; Metzler, *Vikariate*, 58–
     59. Metzler seems to suggest that China is in the "Nordische Missionen" administered
     by Münster.
[118] RAH Jesuitas 16, no. 13, fol. 1v.
[119] See Huonder, *Deutsche Jesuitenmissionäre*, 387.
[120] Castner, "Brevis animadversio circa ea, quae ad Fundationem Monasteriensem Spec-
     tant," [1705?], BNC FG 1247, no. 5, fol. 21r.
[121] Franco, *Synopsis*, 429.
[122] Maas, 704.
[123] Stillig, 36–37.

Hildesheim, and Berchtesgaden.[124] The strength of the House of Wittelsbach appeared clear in 1607, when the estates lent 19,000 gulden to the Elector Ernest, the brother of Maximilian.[125]

The see's ties to the China mission began with Ernest's successor, Ferdinand of Bavaria (1577–1637, r. 1612–50), another brother of Maximilian. Ferdinand presented Trigault with numerous mathematical instruments, "especially when he had learned from our history, which he had read, how much knowledge of mathematics is esteemed among the Chinese," as well as a mechanical apparatus that recreated the nativity of Christ.[126] In turn, Ferdinand's successor, Maximilian Henry (r. 1650–88), established an annual donation of 100 Neapolitan *ducati* for the China mission, to be given to Martini and Dorville or to their agents.[127]

In Bavaria proper, in 1567, at Bishop Friedrich von Wirsberg's (r. 1558–1573) request, Jesuits took over the Würzburg college.[128] When Trigault and Schreck arrived there, the rector wrote that their coming had "put the college ablaze." Trigault received valuable gifts even from Julius Echter von Mespelbrunn, the famously stingy prince-bishop of Würzburg (r. 1573–1617) – a Bavarian report speaks of the bishop's wealth, but adds that "when you speak of giving out money, you grip the bishop at the heart."[129] At Mespelbrunn's court, Trigault and Schreck also met the bishops of Eichstätt and Bamberg. The former, Johann Christoph von Wetterstetten (r. 1612–1636, d. 1637) offered use of his transport vehicles to take the future missionaries to Würzburg.[130]

The bishop of Bamberg, Johann Gottfried von Aschhausen (r. 1609–22), also invited Trigault to dinner, which led to captivating discussions and promises of financial support. He gave 200 gulden for Trigault's

---

[124] Calculations based on Rudolf Reinhardt, "Kontinuität und Diskontinuität. Zum Problem der Koadjutorie mit dem Recht der Nachfolge in der neuzeitlichen Germania Sacra," in *Der dynastische Fürstenstaat: zur Bedeutung von Sukzessionsordnungen fur die Entstehung des frühmodernen Staat*, ed. Johannes Kunisch, Historische Forschungen 21 (Berlin: Duncker & Humblot, 1982), 150. See also ibid., 126–30.

[125] Carsten, 395.

[126] Trigault, "Litterae," 110. *De Christiana Expeditione* (335) includes a chapter entitled, "Ex mathematicis disciplinis magna Nostris auctoritas Nanchini accrescit." See Maurice, 37.

[127] Dusseldorf [?], July 16, 1654, ARSI FG 722/17.

[128] Hans Steininger, "Roman Catholic Missionary Activities Emanating from Würzburg/Bavaria," in 紀念利瑪竇來華四百週年中西文化交流國際學術會議論文集, 731–42. 臺北縣新莊市：輔仁大學出版社, 民國 72 [1983], 733.

[129] Goercke, "Die ersten," 33; Willeke, "Würzburg," 419. A *geheimen Räte* from 1610 declared, "Wirzberg ist gar reich, nichts schuldig, sonder vil ausgelihen gelt, gar geltgeizig und wann man von geltausgeben sagt, so greife man dem bischove ans herz." Friedrich Hefele, "Der Würzburger Fürstbischof Julius Echter von Mespelbrunn und die Liga," (Ph.D. diss. Julius-Maximilians-Universitat Wurzburg, 1912), 34.

[130] Goercke, 33.

travels, expensive equipment, a costly vestment for the about-to-be-named bishop of central China, and he bought for them the technical equipment of a Bamberg mathematician who had recently died. The records of the Bamberger *Hofkammer* for 1617–18 log a series of vestments and liturgical vessels as gifts for both the China and Mexican missions.[131]

Upon the death of Julius Echter, the more generous Aschhausen, then appointed the new bishop of Würzburg (r. 1617–1622), contributed 5,000 gulden and expensive equipment for the mass. Even Bishop Henry V von Knorringen (r. 1598–1646) contributed 400 gulden, although Protestant inroads had impoverished his see of Augsburg.[132]

Lay nobles also demonstrated their generosity. In 1654, Count Palatine Philip William (r. 1653–90) began paying the China Vice-province 100 ducats per year. In addition to supporting the Jesuits locally, Philip William's son and successor, Charles III Philip (r. 1716–42), became a mission patron around 1717, at the prompting of Fonseca.[133] The Count of Kolowrat, provost of the cathedral chapter of Olmütz (Olomouc, in Moravia) also became known for his contributions.[134]

For the 1616 expeditions, a priest named Regens at the Ingolstadt theological seminary gave ten gulden, the *Congregation Latina Maior* another ten gulden, the *Minor* fifteen gulden, and the theology faculty offered a beautiful clock, which one of the priests had inherited, worth twenty gulden. Father Mayrhofer gave the type for a printing press, and the superior contributed to the travel expenses of Trigault and Schreck. Around 1672 the theology faculty at Ingolstadt agreed to offer fifty gulden to support the travels of two of its members, Aigenler and Amrhyn, to China.[135]

The eighteenth century would see other princes contributing to the Jesuit China mission. The archbishop of Cologne Clemens August (r. 1723–61), son of Elector Ferdinand Maria of Bavaria, made a donation.[136] Countess Maria Theresia of Fugger zu Wellenburg stood in regular correspondence with the Chinese missionaries, who told her the uses to which they put her financial support, and sent her a 203-pound chest so full of wonders "that a whole day would not suffice to observe them

[131] Willeke, "Würzburg," 419.
[132] Trigault, "Litterae," 106–7; Steininger, 735–6.
[133] "Rol dos Benifeitores da V Provᵃ da China," Macao, November 8, 1677, ARSI FG 722/17. See biography in Ronny Baier, "Pfalz-Neuburg, Karl Philipp von" in *Biographisch-Bibliographisches Kirchenlexikon* XXI (2003): 1154–60.
[134] Jaksch, 18.
[135] Anton Huonder, "Die erste Aussendung deutscher Jesuiten in die Missionen," *Die Katholischen Missionen* 41 (1912–3): 11; idem, *Deutsche Jesuitenmissionäre*, 184.
[136] Felix Joseph Lipowsky, *Geschichte der Jesuiten in Bayern* (Munich: J. Giel, 1816), II.336.IV.

all."[137] A November 15, 1744, letter by the Jesuit Florian Bahr in Beijing informed the countess that her gift "this year alone bought eternal life for one thousand seven hundred and eighty-nine children."[138]

While evident need and an exotic chic drew such a diverse range of funds to China, the financial ties between Jesuits in Germany and Mexico were far less extensive. Indeed, the German benefactors of Jesuits in Germany served the Mexico mission less as donors than as models for potential donors. For example, the 1578 "Formula Proposed for the Foundation of a Mexican College" discusses the constitutional limitations on securing funding and describes the Society's ideal benefactors, all but one of whom are German princes: the Emperor Ferdinand I, Bavarian Duke Albert V, the Archbishop-elector Daniel Brendel von Homburg of Mainz (r. 1555–82), and the Archbishop-elector Johann von Isenburg of Trier (r. 1547–56). Various formulas urged the king of Spain to take inspiration from these men.[139] Actual financial support, however, was limited to the German Jesuit colleges paying travel expenses to Seville or Cádiz for America-bound missionaries.[140]

Funds did flow east across the Atlantic when the various American provinces sent contributions for the chapel and tomb of Ignatius in the Gesù at Rome.[141] Kino also proposed an idea that would render unnecessary, in some cases, the long-distance exchange of bullion and specie. Rather than having the Mexican province send money back for the sepulchre of San Ignatius and having a European patron send money to found a new mission in Mexico, Kino suggested having the payments cancel each other out. Each amount would thus stay local, being redirected to the other's purpose. The European patron, in consultation with the Jesuit general, would still choose the location of the mission to be endowed. Kino further offered to supplement the money going to the Mexican mission with goods valued at 150 to 200 per cent of the amount of the original donation. He claimed concern with the shipment of donated monies, for some never arrived and others were converted into (not necessarily useful) goods in Mexico City to be sent on to the missions, but perhaps Kino also hoped to circumvent the royal prohibition on the unauthorized exporting of ecclesiastical funds – which was the reason the Portuguese provincial himself gave for not contributing to the Gesù chapel.[142]

---

[137] WB Nr. 684, 690, 693, 706, 711, 721, 722. See Blankenburg, 47.
[138] WB Nr. 648.
[139] "Formulae pro fundado collegio mexicano propositae," in Félix Zubillaga, ed., *Monumenta Mexicana* (Rome: Apud "Monumenta Historica Soc. Iesu," 1946), I.362–3.
[140] Sierra, *Jesuitas*, 116; Jaksch, 18.
[141] "Memoria de las Cantidades, y quienes las han embarcado para la capilla y sepulcro de N. P. Sⁿ Ygnacio," ARSI FG 507, fol. 111r.
[142] Kino, Dolores, to the P. Gen. Tirso González, February 2, 1702, ARSI Mex. 18, fol. 3r–4v, published in Ernest J. Burrus, ed., *Correspondencia del P. Kino con los generales*

Mexico, however, proved to be an additional source for funds supporting the China mission, despite the dangers of transpacific donations arriving extremely late.[143] This is partly explained by the close administrative relations between New Spain and the Philippines. Typically, during the last third of the seventeenth century the crown issued *cédulas* directing Mexican funds to be disbursed to missionaries of various orders (especially Dominicans, like Thomas Gage) heading to the Philippines. In what appears to be an extension of this practice, the Dominicans,[144] Franciscans,[145] and Augustinians[146] in China received stipends from New Spain through the Manila procurator, at the direction of royal *cédulas*. This does not seem to have occurred with the Jesuits, but in the 1690s the Jesuit province in Mexico, at the request of the China Vice-province's procurator, donated 400,000 *réis*.[147]

The most generous individual donor was the Marquis de Villa Puente.[148] Born in Mexico, the Marquis became a great landowner, said to possess some 230,000 head of cattle. He did not hoard his wealth. In addition to giving at least 200,000 pesos to the California missions, he supported Franciscan missionaries in Africa and more generally the strengthening of Catholicism in Syria, India, the Philippines, Caracas, and Havana.[149] Perhaps his interest in China quickened during a trip he took to the Philippines, for in 1707, desiring the "increase in souls," he donated 2,000 pesos for the foundation of a permanent mission there, wherever the superiors preferred.[150] This was supplemented by another 8,000 pesos to missions around Asia in 1723,[151] and 1,800 pesos in 1724 (with 100 pesos earmarked for Macao). His 1725 contributions were greater yet: another 8,000 pesos to Asian missions, 2,000 in *moneda doble mexicana* more for whatever missionary purpose thought best, an annual

---

de la Compañia de Jesús, 1682–1707 (Mexico: Editorial Jus, 1961), 68–72; Kino, Dolores, to the P. Gen. Tirso González, February 3, 1702, ARSI FG 645 Nr. 124; published in Pietro Tacchi Venturi, "Nuove lettere inedite del P. Eusebio Francesco Chino d. l. C. d. G," in *Archivum Historicum Societatis Iesu* 3 (1934), 258, and in Burrus, ed., *Correspondencia*, 73–74; Alden, 641.

[143] Augustin Soler, Mexico, to the P. Provincial Joseph Pires, March 9, 1725, BA/JA/49-V-28, fol. 210r.

[144] AGI Mex. 2730, unfol.

[145] AGI Mex. 2731, fols. 84r, 90r, 94r.

[146] "Religion Calzada de S^n Agustin.," AGI Mex. 2731, fols. 3r, 8r, 9r, 12r, 21r, 39r.

[147] "Contas da v. prov.^{a} começada ao I° de julho de 1690 athe fim de julho de 1691" in ARSI JapSin 23, fols. 170–71. See Alden, 644.

[148] Puente Peña y Castrejon, according to Alegre, iii.385–88.

[149] Venegas, "Empressas Apostólicas," xxiii.

[150] "Transsumptum Contractus initi de fundatione a D Marchione de Villapuente," Mexico, February 15, 1707, ARSI FG 722/17. See Dunne, *Black Robes*, 107, 298.

[151] "Señor Marquez y este año remite a V R para el mismo fin otros mil pesos." Andres Licardi, Mexico, to the P. Provincial of Japan, February 18, 1723, BA/JA/49-V-28 fol. 64v.

sum of 2,000 pesos going to Asia, and another 100 pesos mentioned inci-
dentally in a postscript. The Marquis cited the souls that could be saved
if he would re-route funds spent for vanity and worldly things to the missions.[152] His principal aim, as he stated, was the salvation of souls, but
his goodwill was encouraged by gifts sent back to him, which reportedly
gave him great pleasure.[153] He pleasantly remarked in one letter that his
donations to Asia would continue in the future on the condition of news
of missionary success.[154] Information was at a premium. Most importantly, the Marquis asked that he be remembered in the missionaries'
masses, and after pointed hinting, he gratefully received a relic of Francis
Xavier.[155]

Although relics will be considered more fully in the context of sacred
economy (Chapter 10), it makes sense to survey here the numerous
objects, like the gifts transported by Trigault, that travelled the missionary network. In addition to the money, numerous objects were offered
as gifts.[156] Some of these were sold en route, thus providing the missionary expedition additional funds. Most, however, were twice gifts,
for, once given to the Jesuits, they were meant to be given again to the
Chinese emperor. Indeed, Maximilian explicitly specifies his gifts are for
the "king" of China.[157] Bernhard Diestel brought a letter and gifts from
Leopold I for the Kangxi emperor, but Schall blocked the exchange, for
fear they would be understood as tokens of feudal homage by the Holy
Roman Emperor to his Chinese overlord.

Many of the European princes, thoughtful gift givers in the best aristocratic traditions, had read Trigault's writings for clues as to what

[152] Marquez de Villa Puente, Mexico, to the Provincial of Japan, March 20, 1724, BA/JA/49-V-28, fols. 94r-95v; Augustin Soler, Mexico, to the P. Provincial of Japan Joseph Pires, March 9, 1725, BA/JA/49-V-28, fols. 209v-210v; idem, Mexico, to the P. Provincial of Japan Joseph Pires, March 24, 1725, BA/JA/49-V-28, fol. 208v; Augustin Soler, Mexico, to the P. Provincial of Japan Joseph Pires, March 9, 1725, BA/JA/49-V-28, fol. 209v; Marquez de Villa Puente, Mexico, to the P. Provincial of Japan Joseph Pires, March 24, 1725, BA/JA/49-V-28, fol. 209v.
[153] Augustin Soler, Mexico, to the P. Provincial of Japan Joseph Pires, March 9, 1725, BA/JA/49-V-28, fol. 210r; Marquez de Villa Puente, Mexico, to the P. Provincial of Japan Joseph Pires, March 24, 1725, BA/JA/49-V-28, fol. 208v.
[154] Andres Licardi, Mexico, to the P. Provincial of Japan, February 18, 1723, BA/JA/49-V-28, fol. 64v.
[155] Marquez de Villa Puente, Mexico, to the P. Provincial of Japan Joseph Pires, March 24, 1725, BA/JA/49-V-28, fol. 209r; Augustin Soler, Mexico, to the P. Provincial of Japan Joseph Pires, March 9, 1725, BA/JA/49-V-28, fol. 210r; Marquez de la Villa Puente, Mexico, to the P. Provincial of Japan Joseph Pires, March 20, 1724, BA/JA/49-V-28, fol. 95v.
[156] Francis Xavier Kropf, *Historia Provinciae Societatis Jesu Germaniae Superioris* (Munich: Joannis Jacobi Vötter, 1746), IV.25–26; Lipowsky, II.125; Münsterberg, 13.
[157] Trigault, "Litterae," 104.

gift would be most useful for the missions. Trigault himself had been given instructions by his superior as to what valuables he should secure. Although Longobardo intended some of these to go to lesser mandarins and friends of the missionaries, his main purpose was to locate a gift worthy of the emperor to accompany a request for permission to preach Christianity. The superior's wish list is strikingly international. In addition to manufactured Italian and Flemish goods, he specifically requests a lion, a rhinoceros, a bird of paradise, and several paintings coloured by bird feathers from the Indians of Peru. This selection would offer a clear demonstration of the Society's position, not merely in Europe, but throughout the entire world. All these gifts, even those from Europe, had a globalizing force that surpasses any inherent value, for as Valignano once remarked, the Jesuit presents impressed Chinese officials not for their cost but by being "foreign and never before seen here."[158]

The actual inventory of gifts given is less international but no less striking. William V gave several clocks to Trigault, one in the shape of a cross, another fashioned out of silver with a Virgin and child. Maximilian gave an elaborately constructed wooden cabinet, three feet deep and tall, and two feet wide, with six shelves holding various little compartments covered with silk, each opening with a gilded key and containing some small treasure, usually of silver – perhaps reflecting knowledge of how the Chinese valued it. Other gifts included self-moving figurines, self-playing musical trinkets, diminutive lamps, clocks, surgical and mathematical instruments – including an astrolabe – pictures of Christ and the saints, a wax representation of the three Magi, and a beautifully bound picture book of the life of Christ, wrapped in an envelope sporting the title, "The life of our Lord Jesus Christ, the son of God, the son of the Virgin, according to the four evangelists; to the great and mighty emperor and monarchs of China sent by Maximilian, Count Palatine of the Rhine and Duke of the two Bavarias, in the year of our Lord 1617." The duchess of Bavaria gave two pendant watches, one of gold, and a centaur-clock that moved about on a table, struck the hours, and shot out an arrow with enough force to pierce the wood it held before itself. Prince Albert and Princess Magdalena also gave two pendant watches, and a gold-gilt silver clock in the form of the crucifix. The archbishop of Trier offered a reliquary.[159] Augsburg gave Trigault fifteen tower clocks to be distributed by the emperor of China to his first-rank cities.[160] Trigault's 1616 memorial

[158] Lamalle, 76; Münsterberg, 15.
[159] Väth, 34–36; Lamalle, 104; Maurice, 36; Dunne, *Generation*, 176.
[160] Quoted in ibid., 101. The relevant passage from *De Christiana Expeditione* begins, "sed nihil aeque mirabantur vt horariam machinam grandiorem . . . " Trigault, *De Christiana Expeditione*, 214.

explained routing instructions for the various goods he had collected, and he argued for customs exemptions on boxes from the duke in light of their evangelical purpose.[161]

The collection of depictions of scenes from the life of Christ which Maximilian gave Trigault would have a remarkable fate. Before presenting it to the Chongzhen 崇禎 emperor (r. 1627–44), Schall printed the illustrations in a book called *Jincheng Shuxiang* 進呈書像 [*A Presented Book of Images*], in 1640.[162] He used the preface to explain the book's provenance. The harpsichord Ricci had presented to the court was then in need of repair, and a Latin inscription on the instrument had caught the emperor's eye: "Praise Him with clanging symbols, let them praise His name and make melody to Him with tambourine and dance."[163] Ordered to interpret it, Schall also took the opportunity to present "a Western book from my country translated in Chinese, as well as a collection of images of the Heavenly Lord," the very life of Christ Maximilian had donated.[164]

Indeed, some of the most important gifts proved to be books, which Trigault received from an unnamed relative, from Maximilian and his wife, from Magdalena (the wife of Palatin Wolfgang Wilhelm of Neuburg), and from the College of Ingolstadt. The Bishop of Bamberg gave a book of the flowers of "the most noble garden in all Germany."[165] Some books Trigault acquired himself, especially at the book fairs of Cologne and Frankfurt, which he praises as globally ("*toto orbe*") renowned. Not only did the books themselves come from Germany, but the strategy motivating their acquisition also developed there. Jesuits in the Holy Roman Empire accompanied the foundation of each house with the establishment of a library in order to foster a high Catholic culture in opposition to Protestant humanism. This tactic, which H. Kramm calls their "*Bibliothekenstrategie*," found fertile ground when transplanted to China, where

---

[161] "Memoriale P Nicolai Trigaulii pro $R_x°$ P Rectae Augustano V P Georgio Mayer" [August 23, 1616], ARSI FG 722/17 unfol., no. 4. See "Memoriale P Nicolai Trigaulii pro R° P Rectae Augustano V P Georgio Mayer" [August 23, 1616], ARSI FG 722/17 unfol., no. 1–3.

[162] Eugenio Menegon, "Yang Guangxian's Opposition to Johann Adam Schall: Christianity and Western Science in his Work *Budeyi*," in *Western Learning and Christianity in China: The Contribution and Impact of Johann Adam Schall von Bell, S. J. (1592–1666)*, ed. Roman Malek (St. Augustin: Institut Monumenta Serica, 1998), 317.

[163] Henri Bernard, "L'Encyclopédie astronomique du Père Schall (Tch'ong-tcheng li-cho, 1629, et Si-yang sin-fa li-chou, 1645). La réforme du calendrier chinois sous l'influence de Clavius, de Galilée et de Kepler," *Monumenta Serica* III (1938): 496.

[164] Menegon, 317–18. Menegon's translation. Copies at BStB Cod Sin 23 [printed in Jinjiang (Funjian) 1637; cited in *Jesuiten in Bayern*, 244–46]; BNF Chinois 6756; BNC Mss. 72.

[165] Lamalle, 94–108.

the Jesuits used their knowledge to justify their presence.[166] Even Ricci complained early on of the lack of books. Longobardo in a 1613 memorandum described his hopes for a central library in Beijing, equal to the best of the Society's in Europe, which would serve as an umbrella of protection to missionaries working throughout the empire.[167] Many of the books Trigault brought back are now in China's National Library.

Such gifts, and the financial contributions that accompany them, were balanced by objects being dispatched from the missions to Europe. The sending of something exotic followed news of a monetary contribution in the opposite direction frequently enough that it almost appears obligatory. Sometimes there was a conspicuous absence of gifts offered. Early on, the Jesuits discouraged the Bavarian dukes' desire to acquire curiosities, perhaps because of their reluctance to see money wasted on vanities – rather than on the Society.[168] Although the dukes had other sources, a large portion of their exotica did come from Jesuits abroad, who supplemented their written reports with small gifts such as crockery, lacquer ware, Buddhist rosaries, textiles, or Chinese books.[169] Castner sent back various Chinese objects, including a mother-of-pearl spoon, a knife, and two chopsticks. Scientist Christian Mentzel (1622–1701) gave Leopold I a copy of the Chinese canonical Four Books, which had once belonged to Matteo Ricci, along with a copy Mentzel himself had made of the *Daxue* 大学 [*Great Learning*], with an apparatus including both romanization and translation.[170]

Missionaries also sent to German princes objects, usually made of feathers or turquoise, from New Spain, but confusion over their origins clouds their exact provenance.[171] Not until the nineteenth centuries would these clouds break. A 1774 catalog of the Urban collection errors in the other direction, describing as "Mexican" a clearly Chinese porcelain, which presumably picked up that description as it travelled to Europe across the Pacific and Atlantic Oceans, via Mexico. Thus Albert of Bavaria's global collection included a Mexican feather picture of the

[166] H. Kramm, *Deutsche Bibliotheken unter dem Einfluss von Humanismus und Reformation ein beitrag zur deutschen bildungsgeschichte*. Beiheft . . . zum Zentralblatt für Bibliothekswesen 70 (Leipzig: O. Harrassowitz, 1938), xiii, 90–98.
[167] The Jesuit published some books in China to bolster their intellectual apostolate; Longobardo himself published at least three. Dunne, *Generation*, 111.
[168] Lach and Van Kley, *Asia*, II.ii.1.25.
[169] Claudius Müller, 16–17.
[170] Mungello, *Curious*, 241–43.
[171] Münsterberg, 22; Christian F. Feest, "The Collecting of American Indian Artifacts in Europe, 1493–1750," in *America in European Consciousness, 1493–1750*, ed. Karen Ordahl Kupperman (Chapel Hill: University of North Carolina, 1995), 333; idem, "Vienna's Mexican Treasures: Aztec, Mixtec, and Tarascan Works from Sixteenth Century Austrian Collections," *Archiv für Völkerkunde* 44 (1990), 32.

Madonna, and images of a Mexican idol, of a crocodile, and of a llama (an "indian sheep").[172]

Beyond the missionaries' key role in facilitating the transfer of exoticisms, at a deeper level the very impulse for global mission also encouraged these assortments of curios. A comprehensive collection became a microcosm of the universe. The very title page of Samuel à Quiccheberg's 1565 guide on the acquisition of meaningful and exotic rarities specifies that the planned collection should offer a "fabulous showcase of the entire world." Such a collection visually reflected all human knowledge.[173] Winning foreign objects parallels winning foreign souls. The very act of global collecting was sometimes understood as a form of doing God's work, an illustration of the creation. A contemporary poet praised the world as a "museum announcing God's greatness."[174]

The evidence presented in this chapter gives a sense of the number and nature of ties between the Jesuit missions in Germany, Mexico, and China. Unfortunately, not enough evidence is now available to fully contextualize these findings. For example, the China mission derived a great deal of funding from German sources, and little funding from Iberian or papal sources, but we still have only inexact knowledge of how much any of these made up of the aggregate budget of the Vice-province. The very existence of these ties, even in the absence of a complete understanding of the Jesuits' global network, takes an important step towards correcting the traditional view of connections only running between Rome and a set of independent mission regions, regions as discrete as the chapters in historical studies of the Jesuits. Chapter 10 will explore the exchanges of masses and relics, and their place in the Jesuits' global sacred economy, but in the next chapter we look first at the communication network along which the Marquis de Villa Puente's hints travelled.

---

[172] Münsterberg, 22; Detlef Heikamp, with Ferdinand Anders, "Mexikanische Altertümer aus süddeutschen Kunstkammern," *Pantheon* 28 (1970), 207; Jacob Stockbauer, *Die Kunstbestrebungen am Bayerischen Hofe unter Albrecht V. und seinem Nachfolger Wilhelm V*, Quellenschriften für Kunstgeschichte 8 (Vienna: W. Braunmuller, 1874), 76; John Ayers, "The Early China Trade," in *The Origins of Museums: The Cabinets of Curiosities in Sixteenth- and Seventeenth-Century Europe*, ed. Oliver Impey and Arthur MacGregor (Oxford: Clarendon, 1985), 2.

[173] R. J. Evans, *Rudolf II and His World* (Oxford: Clarendon Press, 1973), 177, 217; Heikamp, 206; Claudius Müller, 12–13.

[174] Claudius Müller, 17.

9   The Jesuit Information Network

> "The night they [the letters] arrived, the bell being sounded, they were read till one past midnight, and in the refectory on all the following ten days. And immediately, a summary of them being copied, they were sent to China, Japan, the Moluccas and Malaca, and all the other places where our Fathers are. And if you knew, dearest ones, how much the news that comes from there resounds here, and how much the people, beyond the brethren, desires and covets it, and how many relics are here made of your letters, doubtless it seems to me that you would offer yourselves to any bodily hardship to give to the brethren here such pleasant recreation."
>
> – Luis Frois, describing the 1552 reception of Brazil missionary Manuel de Nóbrega's 1549 letters[1]

In the early-modern world, missionaries – more so even than sailors or long-distance merchants – conveyed exotic information and effected cultural contact. This chapter's treatment of reports and letters as cargo may not be surprising in an age that recognizes the commodification of information, nor did contemporaries doubt the potential of the written word. Officials of the Spanish and Portuguese crowns routinely considered information from the colonies state secrets. The Fugger firm of Augsburg required their overseas agents to supplement business letters with *avvisi*, gossip about and commentary on local conditions and events. A late seventeenth-century saying from Portuguese India saw less danger in "the point of an Arab's sword" than in "the nib of a Jesuit's pen."[2]

This comparison suggests the special relationship between the Society of Jesus and the written word. Early to recognize information as a "source of mutual consolation and edification in our Lord," the Jesuits' first General Congregation directed the establishment of a network of epistolary exchanges, so that the superiors "in every place . . . should know about the

---

[1] "Fr. Ludovicus Frois S. I. Sociis Conimbricensibus Goa," December 1, 1552, in DI II.488.

[2] Boxer, *Portuguese*, 345.

things that are being done in other places."[3] Ignatius once sent a request to Brazil for *distinctus et exactius* reports of the "region, climate, longitude, latitude, native customs, dress and houses," not out of curiosity, but so that in a crisis he could make informed decisions.[4] As we have seen in Chapter 3, this "consolation and edification" of being well informed was not easy to come by when operating on a global level.

Amidst widespread interest in the Indies, global mission found expression in an astonishing variety of genres, a variety that testifies to its importance. Traditionally historians have emphasized verbal witnesses, in exhortations for missionary enlistments, private letters, and historical accounts – which can include martyrology, hagiography, and general descriptions. Although this chapter focuses on the Jesuits' letters and the publications inspired by them, or directly copied from them, the Society also made use of other media. Not every verbal communication was written (what did Trigault tell his patrons during his travels through Europe?), nor was every written communication verbal (as maps, for example, are not). Unfortunately, we have little access to oral exhortations to mission. Given the physical presence of mission recruiters touring the provinces, this is a key genre that the extant sources rarely preserve. Some sermons, however, survive as published works, like E. de Salazar's 1582 *Veynte discursos sobre el Credo* [*Twenty Discourses on the Creed*].[5]

Much was prosaic. Some was poetic in substance, occasionally also even in form.[6] Perhaps for the first time we witness a body of discourse representing a global conversation, with participating voices from around the world. Naturally, this discourse showed regional variations, but something like the debate over the Jesuits' missionary strategies in China lost little of its intensity in Mexico. The very existence of this informational network is striking, but this chapter will pursue it further by considering its purposes and its intended audiences. The letters exchanged among the German, Chinese, and Mexican Jesuits missions exhibit a striking range of information, covering science, climate, theology, cultural anthropology, martyrs, travel narratives, and descriptions of distant Jesuit colleges.[7]

---

[3] Lach and Van Kley, *Asia*, I.315.
[4] Cummins, *Question*, 184.
[5] Borges Morán, *El envío*, 177; Bolton, *Rim*, 464; *Veynte discursos sobre el Credo, en declaración de nuestra santa fe católica y doctrina cristiana*, cited in Borges Morán, "El sentido," 142.
[6] Otokar Odlozilík, "Missioneros checos in México," *Boletín de la Sociedad Mexicana de Geografia y Estadística* 60 (1945): 428.
[7] Markus Friedrich is conducting a more nuanced analysis of the Jesuits' information network. The first fruit of this work has just appeared, as "Beispielgeschichten in den *Litterae Annuae*: Überlegungen zur Gestaltung und Funktion einer vernachlässigten Literaturgattung," *Das Beispiel, Epistemologie des Exemplarischen*, ed. Nicolas Pethes, Jens Ruchatz, and Stefan Willer (Berlin: Kulturverlag Kadmos, 2007), 143–66.

Circulation of Information

In many respects the most useful sources are letters. Jesuits wrote private letters to colleagues and family, who were sometimes on the other side of the globe. The most striking letters are those from the approximately fifteen thousand Jesuits directing towards Rome their *indipetae*, those formal requests for an assignment in the overseas missions we surveyed in Chapter 6. Typically the general would surrender the received *indipetae* to a procurator for safekeeping.[8] Perhaps this suggests a delegation of decision-making authority as well.

Francis Xavier initiated the custom of sending letters in multiple copies to Europe. Copies of the first letter he wrote from Goa spread throughout the continent, and an autograph copy arrived in Vilnius as late as 1664. Three of his letters from 1543 were published together in Paris two years later in a French translation, and a German edition appeared at Augsburg that same year. The letters' titles suggest that Xavier had addressed them to Jesuits around Europe, including the Germans in Cologne.[9] Jesuit letters of this period famously contradicted each other, but after 1581 Valignano began the practice of collecting the discrete, separate letters into a single, coherent official report.

These official *cartas annuas*, annual letters, became influential, although bold editorial hands complicate their service to historians by removing passages deemed unedifying. Letters from the Indies commanded great interest in Jesuit-influenced areas of Italy, especially in Rome, and Italian translations spread knowledge of the wider world. Jesuits wrote these with what Anya Mali calls the "Ignatian principle of epistolary thrift" – namely, "the idea that letters were meant to inform others of the fruits of missionary labour and were therefore to contain only edifying material."[10]

A single letter could be read by far more people than the addressee alone, which was often the author's intention. Amrhyn's 1672 letter came first to Jodocus Amrhyn in Trent, who forwarded it to Solbad Hall in Tirol with the instructions that it be forwarded again to a Jesuit in Munich.[11] The epistolary excerpt "Chinese Narrative from the Letter of Father Joannis de Haynin" was touring the Upper German province from Regensburg to Mindelheim during the winter of 1726–27 – over half a

---

[8] Hoffmann, "Philipp," 350. Boxer estimates the number at 15,000; Boxer, *Church Militant*, 119.

[9] Francis Xavier, *Epistolae*, I.129. See Lach and Van Kley, *Asia*, I.316, and Wicki, "Der älteste deutsche Druck eines Xaverius-briefes aus dem Jahre 1545, ehemals in Besitz des Basler Humanisten Lepusculus," *Neue Zeitschrift für Missionswissenschaft* IV (1948): 105–9.

[10] Romeo, 335, 336; Mali, 78.

[11] BHStA Jes. 595/V.13.

century after it was written – and was then retired to the Jesuit archive in Munich.[12]

Perhaps most unexpected is the surviving evidence for a lively exchange of Jesuit letters across the Pacific. News of Chinese imperial decrees circulated in Mexico, and as we have seen the Marquis de Villa Puente was particularly keen on gathering news of the Asia missions.[13] Kino received from Castner a letter bragging of the costs incurred in constructing a sepulchre for Francis Xavier.[14] Kappus in Mexico for several years kept up a regular correspondence with Fridelli and Van Hamme in China.[15] Van Hamme himself corresponded with Gilg in Mexico about the salvation of souls, and one of his letters to the procurator for the China mission, in which he mentions the possibility of the emperor expelling all Europeans from China, found its way to Mexico.[16] This correspondence was subject to formidable delays. Kappus (in 1716) and Villa Puente (in 1724)[17] each became concerned only after not hearing from correspondents for three years.

Not all communication was so frustrated. Bishop Palafox kept himself well informed on events in Asia, and even once Navarrete and his fellow Dominicans had arrived in Manila, it was a letter from Palafox in Mexico that informed them of the Dutch capture of Taiwan, which had been serving as a base for mendicant missions intent on bypassing the Jesuits at Macao. That news could travel from Taiwan to mendicants in Manila more rapidly via Mexico than directly shows how circuitous communications could be. Perhaps at Palafox's suggestion, the friars suspected the Jesuits of somehow orchestrating the Dutch conquest to thwart the mendicants' attempts to enter the mainland.[18] News of China was naturally sent on from Mexico to Europe, but communications being as haphazard as they were, occasionally Mexican correspondents would request China news from Europe.[19]

---

[12] "Relatio Chinensis. Ex litteris patris Ioannis de Haynin 5 martii 1669 Macao datis," BHStA Jes. 589.1.

[13] Augustin Soler, Mexico, to Joseph Pires [provincial of Japan], March 9, 1725, BA/JA/49-V-28, fol. 210r; Marquez de Villa Puente, Mexico, to Joseph Pires, March 24, 1725, BA/JA/49-V-28, fol. 209r.

[14] Bolton, *Rim*, 522, 570.

[15] Kappus, Bacanora, to the P. Proc. Gen. Juan de San Martín, January 24, 1716, AHPMCJ México, Nr. 1715.

[16] BRB 16691/16693; Van Hamme, China, to P. Proc., January 13, 1713, AHH México leg. 323, exp. 7, unfol.

[17] Kappus, Bacanora, to the P. Proc. Gen. Juan de San Martín, January 24, 1716, AHPMCJ México, Nr. 1712; Marquez de la Villa Puente to Joseph Pires, March 20, 1724, BA/JA/49-V-28, fols. 94r–95v.

[18] Cortés Ossorio, fol. 17r, sec. 37.

[19] Andreas Mancker, "Schreiben eines österreichischen Jesuitenmissionärs an den Probst zu Pöllau betreffs seiner Reise nach Mexico und seiner Erfahrung daselbt," ed. Josef von

Other information also travelled in the form of printed books brought from Europe to the overseas missions, most famously those collected by Trigault's efforts during his tour of Europe. Trigault left Munich with Schreck on August 8, 1616, to comb the Frankfurt book fair for works to bring back to China. During his travels in Italy and Germany he acquired 200 works in 143 volumes, many bearing the names of donors in Munich, Innsbruck, and Ingolstadt.[20] A few of these books were written in German, and most concerned scientific themes.[21] The Beijing College had a copy of Bodenehr's 1677 *Sacri Imperii Romano Germanici geographica descriptio* [*Geographical Description of the Holy Roman Empire of the Germans*], an atlas whose range stretches from York in the northwest to Belgrade in the southeast.[22] Trigault brought back two works of German history,[23] as well as the ninth part of Theodoré de Bry's *America*, which included Acosta's *De natura novi orbis* [*On the Nature of the New World*].[24] Another history focussed on the conquest of Mexico.[25] The range of this library indicates how important Germany and Mexico was for the China mission, in Trigault's estimation.

Publication of Missionary Works

Even a letter in wide circulation reached a limited audience, and the ultimate goal remained publication. The first book of Jesuit letters was published in Rome in 1552 in Italian, for previously letters appeared only as broadsides.[26] The German Jesuits especially sought the publication of books of letters translated into Latin – a necessity understood and appreciated by their colleagues in Rome. Increasingly Jesuits in the Indies would

---

Zahn, *Steiermärkische Geschichtsblätter* 1 (1880): 40. See Kino to Aveiro, in Burrus, ed., *Kino escribe*, 115.

[20] Hubert Verhaeren, *Catalogue de la Bibliothèque du Pé-t'ang* (Peking: Mission catholique des Lazaristes, 1949), x–xiv.

[21] Ibid., 1130, 1137–8, 1140–1.

[22] Hans Georg Bodenehr, *Sac. Imperii Romano Germanici Geographica Descriptio* (Augsburg: H. G. Bodenehr, 1677), NLC 中国国家图书馆(北堂), 书号 1267.

[23] Marquard Freher, *Germanicarvm rervm scriptores aliqvot insignes, hactenvs incogniti* (Frankfurt/Main: Andreas Wechels Erben, Claude de Marne & Johann Aubry, 1600–1602), NLC 中国国家图书馆(北堂), 书号 01976. Albertus Stadiensis, *Historiographia Alberti Abbatis Stadensis, a condito orbe usque ad auctoris aetatem, id est, annum Iesu Christi M.CC.LVI. deducta & nunc primum evulgata* (Wittenberg: 1608), NLC 中国国家图书馆(北堂), 书号 1892.

[24] Theodorus De Bry, *Americae Nona & postrema Pars. Qva de ratione lementorvm: de novi orbis natvra . . .* (Frankfurt: 1602), NLC 中国国家图书馆(北堂), 书号 3405.

[25] Antonio de Solís, *Istoria della conquista del Messico della popolazione, e de' progressi nell' America Settentrionale Conosciuta sotto nome di Nouva Spagna scritta in Castigliano da Don Antonio de Solis . . .e tradotta in Toscano da un'Accademico della Crusca* (Florence: Stamperia di S.A.S. per G. F. Cecchi, 1699), NLC 中国国家图书馆(北堂), 书号 1887.

[26] Lach and Van Kley, *Asia*, I.318–20.

compose their letters in Latin, thus eliminating this need.[27] The first call for such translations came from Leonardo Kessel, from the college at Cologne, around 1553. For the next few years Canisius lobbied General Laínez for such Latin editions that could reach audiences throughout northern Europe, and Nadal marvelled that "going into Germany I could do great things" with them.[28] Nadal and Polanco exchanged correspondence in December 1562 discussing this same possibility,[29] apparently with success, for in 1563 Sebald Meyer published under imperial privilege the first Latin edition of *Epistolae indicae* at the Jesuit press in Dillingen.[30] The first German edition soon followed, published at Munich in 1571 as *Sendschreiben und warhaffte Zeytungen, Von Aussgang und Verweiterung des Chrisstenthums bey den Hayden in der neuen Welt Auch von Vervolgung und Heiliskeit der Geistlichen Apostolischen Vorsteher* [*Letters and True Papers on the Beginning of the Expansion of Christendom among the Heathen in the New World*].[31] The letters dealing with China appeared in 1586, some three decades before Trigault's arrival.[32]

All the Catholic centres of Germany – Augsburg, Cologne, Dillingen, Ingolstadt, Munich – saw the publication of Jesuit letters, as did Italy, Portugal, Spain, Bohemia, and (especially after 1600) France.[33] Letters appeared in inexpensive editions designed for a wide audience, which students in Jesuit schools read frequently. Publishing such letters fell

---

[27] Polancus, Trent, to Nadal, December 14, 1562, in Braunsberger, ed., III.580. For a discussion of Jesuit translations see Peter Burke, "The Jesuits and the Art of Translation in Early Modern Europe," in *The Jesuits, II: Cultures, Sciences, and the Arts, 1540–1773*, ed. John O'Malley, Gauvin Alexander Bailey, Steven J. Harris, and T. Frank Kennedy (Toronto: Toronto University Press, 2005), 24–32. See also Lach and Van Kley, *Asia*, I.319.

[28] Braunsberger, ed., II.259 (1558, at Ingolstadt), III.580 (Canisius to Nadal, December 16, 1562); Nadal, Innsbruck, to Borja, December 5, 1562, in Leite, ed., *Monumenta Brasiliae*, I.59. See Braunsberger, ed., V.746.

[29] Letter of Nadal, Trent, to Polanco, December 14, 1562, in Nadal, *Epistolae et Monumenta*, II.188.

[30] *Epistolas Indicae, In Quibus Luculenta Extat Descriptio Rerum Nuper in India Orientali praeclare gestarum a Theologis Societatis Iesu: qui paucis ab hinc annis infinita Indorum millia Christo, Iesu Christique Ecclesiae mirabiliter Ecclesiae Catholicae apud Indos & non ita pridem repertas*. See Robert Streit and Johannes Dindinger, *Bibliotheca Missionum* (Aachen: Franziskus Xaverius Missionsverein, 1928–31; Rome: Herder, 1965–), IV.235. See Lach and Van Kley, *Asia*, I.319; Sauer, 37.

[31] Streit and Dindinger, IV.250. As mentioned above, a translation of Xavier's letters came earlier. Sierra, *Jesuitas*, 64, 66.

[32] M. Howard Rienstra, ed. and trans., *Jesuit Letters from China 1583–84* (Minneapolis: University of Minnesota Press, 1982), 5.

[33] Gerhard Stalla, *Bibliographie der Ingolstädter Drucker des 16. Jahrhunderts* (Baden-Baden: Koerner, 1977), I.1722; Lach and Van Kley, *Asia*, I.322, II.ii.349; Jean Balsamo, "Les premières relations des missions de la Chine et leur réception française (1556–1608)," *Nouvelle Revue du Seizième Siècle* 16.1 (1998): 180–84; Streit and Dindinger, IV.436.

within the responsibility of the secretary of the Society at Rome.[34] Trigault largely oversaw his own work, and thus avoided the usual distortions
these sources would undergo at the hands of missionary zeal, translation,
censorship, and the abbreviation both of administrative detail and of any
difficult passages. Trigault himself admitted that much of the information in early letters was unreliable.[35] Unauthorized, spiced-up versions
delighted the reading public and annoyed the Jesuits, and pirated versions of letter collections appeared, while expurgated versions circulated
in Protestant lands.[36] Chrysostom Dabertzhofer published in Augsburg
Drey neue Relationes [*Three New Accounts*], narratives from letters written
by Jesuit missionaries in Japan, India, and Durango, translated carefully
into German and dedicated to the Cathedral Chapter of Augsburg.[37]
These anthologies of letters brought descriptions of far-flung regions
together in a small book.

In late-sixteenth-century Catholic Germany church officials dominated printing, and were not slow to censor. In this climate, not only Jesuit
letter books but other kinds of works on the overseas missions enjoyed
some measure of popularity. In 1588 Valentin Fricus, the Franciscan confessor to Austrian Archduke Matthias, translated Francisco Gonzaga's
history of the Franciscan missions in both Asia and America from Latin
into German. The next year the first German translation of Mendoza's
China *Historia* appeared in Frankfurt.[38] Aegidius Albertinus, secretary
to the elector of Bavaria (and translator of the first Spanish picaresque
novel), composed a small book (Munich, 1608) about Jesuit activity in
China.[39] In 1644 a fellow Jesuit published in Nuremberg a collection
of biographies of Jesuits in Mexico and China.[40] Cologne in particular saw many translations from other languages, and in 1699 a work
on the missions was even published there in Italian.[41] The number of

---

[34] Donald F. Lach & Edwin J. Van Kley, "Asia in the Eyes of Europe in the Seventeenth
Century," *The Seventeenth Century* V (1990): 94; Rienstra, 6.

[35] Trigault, "Ad lectorem," in *De Christiana Expeditione*, iv.

[36] Lach and Van Kley, "Asia in the Eyes," 94. For example, Johannes Rutilius's collections
were published at Louvain in 1566. See idem, *Asia*, I.319.

[37] Peter Masten Dunne, *Pioneer Jesuits in Northern Mexico* (Los Angeles: University of
California, 1944), 190–91.

[38] Lach and Van Kley, *Asia*, II.ii.348–9.

[39] *Histori und eigentliche Beschreibung erstlich was gestaltet, vermittelst sonderbarer Hülff und
Schikung des Allmächtigen das Evangelium und Lehre Christi in dem großen und gewaltigen
Königreich China eingeführt, gepflanzt und gepredigt wird. Am anderen, wie sie alle andere
politische und weltliche Sachen und Gelegenheiten alldort besschaffen sind. Alles lustig und
nützlich zu lesen.* Ursula Aurich, "China im Spiegel der deutschen Literatur des 18.
Jahrhunderts." *Germanischen Studien* 169 (1935): 17.

[40] Streit and Dindinger, vol. I, nos. 210, 212, 216, 262, 714.

[41] *Sehr wehrte und angenehme newe Zeitung Von der Bekehrung zum Catholischen Glauben Des
jungen Königs in China vnd anderer Fürstlichen Personen Und von Der Legation des Ehrw.*

published travel reports, of varying provenance, peaked around 1680.[42] At the same time several novels and dramas appeared that show Baroque Germany's fascination with an idealized, Christianized, China. The end of the century saw the publication of a number of theological works specifically focussed on the rites controversy. In 1710 one theology student's theses on the Chinese Rites incensed G. B. Bussi, the papal nuncio at Cologne, whose outrage in turn became controversial at the university in Würzburg.[43]

Although specific information about the length of press runs and the number of sales of these books remains unavailable, I have assembled information regarding the history of the publications of one of the bestselling authors, Nicolas Trigault.[44] The volume of his publications is impressive. European presses published at least thirty-eight editions of eleven separate works before his death in 1628. This quantity gives him a high status in the world of Jesuit literature. Trigault himself was aware and proud of this success. At Lyon "the same man [Horatius Cordon] also published our history in elegant Latin and Gallic type," he wrote, "the first already translated by a certain relative of mine, each edition of which disappeared so quickly that a new one is being prepared." He also mentioned translations into Spanish, Italian, German, and English.[45]

This record of publication allows us to make some more specific observations about his printed propaganda efforts even without data about press runs. His publications fall into three chronological periods. In the

P. Michaelis Bovyn der Societat IESU Priestern Polnischer Nation zu Ihrer Päbst Heyligkeit nach Rohm. Item Von grosser hoffnung der Bekehrung der Tartaren und deß Königreichs Tunquin welches allein so groß ist als gantz Franckreich. Auß dem Frantzösischen zu Russel vnd Teutschem gedruckten Exemplar. Zu Cöln Bey Wilhelm Griessem im Ertz Engel Gabriel in der Tranckgaß [1653], APF SOCG 193 fol. fol. 266r to 269v; Noel [Natale] Alexandre, Apologia de Padri Domenicani missionarii della China; opure risposta al libro del Padre Le Téllier Giesuita, intitolato difesa de nouvi Christiani, e dilucidationr del P. Le Gobien della stessa Compagnia, sopra gli honori, che li Chinesi prestano à Confusio, ed a i morti. Per un Religioso Dottore, e Professore di Teologia dell' Ordine di S. Domenico (Cologne: heirs of Cornelio d'Egmond, 1699), CBL AA466i.
[42] Paul Hultsch, Der Orient in der deutschen Barockliteratur (Lengerich i.W.: Lengericher Handelsdruckerei, [1938?]), 18.
[43] Streit and Dindinger, vol. VII, nos. 2031, 2037, 2061–4, 2083–5, 2096–100, 2175; Willeke, "Würzburg," 129–30.
[44] I have collected this data from Augustin de Backer, Bibliotheque des ecrivains de la Compagnie de Jesus (Liege: L. Grandmont-Donders, 1853–61), 669–72, as well as from Auguste Carayon, Bibliographie Historique de la Compagnie de Jésus (Paris: Auguste Durand, 1864) and from my own observations. I am excluding from this discussion the 1610 Litterae Statis Jesu and the 1611 De Christiana Expeditione, because their suspicious dates render their existence questionable, and the 1626 Xiru Ermu Zi 西儒耳目資, because it was published outside of Europe.
[45] Trigault, "Litterae," in Lamalle, "La propaganda," 100–1.

first period, from 1609 to 1611, appeared a letter and the *Vita* he wrote of the Belgian Jesuit Gaspar Barzaeus. The second, from 1615 to 1617, falls within the dates of his mission to Europe. A third period runs from 1620 to a peak in 1627 and includes not only six further translations of his famous *De Christiana Expeditione* presentation of the Ricci diaries, but also eleven new editions. The coincidence of his European tour with the peak of his publications in 1615 to 1617 suggests a conscious coordination of his writings with his travels.

Trigault's works display a wide linguistic and geographical range. They appeared not merely in Latin but also in seven vernacular languages, including Flemish and Polish. The places of publication fan out in a correspondingly broad range, from Seville to Krakow. That 61% of these editions were in vernaculars and that 78% were published outside of Italy is unusual for literature of this genre and time.[46]

An even more extraordinary feature of Trigault's publications is the central role Germany played in them. In 1617 *De Christiana Expeditione* appeared in a German translation, entitled *Historia von Einfuehrung der Christlichen Religion, in dass Konigreich China durch die Societ. Jesu* [*History of the Introduction of the Christian Religion in the Kingdom of China through the Society of Jesus*]. Although this seems unsurprising, given the existence of a Polish translation as *Nowiny Chinskie*, the translation of Jesuit literature into German still remained uncommon. Even the best-selling *Life of Francis Xavier* by Horatius Tursellinus appeared in German only in 1674, a full eighty years after its first publication. Nine editions of Trigault were eventually published in Germany, more than in any other land, even Italy, and more than in France and Spain combined. Specifically, five works were published in Augsburg, including the *Historia von Einfuehrung*, three in Cologne, and one each in Münster and Munich.[47]

A printing run of a popular work related to the missions could reach a thousand copies.[48] Beyond the Jesuit presses themselves, some other publishers specialized in missionary themes. For example, the widow Sara Mang continued the publishing enterprises of her husband from 1617, probably to her death in 1624. It was she who published the German *From America* (1620), in addition to *Ausßzug etlicher glaubwürdigen Indianischen, Japonischen und Chinesischen schreiben, was sich ohnlangs in denselben Landen verlauffen* [*Excerpts from Several Credible Indian, Japanese,*

---

[46] All but two lesser works appear first in Latin, and are later translated.

[47] *Vita S. Francisci Xaverii* and *Apostolisches Leben und Thaten dess heiligen Francisci Xaverii*. Georg Schurhammer, *Francis Xavier: His Life, His Times*, trans. M. Joseph Costelloe (Rome: Jesuit Historical Institute, 1973–1982) II.643; Carayon, 371. The most common language-place combination is Latin and Germany.

[48] Lach and Van Kley, "Asia in the Eyes," 95.

and Chinese Writings] (1617), *Indianische Reise von dreyen Ehrwürdigen Priestern Societatis Jesu . . . nach Goa in India . . . in das Königreich China* [*Travels in the Indies of Three Honourable Priests of the Society of Jesus*] (1620), and a *Kurtze Relation, was inn den Königreichen Japon vnd China 1618–1620* [*Short Account of the Kingdoms of Japan and China 1618–1620*] (1621).[49]

These works' long, baroque titles consistently highlight the global nature of the missionary work. In the following representative titles, translated into English, I emphasize expressions of global mission: *Portraits and Names of Those who . . .* through the Four Parts of the World . . . *Expended Their Lives* (Küsell, 1655?), *On the Society of Jesus Fighting in* All Parts of the World (Tanner, 1675), *Catholic Christendom Spread* through the Whole World (Hazart; 1678–1701; German translation by Soutermans), *The Society of Jesus [Whose Members] Have* Moistened the Whole World *with Their Sweat* (Tanner, 1701).[50] Hazart divided his works into regional histories: Japanese, Chinese, Mughal, Vijayanagara, Abyssinian, African, Peruvian, Paraguayan, Brazilian, Floridan, Canadian, Mexican. Like many modern historians', his history of world Christianity consists of a collection of discrete regional descriptions.

Content: Current Events

What kind of information did missionary writings feature? As discussed in Chapter 3, Jesuits tended not to exchange ideas about missionary best practices, although strategies did migrate along the network's best-travelled routes.[51] Scholars have suggested that the reductions of Paraguay were inspired by the newly created villages for converts in India, or that the top-down "hierarchical" approach to conversion migrated from Japan to New France over the course of a century.[52] As we have seen, however, the latter method at least was prescribed by the Constitutions, and missionary methods were largely universal or ad hoc, rather than exchanged between mission regions. Often the most useful information exchanged was descriptions of current events. Already in the 1550s

---

[49] See Sauer, 31.
[50] The original titles are *Effigies et nomina eorum, qui . . .* per quatuor orbis partes . . . *vitam profuderunt, Societatis Jesu . . . militans* in omnibus Mundi partibus, *Catholisches Christenthum,* durch die ganze Welt ausgebreitet, and *Die Gesellschaft Jesu . . .* die gantze Welt *mit ihrem Schweiß befeuchtet haben.*
[51] See Broggio, 107–19.
[52] See Correia-Afonso, 40–41; Takao Abé, "A Japanese Perspective on the Jesuits in New France," in *Proceedings of the Twentieth Meeting of the French Colonial Historical Society, Cleveland, May 1994,* ed. A. J. B. Johnston (Bowmanville: Mothersill Printing, 1995), 14–26.

a letter full of news from the Indies reached Canisius at Ingolstadt.[53] In 1621 Schreck made a point of informing William of Bavaria about the looming "Tartar" (Manchu) invasion of Beijing.[54] Much of the news sent to Germany focussed on topics of special interest. So, when Dimer relays China news to Germany, he dwells on the Cologne-born Schall, "well-known and much loved throughout all China."[55]

Equally important was news collected about other places, such as reports composed in China about Indochina that made their way to Germany.[56] In 1624 Kirwitzer wrote to the Holy Roman Emperor from Goa with a familiarity indicative of a longer correspondence. He described for the emperor the progress of the global mission (including – perhaps pointedly – the Emperor of Ethiopia's turning away from schism), and of the Portuguese struggles against the English and the Dutch, all cast on a global stage that included Ormuz, Madagascar, Goa, Arabia, Surat, Ethiopia, Japan, China, Ceylon, and the Mughal empire. The next letter added news of martyrs in Japan, further Dutch victories, news from Java and Cochinchina, and future prospects in Makassar, Siam, and the Philippines.[57] Similarly, from Beijing Antoine Thomas sent the Duchess of Aveiro news (or reported a lack of news) from Asia, touching on China, Japan, Korea, and even Moscow.[58] Other Chinese intelligence travelled across the Pacific. For example, Gabriel de Curuzelagun y Arriola, president of the Manila Audiencia, supplied the crown with information on the activities of "Nanhoaigin" (Verbiest) in Beijing.[59] Even correspondents still in Europe could be key in relaying extra-European news to Germany. Writing from Portugal, Amhryn addressed a series of letters back to Ingolstadt, conveying news from Mozambique, Brazil, Goa, and China, apparently in the order it came to him in Coimbra. He further reported on matters of particular interest, such as the efforts to repair the clock sent by Maximilian to China.[60]

[53] Canisius, Ingolstadt, to Lainez, February 23, 1558, in Braunsberger, ed., II.206.
[54] Schreck, Hangzhou, to William of Bavaria, September 4, 1621, BStB CLM 27323, fol. 10r.
[55] German extract from Dimer's letter to Germany [the provincial?], 1658, BHStA GR 1256, Nr. 5, [fol. 3v].
[56] Castner, Rome, January 1705, SBB PK Ms. Lat. 640, fol. 58 (extract).
[57] Kirwitzer, Goa, to Emperor Ferdinand II, January 20, 1624, BRB 4169–71, fol. 44r; idem, Japan, to Emperor Ferdinand II, 1624–5, BRB 4169–71, fol. 45r. (excerpt).
[58] Antonius Thomas, Peking, to Aveiro, December 1, 1691, RAH Jesuitas 16, no. 14a, fol. 1r; Letter to Aveiro, Peking, September 15, 1688, RAH Jesuitas 16, no. 14b, fol. 2r.
[59] 1688, AGI Filip. 305, XII.172.
[60] Amrhyn, Lisbon [Evora?], to Ingolstadt, November 25, 1672, BStB CLM 26472 fol. 82r. See also Amrhyn, Coimbra, to Jacob Rassler [rector at Ingolstadt], October 23, 1672, copy of summary at BHStA Jes. 607/92.

Beyond serving as a mere way station for news passing from Asia to Europe, Mexico did much of the collection, editing, and publishing of information on China for American and European audiences. The most successful example of this pattern is Juan González de Mendoza's (1545–1618) *Historia de las cosas más notables, ritos y costumbres del gran Reyno de la China* [*History of the Most Notable Things, Rites, and Customs of the Great Kingdom of China*] (1585).[61] This Spaniard had entered the Augustinian order in Mexico and began composing his *Historia* by drawing from both the 1569 *Tractado* of Gaspar da Cruz as well as the Spanish Augustinian friar Martín de Rada's *Relación* (1575). This was no simple compilation, for Mendoza omitted, or dulled the sharpness of, Rada's more pointed criticisms of China.[62] It worked. The next few decades saw dozens of editions in various European languages, making Mendoza's work the standard and first substantial introduction of China to a European audience.[63] The 1589 German edition in particular proved immensely popular. Additionally, Mendoza later served as the basis for other works, such as Andreas Müller's *Hebdomas observationum de rebus Sinicis* [*Seven Days' Observations on Chinese Things*] (1674).[64] Given the misconceptions of the nearness of the two regions, Mendoza's stay in Mexico presumably gave him sinological authority, though he had never visited China himself.[65]

Mendoza's work was not unique. Guilhelmo de los Ríos, the leading Jesuit at the professed house in Mexico City, wrote and had published locally a work on the state of the China church, thus introducing to America as early as 1628 the story of Aluoben's 啊羅本 first evangelization of China.[66] In 1645 Andrés Pérez de Ribas, the Mexican provincial, wrote a defence of the Society's work in Mexico, the *Historia de los triumphos de nuestra Santa Fe* [*History of the Triumphs of Our Holy Faith*]. Here he defended the Jesuits against charges of a ministry limited to the rich and powerful, of which China stood as the foremost

---

[61] See Streit and Dindinger, IV.362, 533.

[62] AGI Patronato 24, R.22; see Boxer, *Church Militant*, 55.

[63] Rome 1585; other editions 1585, 1586 (x2), 1587, 1588, 1595, 1596; Italian 1586 (x8), 1587 (x2), 1588, 1590; French 1588, 1589 (x2), 1600 (x2), 1606, 1609, 1614; English 1588, 1853; Latin 1589, 1600, 1655; German 1589, 1597; Dutch 1595 (x2), 1656. Lach and Van Kley, *Asia*, I.330, call it "the most comprehensive and popular book on Ming China to appear in Europe." See also Hudson, 242.

[64] Wolfgang Franke, *China und das Abendland* (Göttingen: Vandenhoeck & Ruprecht, 1962), 52; Willy R. Berger, *China-Bild und China-Mode im Europa der Aufklärung* (Cologne: Böhlau, 1990), 44; Mungello, *Curious*, 228.

[65] P. Antonio Sedeño, Manila, to P. Juan de la Plaza, Provincia de Mexico, June 25, 1584, RAH Cortes 562, fol. 380–380r.

[66] "Triumphos, Coronas, Tropheos de la perseguida Iglesia de Japón," RAH Cortes 566, no. 27, fol. 444–499v.

example.[67] Another collection of Jesuit letters from China was published in Mexico in 1650.[68]

Despite German fascination with the Indies, much information flowed in the opposite direction, from Germany overseas. From Germany news – or at least information described as such – circulated through Iberia into Asia and America.[69] In one letter Kino lavishly expressed his gratitude for news from his German province alongside his hope that he be able to reciprocate with clear news from Mexico.[70] Such expectations of reciprocity were common. Communications bypassing Rome went from Germany to Portugal at an early date, from the very beginning of the Society, possibly even then continuing on via Portugal to Asia. Much of it is praise for the Bavarian duke's support for the Jesuits.[71] Announcements of the financial support (described in the previous chapter) from Ferdinand, the bishop of Paderborn, were translated into Spanish and Latin and widely circulated.[72] Mission patrons won prestige on a global scale.

Of course, some remarkable information remained within a single geographical area. Illing wrote Mexican mission news to the Spanish viceroy's wife.[73] Possibly hoping to make Castorano nervous, Stumpf spread within China news of victories over the French in and near Germany, won by John Churchill, the First Duke of Marlborough (1650–1722) and Eugene of Savoy (1663–1736).[74]

Even anecdotal news was chosen for its potential for edification. When "a sad story which was told to me by a Spaniard by the name of Joseph Lopez in the way he had seen it with his own eyes" reached Jesuit Marcus Antonius Kappus (1657–1717) at Mátape, he could not resist passing it on to his brother in Carniola:

In the capital of Mexico . . . one night a firework was lit because of an approaching festival; next to it four dissolute fellows not only played at cards, but one of them

[67] Andrés Pérez de Ribas, *Historia de los triumphos de nuestra Santa Fe entre gentes de las más bárbaras y fieras del nuevo obre: conseguidos por los soldados de la milicia de la Compañia de Jesús en las misiones de Nueva España* (Madrid: Alo[n]so de Paredes, 1645), 408–9, 412.

[68] "Summa del estado del imperio de la China, y christiandad del, por las noticias que dan los padres de la compañia de iesus, que residen en aquel reyno hasta el Año de 1649," APF SOCG 193 fol. 119r–130v.

[69] "Avizos de Alemanha, Vngria, Polonia e outras partes," BA/JA/49-VI-8, fol. 164; "Avzos mais frescos de Alemanha," BA/JA/49-VI-8, fol. 168.

[70] SBB PK Ms. 640, fol. 25r.

[71] Letter from Jay and Canisius, Ingolstadt, to "pater praeposite" [Portugal?], May 28, 1550, BNL PBA 490-F2044 fol. 134r–135r.

[72] RAH Jesuitas 16, no. 13.

[73] Illing, Santa Inés, to "Excelentísima Señora" [wife of viceroy Duke of Albuquerque], October 10, 1706, AGN Jes. I-12 exp. 286, fol. 2061r–2061v.

[74] Stumpf to Castorano, October 15, 1709, BNN (Cast. I) XI B-69, fol. 78r.

also outrageously blasphemed GOD. Yet he had to pay dearly for his curse, for one of the rockets flew, against its nature, not upwards, but straight into the throat of this foulmouthed person, where it exploded with a great detonation and shattered his head into many pieces. It once more brought home to all observers that the Divine Majesty does not allow one to speak with levity about Himself. In order, however, that nobody could deny this horrible event, but instead that everyone would take a lesson from it, it was painted without delay and hung up in the nearby church of Our Dear Lady of Albaneda.[75]

Indeed, family members were frequently recipients of letters from missionaries. Van Hamme wrote a dozen (extant) letters to his mother, and in one three-year period Adam Gerstl (1646–93) wrote twenty-six letters to his father.[76] Other recipients were colleagues back home, and even these could be considered family in a metaphorical sense. Ratkay addresses his "Relatio Tarahumarum Missionum" to the "Aquiline Fathers," a reference to the Habsburg eagle, and stresses how much he owes his "beloved mother" – the Austrian Jesuit province – for his religious education.[77] Van Hamme wrote home to a Jesuit that only two coadjutors in Mexico were from Flandro-Belgian province.[78] Wishing that "Bohemia were closer to us," the rector of the Jesuit college at Santiago marvelled, "With what pleasure I would accept into the noviciate that quantity of youths which in Bohemia present themselves at the religious houses and can not be accepted for the lack of vacancies."[79]

<hr/>

[75] Marcus Antonius Kappus to Johann von Kappus, Mátape, June 20, 1699, original unknown, published as "Brief R. P. Marci Antonii Kappus, der Gesellschafft Jesu Missionarii aus der Oesterreichischen Provintz. Nachmals aber Vorstehers der gesamten Missionen Soc. Jesu in der Landschaft Sonorâ. An Seinen Bruder Herrn Johann von Kappus, Land- und Edelmann in Crain," in WB Nr. 56, and published in Janez Stanonik, "Letters of Marcus Antonius Kappus from Colonial America," *Acta Neophilologica* 22 (1989): 45–8 (German), 48–50 (English).

[76] Van Hamme to his mother, twelve letters dated from 1676 to 1691, with Dutch extracts published in Constant-Philippe Serrure, ed., *Het leven van Pater Petrus Thomas van Hamme, missionaris in Mexico en in China (1651–1727)* (Gent: C. Annoot-Braeckman, 1871), 2–6, 8–9, 36–42, 44, 48–50, 51–55, 57, 66–67, 77–78, 81–82, 96–97. "Auszug aus 26. Briefen, welche Pater Adamus Gerstl, der Gesellschaft Jesu Missionarii aus der Oesterreichischen Provintz an seinem Vatter Herrn von Gerstl, der Röm. Kayserlichen Majestät Beamten in dem Vorderberg in Steuermarck, theils aus Spanien, theils aus West-Indien von dem 30. Junii 1678 bis dem 14. Julii 1681, da er zum letzten mahl aus Engelstadt [Puebla de los Angeles] in Neu-Spanien schriebe, abgesendet hat," in WB Nr. 31.

[77] Ratkay, "Relatio Tarahumarum missionum euisque Tarahumarae nationis terraeque descriptio," Caríchic, March 20, 1683, ARSI Mex. 17, fol. 494r–505r.

[78] Van Hamme, Nanjing, to Van Gallenberghe, May 5, 1691, BRB 16.691/16.693, fol. 19rv at 19r.

[79] Andrés Supecio, Santiago, to the provincial of Bohemia, December 15, 1701, in Matthei, 171.

Content: Scientific Information

Just as important as news updates was the scientific information that criss-crossed the network, for Jesuits enjoyed a high profile as science correspondents. Kircher explicitly thanked missionaries Martini and Grueber in his 1667 *China illustrata*.[80] The same year Henry Oldenburg, the first secretary of the Royal Society of London (founded in 1662), wrote to Robert Hooke to consider the possibility "to procure for the Royal Society a correspondency all over the world by means of missionaries." This would supplement their attempts to compile international weather reports based on reports from correspondents abroad.[81] The Royal Society corresponded with the Jesuits in China, and from 1666 to 1774 its *Philosophical Transactions* featured thirty-four reviews of Jesuit writings from China.[82] In the late seventeenth century the China mission also began corresponding with scientists, such as Joseph-Nicolas Delisle and Theophilus S. Bayer, in the Imperial Academy of St. Petersburg.[83] According to the plans of Jean-Baptiste Colbert, the first expedition of French Jesuits to China was to have obtaining astronomical data as a principal objective.[84] Not all such exchanges were with Europe. Taking advantage of the geographical spread of knowledge of Chinese characters, Van Hamme forwarded locally printed mathematics books from Beijing to a colleague in Cochinchina.[85]

A topic dear to the Jesuits, which only a global network of correspondents could discuss comprehensively, was comets. Astronomy and astrology are inherently universal, as much the same stars are visible in Munich, Mexico, and Beijing (Kino takes care to mention the exceptions).[86] Gaspar da Cruz described the comet of March 1556, which was thought to have forced the abdication of Charles V, noting "it might well be that this sign was *universal to all the world*, and that it signifieth the birth of

---

[80] Athanasius Kircher, *China monumentis, qua sacris, quà profanis, nec non variis naturae & artis spectaculis, aliarumque rerum memorabilium argumentis illustrata* (Antwerp: Jacobum à Meurs, 1667), prooemium [pp. (**v to **2r)]. See also Willeke, "Würzburg," 420.

[81] Han Qi 韓琦, "Sino-British Scientific Relations through Jesuits in the Seventeenth and Eighteenth Centuries," in *La Chine entre amour et haine: actes du VIIIe Colloque de sinologie de Chantilly*, Variétés Sinologiques 87 (Paris: Desclée de Brouwer, 1998), 46, 52.

[82] Joseph Brucker shows Gaubil's mid-eighteenth century correspondence with the Royal Society in "La Chine et l'Extrême-Orient d'après les trauvaux historiques du P. Antoine Gaubil," *Revue des Questions Historiques* 37 (1885): 534–5. See Han Qi, 51.

[83] Standaert, ed., 228.

[84] Catherine Jami, "From Louis XIV's Court to Kangxi's Court: An Institutional Analysis of the French Jesuit Mission to China (1688–1722)," *East Asian Science* (1995): 495.

[85] Petrus Thomas Van Hamme, Beijing, to Conrad Janningus, November 3, 1703, BRB 16691/16693, fol. 55v.

[86] Bolton, *Rim*, 48–9.

Anti-Christ; for the world showeth great signs of ending, and the Scrip-
tures in great part show that they are drawing nigh to being fulfilled."[87]
That comet would pale next to the one of 1680–81, observed by Van
Hamme in Leuven, Kino in Cádiz, and Ratkay and Neumann en route to
the Tarahumara.[88] Ratkay thought it boded ill for Western Europe and for
the Spanish monarchy in particular, but Kino wrote that this universally
observed comet would have universal consequences, with a universality
proportionate to its great size: "Many droughts, hunger, tempests, some
earthquakes, great disorders for the human body, discords, wars, many
epidemics, fevers, pests, and deaths of a great many people."[89]

The most explicitly global scheme for missionary information was
Athanasius Kircher's plan for a Consilium Geographicum (Geographical
Council or Policy). Taking advantage of the Society's worldwide range,
Kircher proposed to collect, via the procurators, data regarding magnetic declination, and longitude and latitude, from colleges spread across
the Jesuit network, "distributed throughout the whole globe, provided
with men skilled in mathematics and, above all, enjoying a unanimous
harmony of minds."[90] His own Jesuits proved more responsive than the
prominent mathematicians he had first tried to recruit, and he was able to
collect magnetic declination information from China, the Middle East,
and Europe. Records of taking latitude readings pepper itinerant Jesuits'
writings.[91] Missionaries thus became active participants in the advance
of longitude and latitude, and taking measurements became a favourite
pastime of Jesuits stationed around the world.[92] Ingolstadt Jesuits (including Adam Aigenler) collaborated on a *Tabula geographico-horologa univer-
salis* [Universal Geographical-Horological Table] which included a "new
table of latitude and longitude" listing coordinates for Munich, Mexico
City, and Beijing, among many others.[93] Edmond Halley's "Tabula

---

[87] My emphasis. *South China in the Sixteenth Century, Being the Narratives of Galiote Pereira,
Fr. Gaspar da Cruz, O. P., Fr. Martin de Rada OESA*, trans. Charles R. Boxer (London:
Printed for the Hakluyt Society, 1953), 227. See Boxer, *Church Militant*, 112.
[88] González Rodríguez, "Un cronista flamenco," 131.
[89] Ratkay, northern Mexico, to the P. Prov. Nikolaus Avancinus, February 25, 1681,
[original unknown] published as "Ein anderer Brief P. Joannis Ratkay, der Gesellschafft
Jesu missionarii aus der Oesterreichsichen Provintz. An R. P. Nicolaum Avancinum,
gedachter Societät in Oesterreich und Hungarn vorgesetzten Provincial, 'Gegeben an
den Gräntzen von Neu-Mexiko' 25. Februar 1681," in WB Nr. 29; Kino, Cádiz, to the
Duquesa de Aveiro, December 28, 1680, published in Burrus, ed., *Kino escribe*, 98–100.
[90] Quoted in Gorman, 242.
[91] For one example, see Adam Gilg, to anonymous Jesuit, Mexico, October 8, 1687, SUA
Prague, Jes. III-419/3, fol. 116r-119r, at 116v.
[92] For example, "Osservazioni de eclissi sino al 1750, in Europa, Asia ed America," SBB
PK Ms. 640, fol. 160r-162v.
[93] BStB CLM 25025 (1663).

Nautica" became popular in the Jesuits' China mission in the eighteenth
century. Castner emphasized that it was a new map of magnetic declina-
tions "for the entire world."[94]

Like current events, scientific information flowed in both directions.
A member of Rome's Lincei Academy, Schreck had discussed sending
a book of eclipse data to his friend and teacher Galileo, who himself
had shown little interest in the China missions' scientific work. In the
same letter Schreck mentioned his plans to use the Jesuit Johann Reinhard Ziegler (1569–1636), a mathematician from Speyer who studied
with Clavius, as his agent in Frankfurt to procure mathematical books.[95]
He had also appealed to the mathematics faculty at Ingolstadt, requesting the literature on the newest astronomical methods – a request that
resulted in Kepler answering Schreck's questions personally, as well as
sending two volumes from his recently published *Rudolphian Tables* to
Beijing.[96] Schreck further contemplated asking Archduke Leopold of
Austria (1586–1632) to appeal to his sister Maria Magdalena, the Grand
Duchess of Tuscany, to obtain astronomical data from Galileo.[97] In 1623
Schreck wrote from Changzhou 常州 to Ingolstadt reporting on Chinese
chronology dating back to Emperor Yao 堯 (of the late third millennium
B.C.), around whose time a solstice occurred near the cusp of Sagittarius –
an event confirmed by the data of Tycho Brahe.[98]

The richest scientific exchanges between Germany and China were
anchored in Berlin. Although few missionaries from China ever toured
Brandenburg to build up enthusiasm for the Orient, it was hardly necessary. The Great Elector Frederick William (r. 1640–88) considered
China a key element in his ambitions for his own realm. As provost of
the St. Nicholai Church, Lutheran pastor Andreas Müller (1630–94)
found royal support when in 1674 he announced to Frederick William
the discovery of a "key" that would accelerate the process of learning to

---

[94] Castner to P. Josef Odermatt, September 21, 1705, SBB PK Ms. Lat. 640, fol. 59r. See
also Castner, Lisbon, to P. Josef Odermett, November 29, 1705, SBB PK Ms. Lat. 640,
fol. 61r.
[95] Schreck, Suzhou in Xiading, to Johannes Faber, April 22, 1622, Bibl. de l'Ecole
de Médicine de Montpellier, no. 104, published in Walravens, 30–35; Bernard,
"L'Encyclopédie," 39, 64–65. See Walravens, Nr. 184.
[96] *Tabulae Rudolphinae quibus Astronomicae scientiae . . . continetur . . .* (Ulm, 1627), BHStA.
See also *China und Europa: Chinaverständnis und Chinamode im 17. und 18. Jahrhundert*,
Ausstellungskatalog (Berlin: Verwaltung der Staatlichen Schlößer und Gärten, 1973),
137; Bernard, "Encylopédia astronomique," 58, 63–8; Walravens, 22.
[97] Schreck, Suzhou in Xiading, to Johannes Faber, April 22, 1622, Bibl. de l'Ecole de
Médicine de Montpellier, no. 104, published in Walravens, 30.
[98] Giuseppe Gabrieli, "Giovanni Schreck Linceo: Gesuita e missionario in Cina e le sue
lettere dall'Asia," *Rendiconti della R. Accademia dei Lincei, Classe di Scienze morali, storiche
e filologiche* ser VI, vol. 12, 5–6 (1936): 510–11.

read Chinese.[99] Christian Mentzel (1622–1701), the Great Elector's personal physician, had more direct contact with China missionaries than did Müller. He enjoyed a close relationship with Couplet (which perhaps helped legitimize his proto-sinology) and obtained Chinese material with the help of Andreas Cleyer (1634–1697/98), who served the Dutch East India Company in Batavia as a physician.[100]

By the end of the century, the central figure in Sino-German scientific relations was Leibniz. His long-held, wide-ranging interest in Chinese philosophy, technology, politics, and science motivated and was motivated by correspondence with Jesuits both in Europe and in China. Leibniz's communication with Jesuit missionaries in Asia lasted from his meeting Claudio Filippo Grimaldi in Rome, in early June 1689 at least until Claude de Visdelou's February 5, 1714, letter from Pondicherry. Bouvet's correspondence with him extended, based on extant sources alone, from his 1697 letter of appreciation for Leibniz's scholarship up to 1707, though perhaps the Spanish succession war caused difficulties for mail.[101] His association with China became so intense that he could joke with his friend the Electress Sophie Charlotte of Brandenburg (1668–1705) that he would soon have to put up a sign over his door, "post office for China."[102] Inspired by the report in Verbiest's *Astronomia Europaea* on the popularity of the state-sponsored calendar in China and its close association with imperial authority, Leibniz recommended the Brandenburg state claim a monopoly on the printing of calendars. Taken up, this suggestion would enrich the coffers of the Prussian Academy. In the 1690s, Brandenburg also began a civil service examination system, probably after the Chinese example.[103]

[99] David E. Mungello, *The Great Encounter of China and the West, 1500–1800* (Lanham, Md.: Rowman & Littlefield Publishers, 1999), 63, 65; idem, *Curious*, 209.

[100] Walter Demel, "The 'National' Images of China in Different European Countries, ca. 1550–1800," in *Images de la Chine: Le contexte occidental de la sinologie naissante*, ed. Edward J. Malatesta and Yves Raguin, Variétés sinologiques – nouvelle série 78 (Tapei and Paris: 1995), 110; Mungello, *Curious*, 232, 237, 239.

[101] Gottfried Wilhelm Leibniz, *Writings on China*, ed. Daniel J. Cook and Henry Rosemont (Chicago: Open Court, 1994), 31; *Die Jesuiten in Bayern*, 242; Aurich, 22–25; Claudia von Collani, *Eine wissenschaftliche Akademie für China: Briefe des Chinamissionars Joachim Bouvet S. J. an Gottfried Wilhelm Leibniz und Jean–Paul Bignon über die Erforschung der chinesischen Kultur, Sprache, und Geschichte* (Stuttgart: Franz Steiner, 1989), 15–16. See Rita Widmaier, ed., *Leibniz korrespondiert mit China: der Briefwechsel mit den Jesuitenmissionaren (1689–1714)*, Veroffentlichungen des Leibniz-Archivs 11 (Frankfurt am Main: V. Klostermann, 1990).

[102] December 14, 1697, Onno Klopp, ed., *Die Werke von Leibniz gemäß seinem handschriftlichen Nachlasse in der königlichen Bibliothek zu Hannover* (Hannover: Klindworth, 1864–84), X.42.

[103] *The Astronomia Europaea of Ferdinand Verbiest, S. J. (Dillingen, 1687): Text, Translation, Notes and Commentaries*, ed. Noël Golvers, Monumenta Serica monograph series 28 (Nettetal: Steyler Verlag, 1993), 75–8, 225; Lach, *Preface*, 37.

China does not make much of an explicit appearance in Leibniz's philosophical works. His one work on China collected various writings as *Novissima Sinica* [*News from China*] (1697–99), for which he wrote a preface that General González would use during the Rites Controversy as an unprejudiced man's point of view.[104] The implicit influence has been a matter of debate, especially the possible origin of Leibniz's philosophy in Zhu Xi's 朱熹 (1130–1200) Neo-Confucianism or in Huayen 華嚴 Buddhism.[105] Arguing that "the Chinese influence went very deep in him, deeper than he knew," E. R. Hughes adopts a positive viewpoint: "To read Chu Hsi's [Zhu Xi's] commentary on *The Mean-in-action* [that is, the Zhongyong 中庸] is to find Leibniz's distinctive ideas staring one in the face."[106] Similarly, A. Zempliner finds analogies from the Neo-Confucian vital energy *qi* 氣 and *li* 理, the law of the individuals, to Leibniz's monads and individualism (that is, the concept of an active substance with internal power and sensitivity leading to individualism).[107] Needham is hardly less enthusiastic: "It is not to be suggested that the stimulus of Chinese organicism was the only one which led Leibniz to his new philosophy."[108] He suggests that the modern "organic" science (as opposed to the "mechanical universe" of early-modern natural science) traces its origins back from Whitehead through Leibniz to "men such as Chuang Chou, Chou Tun-I [周敦頤, 1017–73] and Chu Hsi."[109] David Mungello argues against this, and others have suggested that Leibniz's theoretical system had already been essentially developed when Couplet's 1687 *Confucius sinarum Philosophus* [*Confucius, the Philosopher of the Chinese*] introduced him to Neo-Confucianism.[110]

The spread of Chinese natural religion in Europe corresponded to only half of Leibniz's quest for a universal moral law – and was to be complemented by the export of the revealed Christian message to Asia.[111] During his stay in Paris, Leibniz described to Colbert a "missionary geometry" by which the Persians and the Chinese would discern in the superiority of Western mathematics the truth of Christianity.[112] Still, Leibniz became one of the first Europeans to recognize the possibility of different

---

[104] E. R. Hughes, *The Great Learning and the Mean in Action* (London: J. M. Dent, 1943), 19; Anton Huonder, "Gottfried Wilhelm von Leibniz (1646–1716) und die Missionen," *Die Katholische Missionen* 49 (1927): 158.

[105] Julia Ching and Willard G. Oxtoby, *Moral Enlightenment: Leibniz and Wolff on China* (St. Augustin: Institut Monumenta Serica, 1992), 20.

[106] Hughes, 20, 19.

[107] Arthur Zempliner, "Abhandlung über die chinesische Philosophie," *Studia Leibnitiana* II.3 (1970): 223–31, especially 226–7.

[108] Needham, *Science and Civilisation in China*, II.502.

[109] Ibid., II.496–505.

[110] Mungello, *Curious*, 13–17. See *Jesuiten in Bayern*, 242.

[111] *Jesuiten in Bayern*, 242.

[112] [1675?], Klopp, III.211.

cultures no less valuable for their differences, and thus to contribute to the growing idea of global community.[113] Sometimes this idea expressed itself in an odd mixture of European communion and extra-European belligerence, as did his suggestion to European princes that they release their aggression overseas, rather than on each other: Sweden and Poland could penetrate into Siberia and Tauride, England and Denmark into North America, Spain into South America, Holland into East Asia, and France into Africa.[114]

Leibniz's missionary impulse was strikingly nonconfessional. He wrote to the Protestant theology professor Philipp Müller on August 15, 1698, that "in my view it would always be better that even a not unclouded knowledge of Christ reach those distant peoples as none at all."[115] Hoping to encourage missions to China, Leibniz wrote to Protestants in England, Switzerland, Germany, Netherlands, and Sweden. His voice carried over confessional and national boundaries, but often fell of deaf ears. He remarked, "I do not yet see any such great disposition among with the Dutch or the English even though I have sent my little book to England as food for thought." The Electress Sophie of Hanover (1630–1714) thought the priority should be "to make some good Christians in Germany without going so far away to fashion them," but for his part Leibniz feared that Germany might "fail itself and Christ" by not doing more for the Asian missions. His explanation for why the Protestants had a moral duty to send a mission to China is revealing: Their excellence in science compelled them to spread the gospel.[116]

Prestige and Patronage

Although naturally the content of such scientific reports and news bulletins was eagerly sought, looking more superficially at the information network adds another layer to the analysis. The existence of Chinese-language books in European libraries did not necessarily imply that anyone there could read them,[117] and we should not shy from judging a book by its cover alone. Books can be artefacts as well as texts, especially in the context of princely patronage.

---

[113] See Anton Hilckmann, "Leibniz und die Pluralität der Kulturen: Leibniz und China," *Saeculum* 18 (1967): 317–21.

[114] Jean Baruzi, *Leibniz et l'organization religieuse de la terre* (Paris: F. Alcan, 1907), 9–21.

[115] Huonder, "Gottfried," 160.

[116] Lach, *Preface*, 41; Herrenhausen, June 26, 1700, Klopp, VIII.189; Preface in Lach, *Preface*, 96; Huonder, "Gottfried," 160.

[117] Giovanni Pietro Maffei, *Historiarum indicarum libri XVI* (Cologne: in officina Birckmannica, sumptibus Arnoldi Mylij, 1590), 256.

The most common way to transfer prestige from missionary to mission patron was by the dedication of books. Martini dedicated *De bello Tartarico* [On the Tartar War] to John II Casimir Vasa of "Poland and Sweden," thus acknowledging the Polish king's (r. 1648–68) claim to the throne of Sweden.[118] The first edition of Martini's *Novus atlas sinensis* [*New Chinese Atlas*] (Amsterdam, 1655) is dedicated to Archduke Leopold Wilhelm of Austria, the son of Emperor Ferdinand II, who, as governor (*Statthalter*) of the Habsburg Netherlands, was the highest secular authority of that Jesuit province and was responsible for the approval of the atlas.[119] Schall dedicates his *Historica narratio* (Vienna, 1665) to Emperor Leopold I. The dedication's first sentence emphasizes how far away the missionaries are and how grateful they are to the benevolence of the House of Austria.[120]

In an odd twist, Stumpf commits his treatise "Super remedio conservanda Missionis Sinensis" to the "holy angels," because, he claims, he has been disappointed in his success when writing as a man to men. This suggests that those to whom previous works had been dedicated had failed to meet expectations, but it also establishes something like a continuum between those same people and the angels. Throughout the work he addresses his audience in the vocative with varying terms for the angels: "caelites genii custodes sinarum," "o Superi principes," or "o Amici Dei."[121]

Although only one of Trigault's books was published in Munich, frontispieces of two of his works make explicit the close relationship he enjoyed with the Wittelsbach dukes. The *Litterae Societatis Jesu* [*Letters of the Society of Jesus*], first published in 1615 at Augsburg and Antwerp, is dedicated to the dukes, as is the volume published in Munich, the 1623 *De Christianis apud Japonios triumphis* [*On the Christian Triumphs among the Japanese*]. The Jesuits repaid Duke William V of Bavaria's interest in the Asian missions by dedicating to him in 1570 the third edition of their *Epistolae Indicae et Japonicae* [*Japanese and Indian Letters*].[122] The

[118] Martino Martini, *De bello Tartarico historia, in qua, quo pacto Tartari hac nostra aetate Sinicum imperium invaserint, ac fere totum occuparint, narratur, eorumque mores breviter describuntur*... (Antwerp: ex off. Plantiniana Balthasaris Moreti, 1654), BAV Barberini S XI 32.

[119] Martini, *Novus atlas sinensis* (Amsterdam: Bleau, 1665), BAV Barberini X I 46.

[120] Johann Adam Schall von Bell, *Historica narratio de initio et progressu missionis Societatis Jesu apud chinenses, ac praesertim in regia pequinensis* (Vienna: typis M. Cosmerovij, 1665), BAV H.I78 p. 2rv.

[121] StAK Jesuiten 732, 1–3.

[122] *Epistolae Indicae et Japonicae etx., tertia editio 1570. Epistolae Japonicae de multorum in Variis Insulis gentilium ad Christi fidem conversione. Illustrissimo Principi Comino D. Guilielmo Bavariae Duci dicatae 1570*, cited in Münsterberg, 14.

Wittelsbachs used even those books not dedicated to them, by collecting volumes on or from the Indies as an indication of their piety. Many of these works were collected in the Court Library and are now located in the Staatsbibliothek. Others were sent to Ferdinand Orban (1655–1732), confessor to Maximilian II Emanuel, and were later bequeathed to the Jesuit College in Ingolstadt, whence they have made their way to the Ludwig Maximilian University's library in Munich.[123]

Patrons themselves were often great letter writers, and few were as prolific as the polyglot Duchess of Aveiro, the "Mother of the Missions." Through her correspondence, the duchess' palace in Madrid became Europe's clearinghouse for geographical and ethnographical news. Letters flowed to her from around Europe, as well as from India and China.[124] Verbiest also wrote her at least twice in the 1680s.[125] Perhaps her most constant correspondent was Antoine Thomas, who wrote some thirty-two letters to her. Thomas frequently requested that the Duchess daily commend the salvation of so many souls to God, and intercede with the king to accelerate assistance to the Society.[126] Kino confided in the Duchess about his longing for China,[127] and probably hoped that she would break confidence to use her influence to transfer him.

Not least of the motivations encouraging patrons to become involved in the Jesuits' global network was the desire for prestige. Jesuit missionaries were the rock stars of their century, though possibly only among the social elite, for the sources remain silent as to whether distant missions sparked the imagination of peasants. Missionary fervour was described as a widespread fire, and missionaries traveling through Würzburg for foreign assignments were received as "angels from heaven."[128] A particularly pious theologian in Mainz won the honour of making the beds of the missionaries of the 1616 expedition.[129] In 1646 the eighth general

---

[123] Jane Hwang, "The Early Jesuit-Printings [sic] in China in the Bavarian State Library and the University Library of Munich," in 紀念利瑪竇來華四百週年中西文化交流國際學術會議論文集, ed. Lo Kuang (Taipei, 1983); Münsterberg, 19, 21–2; "Die Raritätenkammer des 18. Jahrhunderts: Pater Ferdinand Orban," in Claudius C. Müller, 16–17.

[124] See Tenri University Library, ed., *The Far Eastern Catholic Missions 1663–1711: The Original Papers of the Duchess of d'Aveiro* (Tokyo: Yushudo, 1975).

[125] Verbiest, Beijing, to the Duchess of Aveiro, November 10, 1685, published in Josson and Willaert, eds., 514–15; Verbiest, Beijing, to the Duchess of Aveiro, September 1, 1686, published in ibid., 522–3.

[126] Antoine Thomas, Beijing, to the Duchess of Aveiro, September 15, 1688, RAH Jesuitas 16, no. 14b, fol. 2v. See Antoine Thomas, Seville, to the Duchess of Aveiro, July 16, 1680. [MS. fol. 2, Maggs Bros., *Bibliotheca Americana* (London, 1923), III.133.] For the thirty-two letters, from July 18, 1678, to October 1, 1694, see III.906–9.

[127] Bolton, *Rim*, 57.

[128] Willeke, "Würzburg," 419.

[129] Huonder, "Die erste," 12.

congregation expressed its gratitude to the Spanish king for his generous financial support of the overseas missions.[130] In an October 20, 1710 letter from China, the Austrian Jesuit Hieronymus Francis declared, "Not just I, but also many other missionaries in China hold that the peace of the entire Christian Church and this China mission depends on the preservation of the radiant House of Austria."[131] From the missionary perspective, the benefits the Habsburgs would win for their patronage were not merely prestige in the eyes of man, but a special place in the eyes of God. Thus not every good delivered through this network was tangible, and in the next chapter we turn at last to the Jesuits' spiritual global economy.

---

[130] 1646, decree 38. Huonder, *Deutsche Jesuitenmissionäre*, 45.
[131] WB Nr. 108.

10 The Jesuit Sacred Economy

A man walks into a Dublin pub and asks for three cold Guinness stouts. The bartender brings him his three, which he drinks one after the other. Watching him drink, the bartender offers, "Sir, you don't have to order three all at once. If you start with one I'll keep an eye on it, and when it gets low I'll bring you a fresh cold one." "Oh, no," the man exclaims, "you don't understand. I have two brothers, one in New Zealand and the other in Canada. We took a vow that whenever any of us drinks, he drinks two more for his two brothers." The idea of this ritual pleases the bartender, and for many weeks his patron orders the three stouts. One Saturday in February the man enters the pub and orders only two. The change in the ritual stops the bartender cold, and he says in a low voice, "My condolences on the loss of your brother." Grinning, the man replies, "My brothers are fine; it's just that I'm after giving up Guinness for Lent."

Our man's drinking custom evokes any rite's openness to multiple interpretations and misinterpretations as well the potential conflicts of new rituals (drinking in threes) with the more traditional ones (Lenten abstinence). It further suggests the power of ritual to bind together a global community, here a community of three brothers on different continents.

As a religion, Christianity has dealt well with space, despite, or because of, the loss of its own sacred sites – Jerusalem fell to the Persians in 614, and has been won and quickly lost by Christian invaders three times since. Sacred locations can sometimes be replicated, as the Catholic observance of the Stations of the Cross recreates the Via Dolorosa. Images, too, can be reproduced by skilled hands, and even copies can retain power. When the Jesuit Wilhelm Gumppenberg compiled his 1657 *Atlas Marianus* [*Marian Atlas*] of over one thousand miracle-producing images of Mary, his list was global.[1] Images and imagining abound in Ignatius's

---

[1] Wilhelm Gumppenberg, *Atlas Marianus, sive, De imaginibus Deiparae per orbem Christianum miraculosis* (Ingoldstadt: Typis Georgii Haenlini typographi academici, 1657). See Andrew Redden and Luke Clossey, "Global Cult of Mary," *World History Encyclopedia* (ABC-Clio, forthcoming).

Spiritual Exercises, which inspired Francisco de Florencia's retreat guide *Las Novenas del Santuario de Nuestra Señora de Guadalupe*, and it was the same Florencia who, as procurator, brought a group of recruits – including the future California missionary Salvatierra – back to Mexico. The Jesuits' mission art academy in Japan, directed by Giovanni Niccolò, may have sent sculptors to Peru (and, in the other direction, at least one painting of the Madonna may have reached China from Mexico).[2]

Images and places can be replicated with greater ease than relics, and are thus perhaps less well suited to economic metaphors. The glue and the goal of the Jesuit global network were sacred. In early-modern Catholicism, however, religion cannot be extracted from economy, human resources, or information creation and exchange.[3] What technologies of ritual did the early-modern Jesuits employ? The previous chapters' analysis of the dynamics of the global Jesuit network have already revealed not only sacraments (baptism, the Eucharist, and ordination to priesthood) and nonsacramental rites (prayers and exorcism) but also activities as mundane as letter writing performed with ceremonial or symbolic affectation. This chapter looks more closely at the most precious commodities of the Jesuits' sacred economy: masses and prayers, relics, and souls.

Masses and Prayers

Prayers and the masses of the liturgy were crucial tools in the missionaries' efforts to save souls. If the modern historian hesitates to describe prayer in terms of economics, it is because the material scarcity usually cited to suggest the appropriateness of economic analysis is here replaced by a temporal opportunity cost – it takes time to pray. That prayers were both important and easily quantifiable is suggested by the frequency with which (often highly) multiplied endowed masses appeared in the wills of wealthy Catholics. With transcendental value and no bulk, prayers were the ultimate luxury item. A letter hastily written by Baptista spends almost as many words asking to be remembered in masses as announcing the Manchu invasion of China.[4]

The Jesuits were no exception. The frequency with which they ended letters with requests for prayers should indicate a sincere need rather

---

[2] Bailey, *Art on the Jesuit Missions*, 71, 91.

[3] For a discussion of the term "sacred economy" see Kathryn Burns, *Colonial Habits: Convents and the Spiritual Economy of Cuzco, Peru* (Durham, North Carolina: Duke University Press, 1999), 3–6.

[4] Juan Baptista de Morales, Mexico, [to Ingoli], November[?] 21, 1646, APF SOCG vol. 145, fol. 300r.

than a hollow rhetorical flourish. Prayer was too central to their central purpose to be dismissed. Even the Constitutions specified that whoever assembles a general congregation, after announcing the place and time for a congregation, should be "prescribing that Masses and prayers be offered everywhere for a good election." The first listed among the many duties of each of the five Jesuit assistants was to "offer special prayer and be mindful in his Masses of the region particularly entrusted to him."[5]

Prayer played a role even before a missionary was selected. When the general decided where to send each missionary, the Constitutions required "commending the matter to his Divine Majesty and causing it to be commended in the prayers and Masses of the house."[6] A successful decision could elicit even more prayers. When Kaspar Rueß found out he had been selected for the overseas mission, he immediately wrote the general and promised to pray for him daily.[7]

Requests for masses must be taken just as seriously as more concrete things. This is rather how they were thought of at the time, and Januske could ask his procurator for both masses and material goods in the same breath.[8] Teaching at Coimbra, Amrhyn wrote to his home college to show how well he was getting on, and still appealed for prayers, as he and Aigenler "need nothing from Germany except for the prayers and sacrifices of our friends, which move our journey forward."[9] Trigault explained that everyone contributes in different ways to this great enterprise, for those without material resources can offer their prayers.[10]

Most often masses were requested for the souls of individuals. This was a frequent request of donors, as when the Marquis de Villa Puente asked that he be remembered in the missionaries' masses.[11] Entire regions could also be included as objects of prayers, alongside individuals. In one letter Canisius commended himself, Germany, and Poland to Ignatius's prayers.[12]

As common as masses were prayers with particular petitions. Haller asked God to grant governor Gabriel del Castillo victories and long life.[13]

---

[5] *Constitutions*, 299 [part VIII, ch. 6, sec. 3, par. 692], 327–28 [part IX, ch. 6, sec. 10, par. 803].

[6] Ibid., 274–72 [part VII, ch. 2, sec. 1, par. 622].

[7] Huonder, *Deutsche Jesuitenmissionäre*, 13; Duhr, *Geschichte*, 2:2.477.

[8] Januske, Oposura, to the P. Proc. Gen. Antonio Garzia, March 31, 1718, AGN Jes. II-29 exp. 25, fol. 26r.

[9] Aigenler, Coimbra, to Ingolstadt, July 3, 1672, BStB CLM 26472 fol. 81v.

[10] RAH Jesuitas 91, no. 28, fol. 7v.

[11] Marquez de Villa Puente, Mexico, to P. Jozé Pires [provincial of Japan], March 24, 1725, BA/JA/49-V-28, fol. 209r.

[12] Canisius, Vienna, to Ignatius, April 16, 1554, in Braunsberger, ed., I.460.

[13] Haller, Parral, to Gov. Gabriel del Castillo, December 3, 1697 [1696?], AGI Guad. 156 fol. 1007r.

When Ratkay requested prayers and sacrifices of the Jesuits of his home province, he specified a purpose – that they might excite his soul into fulfilling its apostolic vocation.[14] With the frequent descriptions of prayers yearning for calm, diary descriptions of storms at seas read like missals.[15] Specific saints, often named as mission patrons, could also be solicited. To counter the powers of the devil, Castner naturally turned to prayer, by which "I put my hope in God, and especially in the powers of St. Joseph and St. [Francis] Xavier, who are the missionaries' protectors."[16] While in Mexico, Jesuit missionary Adam Gilg (1653–1709) wrote his own "Mass for the Conversion of the Infidels."[17]

The requests for prayers ran along almost every path of our network. The China missions requested prayers from Europe and even from America.[18] Kino sent geographical data to the superior of the German province, and added that he commended himself to "my sweetest mother the Upper German province" and to the masses they could perform for him.[19]

Reciprocity of prayer was expected. Emperor Leopold saw off Ratkay with a letter in which he prayed God to grant the missionary fortunate travels and an abundant harvest of souls, but asked to be remembered in the missionary's own prayers.[20] The last paragraph of one of Kappus's letters to his "aunt" ("die frau Mamb") recalls an earlier promise of exchanges of prayers, and illustrates its continued importance for the missionary:

Yet it is already time to hold back the pen desirous to write. And solely and only to add this, my petition: that my aunt and the Sister Maria Teresia do not

[14] Ratkay, "Relatio Tarahumarum missionum euisque Tarahumarae nationis terraeque descriptio," Caríchic, March 20, 1683, ARSI Mex. 17 fol. 505r.

[15] For example, "Libero tercero; En el se refiere el destierro de los Jesuitas Misioneros de la Tarahumara, y su viage por tierra y por mar, y al fin se anade una breve relacion de alguno sucesos notables de este siglo en aquellas partes de las Misiones," BNC FG 1411, fol. 63r. See also Catherine Lugar, "The History of the Manila Galleon Trade," in *Archaeological Report: The Recovery of the Manila Galleon Nuestra Señora de la Concepción*, ed. William M. Mathers, Henry S. Parker III, and Katherine A. Copus (Sutton, Vermont: Pacific Sea Resources, 1990), 39–45; Bolton, *Rim*, 44, 67.

[16] Castner, Rome, to P. Josef Odermett, April 28, 1703, SBB PK Ms. Lat. 640, fol. 55v.

[17] "Missa pro converione infidelium," Mátape[?], 1707[?], ARSI Roma, FG 720/I Nr. 9; published in Walter M. Brüning, "Zur Vorgeschichte der Messe 'Propaganda Fidei.' Eine Bittschrift aus der Sonoramission im Jahre 1707," *Archivum Historicum Societatis Iesu* 8 (1939): 324–6.

[18] RAH Cortes 566, no. 27, "Triumphos, Coronas, Tropheos," fol. 489r.

[19] Kino, Dolores, to the P. Prov. of the Upper German Province, May 14, 1701, SBB PK, Ms. lat., fol. 640, fol. 52v.

[20] Gerard Decorme, *La obra de los Jesuítas mexicanos durante la época colonial, 1572–1767* (México: Antigua Librería Robredo de J. Porrúa e Hijos, 1941), II.307–8.

forget their promise and do not omit to recommend me, the poor sinner, daily to the divine mercy; in fact I have kept steadfastly my promise till the present day, and am remembering daily the aunt and the sister Maria Teresia, as well as the sister Maria Magdalena (my aunt may therefore cordially recommend me and give greetings). I hope also that other acquainted ladies of the convent will occasionally remember me in their holy and innocent prayers. I conclude, and that against my will because I would like to make no end to this writing: recommending me most cordially to the fervent prayers of my aunt.[21]

The best example of long-distance prayer came with the endowment made by Ferdinand von Fürstenberg. The Jesuits' general congregation responded to his generosity with promises of sacrifice and prayer. The newly elected general, Charles de Noyelle, ordered masses and prayers for Fürstenberg in all Jesuit provinces worldwide. When he received the written version of this directive, Fürstenberg performed mass at the altar on which he had put a paper bearing the words written in his own hand: "So that the Chinese and Japanese mission may have fortunate success and bring truly great fruits I offer two thousand holy masses." Writing on his knees, as if in the bishop's presence, Verbiest then penned a thank-you letter that offered twenty-five thousand rosaries said by Beijing's Christians.[22]

Relics

Although in the early-modern period the Jesuits dominated the circulation of relics, their use in proselytizing ventures has a long history. Even Pope Martin I (649–54) sent out relics to bolster the morale of a faltering missionary.[23] Relics had a special relevance for missionaries, as canon law required them for the establishment of new churches. Thus Martini advised the pope of the lack of relics when requesting special dispensations.[24] In a more subtle way, they are handy in the creation of global religion for their capacity for linking two places – the relic's original and present locations – in a way both sacred and physical. It

---

[21] Kappus, Cucurpe, to "Frau Mämb" Francisca Adlmann, abbess of cloister of Clarissas (in Locopolis = Škofja Loka), April 30, 1689, published in Janez Stanonik, ed., "Letters of Marcus Antonius Kappus from colonial America." *Acta Neophilologica* 19 (1986): 54–5.

[22] Quoted in Micus, 68; Metzler, *Vikariate*, 60. See Const. S. J. Decreta Congr. Gen., Congr. XII, d. 27, in Huonder, *Deutsche Jesuitenmissionäre*, 56; De Noyelle, Rome, to Ferdinand, September 19, 1682, ARSI Epp. NN. 7 (Epistolae Generalium ad externos) f. 604v–605v.

[23] Richard E. Sullivan, "The Papacy and Missionary Activity in the Early Middle Ages," *Mediaeval Studies* XVII (1955): 67.

[24] Martini to Pope, [s.p., s.d. but ca. 1656], APF SOCG 193, fols. 262v.

should come as no surprise that the procurators of the overseas missions, most famously those of India, came to Rome specifically seeking relics. Already in 1547 Polanco included this in the duties of a mission procurator.[25]

The typical flow was from Europe, which possessed the highest density of relics. The traffic in relics across the Atlantic began when a fragment of the True Cross was given to the Santo Domingo church.[26] The Jesuits themselves were the force behind the transfer of relics from the "11,000 virgins" (Sts. Ursula and Undecimilla) of Cologne to America.[27] Many available relics had been evacuated from churches in areas won over by the Protestants. The relics Ricci brought to China made such an impression that they merited mention in the official Ming History 明史: "He also brought with him some bones which he said belonged to saints and fairies." The history, however, remained incredulous, as the understood abilities of the saintly contradicted the Chinese theory of their anatomy. It wonders "how could these saints have bones when he himself said that they could fly?"[28]

To a lesser extent, relics also travelled in the other direction. When on January 1, 1782, in the convent of Bom Jesus, Governor Dom Federico Guilherme de Souza, Bishop Manoel de Santa Catarina, and the Intendant General of the Nave Dom Lopo José de Almeida implemented a royal order to examine the body of Francis Xavier, they found the right hand had sometime earlier been sent to Rome by Jesuit priests "as per tradition."[29] In the Mariana Islands Boranga's legs were exhumed in 1695, and sent back to be buried in the Jesuit church in Vienna, his hometown – a truly global burial.[30] Some objects associated with missionaries rather than saints were given a similar treatment, as was a set of chopsticks used by Castner, who stressed that he himself had eaten with them. Such items are analogous to the gifts brought by mission procurators from Europe to the missions, and from the missions to the general and to other patrons.

Obtaining relics was a common perquisite of a missionary patronage. As mentioned in Chapter 8, soon after the Marquis de Villa Puente made a pious gift, a third party wrote the Japan provincial making clear the

[25] November 22, 1547, in DI I.206–8.
[26] Cummins, *Question*, 261.
[27] Christian, 137–38.
[28] Zhang, XIII.8439–62. See Ch'en, 355.
[29] HAG MR 162A, fol 105, cited in P. P. Shirodkar, "Records on Jesuits in Goa Archives," in *Jesuits in India: In Historical Perspective*, ed. Teotonio R. De Souza and Charles J. Borges (Macao: Instituto Cultural de Macau, 1992), 32.
[30] Duhr, *Geschichte*, 3.356. See "Titulus Ultimus Elogialis Defunctorum Commendatio," ÖNB Wien, Handschriften-Sammlung, Cod. 12.227, fol. 79r.

patron's interest in a Francis Xavier relic. A later thank-you letter from the Marquis for such a relic suggested that the blunt hint was taken to heart.

Few were as involved in global relic trade as William V of Bavaria. The duke began in the 1580s to seek out and acquire relics systematically, especially from Protestant areas in northern Germany, and so he could draw from this collection for relics to the China mission.[31] In William's 1616 letter establishing the foundation, he cites the size and power of the Chinese empire, and the Jesuits' zeal in procuring souls for God.[32] The reverse bears a list of relics, and the duke's affirmation of their authenticity, along with his wish that these relics, into whoever's hands they should come, be venerated and kissed with an appropriate honour, just as he had shown them.[33] The placement of this list and this wish suggests that these were being sent to China. Trigault, coming back from Europe, informed the mission procurator of pious William's wish for a head from a Japanese martyr.[34]

Unfortunately, Trigault had to send the duke his regrets that no relics from martyrs from China were available, only those from Japan, for "it has not yet been permitted us to be so blessed."[35] In thanks for the Wittelsbach good turns, in 1620, in the presence of the procurator, Schreck ordered opened the shrine in which the holy relics were guarded, and selected the head of Fayaxinda Leo, who died by fire for the Christian faith in 1613, at Arima near Kobe, along with his children Magdalena and Jacobus. Schreck then wrote that he was sending William's daughter, also named Magdalena, a bone from each, and an additional rib from the Japanese Magdalena. He included for the duchess "Margarete" a cross of Japanese craftsmanship filled with relics.[36]

Receiving Schreck's letter on November 21, 1623, William responded on January 20, 1624, in his own hand. The duke announced that he honoured this letter as if it were itself a relic. He added that the promised

[31] ARSI Jap Sin 117, fol. 1. See Monika Bachtler, "Der verlorene Kirchenschatz von St. Michael," in *St. Michael in München: Festschrift zum 400. Jahrestag der Grundsteinlegung und zum Abschluß des Weideraufbaus*, ed. Karl Wagner and Albert Keller (Munich: Schnell & Steiner, 1983), 127.

[32] "Guilielmus Dei gratia Comes Palatinus Rheni, utriusque Bavariae Dux," August 16, 1616, ARSI FG 722/17, unfol.

[33] "Cum sacra Romana Ecclesia Sanctorum Dei," August 12, 1616, ARSI FG 722/17. See also ARSI JapSin 117, fol. 1.

[34] February 9, 1620, BStB CLM 27323, fol. 7r. On the importance of martyrs' relics, see Gregory, 298–303.

[35] Trigault, Macao, to William, February 2, 1620, BStB CLM 27323, fol. 2r.

[36] Leidinger, 173–4. Leidinger cannot identify Margarete, but I tentatively suggest Mechthild, Albert VI's widow.

relics from Japan had not yet arrived, though they were "more welcome to us than a treasure of gold and silver."[37]

Although it is unclear whether these relics ever reached Bavaria, the St. Michael's Church in Munich featured oil paintings of three Jesuit martyrs crucified in Nagasaki in 1597. Their portraits hung in a side chapel. At least by around 1750, pieces of Francis Xavier's arm bone hung in St. Michael's, near an inscription evocative of MacDonald's, and of a similarly propagandistic purpose: "120,000 baptized."[38]

A Global Ritual Community

Before continuing on to souls, the principal object of this sacred economy, we might take some time to reflect on relics and masses as the technologies that held the Society together. Although broad in geographical range, this Jesuit global community was narrow in membership. Institutional divergences, most notably competition with other religious orders, restricted who could participate in it. Presumably other orders had similar global communities, each defined by who participated with whom in these rituals. Although the drinking habits of the Irish diaspora has remained insufficiently studied, anthropologists have begun to pay attention to rituals that are, in a variety of ways, global. Some rituals have been described as "global" in their ability to indicate for an entire society,[39] or it can be understood to be global (perhaps more accurately, universal) in that it addresses a reality thought to be complete.[40] A rare example of a ritual that is global in the sense we use here comes from the modern Greek diaspora. In the village Olymbos the *glendi* (a celebration of poetry recitation, music, and feasting) is recorded on an audiocassette recorder, and the tapes are mailed to the expatriate Olymbos community in Baltimore. "Through the tape recorder and the print media, *glendia* further create a global community," Anna Caraveli observes, "one defined through activity and perception rather than bounded space or tangible

---

[37] William, Munich, to Schreck, January 20, 1624, BStB CLM 27323, fol. 13r. Schreck's letter was written on September 4, 1621.

[38] Peter Steiner, "Der erhaltene Kirchenschatz von St. Michael," in *St. Michael in München: Festschrift zum 400. Jahrestag der Grundsteinlegung und zum Abschluß des Weideraufbaus*, ed. Karl Wagner and Albert Keller (Munich: Schnell & Steiner, 1983), 158 (ill.) and 159.

[39] See, for example, Amitai Etzioni, "Toward a Theory of Public Ritual," *Sociological Theory* 18 (2000): 45–47. This use originates in Amitai Etzioni and Edward Lehman, "Some Dangers in 'Valid' Social Measurements: Preliminary Notes," *The Annals of the American Academy of Political and Social Science* 373 (1967): 1–15.

[40] Thus the Dreaming (*Tjukurrpa*) among Australian Aborigines, in Sylvie Poirier, "'Nomadic' Rituals: Networks of Ritual Exchange Between Women of the Australian Western Desert," *Man*, New Series 27 (1992): 760.

objects, and one that can be conjured up repeatedly in ever-changing patterns."[41]

Nicolas Standaert has promoted the useful concept of "communities of effective rituals" – rituals effective "both in the sense that they build a group and that they are considered by the group's members as bringing meaning and salvation." Appositely, these communities are specifically described as established at the local level.[42] These local communities of effective rituals, however, were established by religious orders famously international in their geographical range. Did these religious orders form their own communities of effective ritual? In any case they all recognized a common, Catholic set of effective rituals. Not just about maintaining global community, the rituals of early-modern Catholicism were potentially global in meaning. Just as a church may serve as a space for local rituals, so, too, the world becomes the ritual space for global mission.

Although this chapter argues for the importance of these rituals in preserving a global community of Jesuits, such an approach has typically been associated with local societies, at least since A. R. Radcliffe-Brown's fieldwork on the Andaman Islands (1906–8). Anthropologists' interest in ritual as key to social cohesion has a long history and continues to endure. Catherine Bell sums up the social functionalists' appreciation of ritual as "a means to regulate and stabilize the life of this system, adjust its internal interactions, maintain its group ethos, and restore a state of harmony after any disturbance." Perhaps such an association between functionalism and localism is not accidental. The usual explanatory theories, of Arnold van Gennep, Max Gluckman, and Victor Turner, all "appear particularly appropriate to groups whose social, economic and political organizations are sufficiently limited geographically that one can attempt to plot most of it and, in doing so, try to see the connections between symbolic actions and social life."[43]

What differs between global and local ritual? Some types of ritual activity may be more appropriate to one or the other. A relic, as a highly mobile sacred object, is well suited to the role of maintaining a global community. Global ritual may be inherently more cooperative than local ritual. The power struggles described by Pierre Bourdieu do not appear in the

---

[41] Anna Caraveli, "The Symbolic Village: Community Born in Performance," *The Journal of American Folklore*, 98 (1985): 261–2.

[42] Nicolas Standaert, "Workshop 'Court, Ritual Community, and the City: Chinese and Christian Rituality in Late Imperial Beijing' Research questions," 1 (Unpublished manuscript, 2004).

[43] Catherine Bell, *Ritual: Perspectives and Dimensions* (New York: Oxford University Press, 1996), 29, 55.

exchange of gifts among Jesuits and their benefactors.[44] Distance, more than social tensions, is the centrifugal force that threatens to pull apart a global community.

Kirsten Bayes once related an anecdote about a Tibetan spirit who gets little done because he is so distracted by the need to explain the symbolism of the flames surrounding him. This was clearly not the case for the Jesuits. The Jesuits may have understood these rituals as strengthening their global community, but probably not as such, as I have found no explicit evidence of such an understanding. More likely they thought in terms more (salvation) or less (money) rarefied. If for the historian the function of these rituals is to reinforce a global community, for the Jesuit they were essentially all tools for the salvation of souls.

Souls

Bernal Diáz was not being glib when he described the conquistadors' purposes as "to give light to those who were in darkness, and to procure wealth which all men desire," nor was he bringing the spiritual and the material into scandalous juxtaposition.[45] Early-modern Europeans to an impressive degree thought about souls and money in similar ways. Even Kino described the reputation of what was then called the "Island of California" as an enterprise profitable for its "souls and pearls," and Vieira explicitly wrote of a "trade" in souls.[46] More frequent than commercial allusions came descriptions of souls in agricultural terms. Thus Neumann and the Marquis de Villa Puente both spoke of the fruit of harvesting souls, and missionary Johann Baptist Haller (1652–1718) reminded General Juan Fernández de Retana of the rich harvest of souls at stake (*cossecha de Almas*) and of the reward which God is preparing for him.[47]

Although Jesuits could think of souls in something like economic terms, there was little doubt as to which economy, sacred and profane, was

[44] Pierre Bourdieu, *Outline of a Theory of Practice*, trans. Richard Nice (New York: Cambridge University Press, 1977): 10–15.

[45] Bernal Díaz del Castillo, *The True History of the Conquest of New Spain*, trans. Maurice Keatinge (London: John Dean, 1800), 502.

[46] Kino, "Relación puntual de la entrada del almirante Isidro de Atondo y Antillón a la grande isla de California este año de 1683, sacrada de la carta de dicho almirante [April 20, 1683] y de la del padre Eusebio Francisco Kino [April 22, 1683]," BNM AF caja 3, exp. 39, fols. 1r-6v and 7r-14r (two copies), at fol. 7r. See Alden, 528.

[47] "Certificación de los padres José Neumann, Francsico de Celada y Francisco María Pícolo," Sisoguíchic, January 4, 1693, AGI Guad. 156, fol. 1073v; Marquez de la Villa Puente, Mexico, to the P. Provincial of Japan Joseph Pires, March 20, 1724, BA/JA/49-V-28, fol. 94v; Haller, Satevó, to Gen. [Juan Fernández de Retana], December 6, 1696, AGI Guad. 156, fol. 1008v.

more essential. Expanding on his assertion that "our trade is only that of Souls," Vieira continued, "Nor have we any means of assuring our relationship with God and with the world except to remain completely disinterested in material considerations."[48] Likewise, Trigault argued that the needs of the souls were more important than the needs of the body, and knowing the true God was "the most necessary of necessities."[49] Sometimes soteriological processes had very direct effects on the Jesuits, as when souls from purgatory haunted the Society's college in Vienna.[50]

The fundamental importance of souls for the mission can be seen when Kappus gave Kino population reports in terms of numbers of "souls."[51] Similarly, in a telling metonymy, Gilg referred to "souls" being baptized, rather than "people."[52] The use of "soul" to mean person, especially in enumeration, was, and is, also common in English.[53] This was the driving force of the entire missionary network. Thus, when the Marquis de Villa Puente established a mission, he stated explicitly his goal as the "increase in souls."[54] The idea of collective salvation through the world soul had always been marginal in the western religions, though variations of it were held by, for example, the Muslim Abu Bakr Muhammad ibn Zakariya al-Razi (ca. 865–ca.923) and the Jewish Solomon ibn Gabirol (ca. 1022–ca.1058), who looked back to Plato and echoed the Christian universalism of Origen (ca. 185–ca. 254). For our orthodox early-modern Catholics, however, the individuality of the soul and resultant individuality of salvation compel the sacred economy to be quantifiable.

The first Franciscan missionaries in Mexico reported astounding numbers of baptisms. The importance of the salvation of souls appears dramatically in the astonishing numbers reported by these earliest missionaries, who tended, as William B. Taylor has pointed out, to save souls in large, round numbers. Martín de Valencia estimated more than a million

---

[48] Alden, 528.
[49] RAH Jesuitas 91, no. 28, fol. 6r.
[50] "Relaçam do que suçedeo a hum Irmão da Companhia de JESUS com trez almas do Purgatorio no Collegio de Viena de Austria Corte do Serenissmio Emperador no mez de Janeyro de 1634," BA/JA/49-V-10, fl. 355v–362.
[51] Kappus, "Padrón del partido de Cucurpe, enviado al P. Rect. Eusebio Francisco Kino," Cucurpe, November 25, 1690, AHH México, leg. 279 exp. 19, fol. 1r.
[52] Gilg, "Padrón de la misión de Nuestra Señora del Pópulo, enviado al P. Rect. Eusebio Francisco Kino," Pópulo, December 10[?], AHH México, leg. 279 exp. 22.
[53] Myles Coverdale's 1535 translation of Leviticus 11:46 speaks of "All maner of soules yᵗ crepe vpon earth," and in *The Political Anatomy of Ireland* (1691) William Petty writes, "The number of British slain in 11 years was 112 thousand Souls." Both quoted in "soul," *Oxford English Dictionary* Online, Second Edition (1989), www.oed.com (accessed August 12, 2006).
[54] "Transsumptum Contractus initi de fundatione a D Marchione de Villapuente," Mexico, February 15, 1707, ARSI FG 722/17.

baptisms by Franciscans by 1531, and Motolinía reckoned almost 5 million by 1536. Friars were said to baptize fifteen hundred converts daily, and Motolinía reported that a priest in Xochimilco baptized more than 10,000 Indians in a single day. Outdoing this, Pedro de Gante claimed to baptize converts in Mexico City at a daily rate of 14,000, which, excluding breaks, works out to 6.2 seconds per baptism.[55]

The Jesuits' smaller tallies suggest a change in standards rather than a lesser concern for saving souls. Neumann gave baptismal numbers that were far more modest.[56] Kino claimed to have baptized 4,500 Indians during his lifetime. Still, missionaries could take pride in how many baptisms *would* have taken place, if the recipients had had the proper instruction.[57]

The importance of a group of souls could also be stressed by pointing out their dire straits. Trigault described "so many souls that perish without remedy in those remote Chinese kingdoms." The unbelievers' souls were flowing into hell, and needed to be saved from the eternal flame. The souls at stake would populate the chairs of heaven, and remove the sceptre from the hand of the tyranny of Satan.[58] Because of this importance, the worst criticism that could be levelled against something was that it endangered souls. Haller put the loss of souls as the major consequence of Indian rebellion.[59] Baptista explained that division and controversy in the church was horrific because it would speed souls to hell.[60] Even recent converts took up this argument. One record of a heated argument between lay Chinese Catholics and Castorano shows the former repeatedly stressing the number of souls at stake in China. Because of this great number the issues debated were important; because of this great number, the lay Chinese maintained, Castorano was all the more culpable for his wrong views.[61]

Often the Jesuits used numbers of souls to justify the expenses of missionary expeditions, as when Kino writes, "For the Spanish crown the cost

---

[55] Boxer, *Spanish Seaborne*, 162–63; idem, *Church Militant*, 113; Motolinía, 164.

[56] Neumann, Sisoguíchic, to Gen. Juan Fernández de Retana, January 4, 1692, AGI Patronato 236, R.1 (2), fol. 681r.

[57] Kino, Dolores, to the P. Visit. Horacio Pólici [for Cap. Cristóbal Martín Bernal, P. Eusebio Francisco Kino, Francisco de Acuña, Juan de Escalante y Francisco Javier de Barcelón], December 3, 1692, AGN Mis., 26, fol. 325v.

[58] RAH Jesuitas 91, no. 28, fol. 1v, 2r, 9v.

[59] Haller, Satevó, to Gen. [Juan Fernández de Retana], December 6, 1696, AGI Guad. 156, fol. 1008v.

[60] Juan Baptisto de Morales, China, [to Ignoli], November[?] 25, 1650, APF SOCG 193, fol. 358v.

[61] 及千百萬人靈魂之重大。乃出不知道。["A billion souls are a significant number, yet where they go I do not know."] 京都總會長王伯多錄等十八人致外省各堂會長書,告康熙五十五年九月諸人與山東臨清堂代主教康神父談禮儀問題事. ARSI JapSin I, 205, fol. 23.

of all these deeds would be very limited, and in the course of time more than 30,000 souls could be won for Christ."[62] Sometimes the quantification was implicit, as when a missionary made comparisons between the numbers of souls at stake in different situations. In other cases this was an implicit comparison between regions, as when high numbers of converts were foreseen in China.[63] Trigault pointed out that more souls were to be saved inside China than had already been saved everywhere else, and at the same time he stressed the relative scarcity of priests.[64] Another typical use of quantities was in estimates of the number of souls that would be saved, provided a patron would offer a certain level of financial support. Kino insisted that "even many more could have been baptized, if sufficient Jesuits were available."[65] The best way to stress large quantities was to describe a batch of souls as unquantifiable, "infinite souls," or souls "without number."[66]

The Jesuits did not hesitate to quantify souls, and mathematics and religion coexisted harmoniously in the missionary mind. On the occasion of a companion's final profession of faith, Kino gifted him with mathematical instruments, "symbols ... of religious excellence."[67] The vogue for counting souls can be understood in the context of the early-modern vogue for counting more generally. The word "pantometry," meaning the indiscriminate measuring of things, first appeared in English dictionaries in the seventeenth-century.[68] Kino and his companions passed time on ships through measurement as well as missionizing. Sometimes, when Kino assisted in taking latitudes, this measurement contributed to the success of the voyage, but other calculations, such as the height of the mast, are better explained as mathematical recreation.[69] The most prized possession of the missionary Antonio Leal was the clock he used to measure time. Frustrated with the failure of the repairmen in Mexico City to fix it, he bemoaned his loss to the procurator, explaining how much he missed his clock's ticks and tocks, which reassured him on still, lonely nights that time continued to flow. Baegert broke the monotony of California mission life by counting needles on the cholla cactuses (each had a million, he concluded), as well as the number of scorpions he had

[62] Kino, *Crónica*, 88.
[63] Claudius Philippis Grimaldo, Goa, to Jakob Willi, Munich, May 12, 1693, BStB CLM 26472, fol. 122v.
[64] RAH Jesuitas 91, no. 28, fol. 5v.
[65] Kino, *Crónica*, 89.
[66] RAH Jesuitas 91, no. 28, fol. 6v.
[67] Kino, Diary of Travel from Genoa to Sevilla, June 12 to July 27, 1678, BHStA Jes. 607/125.
[68] Patricia Cline Cohen, *A Calculating People* (Chicago: University of Chicago Press, 1982), 16.
[69] Bolton, *Rim*, 48–49.

killed – breaking the five-hundred mark within thirteen years.[70] While cruising on a Chinese river Schreck used his own clock to count boats going in the opposite direction: 129 (from noon to 1 P.M.) and 148 (from 5 to 6 P.M.).[71] These missionaries were eager participants in this new vogue or mania for counting, and they naturally measured what mattered most.

The Jesuits' enthusiasm for quantification thus led them to emphasize numbers of souls. This was not always the case among missionaries. In Franciscan theory, if not in practice, concrete results – numbers of conversions – were less important than one's own adherence to the evangelizing life, though they, too, counted souls.[72] A starker study in contrasts would be the perceived decline of New England Puritanism during the 1650s and 1660s, suggested in sermons asserting that subsequent generations were failing to match the piety of the founders. In fact, these two decades saw an increase in church membership.[73] Despite historians' earlier suppositions, the Puritans must therefore have measured religion qualitatively, in terms of how central it was in their lives, rather than taking the Catholic and Jesuit quantitative approach. Certainly the difference between the Puritan and Jesuit mission was key, but theology also explains the dissimilarity. In keeping with Calvinist predestination, God had already fixed the number of the elect, and the Puritans saw no point in second-guessing Him by keeping an independent census of souls.[74]

The occasional violence of conflict between Protestants and Catholics leads one to expect the greatest missiological differences to arise between these two groups. Yet even the Jesuits, the so-called "shock troops" of the Counter Reformation, worked hard to bridge the intervening gap. When Laínez requested advice for dealing with Protestants, Favre demanded empathy: "If we want to help the heretics of this age we must be careful to regard them with love, to love them in truth and to banish from our heart any thought that might lessen our respect for them.... We must share what unites us, then what gives rise to conflicting views."[75] "What unites us," in the view of Favre and the early Jesuits, was the spiritual pallor and amorality of all Christians, and most importantly

---

[70] Hausberger, *Jesuiten*, 58, 70; Bolton, *Rim*, 412.

[71] Schreck, Hangzhou[?], to Jakob Koller, Munich[?], August 30, 1621, Ms. Monacense 4169–71, fol. 34–5 (extract), published in Walravens, 28–29.

[72] Michel Villey, *La croisade: essai sur la formation d'une théorie juridique*, L'Eglise et l'etat au moyen age 6 (Paris: J. Vrin, 1942), 249.

[73] Robert Pope, *The Half-Way Covenant: Church Membership in Puritan New England* (Princeton: Princeton University Press, 1969).

[74] Cohen, *Calculating*, 79.

[75] Petrus Faber, *Beatri Petri Fabri, epistolae, memoriale et processus: ex autographis aut archetypis potissimum deprompta*, Monumenta historica Societatis Iesu 48 (Rome: Institutum Historicum Societatis Iesu, 1972), 400, sections 1, 2.

of the clergy. Doctrinal error, which separated the Catholics from the heretics, remained secondary to spiritual problems common to both confessions and remained dangerous in so far as it justified the decay of the correct spiritual attitude, the *affectus*.[76] Even for Ignatius, doctrinal aberrations followed from these same "affective and attitudinal" aberrations. The founder of the Society named only one error – the refusal to acknowledge papal authority. A Girolamo Savonarola alarmed Ignatius as much as a Philipp Melanchthon.[77]

The recognition of this essential unity between Protestant and Catholic souls survived the transition from theory into practice. Ignatius advised the Jesuits preaching on the outskirts of Trent during the Council meetings to "be slow and amiable of speech" and in the pulpit to "make no reference to the differences between Protestants and Catholics."[78] Favre was even less of an anti-Protestant crusader. That Jesuit complained, "It hurts me that the earthly Powers have no other activity, no other concern, no other thought, than to extirpate notorious Lutherans." Instead Favre urged returning to a golden age of Christianity, so that he could love the Protestants "all with real love" while "shutting out from his mind all that [could] cool his respect for them."[79] On Pentecost, 1558, the Jesuit Johann Victoria initiated a series of "excursions," or "expeditions," to the countryside around Prague, a mission to Catholics and utraquists and Lutherans alike. (The mission nearly came to premature and deadly failure when the villagers, who had never seen a Jesuit before, mistook them to be Jews in search of converts.)[80] In the next century, in areas of Germany where Protestants and Catholics could legally co-reside, Jesuit schools saw and encouraged the enrolment of sons of Protestants attracted to the quality of the offered education. Once enrolled, Protestant sons and Jesuit novices would receive their instruction together.[81] Some of the former would take up key roles in the Counter

---

[76] Ibid., 402, sec. 8. See Joseph E. Vercruysse, "Jesuit Contribution to Church Unity: A Historical Overview," *CIS: News, Documentation, Abstracts, Bibliography* 20 (1989): 19.

[77] O'Malley, *Fourth Vow*, 11, 17, 21.

[78] Lacouture, 80.

[79] Pierre Favre, *Bienheureux Pierre Favre: Mémorial*, trans. Michel de Certeau (Lyon: E. Vitte, [1960]), 67.

[80] A. Kroess, *Geschichte der böhmischen Provinz der Gesellschaft Jesu* (Vienna: Nachfolger, 1910–27), I.227–8.

[81] N. S. Davidson, *The Counter-Reformation* (Oxford: Basil Blackwell, 1987), 54–5. The same occurred in Poland. See Marvin R. O'Connell, *The Counter-Reformation 1559–1610*, The Rise of Modern Europe 4 (New York: Harper & Row, 1974), 214. For a look at *convivencia* – and its limits – throughout Europe, see Thomas A. Brady, Jr., "Limits of Religious Violence in Early Modern Europe," in *Religion und Gewalt: Konflikte, Rituale, Deutungen (1500–1800)*, ed. Kaspar von Greyerz and Kim Siebenhüner (Göttingen: Vandenhoeck & Ruprecht, 2006), 125–151, especially at 134–5, 138.

Reformation, even as missionaries. Andreas Xavier Koffler was the son of a convert from Lutheranism, and Joachim Calmes himself converted to Catholicism after arriving in Lisbon as a merchant.[82] Favre's subordination of doctrine to *affectus* had its practical side in the Jesuits' principle of *iuvare animas* "helping souls," to provide spiritual assistance regardless of status as Protestant or Catholic. When the spiritual state of Christianity had been improved, they thought, the Protestants' doctrinal aberrations would readily evaporate.[83]

If the missions to Catholics and Protestants share an essential unity, can this unity be extended to the pagan souls? In fact, soteriological imperatives bulldozed through any cultural differences that might have reinforced the distinction between European Catholics and extra-European pagans. Trigault even understood the success of mission among pagans as key to success with the heretics, and with the Turks and the Jews.[84] Two tropes in early-modern Catholic thought make this essential unity clear.

First, the notion that the Catholic Church was compensated for the lost Protestant souls with the newly won souls of newly discovered peoples became a commonplace in the sixteenth century.[85] After reading Francis Xavier's letters of 1545, the Dutch Jesuit Jacobus Lhoost felt gratified that the firm faith of the natives of India recompensed the church for the losses suffered at the hands of Luther and Melanchthon.[86] Gregory XIII's address to Jesuits in 1581 marvelled that the Society that directs "kingdoms, provinces, indeed the whole world . . . came into the world at the very moment when new errors began to be spread abroad."[87] This sentiment of reciprocal correspondence between pagan and Protestant went beyond rhetoric. The Duchess of Aveiro swore an oath to found one church in the overseas missions for every church Elizabeth of England had razed. Even Protestant critics would adapt this idea. Deriding the Jesuits' "Pranckes in Asia," Samuel Purchas wrote of missionaries busily "seeking to repair, with their untempered Mortar, the ruins of their Falling Babylon [at home] and there laying a new foundation of their after-hopes, [finding it] easier to conquer naked Americans and effeminate Indians, than in keeping what they had in Europe."[88]

[82] Pfister, 265, 397; Huonder, *Deutsche Jesuitenmissionäre*, 185. See also Carl Platzweg, *Lebensbilder deutscher Jesuiten in auswärtigen Missionen* (Paderborn: Funtermann'schen, 1882), 43.
[83] Vercruysse, 19–20.
[84] RAH, Jesuitas 91, no. 28, fol. 4v.
[85] Knipping, I.366.
[86] Francis Xavier, 266–67.
[87] Bangert, 97.
[88] Anthony Thomas, Macao, to the Duchess, February 2, 1683, in Sonkeikaku Library, eds., I.164; Cummins, *Question*, 56.

This notion extended beyond the Society of Jesus. In 1546, Marco Laurei gave a sermon at Trent in which he exhorted those "who seem to praise the church in the antipodes, do not let it be wiped out in Europe itself."[89] The Franciscan Gerónimo de Mendieta also recognized this compensation in the Americas, "as if the new World had been called into existence to redress the spiritual balance of the old." Moreover, Mendieta pointed out, incorrectly, that the births of Luther and of Cortés occurred in the same year, as did Cortés's conquest of Mexico and the Leipzig disputation between Luther and Johann Eck. Such specific references to chronological coincidence gave credence to this notion of compensation.[90] Other religious considered Martin Luther and Martín de Valencia as compensating opposites, for the first Martin broke from the Catholic Church the same year the second Martín decided to travel to the Indies.[91] Campanella paired Luther with Columbus and wrote of them together waking the philosophers and theologians from an ignorant and neglectful slumber.[92] Not only were the gains and losses roughly equivalent, but a commonality was also perceived, and their commonality as worthy objects of conversion bridged the cultural differences separating most Protestants from most non-Christians.

The second trope that softened the division between Christian and pagan souls was the idea of an Indies in Europe. It was not the presence of Protestants alone that encouraged Jesuits to consider Europe "another Indies" ("otras Indias").[93] In reply to Philipp Jeningen's letter of November 21, 1687, which requested a missionary posting overseas, General González kindly told the hopeful Jesuit that he had already found his Indies, in Ellwangen.[94] Nadal and Rehm both also made clear the value of German Jesuits staying in their own "Indies."[95] Other "Indies"

---

[89] *Concilium Tridentinum: Diariorum, Actorum, Epistularum, Tractatuum nova collectio* (Freiburg i. Br.: Herder, 1950–2001), V (Act. II) 253 of "Oratio habita in quinta sessione sacri concilii Tridentini per s. theol. magistrum Marcum Laureum Tropeensem ord. Praed" [II.247–530].

[90] Gerónimo de Mendieta, *Historia eclesiástica indiana* (México: Antigua librería [Impr. por F. Diaz de Leon y S. White], 1870), II.12, 13 [174–75]; Torquemada, I.340; Phelan, 32; Brading, 116; Specker, 88; Lach and Van Kley, *Asia*, II.ii.348.

[91] Diego Valades, *Rhetorica christiana: ad concionandi et orandi vsvm accommodata, vtrivsq facvltatis exemplis svo loco insertis* (Perugia: Petrumiacobum Petrutium, 1579), 223.

[92] Tomasso Campanella, *Monarchia Messiae*, ed. Luigi Firpo (Turin: Bottega d'Erasmo, 1960), 87; idem, *Teologia*, ed. Romano Amerio (Milano: Società editrice "Vita e pensiero," 1936–80), XXVII.90, 92.

[93] Adriano Prosperi, "Catholic Reformation," trans. Robert E. Shillenn, *The Oxford Encyclopedia of the Reformation*, ed. Hans J. Hillerbrand (New York: Oxford University Press, 1996), 293.

[94] Hoffmann, "Philipp," 359.

[95] Alphonsus Salmeron, Rome, to Canisius, January 3, 1562, in Braunsberger, ed., III.351–52.

had previously appeared all over the peripheries of Catholic Europe. For Italy, Nadal could speak of an "Indie di Abruzzo," and the Jesuit Michele Navarro could describe his mission in northeastern Sicily as "queste nostre Indie."[96] In 1561 the Jesuits in the college at Monterrey in Galicia reported to Rome that they "have here another Indies."[97] The Polish Jesuit Piotr Skarga (1536–1612) wrote of an Indies in Lithuania.[98] France also had her "Indes de l'intérieur," and the Jesuit Julien Maunoir described his mission field, Ouessant Island off the coast of Brittany, as being so remote from Christianity and all civilization as to be positively "Canadian."[99]

This recognition received confirmation at the Curial level with the founding of the Congregation for the Propagation of the Faith in 1622. The congregation's first thirteen cardinals received from the pope the assignment of "each and every affair pertinent to the propagation of the faith throughout the whole world." Their responsibility thus encompassed not merely the souls of the non-Christians, but also those of the non-Catholics. All areas without an established Episcopal hierarchy, Protestant and pagan, fell under Propaganda's jurisdiction. Strikingly, Propaganda would retain jurisdiction over Protestant England until 1908.[100]

As final evidence suggestive of the unity of vocation for missionaries working with both Christians and pagans, we turn to the transoceanic journeys of the Jesuits dispatched overseas. On Ratkay's Atlantic crossing, every morning, after the captain had relieved the night watch, the drummers had pounded out reveille, and the sailors had set the sails, the missionaries would celebrate mass or a morning service. Everyone on board attended the ceremony. At day's end the chanted Salve Regina and Laurentian litany serenaded the setting sun.[101] Similarly, Trigault took over these duties after the *Nossa Senhora de Jesus*'s chaplain died. On Sundays and feast days the festival office was sung on the back deck.[102] Every morning the chaplain's duties included a "dry Mass," without the

[96] Nadal to the rector of the college of Teramo, November 23, 1571, in Pietro Tacchi-Venturi, *Storia della Compagnia di Gesù in Italia* (Rome: Civiltà cattolica, 1930–1951), I.i.324, note 3, quoted in Carla Faralli, "Le missioni dei Gesuiti in Italia," *Bolletino della Società di Studi Valdesi* 138 (1975): 100; Tacchi-Venturi I.i.325–26 and II.92–95, quoted in Faralli, 100.
[97] ARSI Hisp. 98, fol. 183, quoted in Broggio, 59.
[98] David Frick, personal communication.
[99] Deslandres, "Mission et altérité," 1; Louis Châtellier, *The Religion of the Poor: Rural Missions in Europe and the Formation of Modern Catholicism, c. 1500-c.1800*, trans. Brian Pearce (Cambridge: Cambridge University Press, 1997), 35–36; R. Hoffmann, 903.
[100] Jedin, "Weltmission," 397, 401.
[101] WB Nr. 28.
[102] Väth, 40–41.

consecration of bread and wine. A chaplain's most critical obligation was to recite litanies of the Blessed Virgin and the Rosary during storms.[103] As Willa Cather once wrote, sailors "lived too near the next world not to wish to stand well with it," and Jesuits responded to this situation.[104] Mancker reported on board his ship a full-blooded "public mission" ("öffentliche Mission") consisting of frequent sermons, prayers, and confessions.[105] Gilg wrote of an eight-day "mission" on his journey.[106] Nor were these "transition" missions merely nautical, for Diestel and Grueber were told to look en route to China for mission opportunities among the nations through which they travelled.[107] Thus missionaries, their hearts set on non-Christian souls, eagerly took advantage of the opportunity to shore up the faith of their fellow passengers and the rough but Catholic crew.

All this is not to say that an early-modern Catholic could not distinguish between an Indian, a Huguenot, and an "unreformed" Catholic prostitute. The division certainly appeared in contemporary literature. Nadal could write of Jesuits going "to the Indies among the unbelievers, to Germany among the heretics, to Prester John and to Egypt among the schismatics."[108] The division had practical consequences as well. The Jesuits in Goa, for example, were divided between those who convert unbelievers and those who maintain them in the faith.[109]

These distinctions were never so great as to justify the historiographical walls that have calcified around them. Often the political situation was more relevant than the religious orientation of the targets. The clandestine Catholicism the Norwegian Jesuit Laurentius Norvegus (1539–1622) encouraged at a Protestant seminary in Sweden was not dissimilar to Ricci's position in Beijing. Debates over whether to allow the Bavarian and Bohemian laity to receive communion in both kinds echoed those of the Chinese rites controversy.

A recruiting circular attempted to rebut the argument that one could be a missionary just as well in Spain as in America by saying that the doctor should first go to those who need his assistance most – clearly indicative of a continuity of vocation between evangelizing the Indians

[103] Caterino, 77; Cummins, *Question*, 170.
[104] Willa Cather, *Shadows on the Rock* (New York: Knopf, 1980), 209.
[105] WB Nr. 30.
[106] WB Nr. 33.
[107] Wessels, "New Documents," 283, 290.
[108] Hieronymus Nadal, "Exhortationes Complutense," 1561, in *Epistolae et Monumenta*, V.443.
[109] Amrhyn, Coimbra, to Jacob Rassler, rector at Ingolstadt, October 23, 1672, MZA 17, 293/94.

and maintaining the Spanish in their religion.[110] Rather than partition-
ing the missionary targets into three discrete groups, a model truer to
the missionaries' understanding would take the form of a continuum,
upon which Catholics, Protestants, and pagans are placed according to
the development of their faith. According to Paul III's 1537 bull *Altitudo
divini consilii*, once an Indian was baptized and had demonstrated a basic
understanding and a satisfactory piety, he could participate in communion.[111] The appropriate distinction derives from the two-step process
of conversion. First, baptism brought the convert (or newborn Catholic)
into the church. Second, his or her faith was developed further and made
conscious and deliberate. We see here echoes of the medieval distinction
between formed and unformed faith. First, one's belief in the church suffices at a certain level (quantitative aspects of conversion), but then one's
piety continues to deepen (qualitative aspects of conversion).

This continuum also describes how conversion efforts played out in
practice. For example, in 1522 the first Catholic bishop of Goa provided the clearest articulation of this understanding of a spectrum ranging from non-Christians, through "bad" Christians, up to "good" Christians. Arguing for the expulsion from Portuguese territory of anyone who
refused to profess Christianity, the bishop admitted that baptism under
these circumstances would yield only nominal Christians, not "good"
ones. "Yet," he continued wryly, "their children will become so." Subsequent history conformed to his prediction.[112]

The overriding goal of the Society, and of all early-modern Catholicism,
was the care of souls, *auxilium animarum*, or as one motto puts it, "the
salvation of souls is the supreme law" (*salus animarum suprema lex*).[113]
The Jesuit Johannes Dirckinck, in his 1708 booklet for missionaries in
the Rhineland describes the goal of the mission as "untiring zeal for the
salvation and perfection of itself and others, and especially the help of
so many souls who through ignorance of things necessary for salvation,
in the state of sin, as they abide in the danger of eternal damnation," a

---

[110] Cádiz, April 10, 1785, Cesareo de Armellada, *Por la Venezuela indigena de ayer y de hoy:
Relatos de misioneros capuchinos en viaje por la Venezuela indigena*, Sociedad de Ciencias
Naturales La Salle, Monografias, no. 5 (Caracas: Sociedad de Ciencias Naturales La
Salle, 1960), 29–36.

[111] Perry, *Spanish Seaborne Empire*, 163.

[112] Boxer, *Portuguese Seaborne*, 72.

[113] Scaduto, 323–90; J. O'Malley, *Trent and All That: Renaming Catholicism in the
Early Modern Era* (Harvard: Harvard University Press, 2000), 52. See *Codex
Iuris Canonici*, canon 1752 ("In causis translationis applicentur praescripta cano-
nis 1747, servata aequitate canonica et prae oculis habita salute animarum,
quae in Ecclesia suprema semper lex esse debet") IntraText Digital Library
http://www.intratext.com/IXT/LAT0010/_P6Z.HTM (accessed May 8, 2006).

locution he borrowed from General Aquaviva.[114] For many early-modern Catholics the soul commanded paramount importance. The proposal for a Propaganda-like congregation in Tomás de Jesús's *De procuranda salute omnium gentium* [*On Attending to the Salvation of All Peoples*] (1613) makes clear that "the saving of a single soul is more important than acquiring all the kingdoms of this earth."[115] Ignatius succeeded in reviving *Cum infirmitas*, canon twenty-two of the Constitution of the Fourth Lateran Council (1215), which declared that no doctor might treat a patient who refused to confess to a priest.[116] This canon had slowly fallen into disuse and had become widely ignored, but for Ignatius the health of the body was insignificant compared to that of the soul. For this same reason, Jesuit missionary Wenzel Eymer (1661–1709) carefully noted that condemned Tarahumara rebels were executed as good Christians.[117]

This widespread salvific urgency often made appearances in unexpected places. In a discussion of the conceptual approach the early Jesuits took to furnishing churches, the art historian Chipps Smith describes the beginning: "First, a central thesis or theme is determined, one that is in keeping with the Society's mission to propagate faith and aid 'the progress of souls in Christian life and doctrine.'"[118] Attempting to block a movement in the 1556 Diet of the Bavarian *Landschaft* (estates) to introduce communion in both kinds, Duke Albert V pointed out the danger this move would do to the souls of the members of the estates.[119] Ignatius made the ultimate purpose of the Jesuits' celebrated "modern" schools explicit in his "Regulations for the Rector of the Roman College" (1551), for the "rector's chief care should be to promote the study of literature for no other ends but the glory of God and the assistance of souls."[120] Political circumstances may well have given birth to the Catholic League, yet its members' eyes constantly drifted from the field of battle toward

---

[114] "Instructio pro pp. missionariis Societatis Jesu Provincae Rheni inferioris," BS & B CLM 26472, fol. 285 (at p. 3–4). See also Prosperi, "L'Europa cristiana," 214.

[115] John Patrick Donnelley, "Antonio Possevino's Plan for World Evangelization," *Catholic Historical Review* 74.2 (1988): 182. The proposal is at Thomas á Jesu, *De procuranda salute omnium gentium* (Rome: Collegio Internazionale S. Teresa, 1940) Book III, 165–84.

[116] Ignatius, *Monumenta*, I.261 (June 24, 1543 to Cardinal Marcello Cervino, Rome) and 286 (early 1544, "Sociis in Hispania versantibus," Rome); José García Madariaga, "¿Entra la materia doctrinal como objectivo proprio del 4° Voto (y II)?" *Manresa* 53 (1981): 236; Pietro Tacchi-Venturi, II.ii.190–95; O'Malley, *Fourth*, 5.

[117] "Sentencia," Matáchic, April 28, 1687, AGI Guad. 156 fol. 180r-181v, at fol. 181r.

[118] Jeffrey Chipps Smith, "The Art of Salvation in Bavaria," in *The Jesuits: Cultures, Sciences, and the Arts, 1540–1773*, ed. John W. O'Malley, Gauvin Alexander Bailey, Steven J. Harris, and T. Frank Kennedy (Toronto: University of Toronto Press, 1999), 574.

[119] Carsten, 375.

[120] Mullett, 95.

the heavens, and Schreck regarded the League's purpose as primarily the spread of the Catholic faith.[121] Often the underlying soteriological motivation remains implicit. Michael Mullett refers to Jesuits work on Italy's "appalling social problems" in contrast to their foreign missionary work, but the refuges for orphans and ex-prostitutes were also the means to rescue their souls.[122] The soteriological urgency of these missions prevents neat distinctions between mission work and social work.

The next, concluding chapter of this book explores how the global Jesuit mission impacts not just studies of the missions, but has the potential to reconfigure historians' understandings of early-modern Catholicism in the context of globalization.

[121] Schreck, Suzhou in Xiading, to Johannes Faber, April 22, 1622, published in Walravens, 30.
[122] Mullett, 88.

11   An Edifying End: Global Salvific Catholicism

"Both had an edifying end, dying on the high seas before arriving at Goa."

– Eusebius Kino, on Amrhyn and Aigenler[1]

Kino's obituary for his colleagues characterized their deaths as "edifying" because they departed this life only after leaving Europe to work as missionaries in Asia. A modern observer unsympathetic to their prose-lytizing mission might recognize these deaths as appalling ends to mis-guided lives, while even a modern Catholic might regard them as tragic failures that aborted worthy missionary work before it began. Why did Kino cast them in such a positive light? This study's findings have sug-gested an answer. Contracting the plague while ministering to its victims, Beatus Amrhyn and Adam Aigenler died as missionaries, and indeed as missionaries who would be working far from home. As we have seen, in the early-modern Jesuit understanding both these factors could have pos-itive and crucial soteriological consequences. Ultimately their missions were at least partially successful in that they worked toward the salva-tion of their own souls. What wider consequences does the attitude and behaviour of these Jesuit missionaries have for the Catholicism of that time? Although the Protestant Reformation achieved early a remarkable stability as a historical concept, historians have never achieved a similar consensus about what has been called the Catholic Reformation, Catholic Renewal, Catholic Renaissance, and Catholic Refashioning. Within the last fifty years historians have suggested three major approaches: the pair of Counter Reformation and Catholic Reform, Confessionalization, and Early Modern Catholicism. This concluding chapter uses the Jesuits' global mission as a lens to reexamine each of these three ways of under-standing this entire phenomenon.

---

[1] Burrus, ed., *Kino escribe*, 113.

Counter Reformation and Catholic Reform:
The Unity of Mission

Johann Stephan Pütter first used the term "Counter Reformations" (*Gegenreformationen*) in 1776, to indicate Catholics' specific efforts to retake a given locale from the Protestants.[2] Its most influential formulation came from Hubert Jedin, who broadened the concept's scope by making it a unified development and reversed its sense by recasting it as a defensive movement. For Jedin, the Counter Reformation was the entire Catholic Church's defence against Protestant attack. Jedin also elevated to a similar standing the concept of Catholic Reform, which he explained as those impulses toward church reform that began in the late medieval period and continued into the eighteenth century. Although Jedin understood these two phenomena, Counter Reformation and Catholic Reform, to be sometimes separate and sometimes united, he argued that this period of church history was best understood by combining the two into one designation: "Catholic-Reform-and-Counter-Reformation."[3]

This project could not have been completed in terms of Jedin's concept, which would artificially divide the missions by seeing those in German lands as a crucial part of the Counter Reformation while locating the Mexico and China missions within Catholic Reform. The last chapters of this study, however, illustrate how closely the German missions were linked to the missions in the Indies. The fundamental institutional unity of the missions makes Jedin's conceptual distinction seem artificial.

A weightier argument against it arises from considering the historiographical tradition of the missions themselves. Historians have divided the missions into three different categories, based on the religious identity of the targeted peoples. Students of missions as such look to the attempted conversions of non-Christians, usually outside of Europe, excepting some Jews, Muslims, and the Sami of the far north. Historians of the "Counter Reformation" consider church efforts to win Protestants over to Rome. In turn, those tracing "Catholic Reform" or "Catholic piety" look at efforts to bolster the faith of Catholics.[4] Historians tend not to work in

---

[2] See Albert Elkan, "Entstehung und Entwicklung des Begriffs 'Gegenreformation,'" *Historische Zeitschrift* 112 (1914): 475.

[3] Hubert Jedin, "Ein Vorschalg für die Amerika-mission aus dem Jahre 1513," *Neue Zeitschrift für Missionswissenschaft* 2 (1946): 81–4.

[4] The missions to Catholics have enjoyed little conceptual continuity, and have appeared under a variety of names: popular missions, *Volksmissionen*, home missions, *missions à l'intérieur*, and parish or parochial missions – along with several modern terms occasionally applied anachronistically (area mission, *Gebietsmission*, and *Mission Général*). The reason for this scattered conceptualization most likely derives from these missions' lack of organization. Many missions to Protestants also laboured under a freedom from organization and direction. The work of Norvegus, for example, appears to be self-initiated and

more than one of these fields. In part, the division stems from, and fuels, varied thematic emphases. The historiography of non-Christian missions focuses on cultural – rarely exclusively religious – "negotiation" coloured by relations of power. That of the Counter Reformation has adopted a more political and, decreasingly, legal approach, proceeding from the formula of *cuius regio, eius religio* ("whoever's region, *his* religion"). To locate the currents of the Catholic reform one typically dives deeper, into the waters of a more socially and culturally oriented history. This trifurcated historiography does indeed reflect different missionary environments, and excellent history has been written in each area, with the extra-European missions recently receiving the most attention.[5]

By emphasizing the missionaries over the potential converts, and by focusing on the process of salvation at the core of the attendant power plays and cultural negotiation, we restore the essential unity of these seemingly disparate missions. This final chapter argues that this unity reflects a historical reality, for contemporaries could and did appreciate the ultimate similarity among a pagan, a Lutheran, and a straying Catholic. In the following section I show how this understanding suggests a new interpretation of the Catholic Reformation, an interpretation appealing in its coherence and unfaltering in its loyalty to the understanding of its participants.

A handful of historians have already recognized this unity, which is most comprehensively described for the Spanish-world case by Paolo Broggio.[6] In his discussion of the early Jesuits, John O'Malley hails the "vineyard of the Lord" as the most "pervasive metaphor for where their 'missions' were exercised." This suggests, he continues, an ecclesiology that is pastoral and outgoing, and one remarkable in its "*fuzzy lines of demarcation*, for surely included in the 'vineyard' were infidels, heretics, schismatics and pagans – for it was often to these people that the Jesuits were sent."[7] Dominique Deslandres probes the cause of the French missionaries' "equally dim view of lukewarm Catholics, ignorant

---

self-directed. Contemporary French missiology opposes two terms, *pastorat* (internal) and *mission* (or the *apostolat*, to non-believers). After World War II the French religious leaders realized how unchristian their co-nationals had become and the absurdity of sending missionaries overseas. The meaning of "mission," as well as its priorities, became internal to France. See R. Hoffmann, 10.

[5] Châtellier discusses the greater attention extra-European missions have received. Richard gives no explanation for his exclusion of the orthodox Christians from "*la mission proprement dire*," nor does the evidence demand one. Châtellier, xi–xii, 1; Jean Richard, *La Papauté et les missions d'Orient au Moyen Age (XIIIe–XVe siècles)*, Collection de l'École française de Rome 33 (Rome: École française de Rome, 1977), 4.

[6] See Broggio, especially at 33 and 48–9.

[7] O'Malley, "Mission," 9. O'Malley's italics.

peasants, French heretics, pagans from the Middle East and the East Indies, Turks, and the 'Savages' of Canada": "For them, the apostolic mission of winning souls to God . . . was the same throughout the world, since satanic sovereignty was equally menacing everywhere. The nature of the enterprise was the same because, in the missionaries' view, the fundamental nature of the people they sought to convert was the same, despite their apparent diversity." All peoples had souls in need of salvation.[8]

The division between Counter Reformation and Catholic Reform is ill equipped to take account of either this continuum of religious identity or the unified mission operations suggested by this study. Indeed, it may well be advantageous for each term to resume an earlier meaning. Rather than describing one half of this entire phenomenon, "Counter Reformation" would gain new life by taking back its old meaning of specific and institutional movements against Protestantism, as, for example, the Jesuits' repossession of former religious houses won back from the Protestants. In contrast "Catholic Reform" could expand its scope and take centre stage by understanding "reform" in its early medieval sense, as the conversion and self-reformation of an individual. Only since the eleventh century was "reform" clearly applied to the church as a corporate body – which would become the primary sense of the word.[9] A Catholic Reform centred on personal conversion, and extended to encompass institutional mechanisms for its realization, more truly reflects the Catholicism of the early-modern Jesuits.

Confessionalization: Jesuits between Modernity and the Devil

A second approach to this phenomenon recognized the essential similarities between the Protestant Reformation and its Catholic counterpart. In 1958 Ernst Walter Zeeden introduced the concept of *Konfessionsbildung*, the creation of confessions, to describe the institutional formation of stable churches. More recently the idea of confessionalization (*Konfessionalisierung*), formulated by Heinz Schilling and Wolfgang Reinhard, shifted emphasis onto the social effects of these processes and gained a widespread currency.[10]

---

[8] Deslandres, "Mission et altérité," 4, 9–10.

[9] O'Malley, *Trent*, 16.

[10] For background, see Thomas A. Brady, Jr., "Confessionalization – The Career of a Concept," in *Confessionalization in Europe, 1550–1700: Essays in Honor and Memory of Bodo Nishan*, ed. John M. Headley, Hans J. Hillerbrand, and Anthony J. Papalas (Burlington, Vt.: Ashgate, 2004), 1–20.

Although the results of this project indicate an often symbiotic relationship between state and church, the picture of the Society of Jesus
presented here suggests three disjunctures with the Confessionalization
thesis – especially as outlined by Reinhard, in whose formulations the
Jesuits play the central role.

First, it questions the extent to which the Counter Reformation was
"modern" in its rationality and individualism, just like its Protestant ana-
logue.[11] Just as the late Heiko Oberman has taught us of Luther's enduring medievalness, so, too, can even Catholic partisans accept a lack of
modernity on their own side.[12] The showcase example of this alleged
modernity is the "positively revolutionary" Jesuit order. Of all the "modern" attributes Reinhard lists, I see only the "internalization of the group's
central values" and the "extremely careful training" as being potentially
innovative. (Surely medieval Benedictines internalized the Benedictine
central values, for are not Benedictine central values just those that Benedictines do internalize?) The Jesuits, no less than Luther, found themselves situated between God and the devil. A good deal of what looks
irrational from a nonreligious perspective remained, and their individualism was singularly concerned with the salvation of their own souls.

The Jesuits' other "modern" attributes are also questionable. The internalization of central values may have "concentrated on individuals in an
entirely new way," but the present study – as well as those by Thomas V.
Cohen and A. Lynn Martin – indicates that individuals met Jesuit central
values in terms of personal salvation. Reinhard takes the failure of efforts
to form a parallel female Jesuit order (which he would consider a modern-
izing "ecclesiastical emancipation of women") as evidence for the Jesuits'
modernity, for the Society would then be so modern that the church
would not have tolerated in it a modern outlook on women. He finds the
Jesuits' training innovative, but at its core remained the Spiritual Exercises, which Reinhard himself calls "anything but 'modern.'" In any case,
even if the Jesuits were so modern, does not the fierce opposition they
engendered among Catholics (Reinhard points out Gian Pietro Carafa,
Pope Paul IV) indicate how unsuited this modernity is as an attribute
of the Catholic Reformation as a whole?[13] The Jesuits' modernity lies

---

[11] Wolfgang Reinhard, "Pressure towards Confessionalization? Prolegomena to a Theory
of the Confessional Age," in *The German Reformation: The Essential Readings*, ed. C.
Scott Dixon (Oxford: Blackwell, 1999), 174.
[12] Heiko A. Oberman, *Luther: Man between God and the Devil*, trans. Eileen Walliser-
Schwarzbart (New Haven: Yale University Press, 1989).
[13] Reinhard, "Pressure," 176.

more in specific areas, such as educational method, than in their general religious sensibility.[14]

What about the "modern economic organization" of the Jesuits? Reinhard seems to link "modern" here with the ability to "deal . . . with financial transactions" and points to the papacy as "the major financial power in the Middle Ages" which "remained one of the most important borrowers." This makes financial efficiency look medieval, or at least severs the ties between it and modernity, and the ability to borrow massively seems an inadequate criterion for economic prowess. Rather, widespread debt, which certainly characterized the Jesuit missions in Asia, indicates inefficient economic management, and the confusion of the China mission's financial records betrays little clear-headed managing in the face of local and global obstacles. There is good reason to see in the Jesuits an economic modernism, for their success speaks for itself. The classic argument for this comes from H. M. Robertson, who saw probabilism as the key to "unrestrained individualism in economic affairs." The moral system of probabilism accepts a belief that is probable even if another, contradictory belief is yet more probable. For example, a merchant with a probable opinion of the injustice of a maximum commodity price could cheat his customers to recoup his losses.[15] Still, the very idea of resorting to a theological doctrine suggests a marked lack of modernity, as does the pious refusal to ship playing cards across the Pacific.[16]

In addition to modernity, Reinhard points to the use of the formulation and dissemination of dogma and confessional propaganda, training and education, discipline, ritual, and language as key to the formation of confessional identity.[17] Confessional identity, however, was not the sole attribute of an individual, and it was the most important only in certain situations. Members of all confessions could trespass confessional boundaries when the situation warranted. We have witnessed Leibniz's scientific, and missionary, aspirations as they cross confessional lines. English Protestant captains taxied Jesuits around the Far East.[18] Social status bound together individuals of differing confessions. Bishop Julius Echter von Mespelbrunn of Bamberg, a famously zealous Catholic reformer, sent a wedding gift to a former Bamberg canon and his Protestant wife. Protestant nobles implemented the Counter Reformation in the

---

[14] See Rainer A. Müller, 272–3.
[15] Hector Menteith Robertson, *Aspects of the Rise of Economic Individualism: a Criticism of Max Weber and His School* (Cambridge: Cambridge University Press, 1935), 104, 107.
[16] See Clossey, "Merchants," 46.
[17] Reinhard, "Pressure," 177–8.
[18] WB Nr. 34.

prince-bishopric of Bamberg.[19] In the late sixteenth century the magistrates of Wesel did not turn away Dutch Calvinist exiles but found another distinction more important than confession – namely, which exiles were potentially seditious and which deserved compassion.[20] Confession-crossing reached a sublime extreme in 1773, when Frederick II refused the pope's directive to suppress the Jesuits in Prussia by citing his Breslau Treaty obligations to maintain Catholicism in his domains. The Lutheran king could not resist adding that if he were Catholic the pope could release him from the responsibility to defend Catholicism and the Jesuits.[21]

Finally, this research has shown that the early-modern state's use of religion went far beyond the desire to establish a strict social control over its subjects and to consolidate its territory. Religion was no mere tool. At one turn in his wrangling with the Bavarian Estates, Duke Albert V of Bavaria allowed the nobility to expand their exercise of low justice rather than suffering lay access to the chalice in communion.[22] The long-distance financial support of global missions brings this point home, for what was the immediate use of diverting resources to the ends of the earth? Certainly the prestige value of funding distant missions enhanced the status of Catholic rulers. Then again, Duke Maximilian was not plotting to turn the Chinese into loyal Bavarian subjects, and more is at work than "the confession as a means of political demarcation."[23] This project admits the use of religion by the early-modern state toward the incorporation of the church into the state bureaucracy, but pushes it further. In fact, the Bavarian dukes could and did influence doctrinal issues, and Bavarian marriage regulations were stricter than those outlined at Trent.[24]

Were the Jesuit missionaries acting as agents of confessionalization in their intrusion "into the private lives of the people, regulating their sexual behaviour, family life, and church attendance"?[25] As Bernd Hausberger

---

[19] Richard Ninness, "Gegenreformatorische Fürstbischöfe und ihr Dilemma," paper presented at the Ninth Transatlantic Doctoral Seminar in German History, Washington, D.C., April 2003.

[20] Jesse Spohnholz, "Strangers and Neighbors: The Tactics of Toleration in the Dutch Exile Community of Wesel, 1550–1590" (Ph.D. dissertation, University of Iowa, 2004), 148–202.

[21] J. Crétineau-Joly, *Histoire religieuse, politique et littéraire de la Compagnie de Jésus* (Paris: Paul Mellier, 1844–46), V.465.

[22] Carsten, 376.

[23] Reinhard, "Pressure," 184.

[24] Carsten, 379, 389. For a nuanced discussion of religion and state building in Bavaria see Ulrike Strasser, *State of Virginity: Gender, Religion, and Politics in an Early Modern Catholic State* (Ann Arbor: University of Michigan Press, 2004).

[25] R. Po-Chia Hsia, *Social Discipline in the Reformation: Central Europe, 1550–1750* (London: Routledge, 1989), 7.

points out, the intent of the Jesuits' work in the Spanish colonies was to achieve among the Indians a comprehensive revolution in mentality, along with discipline in the Weberian sense.[26] Although the Jesuits did intrude in these ways, their objective was not to distinguish their Indian "subjects" in Mexico from Calvinists in a neighbouring territory, for there were none. If the missionaries adopted the same methods as promoters of confessionalization, but without the attributed motivation, perhaps a soteriological motivation is in fact key to confessionalization as well. Social disciplining was the salvation of souls.

Early-Modern Catholicism: The Centrality of Mission

The most recent conceptualization of these subjects is John O'Malley's "Early Modern Catholicism," which he defines as the Catholicism that happened in the early-modern period. In this sense, the "Early Modern" of "Early Modern Catholicism" refers back to the "Early Modern" of "Early Modern Europe." If this is so, then it has no inherent meaning and is as "bland and faceless" as O'Malley acknowledges.[27] More likely "Early Modern Catholicism" cannot arrive without carrying in tow the parameters of interpretation implicit in "Early Modern Europe" – itself a debatable historical category.[28] The results of this study, moreover, suggest the centrality of soteriology in early-modern Catholicism, and this could give the O'Malley concept an organizing principle.

The importance of the care of souls provides early-modern Catholicism with a unifying heart. Its artists typically – in a departure from earlier practice – crowned allegorical images of the church with the papal tiara.[29] Modern historians have followed their lead by accepting the papacy's arguments for its own importance. They have accepted the decrees of Trent as the entire movement's manifesto. Almost every study of the Catholic Reformation, under any of its aliases, has institutional history at its heart. The Catholic Church appears unified institutionally because, when compared with the Protestant churches, it was, and is, unified.

In fact, the missionary ideal was a central concern of the papacy itself. Already in the incipit of his bull *Orthodoxe fidei propagationem* (December 13, 1486) Pope Innocent VIII (1484–92) declared, "Our chief concern and commission from heaven is the propagation of the orthodox faith, the

---

[26] Hausberger, *Für Gott und König*, 26.
[27] O'Malley, *Trent*, 8–9, 140.
[28] See Randolph Starn, "The Early Modern Muddle," *Journal of Early Modern History* 6.3 (2002): 296–307. For a sensible and sensitive discussion of the implications of "early modern," see Terence Cave, "Locating the Early Modern," *Paragraph* 29 (2006): 12–26.
[29] Knipping, 351.

increase of the Christian religion, the salvation of barbarian nations, and the repression of the infidels and their conversion to the faith." Gregory XIII made explicit in a letter to Canisius that

among the cares by which We are extraordinarily troubled in this pastoral office assigned to Us by God, that has always been regarded by Us as the first and heaviest which We know to belong to this office in the highest degree and to be the object of God's chief solicitude, namely whatever appertains to the salvation of souls by the employment of all zeal and resources.[30]

This understanding was not limited to the papacy. Tomás de Jesús's *Stimulus missionum [Incentive for Mission]* (1610) announced that the "extreme spiritual necessity" of the newly found peoples was designed by God to attract papal attention to the need to prioritize global mission.[31]

The coherence of early-modern Catholicism does not derive from the institutional integrity of the Catholic Church. This institutional integrity lurks mostly in historical studies and in the propaganda – or better, pro-pagandas – of the church itself. In reality, the church's unity was com-promised by (1) lower-level institutional divisions (e.g. secular vs. reli-gious, or Jesuits vs. Dominicans), (2) nationalizing sentiments, and (3) vast distances which overwhelmed the logistical technologies of the time (overextended "supply lines"). Rather, the coherence of early-modern Catholicism is theological and programmatic, specifically, soteriologi-cal. Within this soteriological agenda most were first concerned for their own souls, in a way usually associated with Luther, or with medieval Catholicism, and secondarily for those of others. Because the Protes-tant concern was also intensely soteriological, both Reformations partic-ipate in a single organizing principle, and diversity occurs either through variations on this principle (Luther does not pursue non-Christian peo-ples) or through institutional differences. Although this sounds straight-forward, the soteriological aspect is rarely highlighted in treatments of early-modern Catholicism.

Understanding early-modern Catholicism in terms of salvation should help prevent misinterpretations such as those outlined in Chapter 1. Jesuit missionaries earned such success in such a variety of endeavours, from mathematics to medicine to linguistics, that historians forget they were missionaries at all – perhaps because in our ecumenical and scientific age landing on the moon quickens the pulse more than a prominent conversion. Dualistic explanations that separate religion from politics or

---

[30] Braunsberger, ed., VII.106–7.
[31] His appeal was reprinted in *De procuranda salute omnium gentium*, 67–98.

from science distort the reality of this Catholicism.[32] The 1614 order of Japan provincial Valentino Carvalho that the Chinese not be taught science or mathematics, but only religion, was revoked almost immediately.[33] As H. E. Bolton insisted, to doubt the priority of the mission for the missionaries is "to confess complete and disqualifying ignorance of the great mass of existing missionary correspondence, printed and unprinted, so fraught with unmistakable proofs of the religious zeal and devotion of the vast majority of the missionaries."[34]

The missionary sources make clear this subordination of science to religion. Martino Martini himself explained his motivation in compiling the *Atlas* "so that the Christian reader can infer from the size and densities [of the cities and regions] how much the field spreads itself out here through the labours of the apostolic workers for the spreading divine glory.... The harvest is great, but the workers are few [Matthew 9]."[35] In the *Espejo rico del claro corazón* [*Treasured Mirror of the Clear Heart*], his translation of the *Beng Sim Po Cam* 明心寶鑑, the Dominican Juan Cobo brought Chinese "riches" of knowledge and virtue to a Castilian audience in order to encourage them to bring the "true richnesses" of the Christian faith to the Chinese. This is not mere sinology.[36] The very title of Pedro Chirino's dictionary expresses the fundamental purpose for learning Chinese "for the conversion of the Chinese" ("ad convertendos eos Sinenses").[37] In his *Historia natural*, Acosta also explained the missiological motivation behind the Jesuits' efforts to master languages, and the missionary purpose always stood behind his ethnography.[38]

---

[32] Jacques Gernet, "Christian and Chinese Visions of the World in the Seventeenth Century," *Chinese Science* IV (1980): 1. Paolo Prodi opposes the dualistic religion-versus-politics explanations. See *Papal Prince: One Body and Two Souls: The Papal Monarchy in Early Modern Europe*, trans. Susan Haskins (Cambridge: Cambridge University Press, 1987), 5.

[33] Daniello Bartoli, *Opere del P. Daniello Bartoli, della Cina* (Turin: B. Marietti, 1825), III.150 [chapter 63].

[34] Herbert Eugene Bolton, "The Mission as a Frontier Institution in the Spanish-American Colonies," *American Historical Review* 23 (1917): 47.

[35] "Praefatio ad lectorem" of *De Bello* (Antwerp: 1654), BAV Barberini S XI 32.

[36] John Cobo, *Beng Sim Po Cam/Espejo rico del claro corazon* [Castillian translation of the 明心寶鑑 by Fan Liben 范立本], [ca. 1592], BN 6040, fol. 2v–3r.

[37] Pedro Chirino, *Dictionarium Sinohispanicum. Quo P. Petrus Chirino Societatis Jesu linguam Sinensium in Filipinis addiscebat ad convertendos eos Sinenses qui Filipinas ipsas incolunt, et quadraginta millium numerum excedunt*, [1604], B. Ang. MS 60.

[38] José de Acosta, *Historia natural y moral de las Indias*, ed. Edmundo O'Gorman (Mexico: Fondo de Cultura Economica, 1962), 285. See Michael Sievernich, "Vision und Mission der Neuen Welt Amerika bei José de Acosta," in *Ignatianisch: Eigenart und Methode der Gesellschaft Jesu*, ed. Michael Sievernich and Günter Switek (Freiburg: Herder, 1990), 293.

To emphasize salvation as the key to this phenomenon is not a new interpretation. Indeed, Jedin himself hailed the role of the Council of Trent in transforming the church into a *Seelsorgskirche*, a church concerned with the pastoral care of souls. More recently, historians have used non-parochial aspects of earlier Christianity, such as the activities of confraternities, to correct his perception of a pre-Tridentine church almost indifferent to the care of souls, and Jedin's transformation no longer appears quite as dramatic as the Copernican changes in science to which he had compared it.[39]

The Tridentine decrees themselves are a potential objection to understanding the early-modern church as focussed on mission, for they contain no mention of the missions. Jedin solved this complication by pointing to the founding of Propaganda as a later consequence of Trent, but this move seems unnecessarily timid.[40] The mission was not mentioned in the decrees because they were the central point of the decrees. Every decree deals with the salvation of souls. To hive the mission off as a separate ecclesiastical category is to make the mistake of many modern historians.

Global Salvific Catholicism

Ernest Lepore once said that old philosophies rarely die from being disproved: They simply stop attracting debate. So far "Early Modern Catholicism" has won more acceptance than examination, and its usefulness and blandness will ensure it a long life.[41] At first glance, the term "Early Modern Catholicism" looks like an improved version of "Counter Reformation" or "Catholic Reform." In fact, it is a very different sort of thing altogether. Its predecessors all had explanatory power; each presented a theory to illuminate some aspect of this Catholicism. "Early Modern Catholicism" is a name like "Bob," for it merely identifies. "Counter Reformation" and "Catholic Reform" are names like "Atatürk" ("Father of the Turks") or "Hongwu" 洪武 ("Immensely Martial"), charged with meaning though not necessarily accurate. The tremendous virtue of "Early Modern Catholicism" is that it is all-embracing – catholic, even. It does not dismember or distort the historical reality, but only because it declines to engage the historical reality at all, even as it

---

[39] Hubert Jedin, *Katholische Reformation oder Gegenreformation?* (Lucerne: Josef Stocker, 1946), 59.

[40] Ibid., 62.

[41] To my knowledge, the only sustained evaluation of the term since O'Malley proposed it comes in Jesse Kuester, "Penitents, Militants, Scoundrels, and Saints: Early Modern Catholicism and the French Catholic League," (Master's project, Simon Fraser University, 2006).

envelopes it. Unlike all of its predecessors "Early Modern Catholicism" tells no story and offers no explanation; it imposes no artificial analytical divides because it attempts no analysis.

For all its diversity, the history of Catholicism is too dynamic and too directed to require so bland a name as "Early Modern Catholicism." If the "Early Modern" here refers to "Early Modern Europe," it is either vacuous (if neutral) or problematic (if it brings in unhelpful parameters of interpretation from "Early Modern Europe"). Differently understood, however, the name can take on new life: What if "Early Modern" referred not to Europe but to the "Early Modern World"?

The sixteenth century surpassed Columbus with several momentous crossings of the Pacific Ocean that transformed the very topology of the largest known world – that of the Europeans' information network – by linking its far eastern and western frontiers. With the undoing of the Pacific limit, the earlier two-dimensional circumscribed disc became a three-dimensional band bound only by the polar regions. Such a world has no geometrical centre, and the nuclei of the traditional networks shared the stage with new focal points. The world became round, and history became global.

Global history between the medieval (or premodern) and late modern eras is sometimes described as the "Early Modern World." This was an era marked by a world increasingly united by the projection of European power abroad, especially in the Americas. Although early-modern Europeans still had little knowledge of, let alone hegemony over, the inland regions of Africa and Asia, the links created and dominated by Europeans made all the world a single stage for fundamental historical processes.

Although the "Early Modern World" shares a genealogy with "Early Modern Europe," the most salient features of early modernity change as the geographical scope in question changes. In modern scholarship the concept of an "early-modern" period matured in Joseph Fletcher's posthumously published article "Integrative History: Parallels and Interconnections in the Early Modern Period, 1500–1800" and developed further in the works of Sanjay Subrahmanyam, Victor Lieberman, and Anthony Reid, among others.[42] The concept of the early-modern world

---

[42] Joseph Fletcher, "Integrative History: Parallels and Interconnections in the Early Modern Period, 1500–1800," in *Niğuča Bičig / Pi Wên Shu* 秘文書 / *Journal of Turkish Studies / Türklük Bılgısı Araştirmalari* 9 (1985): 37–57; Victor Lieberman, "Transcending East-West Dichotomies: State and Culture Formation in Six Ostensibly Disparate Areas," *Modern Asian Studies* 31 (1997): 463–546; Sanjay Subrahmanyam, "Connected Histories: Notes towards a Reconfiguration of Early Modern Eurasia," *Modern Asian Studies* 31 (1997): 735–62. See also Luke Clossey, "Early Modern World," *Berkshire*

survived criticism by Jack Goldstone and Søren Clausen to serve as a useful concept in the work of John F. Richards and to provide a global framework for regional studies, especially of Japan.[43] Fletcher and Richards each located their own sets of defining attributes. Expensive and complex, the most advanced weapons became a monopoly of centralized states, which brought them to bear against local rivals. Administrative procedures also became increasingly routinized and efficient. Ever more abstract notions of state authority accompanied the evolution of new sources of legitimacy. From the Irrawaddy to the Seine, religious uniformity served to reinforce and confirm centralized rule. The ideal of universal empire was native to America, Africa, and Eurasia.[44] One of Fletcher's seven "parallelisms" is "Religious Revival and Missionary Movements." Although Richards does not give the same formal importance to early-modern missionaries, three of his most important large-scale processes defining the early-modern world are necessary prerequisites for the Jesuits' global mission: the creation of global sea passages, the rise of a true world economy, and the growth of large, stable states.[45]

Sociologists have recently paid much attention to contemporary globalization, with the attendant issues of syncretism, agency, and cultural consumption, yet few discrete, transnational, and institutionally sophisticated phenomena have been as wide-ranging as the early-modern Catholic missions.

The Jesuits' globalizing range is not entirely without precedent. In the ninth century the Persian geographer Istakhri described the Radanite Jews' trading network, which stretched from Lyon to Canton, with four main

Encyclopedia of World History (Berkshire Publishing Group: Great Barrington, Mass., 2004), 592–98. For early modernity in European historiography, see Wolfgang Reinhard, "The Idea of Early-Modern History," in *Companion to Historiography*, ed. Michael Bentley (London: Routledge, 1997), 281–92.

[43] Jack Goldstone, "The Problem of the 'Early Modern' World," *Journal of the Economic and Social History of the Orient* 41 (1998): 249–84; Søren Clausen, "Early Modern China – A Preliminary Postmortem," <www.hum.au.dk/ckulturf/pages/publications/sc/china.htm>; John F. Richards, "Early Modern India and World History," *Journal of World History* 8 (1997): 197–209; idem, *The Unending Frontier: An Environmental History of the Early Modern World*, California World History Library 1 (Berkeley: University of California Press, 2003). See also Kären Wigen, "Japanese Perspectives on the Time/Space of 'Early Modernity,'" paper for the XIX International Congress of Historical Sciences, Oslo, Norway, August 7, 2000. <www.oslo2000.uio.no/program/papers/m1a/M1a-wigen.pdf>; Jack A. Goldstone, "Efflorescences and Economic Growth in World History: Rethinking the 'Rise of the West' and the Industrial Revolution," *Journal of World History* 13.2 (Fall 2002), 323–89.

[44] See Luke Clossey, "Faith in Empire: Religious Sources of Legitimacy for Expansionist Early-Modern States," in *Politics and Reformations: Communities, Polities, Nations, and Empires*, ed. Christopher Ocker, Michael Printy, Peter Starenko, and Peter Wallace (Leiden: Brill, 2007), 571–87.

[45] Fletcher, 25–28; Richards, 198–201.

routes ranging from the Crimean Jewish kingdom of Khazaria in the north down to the Indian subcontinent. Not only did the various commodities (eunuchs, slaves, swords, and furs) crisscross Eurasia, but so, too, did the merchants themselves, enjoying a peculiar freedom of movement as non-Christians in Muslim lands and as non-Muslims in Christian lands.[46]

A closer analogy to the Jesuits comes with Roman Catholicism's first, medieval presence in China, with papal legates, Franciscan missionaries, and their converts, alongside the Christians enslaved and deported during the Mongol invasion of Hungary. Italian merchants residing in China provided the missionaries with financial support, crucial to the mission's expensive conversion strategy: From Beijing the archbishop Giovanni da Montecorvino (1247–ca.1329) reported that he had "purchased by degrees forty boys of the sons of the pagans, between seven and eleven years old, who as yet knew no religion."[47] The merchants also kept the Franciscans in touch with their superiors in Europe, and relayed correspondence between eastern and western potentates.[48] The Genoese merchant Andalo de Savignano, for example, served the Shundi 順帝 emperor (1333–1370, also known as Toghôn Temür) as his ambassador to the pope. Such transcontinental connections were only possible during the *Pax Mongolica*, when Mongols boasted that a maiden, alone, could carry a bag of gold across the empire without fear. Its collapse broke contact with Rome, and of the twelve archbishops sent east between 1342 and 1490 to take up their see in Khanbaliq (Beijing), none were, or are, known to have arrived.[49] Late-medieval Catholicism was global only in the most fragile sense.

To match the Jesuits' truly global presence, acknowledgement of local cultural circumstances, and ability to affect cultural change, we have to wait for the twentieth century, for the globally iconic Music Television (MTV) networks and their propagation of the cult of a very different Madonna (or مادونا, or 麥當娜). The years 1987–95 saw the birth of MTV

[46] L. Rabinowitz, *Jewish Merchant Adventurers: A Study of the Radanites* (London: Edward Goldston, 1948), 98, 112–50, 163–71, 231.

[47] Ibid., 68–70, 78; *The Mongol Mission: Narratives and Letters of the Franciscan Missionaries in Mongolia and China in the Thirteenth and Fourteenth Centuries*, ed. Christopher Dawson (London: Sheed and Ward, 1955; reprinted as *Mission to Asia*, New York: Harper & Row, 1966), 225; Luciano Petech, "Les marchands italiens dans l'empire mongol," *Journal asiatique* 250.4 (1962) (reprinted in *Selected Papers on Asian History* [Rome: ISMEO, 1988], 166–67); second letter of John of Monte Corvino, Cambaluc, January 8, 1305, in Dawson, 225. This missionary strategy dates back at least to the sixth century with Gregory I. See Sullivan, 52.

[48] Henry Hosten, "Letter of Friar Peregrine, Second Bishop of Zayton, China (December 30, 1318)," *Journal and Proceedings of the Asiatic Society of Bengal* (n.s.) 26 (1930): 454–55.

[49] Sebes, "Jesuit Attempts," 67; Latourette, *History of Christian Missions*, 71–72.

Europe, MTV Brasil, MTV Asia, MTV Latino, and MTV Mandarin. If the Jesuits made the world more real to their patrons and global correspondents, MTV made Europe more real, through the fashioning of the first pan-European advertising market, coinciding conspicuously with the collapse of the Iron Curtain. Now each of the thirty-eight MTV channels adapts global music to a local audience. MTV Indonesia takes a "funky but respectful" approach to Islam.[50] The analogy between the Society of Jesus and Music Television may seem mischievous, but it strikes me as more accurate than the other metaphors we have seen scholars propose, such as the United Nations or the United States Marines. This develops the idea that the missionary orders were "surely among the world's first transnational, nonprofit corporations"[51] by including the globalizing aspect.

The best modern survey of long-distance trading and missionary enterprises in the pre-modern world is Jerry H. Bentley's *Old World Encounters* (1993), and its descriptions of the dynamic frontiers of religious identity. Although lacking the same scope and quality of evidence, Frederick Teggart's *Rome and China* (1939) is the real antecedent of Bentley's work. Reaching beyond comparison, Teggart is most virtuoso at teasing out correlations. His *tour de force* follows chain reactions – fuelled by interruptions of trade – across Eurasia, tracing the evacuation of Roman troops from Scotland (A.D.106–8) back to the retirement of Ban Chao 班超 (A.D. 102), a monetary crisis in Rome back to Han policy, and the third-century barbarian invasions of Rome back to the collapse of the Han dynasty.[52]

World historians assert that the world has been sufficiently united to yield a single history for some time, whether from 5000 B.C. or from A.D. 1250. Thus, when the silver discovery in America echoes through Europe to affect inflation in China, this link of causality is of a familiar sort, though enhanced by the addition of another continent to the game. Indeed, all but the most positivistic of historians would readily admit to the existence of global causal connections too subtle for detection. James Gleich's American butterfly, after all, needs neither longitude nor

---

[50] Tom McGrath, *MTV: The Making of a Revolution* (Philadelphia: Running Press, 1996), 161–63, 182, 187, 191, 202; "The One Where Pooh Goes to Sweden: Anti-Americanism and Television," *The Economist* (April 25, 2004) http://www.economist.com/business/displayStory.cfm?story_id=1682750 (accessed April 25, 2004).

[51] Max L. Stackhouse, "Missionary Activity," *Encyclopedia of Religion* (New York: Macmillan, 1987), IX.568.

[52] Jerry H. Bentley, *Old World Encounters: Cross-Cultural Contacts and Exchanges in Pre-Modern Times* (Oxford: Oxford University Press, 1993); Frederick Teggart, *Rome and China: A Study of Correlations in Historical Events* (Berkeley: University of California, 1939), viii–xi, 134, 146–48.

the magnetic compass to stir up a storm in China. Nor, to return to Teggart, was Ban Chao an early Scottish nationalist. What distinguishes the Radanites, the Jesuits, and MTV from other world-spanning phenomena is an awareness of causality. Blaming the Spanish in Potosí might not occur to the Ming merchant harassed by inflation, but the missionary who travels from New Spain to China would be intensely and necessarily aware of the Chinese stimulus of his travels. The cause would be so alive to him that he would die for it.

This world mission had affinities to – and probably was inspired by – the neostoic ideal of a universal community of equals, based on a common natural law. With its cosmopolitan attitude of a brotherhood of humanity, Stoicism had militated against national and racial barriers. If the humanistic revival of Stoicism did thus feed the early-modern missionary movement, we then are witnessing the Renaissance laying the foundation for the Catholic Reformation. The other side of the Stoic coin, reinforced by Renaissance Platonism, was the "syncretistic notion that all religions say the same thing in different terms," which presumably retarded the missionary impulse.[53] The neostoic sense of the world's unity drew on the idea that not only all religions, but also all languages, were essentially the same. For example, the seventeenth century saw several attempts at a universal language – some thought Chinese a likely candidate, although missionaries tended to discourage the notion.[54] The upshot is ambiguous. Neostoicism potentially fuelled global empathy while at the same time took the edge off the soteriological drive.

Neostoic natural law, and rationality, reappeared in the *De Indis* [*On the Indies*] of Francisco de Vitoria (ca. 1486–1546). Vitoria justified the missionary's universal access to potential converts on a point from natural law, the *titulus naturalis societatis et communicationis*, that is, the right to unhindered *communicatio* – communication and trade – among all peoples. Thus Spaniards could legally confiscate the property of any Indians who restrict the travels of missionaries, or of merchants.[55] However, Vitoria understood the papacy as also being subject to natural law and

---

[53] Seymour Cain, "Study of Religion: History of Study," *Encyclopedia of Religion*, XIV.68. For Renaissance Platonism see Headley, 243–71.

[54] Mungello, *Curious*, 16.

[55] Franciscus de Vitoria, *De Indis et de iure belli relectiones*, ed. Ernest Nys, Classics in International Law (New York: Oceana, 1964), 705–6 [or 77–80], cited in Anthony Pagden, "Dispossessing the barbarian: the language of Spanish Thomism and the debate over the property rights of the American Indians," in *The Languages of Political Theory in Early-modern Europe* (New York: Cambridge University Press, 1987), 86; Vitoria, *De Indis*, 257, 260. See also Anthony Pagden, "The School of Salamanca and the 'Affairs of the Indies,'" *History of Universities* 1 (1981): 71–112.

therefore unable to claim universal governance.[56] Drawing upon a universal love that transcended national and racial divisions, the Jesuit theologian Francisco Suárez (1548–1617) propounded the doctrine of *ius gentium* – the moral laws that allow and promote the peaceful coexistence of the open society of nations. Suárez writes,

> The human race, howsoever divided into various peoples and kingdoms, always has a certain unity, not only specific, but also as it were political and moral, which is indicated by the natural precept of mutual love and mercy, a precept extended to all, even strangers and of whatsoever reason. Therefore, although each perfect city, state or kingdom constitutes in itself a perfect community consisting of its own members, nevertheless each of them is also a member in a certain fashion of this universe, so far as it concerns the human race.[57]

Thus Suárez follows Vitoria on mission issues. Both men's contributions to the development of international law have received notice. Here we stress their role in the development of global mission, but equally important are the commercial issues involved, to which Ivan Strenski has traced the religious roots of the modern legitimization of economic globalization.[58] There is indeed a fundamental correspondence between religious and commercial globalization. Seeking to explain Franciscans' approach to religious conversion in Mexico, Inga Clendinnen describes, appropriately, a "trade-store model" in which "with time and enough penetration of the market, 'undesirable' native products and preferences are displaced, to be replaced by European products and learnt European preferences."[59]

Even contemporaries recognized the missionary enterprise's special relationship with trade. In New Spain, the missionary Andreas Mancker (1648–1702) decided to apply for a transfer to the China mission, with optimism largely because "every year ships come from China and go back for commercial reasons."[60] Jesuit Antoine Thomas (1644–1709)

---

[56] Thomas A. Brady, Jr., "The Rise of Merchant Empires, 1400–1700: A European Counterpart," in *The Political Economy of Merchant Empires: State Power and World Trade 1350–1750*, ed. James D. Tracy (New York: Cambridge University Press, 1991), 130.

[57] *De legibus* (1612, Coimbre). l. II, c. xix, n. 9, p. 169, quoted in René Brouillard, "Suarez, François," in *Dictionnaire de théologie catholique* (Paris: Letouzey et Ane, 1903–50), 14:2.2646, 2719–22.

[58] Ivan Strenski, "The Religion in Globalization," *Journal of the American Academy of Religion* 72 (2004): 631–52.

[59] Inga Clendinnen, "Franciscan Missionaries in Sixteenth-Century Mexico," in *Disciplines of Faith: Studies in Religion, Politics, and Patriarchy*, ed. J. Obelkevich, L. Roper, and R. Samuel (New York: Routledge and Kegan Paul, 1987), 231.

[60] Letter, México, February 25, 1681, to the Probst of Pöllau, Steiermärkisches Landesarchiv – Archiv Stift Pöllau, Schuber 7, Heft 20, fol. 25r-26r (copy); published

sent the Duchess of Aveiro a cipher key in which missionaries were "merchants" and the Christian faith "commerce."[61] His colleague António Vieira (1608–1697) put the matter more directly in the *Historia do futuro* [*History of the Future*]: "If there were not merchants who go to seek for earthly treasures in the East and West Indies, who would transport thither the preachers who take heavenly treasures? The preachers take the Gospel and the merchants take the preachers."[62]

Merchants and missionaries fashioned the early-modern world and the globalization that integrated it. The sociologist Anthony Giddens understands globalization as an evolving modernity, for "modern organisations are able to connect the local and the global in ways which would have been unthinkable in more traditional societies."[63] In the early-modern world the Society of Jesus, and to a lesser extent the other missionary orders, was exactly such an organization. The parameters of interpretation implied by "Early Modern" in fact do fit "Early Modern Catholicism" if we read this name as "Early Modern [World] Catholicism." Early-modern Catholicism was a world Catholicism because of the centrality of the missions. The missions were central because of the overriding importance of soteriology. Thus the name "Early Modern [World] Catholicism" in two steps arrives at the heart of the concept: salvation.

"Salvific" characterizes early-modern Catholicism just as intensely as "global." Certainly the idea of salvation endures in Catholicism today. At some time and some place in the last two centuries, however, it has faded. For Christianity as a whole, the change began at least before the 1928 International Missionary Council meeting in Jerusalem; for Roman Catholicism, it came no later than the Second Vatican Council (1962–65), and its roots stretch back earlier. According to the 1964 Dogmatic Constitution of the Church (*Lumen gentium*), the "plan of salvation" now "includes" not only Muslims, but even those who "without blame on their part, have not yet arrived at an explicit knowledge of God and with His

---

as "Schreiben eines österreichischen Jesuitenmissionärs an den Probst zu Pöllau betreffs seiner Reise nach Mexico und seiner Erfahrung daselbt," ed. Josef von Zahn, *Steiermärkische Geschichstblätter* 1 (1880): 29–40.

[61] 1679 or 1680. Maggs Bros., *Bibliotheca Asiatica Part II*, 79. In the late first millennium A.D., near the southern ends of the trans-Saharan trade routes, the Hausa words for "Muslim" and "trader" were the same. Alice Willard, "Gold, Islam, and Camels: The Transformative Effects of Trade and Ideology," *Comparative Civilizations Review* 28 (1993): 99.

[62] Quoted in Boxer, *Portuguese Seaborne*, 65. For further reflection on the connection between merchants and missionaries, see Joseph Dahlmann, *Die Sprachkunde und die Missionen* (Freiburg im Breisgau: Herder, 1891), 24.

[63] Anthony Giddens, *The Consequences of Modernity* (Stanford: Stanford University Press, 1990) 29, 63.

grace strive to live a good life."[64] Today the Vatican's pronouncements on salvation sound defensive. Explaining a line in his coauthored declaration *Dominus Iesus* ("the followers of other religions can receive divine grace"), Joseph Cardinal Ratzinger, now Benedict XVI, has to insist, "I did not say that salvation can be achieved by every path. The way of conscience, the keeping of one's gaze focused on truth and the objective good, is one single way, although it can take many forms because of the great number of individuals and situations."[65] The Jesuits continue missionary activity today, but the main menu on the Society's webpage includes "interreligious dialogue" rather than "mission." Over three hundred Jesuits became martyrs in the twentieth century, yet the vast majority (over 75%) of these martyrdoms occurred within Europe, and most of these in Spain, rather than in distant missions.[66] The church has come a long way since the Council of Trent's pregnant silence on missions, when it occurred to no one to assert, led alone defend, the necessity of mission for the salvation of souls. Its necessity was obvious, and to thousands of Jesuits it was absolutely urgent.

What is distinctive about early-modern Catholicism? The centrality and scope of the Jesuit missions suggest an answer. Early-modern Catholicism was more extensively global than anything previous, and early-modern Catholicism was more intensively salvific than it is today. Go back before the fifteenth century and Catholicism is not so global; come ahead to the present and Catholicism is not so salvific. Such distinctions are indeed largely a matter of degree. Nevertheless, only in the early-modern period was Catholicism simultaneously both extremely global and extremely salvific. This project has shown how the global and the salvific elements fed into each other to create a moment unique in the history of Christianity. If Giddens is correct in linking modernity to globalization, this global, salvific moment of Catholicism is inherently unstable, as the global erodes the salvific. In any case, the urgency of global

---

[64] The quotation comes from section 16. For the full text, see "Dogmatic Constitution of the Church *Lumen Gentium*," <http://www.vatican.va/archive/hist_councils/ii_vatican_council/documents/vat-ii_const_19641121_lumen-gentium_en.html> (accessed August 17, 2006).

[65] "Die Zukunft der Ökumene im Rhein-Main-Gebiet: Reaktionen auf die Vatikan-Erklärung 'Dominus Iesus,'" *Frankfurter Allgemeine Zeitung* (October 28, 2000), as quoted in the translation of *L'Osservatore Romano* [Weekly Edition in English] (November 22, 2000), p. 10. The interview is also available at "Answers to Main Objections against *Dominus Iesus*," (August 17, 2006). http://www.ewtn.com/library/Theology/OBDOMIHS.HTM/. For the text, see "*Dominus Iesus*," http://www.vatican.va/roman_curia/congregations/cfaith/documents/rc_con_cfaith_doc_20000806_dominus-iesus_en.html (accessed August 17, 2006).

[66] I base my calculations on "Jesuit Martyrs of the 20th Century," March 28, 2000, http://www.companysj.com/news/martyrs20.html (accessed August 16, 2006).

mission made early-modern Catholicism essentially global. This was the era of "Global Salvific Catholicism."

This is not to say that Global Salvific Catholicism captures all, or even most, aspects of this Catholicism. Dunking an image of St. Peter in a local river to solicit rain is neither global nor salvific, and little evidence until the nineteenth century suggests popular enthusiasm for distant missions. Probably nothing less inclusive than "Early Modern Catholicism" will ever have that range. Nevertheless, Global Salvific Catholicism does distinguish this from earlier and later Catholicism, and in a natural, non-reactionary way from contemporary Protestantism, with exceptions like the ill-starred Calvinist mission to "French Antarctica" proving the rule.

As subjects of historical study, the Jesuit missions and the early-modern world have much to offer each other. Early globalization colours so many of the historically important facets of the early-modern world, and the missions of the Society of Jesus were the globalizing institution *par excellence*. The great advantage of regarding early-modern Catholicism as fundamentally global is that no other attribute leads us more directly to the soul of the movement – salvation.

Appendix A: Abbreviations for Document Sources

AGI	Archivo General de Indias, Seville
C.C.	sección Casa de Contratación
Filip.	sección Filipinas
Guad.	sección Papeles de Simancas . . . Guadalajara
Mex.	sección México
MP-DR	sección Mapas y Planos – Documentos Reales
Patronato	sección Patronato Real
AGN	Archivo General de la Nación, México
AHH	Archivo Histórico de Hacienda
Jes.	ramo Jesuitas
Mis.	ramo Misiones
AHN	Archivo Histórico Nacional, Madrid
Jes	Jesuitas
AHPMCJ	Archivo Histórico de la Provincia Mexicana de la Compañía de Jesús, México
AMSJ	Archivum Monacense Societatis Jesu [Oberdeutsche Provinz SJ], Munich
APF	Archivio della Santa Congregazione per l'Evangelizzazione dei Populi, Rome
SOCG	Scritture Originali riferite nelle Congregazioni Generali
ARSI	Archivum Romanum Societatis Jesu, Rome [Archivio Antico]
Ang.	Provincia Angliae
Austr.	Provincia Austriae
Boh.	Provincia Bohemiae
FG	"Fondo Gesuitico," section restored in 1924 [see Lamalle]
Gall.	Assistentia Galliae
G. Sup.	Provincia Germaniae Superioris
Goa	Provincia Goana et Malabarica
Hisp.	Assistentia Hispaniae
JapSin	Provincia Japoniae et vice provincia Sinensis

Lus.	Assistentia Lusitaniae
Mex.	Provincia Mexicana
Phil.	Provincia Philippinarum
Pol.	Provincia Polaniae
Rhen. Sup.	Provincia Rheni Superioris
ASV	Archivio Secreto Vaticano, Città del Vaticano
B. Ang.	Biblioteca Angelica, Rome
B. Cas.	Biblioteca Casanatense, Rome
BA/JA	Biblioteca da Ajuda, Lisbon, Jesuítas na Asia collection
BAV	Biblioteca Apostolica Vaticana
Barberini	Barberini Orientale Collection
Racc	Gen Or. Raccolta Generale Oriente
BHStA	Bayerisches Hauptstaatsarchiv, Munich
G.R.	General Registration
Jes.	section Jesuitica
BL	British Library, London
BLB	Bancroft Library, Berkeley
BN	Biblioteca Nacional, Madrid
BNC	Biblioteca Nazionale Centrale Vittorio Emanuele II, Roma
FG	Fondo Gesuitico
Mss.	Manuscritti e Documenti
BNF	Bibliothèque Nationale de France
All.	Département des Manuscrits, Allemand
BNL	Biblioteca Nacional, Lisbon, Manuscript Section
FG	Fundo Geral
PBA	Pombalina
BNM	Biblioteca Nacional, México
AF	Archivo Franciscano
BNN	Biblioteca Nazionale Napoli
BRB	Bibliothèque Royale de Belgique, Brussels
BStB	Bayerische Staatsbibliothek, Munich
CLM	Codd. MSS. latinor.
CodSin	Codices sinenses
CBL	Chester Beatty Library, Dublin
DI	*Documenta indica*, Josef Wicki, ed., 18 vols. Rome: 1948–88.
HAG	Historical Archives of Goa
MR	Livros das monções do Reino series
MDC	Museo Diocesano, Catania
MZA	Moravský Zemský Archiv v Brně
ÖNB	Österreichische Nationalbibliothek, Wien
RAH	Biblioteca de la Real Academia de la Historia, Madrid

RBM	Real Biblioteca [del Palacio], Madrid
SBB PK	Staatsbibliothek zu Berlin, Stiftung Preußischer Kulturbe-sitz
StAK	Stadtarchiv Köln
SUA	Státni Ústřední Archiv v Praze
Jes.	Jesuitica
UCSD Man.	University of California, San Diego, Mandeville Special Collections Library
WB	Stöcklein, Joseph, et alia, ed., *Der Neue Welt-Bott*. 5 vols. Augsburg, Graz: 1726–55.

Appendix B: Chronological Tables (1540–1722)

Popes	Holy Roman Emperors	Kings of Spain	Kings of Portugal	Dukes of Bavaria	Emperors of China
Paul III 1534-49	Charles V 1530-56	Charles I 1516-56	John III 1521-67	William IV 1508-50 *with* Louis X 1516-40	The Jiājìng 嘉靖 Emperor 1521-66
Julius III 1550-55[1]				Albert V 1550-79	
Paul IV 1555-59	Ferdinand I 1556-64	Philip II 1556-98	Sebastian 1557-78		
Pius IV 1559-65					
	Maximilian II 1564-76				
Pius V 1566-72					The Lóngqìng 隆慶 Emperor 1566-72
Gregory XIII 1572-85					The Wànlì 萬曆 Emperor 1572-1620
	Rudolf II 1576-1612				
			Cardinal Henry 1578-80	William V 1579-97	
			Anthony 1580 *as* Philip I 1581-98		

[1] Marcellus II, 1555

Jesuit Generals		
	1540	Founding bull of the Society of Jesus, *Regimini militantis ecclesiae*
Ignatius Loyola 1541-56		
	1545	*Constitutiones circa missiones*; Council of Trent opens
	1547	Battle of Mühlberg
	1549	Jay, Canisius, and Salmerón arrive at Ingolstadt; Province of the East Indies founded
	1552	First book of Jesuit letters appears in Rome; Francis Xavier dies
	1554	Godinho takes office as first mission procurator for the Portuguese province
	1555	Peace of Augsburg
	1556	Upper Germany and Lower Germany provinces founded
James Lainez 1558-65	1558	Society's first congregation approves the Constitutions
	1563	Austrian Province founded; first Latin edition of *Epistolae indicae*, at Dillingen
Francis Borgia 1565-72		
	1572	Sánchez de Canales establishes Mexican province
Everard Mercurian 1573-80	1573	*Ordenanzas sobre Descubrimientos*; plenary indulgence to Jesuits dying en route
	1574	*Ordenanzas del Patronato*; Spain prohibits religious orders from sending recruiters
	1578	Jesuits begin major investments in Macao-to-Nagasaki silk trade
	1580	First Jesuits left Mexico for the Philippines
Claudius Aquaviva 1581-1615	1582	Matteo Ricci arrives at Macao

Popes	Holy Roman Emperors	Kings of Spain	Kings of Portugal	Dukes of Bavaria	Emperors of China
Sixtus V 1585-90	Rudolf II 1576-1612	*as* Philip II 1556-98	*as* Philip I 1581-98	William V 1579-97	The Wànlì 萬曆 Emperor 1566-1620[2]
varia[3]					
Clement VIII 1592-1605[4]					
		as Philip III 1598-1621	*as* Philip II 1598-1621	Maximilian I 1597-1651	
Paul V 1605-21					
	Matthias 1612-19				
	Ferdinand II 1619-37				The Tiānqǐ 天啓 Emperor 1620-27
Gregory XV 1621-23		*as* Philip IV 1621-65	*as* Philip III 1621-40		
Urban VIII 1623-44					
					The Chóngzhēn 崇禎 Emperor 1627-44

[2] The Taichang Emperor (1627)
[3] Urban VII (1590), Gregory XIV (1590-91), Innocent IX (1591)
[4] Leo XI (1605)

Jesuit Generals		
Claudius Aquaviva 1581-1615	1585	Third Catechism of Lima; royal *cédula* restricts missionaries' going to China
	1588	Acosta's *De Procuranda Indorum Salute*
	1589	Jesuits begin work among the Mexican Indians
	1593	Fifth General Congregation begins; Cesare Ripa's *Iconologia*
	1600	*Onerosa pastoralis officii* disputes Portugal's right to route missionaries via Lisbon
	1603	Francisco de Figueroa becomes mission procurator for America in Spain
	1605	Campanella's *Atheismus Triumphantus*
	1609	Nicolas Trigault arrives in China
	1610	Death of Matteo Ricci
	1611	Louis Richeôme's *La peinture spirituelle*
	1612	Francisco Suárez's *De legibus ac Deo legislatore*; Trigault sent to Europe
Mutius Vitelleschi 1615-45	1615	*Romanae ecclesiae antistes* grants concessions to Christians in China
	1616	Bavaria begins donations to China mission
	1617	German translation of *De Christiana Expeditione*
	1618	Thirty Years' War begins; Trigault returns to China
	1619	Catarina de San Juan ("La China Poblana") brought to Mexico as a slave
	1620	German edition of *Auß America*
	1621	Approval of Jesuits' investment in houses in Macao
	1622	Congregatio de Propaganda Fidei established; Ignatius & Xavier canonized
	1623	China bcomes independent Vice-province
	1626	Maximilian confirms 500-gulden annual donation to China mission
	1628	Trigault dies
	1630	Schreck dies

Popes	Holy Roman Emperors	Kings of Spain	Kings of Portugal	Dukes of Bavaria	Emperors of China
Urban VIII 1623-44	Ferdinand II 1619-37	*as* Philip IV 1621-65	*as* Philip III 1621-40	Maximilian I 1597-1651	The Chóngzhēn 崇禎 Emperor 1627-44
	Ferdinand 1637-57				
			John IV 1640-56		
Innocent X 1644-55					The Shùnzhì 順治 Emperor 1644[43]-61
				Ferdinand Maria 1651-79	
Alexander VII 1655-67			Afonso VI 1656-67		
	Leopold I 1658-1705				The Kāngxī 康熙 Emperor 1661-1722
		Charles II 1665-1700			
Clement IX 1667-69			Peter II 1667-1706		
Clement X 1670-76					
Innocent XI					

Jesuit Generals		
Mutius Vitelleschi 1615-45	1634?	Didace Barreto leaves Mexico for China
	1638	Cypriano preaching at Macao
	1642	Juan de Palafox y Mendoza becomes acting viceroy
	1645	Pérez de Ribas's *Historia de los triumphos*; Eighth General Congregation begins
Vincent Caraffa 1646-49	1646	Athanasius Kircher's *Ars magna lucis et umbrae*
	1648	Thirty Years' War ends
Francis Piccolomini 1649-51	1649	Lisbon restricts non-Portuguese missionaries' travels
Goschwin Nickel 1652⁵-64	1654	Spain outlaws the sending of foreign missionaries to the colonies
	1655	Ferdinand Maria renews 500-gulden annual donation to China mission
	1656	Diestel and Grueber overland trip to China
	1661	Martini dies
John Paul Oliva 1664-81	1666	Schall Von Bell dies
	1667	Kircher's *China Monumentis illustrata*
	1674	Andreas Müller announces discovery of Chinese "key"

---

[5] Aloysius Gottifredi (1652)

Popes	Holy Roman Emperors	Kings of Spain	Kings of Portugal	Dukes of Bavaria	Emperors of China
Innocent XI 1676-89	Leopold I 1658-1705	Charles II 1665-1700	Peter II 1667-1706	F. Maria 1651-79	The Kângxi 康熙 Emperor 1661-1722
				Maximilian II Emanuel 1679-1726	
Alexander VIII 1689-91					
Innocent XII 1691-1700					
Clement XI 1700-21		Philip V 1700-24			
	Joseph I 1705-11		John V 1706-50		
	Charles XI 1711-40				
Innocent XIII 1721-24					Yongzheng 雍正

Jesuit Generals		
John Paul Oliva 1664-81	1679	Jesuits assigned the mission of the proposed colony of California
	1680	Comet observed by Jesuit missionaries globally; Eusebius Kino arrives in Mexico
Charles de Noyelle 1682-86	1682	Ferdinand von Fürstenberg establishes a special foundation for missions
	1684	Louis XIV sends Jesuit missionaries to China
Thyrsus González 1687-1705	1689	Last payment of 500-gulden annual donation to China mission
	1691	Pozzo painting the ceiling of the S. Ignazio (early 1690s)
	1692	The Kangxi Emperor formally tolerates Christianity
	1696	Pious Fund for California begins
	1697	Earliest missionizing of Baja California; Leibniz's *Novissima Sinica*
	1699	"caritas pura" condemned by pope
	1701	Outbreak of the War of the Spanish Succession
	1704	Papal decree against Jesuit position in Chinese Rites controversy
Michelangelo Tamburini 1706-30	1707	Increased quota of foreign missionaries to Spain; Villa Puente's first donation
	1710	Controversy at the university in Würzburg over Chinese Rites
	1711	Kino dies
	1713	Peace of Utrecht
	1715	*Ex illa die* confirms 1704 decree
	1721	The Kangxi Emperor prohibits Christian mission in China

Appendix C: Principal Prosopographical Information

for Jesuits active on the Germany/China/Mexico network before 1705

This chart is based primarily on Joseph Dehergne, Répertoire des Jésuites de Chine de 1552 à 1800 (Rome: Institutum Historicum S. I., 1973) and Bernd Hausberger, Jesuiten aus Mitteleuropa im kolonialen Mexiko (Munich: R. Oldenbourg, 1995). The reader is invited to refer to these sources, and to the Ricci Roundtable Database (ricci.rt.usfca.edu) for further biographical and bibliographical details.

	Birth		S.J.[1]	Miss.[2]	Death	
Aigenler, Adam	1633	Tramin, Tyrol	1653	1673	1673	en route to China
Alberich, Johann	1586	Dorenbüren (near Constance)	1605	1618	1618	en route to China
Amarell, Maximillian	1651?	Bohemia	1667	1686	1696	Tehueco, Sinaloa
Amrhyn, Beatus	1632	Lucerne	1649	1673	1673	en route to China
Barreto, Didace	?	"Nova Hispania"	1641?	1634?	?	China?
Boranga, Karl	1640	Vienna	1656	1678	1684	Rota, Mariana Islands
Boruhradský, Simon	1650?	Polná, Moravia	1670	1678	1697?	en route to the Mariana Islands
Brack, Christof	1652	Rottenburg am Neckar	1672	1692	1693	en route to China
Calmes, Joachim	1652	Hamburg	1678	1682	1686	Hainan
Castner, Kaspar	1665	Munich	1681	1696	1709	Beijing
Charandy, Jean-Baptiste	1659	Solothurn	1680	1692	1692	en route to China
Diestel, Bernhard	1621	Vipava [Wippach], Carniola/Slovenia	1639?	1650	1660	Jinan 济南 (Shandong)
Dimer, Jacob	1626	Hötting-Innsbruck	1646	1657	1658	Makassar (Sulawesi)
Eymer, Wenzel	1661	Mělník, Bohemia	1678	1692	1717?	Papigóchic

	Birth		S.J.[1]	Miss.[2]	Death	
Fiva, Nikolaus	1609	Fribourg [Freiburg im Üechtland]	1628	1635	1640	Hangzhou 杭州
Gerstl, Adam	1646	Styria	1664	1678	1693?	Manila
Gilg, Adam	1653?	Rýmařov [Römerstadt], Moravia	1670?	1687	1709	NW Mexico
Grueber, Johannes	1623	St. Florian, Upper Austria	1641	1656	1680	Sárospatak, Hungary
Haller, Johann Baptist	1652?	Gemona del Friuli	1674	1687	1718	Mexico City
Herdtrich, Christian Wolfgang Heinrich	1625?	Peggau, Styria	1641	1657	1684	Xinjiang 新绛 (Shanxi)
Hostinský, Georg	1654?	Valašské Klobouky [Walachisch Klobouk], Moravia	1670?	1687	1726	Papigóchic
Illing, Wilhelm	1648	Žatec [Saaz], Bohemia	1664	1686	1712?	Caríchic or Loreto, Chínipas
Januske, Daniel	1661	Wrocław [Breslau], Silesia	1676?	1690	1724	Oposura, Sonora
Kall, Adam	1657?	Cheb [Eger], Bohemia	1673	1687	1702	Manila
Kappus, Marcus Antonius	1657?	Ljubljana [Laibach], Slovenia	1676	1687	1717	Mátape, Sonora
Kino, Eusebius Franciscus	1645	Segno (near Trent)	1665	1678	1711	Santa Maria Magdalena, Sonora
Kirwitzer, Wenzel Pantaleon	1588?	Kadaň [Kaaden], Bohemia	1606?	1618	1626?	Macao
Klein, Paulus	1652	Eger [Cheb], Bohemia	1669	1678	1717	Manila
Koffler, Andreas Xavier	1607?	Krems, Lower Austria	1627	1639	1652?	Tianzhou 田州 (Tianyang 田阳 in Guangxi)
Mancker, Andreas	1648?	Herzogenburg, Lower Austria	1664	1678	1682?	en route to China
Martini, Martino	1614	Trent	1632?	1639	1661	Hangzhou 杭州
Möers, Jakob	1658	Cologne	1674	1689	1691?	Mozambique
Monte, Walter Ignacio de ("Sonnenberg")	1612	Lucerne	1628	1641?	1680?	抚州 Fuzhou (Jiangxi)
Neumann, Joseph	1648?	Brussels	1673	1678	1732	Caríchic, Tarahumara
Ratkay, Johann Maria	1647?	Ptuj [Pettau], Styria	1664	1678	1683?	Caríchic, Sierra Tarahumara

(*continued*)

	Birth		S.J.[1]	Miss.[2]	Death	
Revell, Thomas	1643	Brussels	1664?	1678	1692?	Sierra de Chínipas
Schall Von Bell, Johann Adam	1592	Cologne	1611?	1618	1666	Beijing
Scheffelmayr, Franz Xaver	1624	Wangen, Swabia	1641	1656	1666	Macao
Schreck, Johann Terrenz	1576	Diocese of Constance	1611	1617	1630	Beijing
Schuch, Moritz	1650	Donauwörth, Bavaria	1675	1691	1692	Shiraz (Persia)
Spillebeen, Martin	1589	Bruges	1609	1617	1629	Nanjing 南京
Staubach, Johann Balthasar	1659	Fulda	1676	1690	1691	Goa
Steinhöffer, Johann	1664	Jihlava [Iglau], Moravia	1686?	1692	1716	Yécora, Sinaloa
Strohbach, August Ignaz Alois	1649?	Jihlava [Iglau], Moravia	1667	1678	1684	Tinian, Mariana Islands
Stumpf, Kilian	1655?	Würzburg	1673	1691	1720	Beijing
Trigault, Nicolas	1577	Douai	1594	1607	1628	Hangzhou 杭州
Ureman, Johann	1583?	Split, Dalmatia	1600	1615	1621?	Nanjing 南京
Van Hamme, Petrus Thomas	1651	Ghent	1672	1687	1727	Songjiang 松江 (Jiangsu, China)
Verdier, Ferdinand	1649	Klagenfurt, Carinthia	1678	1687	1707?	Sonora
Walta, Michael	1606	Munich	1623	?	1644?	Pujiu 普救 (Shanxi)
Weidenfeld, Adam	1645	Cologne	1663	1680	1680	At sea, near Brazil
Welser, Anton	1564?	Augsburg	1587?	1611?	1640?	Neuburg an der Donau
Wit, Bernhard de	1658	Emmerich	1677	1691	1692?	En route to China

[1] Year of entry into the Society
[2] Year of departure for the missions

Appendix D: Monetary Systems[†]

Northern Europe

The thaler was a German silver coin. The gulden (guilder, florin, florijn) was a Dutch coin and money of account.

Chinese

A tael (liang 兩) was a Chinese unit of weight used in measuring silver. During the Ming Dynasty a liang was the equivalent of 37 grams (1.3 oz).

Spanish

The maravedi was the basic unit of the Spanish money of account. The peso (de cambio) was a Spanish money of account, equal to 272 maravedies. (The peso was also a silver coin, the value of which varied relative to the peso de cambio). The ducat (ducado, ducado de cambio) was a Spanish money of account, equal to 375 maravedies.

Portuguese

The real (plural "réis") was the basic unit of the Portuguese money of account. It was also a coin. The cruzado was a Portuguese money of account (also a coin) worth 400 réis at the beginning of the seventeenth

[†] Sources: Charles R. Boxer, ed., *The Tragic History of the Sea, 1589–1622* (Cambridge: Hakluyt Society, 1959); John J. McCusker, *Money and Exchange in Europe and America, 1600–1775: A Handbook* (Chapel Hill, N.C.: University of North Carolina Press, 1978); Richard Von Glahn, *Fountain of Fortune: Money and Monetary Policy in China, 1000–1700* (Berkeley: University of California Press, 1996); Endymion Wilkinson, *Chinese History: A Manual*, rev. ed., Harvard-Yenching Institute monograph series 52 (Cambridge, Mass.: Harvard UP, 2000).

century. The conto was a Portuguese money of account equal to one million réis.

Calculations based on Sir Isaac Newton's Assay Report (1702) suggest rough equivalences: 1 gulden = 0.65 thalers = 0.71 cruzados = 0.45 pesos.

Works Cited

The nature of this project makes a traditional, comprehensive bibliography unfeasible. For additional references, see the bibliographies of the regional missionary histories discussed in Chapter 1 above, and of my "Distant Souls" dissertation.

Abé, Takao. "A Japanese Perspective on the Jesuits in New France." In *Proceedings of the Twentieth Meeting of the French Colonial Historical Society, Cleveland, May 1994*, ed. A. J .B. Johnston, 14–26. Bowmanville: Mothersill Printing, 1995.

Acosta, José de. *De natvra Novi orbis, libri dvo, et de promvlgatione evangelii, apvd barbaros, sive De procvranda Indorvm salvte, libri sex*. Salamanca: Apud Guillelmum Foquel, 1638.

———. *De Procuranda Indorum Salute*. Collecion España misionera. Madrid: [s.n.], 1952.

———. *De temporibus novissimis libri quatuor*. Rome: Ex Typographia Iacobi Tornerij, 1590.

———. *Historia natural y moral de las Indias*, edited by Edmundo O'Gorman. Biblioteca americana. Serie de cronistas de Indias 38. Mexico: Fondo de Cultura Economica, 1962.

Albrecht, Dieter. *Die auswärtige Politik Maximilians von Bayern 1618–1635*. Göttingen: Vandenhoeck & Ruprecht, 1962.

———. *Maximilian I. Von Bayern 1573–1651*. Munich: Oldenbourg, 1998.

Alden, Dauril. *The Making of an Enterprise, The Society of Jesus in Portugal, Its Empire, and Beyond, 1540–1750*. Stanford: Stanford University Press, 1996.

Alegre, Francisco Javier. *Historia de la provincia de la Compañia de Jesús de Nueva España*, edited by Ernest J. Burrus and Felix Zubillaga. 4 vols. Rome: Institutum Historicum, 1956–60.

Altová, Blanka, and Jan Kulich. *St. Barbara Cathedral*. Libice nad Cidlinou: Gloriet, 2003.

Amrhyn, Franz Xaver (1655–1731). "Documenta pro Candidatis ad Missiones Indicas." In "Missionsaszetische Anweisungen aus dem 17. Jahrhundert." *Zeitschrift für Aszese und Mystik* 13 (1938): 202–15.

Anderson, Andrew Runni. *Alexander's Gate, Gog and Magog, and the Inclosed Nations*. Monographs of the Medieval Academy of America, no. 5. Cambridge, Mass.: The Medieval Academy of America, 1932.

Angel, Santos Hernández. *Los Jesuitas en América*. Colección Iglesia Católica en el Nuevo Mundo 5. Madrid: Editorial MAPFRE, 1992.

"Answers to Main Objections against Dominus Iesus." (August 17, 2006). http://www.ewtn.com/library/Theology/OBDOMIHS.HTM/.

Anzures y Bolaños, María del Carmen. "El Florilegio Medicinal de Johannes Steinhöffer: una contribución a la entobotánica mexicana." *Ibero-Americana Pragensia* 21 (1987):103–23.

———, ed. *Florilegio Medicinal*. Mexico: Academia Nacional de Medicina, 1978.

Appuhn-Radtke, Sibylle. *Das Thesenblatt im Hochbarock: Studien zu einer graphischen Gattung am Beispiel der Werke Bartholomaus Kilians*. Weissenhorn: A. H. Konrad, 1988.

Aristotle. *Aristotle's Physics, Books III and IV*, translated by Edward Hussey. New York: Oxford University Press, 1983.

Armellada, Cesareo de. *Por la Venezuela indigena de ayer y de hoy: Relatos de misioneros capuchinos en viaje por la Venezuela indigena*. Sociedad de Ciencias Naturales La Salle, Monografias, no. 5. Caracas: Sociedad de Ciencias Naturales La Salle, 1960.

Astráin, Antonio. *Historia de la Compañia de Jesús en la Asistencia de España*. Vols. 3–7. Madrid: 1909–25.

Atwell, William. "Ming China and the Emerging World Economy, c.1470–1650." In *The Ming Dynasty, 1368–1644, Part 2, Vol. 8, The Cambridge History of China*, edited by Frederick W. Mote and Denis Twitchett, 376–416. Cambridge: Cambridge University Press, 1998.

Audenaert, Willem. *Prosographia Iesuitica Belgica Antiqua (PIBA): A Biographical Dictionary of the Jesuits in the Low Countries, 1542–1773*. 4 vols. Leuven-Heverlee: Filosofisch en Theologisch College, S. J., 2000.

Aurich, Ursula. *China im Spiegel der deutschen Literatur des 18. Jahrhunderts*. Germanischen Studien 169. Berlin: Ebering, 1935.

Ayers, John. "The Early China Trade." In *The Origins of Museums: The Cabinets of Curiosities in Sixteenth- and Seventeenth-Century Europe*, edited by Oliver Impey and Arthur MacGregor, 259–66. Oxford: Clarendon, 1985.

Bachtler, Monika. "Der verlorene Kirchenschatz von St. Michael." In *St. Michael in München: Festschrift zum 400. Jahrestag der Grundsteinlegung und zum Abschluß des Weideraufbaus*, edited by Karl Wagner and Albert Keller, 127–35. Munich: Schnell & Steiner, 1983.

Backer, Augustin de. *Bibliotheque des ecrivains de la Compagnie de Jesus, ou, Notices bibliographiques*. Liege: L. Grandmont-Donders, 1853–61.

Baddeley, J. F. "Father Matteo Ricci's Chinese World Maps, 1584–1608." *The Geographical Journal* 50.4 (1917): 254–70.

Baier, Ronny. "Pfalz-Neuburg, Karl Philipp von." In *Biographisch-Bibliographisches Kirchenlexikon*, edited by Friedrich Wilhelm Bautz and Traugott Bautz, XXI.1154–60. Hamm: Bautz, 1970–.

Bailey, Gauvin A. *Art on the Jesuit Missions in Asia and Latin America, 1542–1773*. Toronto: University of Toronto Press, 1999.

———. *Between Renaissance and Baroque: Jesuit Art in Rome, 1565–1610*. Toronto: University of Toronto Press, 2003.

Balsamo, Jean. "Les premières relations des missions de la Chine et leur réception française (1556–1608)." *Nouvelle Revue du Seizième Siècle* 16.1 (1998): 155–84.

Bangert, William V. *A History of the Society of Jesus*. St. Louis: Institute of Jesuit Sources, 1972.

Bannon, John Francis. "The Jesuits in Sonora, 1620–1687." Ph.D. diss., University of California, Berkeley, 1939.

Barnadas, Joseph M. "The Catholic Church in Colonial Spanish America." In *The Cambridge History of Latin America*, I.511–40. Cambridge: Cambridge University Press, 1984.

Bartoli, Daniello. *Dell'historia della Compagnia de Giesu*. Rome: 1653.

———. *Opere del P. Daniello Bartoli, della Cina*. Turin: B. Marietti, 1825.

Baruzi, Jean. *Leibniz et l'organization religieuse de la terre* Paris: F. Alcan, 1907.

Bauerreiß, Romuald. *Kirchengeschichte Bayerns*. 5 vols. St. Ottilien: EOS Verlag, 1965.

Beckmann, Johannes. *China im Blickfeld der mexikanischen Bettelorden im 16. Jahrhundert*. Schöneck-Beckenried: Neue Zeitschrift fur Missionswissenschaft, 1964.

———. "Die Glaubensverbreitung und der europäische Absolutismus." In *Handbuch der Kirchengeschichte*, edited by Hubert Jedin, 5.255–350. Freiburg: Herder, 1965–1979.

———. "Missionsaszetische Anweisungen aus dem 17. Jahrhundert." *Zeitschrift für Aszese und Mystik* 13 (1938): 202–15.

———. "Utopien als missionarische Stoßkraft." In *Vermittlung zwischenkirchlicher Gemeinschaft: 50 Jahre Missionsgesellschaft Immensee*, edited by Jakob Baumgartner, 361–407. Schöneck-Beckenried: Neue Zeitschrift fur Missionswissenschaft, 1971.

Beidelman, T. O. "Social Theory and the Study of Christian Missions in Africa." *Africa* 44 (1974): 235–47.

Bell, Catherine. *Ritual: Perspectives and Dimensions*. New York: Oxford UP, 1996.

Bellah, Robert N. "Religious Evolution." *American Sociological Review* 29 (3): 358–74.

Bentley, Jerry H. *Old World Encounters: Cross-Cultural Contacts and Exchanges in Pre-Modern Times*. Oxford: Oxford University Press, 1993.

Berger, Willy R. *China-Bild und China-Mode im Europa der Aufklärung*. Cologne: Böhlau, 1990.

Bernard, Henri. "L'Encyclopédie astronomique du Père Schall (Tch'ong-tcheng li-cho, 1629, et Si-yang sin-fa li-chou, 1645). La réforme du calendrier chinois sous l'influence de Clavius, de Galilée et de Kepler." *Monumenta Serica* III (1938): 35–77, 441–527.

———. *Le Père Matthieu Ricci et la Société Chinoise de son temps (1552–1610)*. 2 vols. Tientsin: Hautes études, 1937.

Bettray, Johannes. "Österreichische Missionare in Lateinamerika." *Zeitschrift für Lateinamerika* 8 (1976): 54–67.

Bhardwaj, Surinder M. and Pillai Lokacarya. "Hindu Pilgrimage." *Encyclopedia of Religion*, vol. 11, 353–54. New York: Macmillan, 1987.

Bireley, Robert. *Maximilian von Bayern, Adam Contzen S. J. und die Gegenreformation in Deutschland 1624–1635*. Gottingen: Vandenhoeck und Ruprecht, 1975.

Blair, Emma Helen and James Alexander Robertson. *The Philippine Islands, 1493–1803*. 28 vols. Cleveland, OH: The A. H. Clark Company, 1903–09.

Blankenburg, [Mary] Angela. "German Missionary Writers in Paraguay." *Mid-America* 29 (1947): 34–68 and 122–31.

Bodenehr, Hans Georg. *Sac. Imperii Romano Germanici Geographica Descriptio.* Augsburg: H. G. Bodenehr, 1677.

Boehmer, Heinrich. *The Jesuits: An Historical Study*. Translated by Paul Zeller Strodach. Philadelphia: Castle Press, 1928.

Bolton, Herbert Eugene. "The Mission as a Frontier Institution in the Spanish-American Colonies." *American Historical Review* 23 (1917): 42–61.

———. *Rim of Christendom: A Biography of Eusebio Francisco Kino, Pacific Coast Pioneer.* New York: Macmillan, 1936.

Bordeau, F. "Le vocabulaire de la mission." *Parole et mission* 3 (1960): 9–27.

Borges Morán, Pedro. "Características sociológicas de las órdenes misioneras americanas." In *Evangelización y Teología en América* (Siglo XVI), I.619–25. X Simposio International de Teología de la Universidad de Navarra. Pamplona: Servicio de Publicaciones, Universidad de Navarra, 1990.

———. *El envío de misioneros a américa durante la época española*. Biblioteca Salmanticensis, 18. Salamanca: Universidad Pontificia, 1977.

———. "El sentido trascendente del descubrimiento y conversión de Indias." *Missionalia Hispanica* 13 (1956): 141–77.

———. *Métodos Misionales en la Cristianización de América. Siglo XVI*. Madrid: 1960.

Bösel, Richard. "Pozzo, Andrea." *Dictionary of Art*, edited by Jane Turner, 25.413–17. New York: Grove, 1996.

Bossy, John. "Catholicity and Nationality in the Northern Counter-Reformation." In *Religion and National Identity*, edited by Stuart Mews, 285–96. Studies in Church History 18. Oxford: Basil Blackwell, 1982.

———. "Postscript." In H. Outram Evennett, *The Spirit of the Counter-Reformation*. Cambridge: Cambridge University Press, 1968.

Bourdieu, Pierre. *Outline of a Theory of Practice*, translated by Richard Nice. New York: Cambridge University Press, 1977.

Boxer, Charles Ralph. "The *Carreira da India*: Ships, Mens, Cargoes, Voyages." In *From Lisbon to Goa, 1500–1750: Studies in Portuguese Maritime Enterprise*, I.33–61. London: 1984.

———. *The Christian Century in Japan, 1549–1650*. Berkeley: University of California, 1951.

———. *The Church Militant and Iberian Expansion*. Baltimore: Johns Hopkins UP, 1978.

———. "European Missionaries and Chinese Clergy, 1654–1810." In *The Age of Partnership: Europeans in Asia before Dominion*, edited by Blair B. Kling and M. N. Pearson, 97–121. Honolulu: University Press of Hawaii, 1979.

———. *The Great Ship from Amacon, Annals of Macao and the Old Japan Trade, 1555–1640*. Lisbon: Centro de Estudos Históricos Ultramarinos, 1959.

———. "Macao as a Religious and Commercial Entrepôt in the Sixteenth and Seventeenth Centuries." *Acta Asiatica* 26 (1974): 64–90.

———. "Notes on Chinese Abroad in the Late Ming and Early Manchu Periods." *T'ien Hsia Monthly* IX (1939): 447–68.

———. *The Portuguese Seaborne Empire, 1600–1800*. London: Hutchison, 1965.

———. *The Tragic History of the Sea, 1589–1622.* Cambridge: Hakluyt Society, 1959.

Brading, David A. *The First America: The Spanish Monarchy, Creole Patriots, and the Liberal State 1492–1867*. Cambridge: Cambridge University Press, 1991.

Brady, Thomas A., Jr. "Confessionalization—The Career of a Concept." In *Confessionalization in Europe, 1550–1700: Essays in Honor and Memory of Bodo Nishan*, edited by John M. Headley, Hans J. Hillerbrand, and Anthony J. Papalas, 1–20. Burlinton, VT: Ashgate, 2004.

———. "Limits of Religious Violence in Early Modern Europe." In *Religion und Gewalt: Konflikte, Rituale, Deutungen (1500–1800)*, edited by Kaspar von Greyerz and Kim Siebenhüner, 125–51. Göttingen: Vandenhoeck & Ruprecht, 2006.

———. "The Rise of Merchant Empires, 1400–1700: A European Counterpart." In *The Political Economy of Merchant Empires: State Power and World Trade 1350–1750*, edited by James D. Tracy, 117–60. New York: Cambridge University Press, 1991.

Braun, Joseph. *Die Kirchenbauten der Deutschen Jesuiten: Ein Beitrag zur Kultur- und Kunstgeschichte des 17. und 18. Jahrhunderts*. Freiburg im Breisgau: Herder, 1908.

Braunsberger, Otto, ed. *Beati Petri Canisii Epistulae et Acta*. 8 vols. Freiburgi Brisgoviae: S. Herder, 1896–1923.

Brockey, Liam. *Journey to the East: The Jesuit Mission in China, 1579–1724*. Cambridge: Harvard University Press, 2007.

Brodrick, James. *Origines et expansion des Jésuites*. Paris: SFELT, 1950.

———. *Saint Peter Canisius, S. J., 1521–1597*. London: Sheed and Ward, 1935.

Broggio, Paolo. *Evangelizzare il mondo: Le missioni della Compagnia di Gesù tra Europa e America (secoli XVI–XVII)*. Rome: Carocci: 2004.

Brou, Alexandre. *Les Jésuites de la légende*. 2 vols. Paris: Victor Retaux, 1906–7.

Brouillard, René. "Suarez, François." In *Dictionnaire de théologie catholique*. Vol. 14:2. Paris: Letouzey et Ane, 1903–50.

Brucker, Joseph. "La Chine et l'Extrême-Orient d'après les trauvaux historiques du P. Antoine Gaubil." *Revue des Questions Historiques* 37 (1885): 485–539.

Brüning, Walter M. "Zur Vorgeschichte der Messe 'Propaganda Fidei.' Eine Bittschrift aus der Sonoramission im Jahre 1707." *Archivum Historicum Societatis Iesu* 8 (1939): 319–27.

Bryce, James. *The Holy Roman Empire*. New York: Macmillan, 1877.

Burke, Peter. "America and the Rewriting of World History." In *America in European Consciousness, 1493–1750*, edited by Karen Ordahl Kupperman, 33–51. Chapel Hill: University of North Carolina, 1995.

———. "The Jesuits and the Art of Translation in Early Modern Europe." In *The Jesuits, II: Cultures, Sciences, and the Arts, 1540–1773*, edited by John O'Malley, Gauvin Alexander Bailey, Steven J. Harris, and T. Frank Kennedy, 24–32. Toronto: Toronto University Press, 2005.

Burns, Kathryn. *Colonial Habits: Convents and the Spiritual Economy of Cuzco, Peru.* Durham, North Carolina: Duke University Press, 1999.

Burrus, Ernest J., ed. *Correspondencia del P. Kino con los generales de la Compañia de Jesús, 1682–1707.* Testimonio histórico 5. Mexico: Editorial Jus, 1961.

———. *Kino and the Cartography of Northwestern New Spain.* Tucson: Arizona Pioneers' Historical Society, 1965.

———. *Kino escribe a la duquesa. Correspondencia del P. Eusebio Francisco Kino con la duquesa de Aveiro y otros documentos.* Colección Chimalistac 18. Madrid: J. Porrúa Turanzas, 1964.

———. "Kino's Relative, Father Martino Martini, S. J.: A Comparison of Two Outstanding Missionaries." *Neue Zeitschrift für Missionswissenschaft* 31 (1975): 100–109.

———. *La obra cartográfica de la Provincia Mexicana de la Compañia de Jesús (1567–1967).* 2 vols. Madrid: Ediciones Jose Porrua Turanzas, 1967.

Buser, Thomas. "Jerome Nadal and Early Jesuit Art in Rome." *Art Bulletin* LVIII (1976): 424–33.

Buxbaum, Engelbert Maximilian. *Petrus Canisius und die Kirchliche Erneuerung des Herzogtums Bayern, 1549–1556.* Rome: Institutum Historicum S. I., 1973.

Cabantous, Alain. *Le Ciel dans la mer: christianisme et civilisation maritime (XVe–XIXe siècle).* Paris: Fayard, 1990.

Cain, Seymour. "Study of Religion: History of Study." *Encyclopedia of Religion*, vol. 12, 153–55. New York: Macmillan, 1987.

Campanella, Tommaso. *Articuli prophetales*, edited by Germana Ernst. Florence: La nuova Italia, 1977.

———. *Atheismus Triumphatus seu Reductio ad religionem per scientiarum veritates . . . contra Antichristianismum Achitophellisticum.* Rome: 1631.

———. *Lettere*, edited by Vincenzo Spampanato. Bari: G. Latera, 1927.

———. *Monarchia Messiae*, edited by Luigi Firpo. Turin: Bottega d'Erasmo, 1960.

———. *Quod reminiscentur et convertentur ad dominum universi fines terrae* (Ps. 21), edited by Romano Amerio. Padua: Ex officina libraria Cedam, 1939.

———. *Teologia.* Edited by Romano Amerio. 30 vols. Milano: Società editrice "Vita e pensiero," 1936–80.

Campeau, Lucien. *L'évêché de Québec, 1674: aux origines du premier diocèse érigé en Amérique française.* Québec: Société historique de Québec, 1974.

Canny, Nicholas. "Early Modern Ireland c.1500–1700." In *The Oxford Illustrated History of Ireland*, edited by R. F. Foster, 104–60. New York: Oxford University Press, 1989.

Caraveli, Anna. "The Symbolic Village: Community Born in Performance." *Journal of American Folklore* 98 (1985): 259–86.

Carayon, Auguste. *Bibliographie Historique de la Compagnie de Jésus ou Catalogue des ouvrages relatifs a l'histoire des Jésuites depuis leur origine jusqu'a nos jours.* Paris: Auguste Durand, 1864.

Carrasco, Davíd. *Religions of Mesoamerica: Cosmovision and Ceremonial Centers.* San Francisco: Harper & Row, 1990.

Carsten, F. L. *Princes and Parliaments in Germany: From the Fifteenth to the Eighteenth Century.* Oxford: Clarendon Press, 1963.

Castillo Graxeda, José del. *Compendio de la vida y virtudes de la venerable Catarina de San Juan.* Bibliotheca Angelopolitana 3. Puebla: Gobierno del Estado de Puebla, Secretaria de Cultura, 1987.

Caterino, Aldo. "Transoceanic Navigation in the Seventeenth Century: The Portuguese Route to the Indies." In *Martino Martini: A Humanist and Scientist in Seventeenth Century China,* edited by Franco Demarchi and Riccardo Scartezzini, 65–90. Trento: Università degli Studi di Trento, 1996.

Cather, Willa. *Shadows on the Rock.* New York: Knopf, 1980.

Cave, Terence. "Locating the Early Modern." *Paragraph* 29 (2006): 12–26.

Ch'en, Kenneth. "Matteo Ricci's Contribution to and Influence on Geographical Knowledge in China." *Journal of the American Oriental Society* 59 (1939): 325–59 and 509.

Châtellier, Louis. *The Religion of the Poor: Rural Missions in Europe and the Formation of Modern Catholicism, c. 1500-c.1800,* translated by Brian Pearce. Cambridge: Cambridge University Press, 1997.

Chaunu, Pierre, and Huguette Chaunu. *Séville et l'Atlantique.* 8 vols. Paris: A. Colin, 1955–56.

Chaves, Jonathan. "Inculturation versus Evangelization: Are Contemporary Values Causing Us to Misinterpret the 16–18th Century Jesuit Missionaries?" *Sino-Western Cultural Relations Journal* 22 (2000): 56–60.

Chen Minsun. "Ferdinand Verbiest and the Geographical Works by Jesuits in Chinese 1584–1674." In *Ferdinand Verbiest (1623–1688): Jesuit Missionary, Scientist, Engineer and Diplomat,* edited by John W. Witek, 124–33. St. Augustin: Institut Monumenta Serica, 1994.

Chevalier, Francois. *Land and Society in Colonial Mexico: The Great Hacienda.* Berkeley: University of California Press, 1963.

China und Europa: Chinaverständnis und Chinamode im 17. und 18. Jahrhundert. Ausstellungskatalog. Verwaltung der Staatlichen Schlößer und Gärten. Berlin: 1973.

Ching, Julia and Willard G. Oxtoby. *Moral Enlightenment: Leibniz and Wolff on China.* St. Augustin: Institut Monumenta Serica, 1992.

Christian, David. "Silk Roads or Steppe Roads? The Silk Roads in World History." *Journal of World History* 11 (2000): 1–26.

Christian, William A., Jr.. *Local Religion in Sixteenth-Century Spain.* Princeton: Princeton University Press, 1981.

Church St. Ignatius of Loyola, Rome. Rome: Chiesa di Sant'ignazio, 1991.

Ciolek, T. Matthew. "Old World Traditional Trade Routes (OWTRAD) Project." May 6, 2004. http://www.ciolek.com/owtrad.html.

Clausen, Søren. "Early Modern China—A Preliminary Postmortem." www.hum.au.dk/ckulturf/pages/publications/sc/china.htm.

Clendinnen, Inga. "Franciscan Missionaries in Sixteenth-Century Mexico." In *Disciplines of Faith: Studies in Religion, Politics, and Patriarchy,* edited by J. Obelkevich, L. Roper, and R. Samuel, 229–45. New York: Routledge and Kegan Paul, 1987.

Clossey, Luke. "Distant Souls: Global Religion and the Jesuit Missions of Germany, Mexico, and China, 1595–1705." PhD dissertation, University of California, Berkeley, 2004.

———. "The Early-Modern Jesuit Missions as a Global Movement." UC World History Workshop, Working Papers from the World History Workshop Conference Series 3. http://repositories.cdlib.org/ucwhw/wp/3.

———. "Early Modern World." In *Berkshire Encyclopedia of World History*, 592–98. Great Barrington, MA: Berkshire Publishing Group, 2004.

———. "Faith in Empire: Religious Sources of Legitimacy for Expansionist Early-Modern States." In *Politics and Reformations: Communities, Polities, Nations, and Empires*, edited by Christopher Ocker, Michael Printy, Peter Starenko, and Peter Wallace, 571–87. Studies in Medieval and Reformation Traditions, 128. Leiden: Brill, 2007.

———. "Merchants, Migrants, Missionaries, and Globalization in the Early-Modern Pacific." *Journal of Global History* 1 (2006): 41–58.

Codignola, Luca. *The Coldest Harbour of the Land: Simon Stock and Lord Baltimore's Colony in Newfoundland, 1621–1649*. Montreal: McGill-Queen's University Press, 1988.

———. "The Holy See and the Conversion of the Indians in French and British North America, 1486–1760." In *America in European Consciousness, 1493–1750*, edited by Karen Ordahl Kupperman, 195–242. Chapel Hill: University of North Carolina, 1995.

Cohen, Patricia Cline. *A Calculating People*. Chicago: University of Chicago Press, 1982.

Cohen, Thomas V. "Why the Jesuits Joined, 1540–1600." *Historical Papers* [Canadian Historical Association] (December 1974): 237–57.

Colección de documentos inéditos relativos al descubrimiento, conquista y organización de las antiguas posesiones españolas de ultramar. 2. ser. Madrid: Real Academia de la Historia. Madrid, Est.tip. "Sucesores de Rivadeneyra," 1885–1932.

Collani, Claudia von. "*Der Neue Welt-Bott*: A Preliminary Survey." *Sino-Western Cultural Relations Journal* 25 (2003): 16–43.

———. *Eine wissenschaftliche Akademie für China: Briefe des Chinamissionars Joachim Bouvet S. J. an Gottfried Wilhelm Leibniz und Jean-Paul Bignon über die Erforschung der chinesischen Kultur, Sprache, und Geschichte*. Stuttgart: Franz Steiner, 1989.

———. "P. Kilian Stumpf SJ—Nachfolger des hl. Kilian in China." *Würzburger Diözesangeschichtsblätter* 51 (1989): 545–67.

Columbus, Christopher. *The Libro de las profecías of Christopher Columbus*, translated by Delno C. West and August Kling. Gainesville, Fla.: University of Florida Press, 1991.

Correia-Afonso, J. "Indo-American Contacts through Jesuit Missionaries." *Indica* 14.1 (1977): 29–42.

Corsi, Elisabetta. "Late Baroque Painting in China Prior to the Arrival of Matteo Ripa Giovanni Gherardini and the Perspective Painting Called Xianfa." In *La missione cattolica in Cina tra i secoli XVIII–XIX: Matteo Ripe e il Collegio dei Cinesi*, ed. Michele Fatica and Francesco D'Arelli, 102–22. Naples: Istituto Universitario Orientale, 1999.

Cortés Ossorio, Juan. *Reparos historiales apologeticos dirigidos al excelentissimo Señor Conde de Villavmbrosa . . .: propvestos de parte de los missioneros apostolicos del imperio de la China. Representando los descvidos, qve secometen en vn libro, que le ha publicado en Madrid, en grave perjuizio de aquella mission.* Pamplona: 1677.

Couclelis, Helen. "Aristotelian Spatial Dynamics in the Age of Geographic Information Systems." In *Spatial and Temporal Reasoning in Geographic Information Systems,* edited by Max J. Egenhofer and Reginal G. Golledge, 109–18. New York: Oxford University Press, 1998.

Crétineau-Joly, J. *Histoire religieuse, politique et litteraire de la Compagnie de Jésus.* 6 vols. Paris: Paul Mellier, 1844–46.

Crivelli, Camillus. "Mexico." In *The Catholic Encyclopedia.* September 15, 2003. http://www.newadvent.org/cathen/.

Crone, G[erald] R[oe]. *Maps and Their Makers: An Introduction to the History of Cartography.* 5th ed. Hamden, Conn.: Archon Books, 1978.

Crosby, Alfred W. *The Measure of Reality: Quantification and Western Society, 1250–1600.* Cambridge: Cambridge University Press, 1997.

Crucé, Emeric. *Le Nouveau Cynée: ou, discours des occasions et moyens d'établir une paix générale et la liberté du commerce par tout le monde.* Paris: EDHIS, Éditions d'histoire sociale, 1976.

Cummins, J. S. *A Question of Rites: Friar Domingo Navarrete and the Jesuits in China.* Hants: Scolar Press, 1993.

———. "Two Missionary Methods in China: Mendicants and Jesuits." *Archivo Ibero-America* 38 (1978): 33–108.

Dahlmann, Joseph. *Die Sprachkunde und die Missionen.* Freiburg im Breisgau: Herder, 1891.

Davenport, Frances G., ed. *European Treaties Bearing on the History of the United States and Its Dependencies to 1648.* 4 vols. Washington, D. C.: Carnegie Institution, 1917–37.

Davidson, N[icholas] S. *The Counter-Reformation.* Oxford: Basil Blackwell, 1987.

Davidson, Peter. "The Jesuit Garden." In *The Jesuits II: Cultures, Sciences, and the Arts, 1540- 1773,* edited by John W. O'Malley, Gauvin Alexander Bailey, Steven J. Harris, and T. Frank Kennedy, 86–107. Toronto: University of Toronto Press, 2006.

Dávila Padilla, Agustín. *Historia de la fundación y discurso de la provincia de Santiago de México, de la Orden de Predicadores.* 3d ed. Colección de grandes cronicas mexicanas 1. Mexico: Editorial Academia Literaria, 1955.

Dawson, Christopher, ed. *The Mongol Mission: Narratives and Letters of the Franciscan Missionaries in Mongolia and China in the Thirteenth and Fourteenth Centuries.* London: Sheed and Ward, 1955; reprinted as *Mission to Asia,* New York: Harper & Row, 1966.

De Bry, Theodor. *Americae Nona & postrema Pars, qva de ratione lementorvm: de novi orbis natvra . . .* Frankfurt: Matthias Becker, 1602.

De Vries, Jan. *Economy of Europe in an Age of Crisis.* New York: Cambridge University Press, 1988.

Decorme, Gerard. *La obra de los Jesuitas mexicanos durante la época colonial, 1572–1767.* Mexico: Antigua Librería Robredo de J. Porrúa e Hijos, 1941.

Dehaisnes, Chretien. *Vie du Pere Nicolas Trigault de la Compagnie de Jesus*. Paris: P. Lethielleux, 1864.

Dehergne, Joseph. *Répertoire des Jésuites de Chine de 1552 à 1800*. Rome: Institutum Historicum S. I., 1973.

Delacroix, S. *Histoire Universelle des Missions Catholiques*. 4 vols. Paris: Grund, 1956–59.

Demel, Walter. "The 'National' Images of China in Different European Countries, ca. 1550–1800." In *Images de la Chine: Le contexte occidental de la sinologie naissante*, edited by Edward J. Malatesta and Yves Raguin, 85–125. Variétés sinologiques—nouvelle série 78. Tapei and Paris: 1995.

Deslandres, Dominique. "The French Jesuits' Missionary World." In *The Jesuits: Cultures, Sciences, and the Arts, 1540–1773*, edited by John W. O'Malley, Gauvin Alexander Bailey, Steven J. Harris, and T. Frank Kennedy, 258–73. Toronto: University of Toronto Press, 1999.

————. "Mission et altérité: Les missionnaires français et la définition de l''Autre' au XVIIe siècle." In *Proceedings of the Nineteenth Meeting of the French Colonial Historical Society, Providence, R. I., May 1993*, edited by James Pritchard, 1–13. Cleveland: French Colonial Historical Society, 1993.

Díaz del Castillo, Bernal. *The True History of the Conquest of New Spain*, translated by Maurice Keating. London: John Dean, 1800.

Dickens, Charles. *Pictures from Italy*. London: Penguin Classics, 1998.

Die Jesuiten in Bayern, 1549–1773: Ausstellung des Bayersiches Hauptstaatsarchiv und der Oberdeutschen Provinz der Gesellschaft Jesu. Ausstellungskataloge der Staatlichen Archive Bayerns 29. Weissenhorn: A. H. Konrad, 1991.

"Die Zukunft der Ökumene im Rhein-Main-Gebiet: Reaktionen auf die Vatikan-Erklärung 'Dominus Iesus,'" *Frankfurter Allgemeine Zeitung* (October 28, 2000), translation of *L'Osservatore Romano* [Weekly Edition in English] (November 22, 2000), p. 10.

Dimler, G. Richard. *Friedrich Spee's Trutznachtigall*. German Studies in America 13. Bern: Herbert Lang, 1973.

Doctrina cristiana en lengua española y mexicana, por los religiosos de la Orden de Santo Domingo, obra impresa en México por Juan Pablos en 1548, y ahora editada en facsímil. Colección de incunables americanos, siglo XVI, 1. Madrid: Ediciones Cultura Hispánica, 1944.

"Dogmatic Constitution of the Church Lumen Gentium," (August 17, 2006). http://www.vatican.va/archive/hist_councils/ii_vatican_council/documents/vat-ii_const_19641121_lumen-gentium_en.html.

Dollinger, Heinz. *Studien zur Finanzreform Maximilian I. von Bayern: Ein Beitrag zur Geschichte des Fruhabsolutismus*. Schriftenreihe der Historischen Kommission bei der Bayerischen Akademie der Wissenschaften 8. Göttingen: Vandenhoeck u. Ruprecht, 1968.

"Dominus Iesus," (August 17, 2006). http://www.vatican.va/roman_curia/congregations/cfaith/documents/rc_co n_cfaith_doc_20000806_dominus-iesus_en.html.

Donnelly, John Patrick. "Antonio Possevino's Plan for World Evangelization." *Catholic Historical Review* 74.2 (1988): 179–98.

————. "Art and the Early Jesuits: The Historical Context." in *Jesuit Art in North American Collections: Milwaukee Haggerty Art Museum*. Milwaukee: Marquette University, 1991.

Döring, Jürgen. "Weltkugel und Landkarte als Motive." In *Mittel und Motive der karikatur in fünf Jahrhunderten: Bild als Waffe*, edited by Gerhard Langemeyer, 221–24. Munich: Prestel, 1985.

Dörrie, Heinrich. *Drei Texte zur Geschichte der Ungarn und Mongolen: Die Missionreisen des fr. Julianus O. P. ins Uralgebiet (1234/5) und nach Rubland (1237) und Bericht der Erzbiscofs Peter uber die Tartaren*. Nachrichten der Akademie der Wissenschaften in Göttingen. I., Philologisch-Historische Klasse 6. Göttingen: Vandenhoeck & Ruprecht, 1956.

Dubowy, Ernst. "Felix Anton Scheffler: ein Beitrag zur Kunstgeschichte des 18. Jahrhunderts." *Jahrbuch des Vereins für christliche Kunst in München* 6 (1925/6): 89–281.

Duhr, Bernhard. *Deutsche Auslandsehnsucht im achtzehnten Jahrhundert aus der überseeischen Missionsarbeit deutscher Jesuiten*. Stuttgart: Ausland und Heimat Verlags-Aktiengesellschaft, 1928.

————. *Geschichte der Jesuiten in den Länder Deutscher Zunge*. 4 vols. Freiburg im Breisgau: Herder, 1907–28.

————. "Zur Geschichte der deutschen Volksmissionen in der 2. Hälfte des 17. Jahrhunderts." *Historisches Jahrbuch* 37 (1916): 593–623.

Dunne, George H. *Generation of Giants: The Story of the Jesuits in China in the Last Decades of the Ming Dynasty*. London: Burns and Oates, 1962.

Dunne, Peter Masten. *Black Robes in Lower California*. Berkeley: University of California, 1952.

————. *Pioneer Jesuits in Northern Mexico*. Los Angeles: University of Cailifornia, 1944.

Edgerton, Samuel Y. *The Renaissance Rediscovery of Linear Perspective*. New York: Basic Books, 1975.

Egaña, Antonio, ed. *Monumenta Peruana*. 8 vols. Rome: Institutum Historicum Societatis Jesus, 1954–86.

Eliot, T. S. *Sweeney Agonistes, in The Complete Poems and Plays, 1909–1950*, 74–85. New York: Harcourt Brace & Company, 1980.

Elkan, Albert. "Entstehung und Entwicklung des Begriffs 'Gegenreformation.'" *Historische Zeitschrift* 112 (1914): 473–93.

Engelhardt, Zephyrin. *Lower California*. Vol. 1, *The Missions and Missionaries of California*. San Francisco: James H. Barry Co., 1908.

Ettelt, Beatrix, ed. *Die Jesuiten in Ingolstadt, 1549–1773: Austellung in Ingolstadt 12. Oktober 1991 bis 12. Januar 1992*. Ingolstadt: Stadtsarchiv Ingolstadt, 1991.

Etzioni, Amitai. "Toward a Theory of Public Ritual." *Sociological Theory* 18 (2000): 44–59.

———— and Edward Lehman. "Some Dangers in 'Valid' Social Measurements: Preliminary Notes." *The Annals of the American Academy of Political and Social Science* 373 (1967): 1–15.

Evans, R. J. *Rudolf II and His World*. Oxford: Clarendon Press, 1973.

Faber, Petrus. *Beatri Petri Fabri, epistolae, memoriale et processus: ex autographis aut archetypis potissimum deprompta.* Monumenta historica Societatis Iesu 48. Rome: Institutum Historicum Societatis Iesu, 1972.

Faralli, Carla. "Le missioni dei Gesuiti in Italia." *Bolletino della Società di Studi Valdesi* 138, 1975.

Farrugia, Edward. "Im Banne des Orients: Werdegang und Zukunftsorientierung des hl. Ignatius von Loyola." In *Ignatius von Loyola und die Gesellschaft Jesu 1491–1556*, edited by Andreas Falkner and Paul Imhof, 397–408. Würzburg: Echter, 1990.

Favre, Pierre. *Bienheureux Pierre Favre: Mémorial.* Translated by Michel de Certeau. Lyon: E. Vitte, [1960].

Feest, Christian F. "The Collecting of American Indian Artifacts in Europe, 1493–1750." In *America in European Consciousness, 1493–1750*, edited by Karen Ordahl Kupperman, 324–60. Chapel Hill: University of North Carolina, 1995.

———. "Vienna's Mexican Treasures: Aztec, Mixtec, and Tarascan Works from Sixteenth Century Austrian Collections." *Archiv für Völkerkunde* 44 (1990): 1–64.

Fletcher, Joseph. "Integrative History: Parallels and Interconnections in the Early Modern Period, 1500–1800." In *Niǵuća Bičig / Pi Wên Shu* 秘文書 */ Journal of Turkish Studies / Türklük Bilgisi Araştırmalari* 9 (1985): 37–57.

Foley, Henry. *Records of the English Province of the Society of Jesus.* 6 vols. London: Burns and Oates, 1880.

Foresta, Patrizio. "Die 'Mission in Germaniam.' Die Wahrnehmung des Apostolats durch den jungen Canisius." In *Sendung – Eroberung – Begegnung: Franz Xaver, die Gesellschaft Jesu und die katholische Weltkirche im Zeitalter des Barock*, edited by Johannes Meier, 31–66. Wiesbaden: Harrassowitz, 2005.

Foss, Theodore N. "A Western Interpretation of China: Jesuit Cartography." In *East Meets West: The Jesuits in China, 1582–1773*, edited by Charles Ronan and Bonnie Oh, 209–51. Chicago: Loyola University Press, 1988.

Francis Xavier. *Epistolae S. Francisci Xaverii aliaque eius scripta: Nova editio ex integro refecta textibus, introductionibus, notis, appendicibus aucta*, edited by Georgius Schurhammer et Iosephus Wicki. Monumenta historica Societatis Iesu 67–68. 2 vols. Rome: "Monumenta Historica Soc. Iesu," 1944–45.

Franco, Antonio. *Synopsis Annalium S. J. in Lusitania ab anno 1540 usque ad annum 1725.* Augustae Vindel.: Sumptibus Philippi, Martini, & Joannis Veith, Hæredum, 1726.

Franke, Wolfgang. *China und das Abendland.* Göttingen: Vandenhoeck & Ruprecht, 1962.

Freher, Marquard. *Germanicarvm rervm scriptores aliqvot insignes, hactenvs incogniti.* Frankfurt/Main: Andreas Wechels Erben, Claude de Marne & Johann Aubry, 1600–02.

Friedman, John Block. *The Monstrous Races in Medieval Art and Thought.* Cambridge, Mass.: Harvard University Press, 1981.

Friedman, Jonathan. "Religion as Economy and Economy as Religion," *Ethnos* 40.1–4 (1975): 46.

Friedrich, Markus. "Beispielgeschichten in den *Litterae Annuae*: Überlegungen zur Gestaltung und Funktion einer vernachlässigten Literaturgattung." In

Das Beispiel, Epistemologie des Exemplarischen, edited by Nicolas Pethes, Jens Ruchatz, and Stefan Willer, 143–66. Berlin: Kulturverlag Kadmos, 2007.

Fröschle, Hartmut. *Die Deutschen in Lateinamerika: Schiksal und Leistung.* Tübingen-Basel: Erdmann, 1979.

Funkenstein, Amos. *Theology and the Scientific Imagination from the Middle Ages to the Seventeenth Century.* Princeton: Princeton University Press, 1986.

Gabrieli, Giuseppe. "Giovanni Schreck Linceo: Gesuita e missionario in Cina e le sue lettere dall'Asia." *Rendiconti della R. Accademia dei Lincei, Classe di Scienze morali, storiche e filologiche* ser VI, vol. 12, 5–6 (1936): 462–514.

Galán García, Augustín. "La organización misional jesuita y su hospicio de Indias en Sevilla (1566–1717): Notas para su estudio." *Archivo Hispalense* 220 (1989): 105–13.

García, Genaro. *Don Juan de Palafox y Mendoza, obispo de Puebla y Osma, visitador y virrey de la Nueva Espana.* Mexico: Libreria de Bouret, 1918.

García, Gregorio. *Origen de los indios del Nuevo Mundo*, edited by Andrés González de Barcia. Biblioteca americana. Mexico: Fondo de Cultura Económica, 1980.

García Icazbalceta, Joaquin, ed. *Nueva colección de documentos para la historia de Mexico.* 5 vols. Mexico: Andrade y Morales, sucesores, 1886–92.

Geoffroy de Grandmaison. *Saint Ignace de Loyola.* Paris: Laurens, 1930.

Gerlich, R., and T. van Oorschot. "Spee von Langenfeld, Friedrich." In *Diccionario histórico de la Compañia de Jesús: biográfico-temático.* Rome: Institutum Historicum, 2001.

Gernet, Jacques. *Chine et christianisme: action et reaction.* Paris: Gallimard, 1982.

———. "Christian and Chinese Visions of the World in the Seventeenth Century." *Chinese Science* IV (1980): 1–17.

Giddens, Anthony. *The Consequences of Modernity.* Stanford: Stanford University Press, 1990.

Ginzburg, Carlo. "Killing a Chinese Mandarin: The Moral Implications of Distance." *New Left Review* 208 (1994): 107–19.

Gliozzi, Giuliano. *Adamo e il Nuovo Mondo.* Florence: La nuova Italia, 1977.

Goddard, Peter A. "The Devil in New France: Jesuit Demonology 1611–1650." *Canadian Historical Review* 78 (1997): 40–62.

Godinho, Vitorino Magalhães. *L'économie de l'empire portugais aux XVe et XVIe siècles.* Paris: SEVPEN, 1969.

Goercke, E. "Die ersten deutschen Überseemissionare der Jesuiten stellte das Ingolstädter Kolleg der Societät Jesu." *Ingolstädter Heimatblätter* 49 (1986): 33–36.

Goetstouwers, J. B., ed. *Synopsis historiae Societatis Jesu.* Leuven: Typis ad Sancti Alphonsi, 1950.

Goldstone, Jack A. "Efflorescences and Economic Growth in World History: Rethinking the 'Rise of the West' and the Industrial Revolution." *Journal of World History* 13.2 (Fall 2002): 323–89.

———. "The Problem of the 'Early Modern' World." *Journal of the Economic and Social History of the Orient* 41 (1998): 249–84.

Golvers, Noël, ed. *The "Astronomia Europaea" of Ferdinand Verbiest, S. J. (Dillingen, 1687). Text, translation, notes.* St. Augustin: Institut Monumenta Serica, 1992.

———. *François de Rougement, S. J., Missionary in Ch'ang-shu (Chiang-nan): A Study of the Account Book (1674–1676) and the Elogium.* Leuven: Leuven University Press, 1999.

Gómez Canedo, Lino. "Fuentes Mexicanas para la historia de las misiones en el Extremo Oriente." In *La expansión hispanoamérica en Asia, siglos XVI y XVII,* edited by Ernesto de la Torre Villar, 15–30. Fondo de cultura Mexico, economica, 1980.

González Rodríguez, Luis. "Un cronista flamenco de la Tarahumara en 1688: Petrus Thomas van Hamme." *Estudios de historia novohispana* 3 (1970): 129–47.

Gorman, Michael John. "The Angel and the Compass: Athanasius Kircher's Geographical Project." In *Athanasius Kircher: The Last Man Who Knew Everything,* ed. Paula Findlen, 239–62. London: Routledge, 2004.

Gregory, Brad. *Salvation at Stake: Christian Martyrdom in Early Modern Europe.* Cambridge, Mass.: Harvard University Press, 1999.

Grueber, Johann. *Als Kundschafter des Papstes nach China 1656–1664: Die erste Durchquerung Tibets,* edited by Franz Braumann. Stuttgart: K. Thienemann, 1985.

Grulich, Rudolf. *Der Beitrag der böhmischen Länder zur Weltmission des 17. und 18. Jahrhunderts.* Königstein: Institut für Kirchengeschichte von Böhmen, Mähren, Schlesien, 1981.

Guibert, Joseph de. *La spiritualité de la Compagnie de Jésus; esquisse historique.* Edited by Edmond Lamalle. Bibliotheca Instituti Historici S. I. vol. 4. Rome: Institutum Historicum S. I., 1953.

Gumppenberg, Wilhelm. *Atlas Marianus, sive, De imaginibus Deiparae per orbem Christianum miraculosis.* Ingoldstadt: Typis Georgii Haenlini typographi academici, 1657.

Han Qi 韓琦. "Sino-British Scientific Relations Through Jesuits in the Seventeenth and Eighteenth Centuries." In *La Chine entre amour et haine: actes du VIIIe Colloque de sinologie de Chantilly,* 43–59. Variétés Sinologiques 87. Paris: Desclée de Brouwer, 1998.

Hansen, Joseph, ed. *Rheinische Akten zur Geschiche des Jesuitenordens, 1542–1582.* Publikationen der Gesellschaft für Rheinische Geschichtskunde 14. Bonn: Hermann Behrendt, 1896.

Hantzsch, Viktor. "Der Anteil der deutschen Jesuiten an der wissenschaftlichen Erforschung Amerikas." In *Studium Lipsiense,* 270–85. Berlin: Weidmann, 1909.

Harvey, P. D. A. "Local and Regional Cartography in Medieval Europe." In *Cartography in Prehistoric, Ancient, and Medieval Europe and the Mediterranean,* edited by J. B. Harley and David Woodward, 464–501. Vol. 1, *The History of Cartography.* Chicago: University of Chicago Press, 1987.

Haskell, Francis. *Patrons and Painters: A Study in the Relations between Italian Art and Society in the Age of the Baroque.* New York: Knopf, 1963.

Hattler, Franz. *Der ehrwüridge Pater Jakob Rem aus der Gesellschaft Jesu und seine Marienconferenz*. Regensburg: Manz, 1881.

Hausberger, Bernd. *Für Gott und König: Die Mission der Jesuiten im kolonialen Mexiko*. Studien zur Geschichte und Kultur der Iberischen und Iberoamerikanischen Länder 6. Munich: R. Oldenbourg, 2000.

———. *Jesuiten aus Mitteleuropa im kolonialen Mexiko: Eine Bio-Bibliographie*. Studien zur Geschichte und Kultur der Iberischen und Iberoamerikanischen Länder 2. Munich: R. Oldenbourg, 1995.

Headley, John M. "Campanella, America, and World Evangelization." In *America in European Consciousness, 1493–1750*, edited by Karen Ordahl Kupperman, 243–71. Chapel Hill: University of North Carolina, 1995.

Hefele, Friedrich. "Der Würzburger Fürstbischof Julius Echter von Mespelbrunn und die Liga." Ph.D. diss., Julius-Maximilians-Universitat Wurzburg, 1912.

Hefner, Robert W. "Introduction: World Building and the Rationality of Conversion." In *Conversion to Christianity: Historical and Anthropological Perspectives on a Great Transformation*, 3–44, edited by Robert W. Hefner. Berkeley: University of California Press, 1993.

Heikamp, Detlef, with Ferdinand Anders. "Mexikanische Altertümer aus süddeutschen Kunstkammern." *Pantheon* 28 (1970): 205–20.

Helms, Mary W. "Essay on Objects: Interpretations of Distance Made Tangible." In *Implicit Understandings: Observing, Reporting, and Reflecting on the Encounters between Europeans and Other Peoples in the Early Modern Era*, edited by Stuart B. Schwartz, 355–77. Cambridge: Cambridge University Press, 1994.

Henrion, M. R. *A Histoire Générale des Missions Catholiques*. Paris: 1847.

Hernández, Pablo. *Organización social de la doctrinas guaranies de la Compañia de Jesús*. Barcelona: G. Gili, 1913.

Herz, Alexandra. "Imitators of Christ: The Martyr-Cycles of Late Sixteenth-Century Rome Seen in Context." *Storia dell'arte* 62 (1988): 53–70.

Hibbard, Howard. "*Ut picturae sermones*: The First Painted Decorations of the Gesù." In *Baroque Art: The Jesuit Contribution*, edited by Rudolf Wittkower and Irma B. Jaffe, 29–41. New York: Fordham University Press, 1972.

Hilckmann, Anton. "Leibniz und die Pluralität der Kulturen: Leibniz und China." *Saeculum* 18 (1967) 317–21.

Hoffmann, Hermann. "Philipp Jeningens Missionssehnsucht." *Theologische Quartalschrift* 30 (1930): 349–73.

———. *Schlesische, mährische und böhmische Jesuiten in der Heidenmission*. Zur schlesischen Kirchengeschichte 36. Breslau: 1939.

Hoffmann, R. "Missiology." In *The New Catholic Encyclopedia*, IX.900–904. New York: McGraw-Hill, 1967.

Högner, Herman-Ludwig. "Philosophie und Medizin in Ingolstadt: Professoren der Philosophischen Fakultät von 1641 bis 1720." Ph.D. diss., Erlangen, 1976.

Hosten, Henry. "Letter of Friar Peregrine, Second Bishop of Zayton, China (December 30, 1318)." *Journal and Proceedings of the Asiatic Society of Bengal* (n.s.) 26 (1930): 437–56.

Hsia, R. Po-Chia. *Social Discipline in the Reformation: Central Europe, 1550–1750*. London: Routledge, 1989.

Hudson, Geoffrey Francis. *Europe and China: A Survey of their relations from Earliest times to 1800*. London: E. Arnold, 1931.

Hughes, E. R. *The Great Learning and the Mean in Action*. London: J. M. Dent, 1943.

Hultsch, Paul. *Der Orient in der deutschen Barockliteratur*. Lengerich i.W.: Lengericher Handelsdruckerei, [1938?].

Huonder, Anton. *Der hl. Ignatius von Loyola und der Missionsberuf der Gesellschaft Jesu*. Abhandlungen aus Missionskunde und Missionsgeschichte 35. Aachen: Xaverius verlagsbuchhandlung, 1922.

———. *Deutsche Jesuitenmissionäre des 17. und 18. Jahrhunderts: Ein Beitrag zur Missionsgeschichte und zur deutschen Biographie*. Freiburg im Breisgau: Herder'sche Verlagshandlung, 1899.

———. *Deutsche Jesuitenmissionäre*. [unpublished manuscript of second edition; Archiv der Oberdeutschen Provinz, Munich: Anton Huonder, *Deutsche Jesuitenmissionäre des 17. und 18. Jahrhunderts*, AMSJ, Abt. 47 (Huonder)]

———. "Die erste Aussendung deutscher Jesuiten in die Missionen." *Die Katholischen Missionen* 41 (1912–13): 10–12.

———. "Eine Todesfahrt." *Die Katholische Missionen* (1918–19): 77–79.

———. "Gottfried Wilhelm von Leibniz (1646–1716) und die Missionen." *Die Katholische Missionen* 49 (1927): 156–160.

Hwang, Jane. "The Early Jesuit-Printings in China in the Bavarian State Library and the University Library of Munich." In 紀念利瑪竇來華四百週年中西文化交流國際學術會議論文集, 281–93. 臺北縣新莊市: 輔仁大學出版社, 民國 72 [1983].

Ibero-Mundo Regional Atlas Team. "Project Description." 21 November 2001. http://redgeomatica.rediris.es/ecai/atlas_iberomundo/.

Ignatius of Loyola. *Monumenta Ignatiana, ex autographis vel ex antiquioribus exemplis collecta, series prima: Sancti Ignatii de Loyola Societatis Jesu fundatoris epistolae et instructiones*. 12 vols. Monumenta Historica Societatis Jesu 22, 26, 28, 29, 31, 33, 34, 36, 37, 39, 40, 42. Rome: [Institum historicum S. I.], 1964–68.

———. "On Perfect Obedience." http://www.georgetown.edu/centers/woodstock/ignatius/letter25.htm 9 April 2004.

———. *The Spiritual Exercises of St. Ignatius: Based on Studies in the Language of the Autograph*, translated by Louis J. Puhl. Chicago: Loyola University Press, 1951.

Imago Primi Saeculi Societatis Iesu a Provincia Flandro-Belgica eiusdem societatis repraesentata. Antwerp: Moretus, 1640.

Israel, Jonathan I. *Race, Class, and Politics in Colonial Mexico, 1610–1670*. Oxford: Oxford University Press, 1975.

Izikowitz, Karl Gustav. *Lamet: Hill Peasants in French Indochina*. Göteborg: [Elanders boktr.], 1951.

Jacques, Roland. *Des nations à évangéliser: Genèse de la mission catholique pour l'Extême-Orient*. Paris: Cerf, 2003.

Jaffé, Michael. "Rubens before 1620, with Particular Reference to Aspects of His Commissions for the Company of Jesus." In *Rubens dall'Italia all'Europa*, 13–20. Vicenza: Neri Pozza, 1992.

Jaksch, Josef. *Sudetendeutsche in der Weltmission des 17. und 18. Jahrhunderts.* Königstein i. Taunus.: Sudetendeutsches Priesterwerk, 1957.

Jami, Catherine. "From Louis XIV's Court to Kangxi's Court: An Institutional Analysis of the French Jesuit Mission to China (1688–1722)." *East Asian Science* (1995): 493–99.

Jann, Adelhelm. *Die katholischen Missionen in Indien, China, und Japan: Ihre Organisation und das portugiesische Patronat vom 15. bis ins 18. Jahrhundert.* Paderborn: F. Schöningh, 1915.

Jedin, Hubert. "Ein Vorschalg für die Amerika-mission aus dem Jahre 1513." *Neue Zeitschrift für Missionswissenschaft* 2 (1946): 81–4.

————. *Katholische Reformation oder Gegenreformation?* Lucerne: Josef Stocker, 1946.

————. "Weltmission und Kolonialismus." *Saeculum* 9 (1958): 393–404.

Jesuit Art in North American Collections: Milwaukee Haggerty Art Museum. Milwaukee: Marquette University, 1991.

"Jesuit Martyrs of the 20th Century," March 28, 2000 (August 16, 2006). http://www.companysj.com/news/martyrs20.html.

Jones, E. R. "The Image of the Barbarian in Medieval Europe." *Facing Each Other: The World's Perception of Europe and Europe's Perception of the World*, edited by Anthony Pagden, 21–52. Aldertshot: Ashgate Variorum, 2000.

Josson, H. and Léopold Willaert, eds. *Correspondance de Ferdinand Verbiest de la compagnie de Jésus (1623–1688), directeur de l'observatoire de Pékin.* Brussels: Palais des académies, 1938.

Jouanen, José. *Historia de la Compañia de Jesús en la antigua Provincia de Quito, 1570–1774.* 2 vols. Quito: Editorial Ecuatoriana, 1941–43.

Juan de Ávila. *Dos memoriales ineditos del Juan de Avila para el Concilio de Trento* Miscelanea Comillas 3. Comillas, Santander: Universidad Pontificia, 1945.

Kalista, Zdeněk. *Cesty ve znameni kříže: Cartas e informes de misioneros checos de los siglos XVII y XVIII del ultramar.* 2nd edition. Prague: Evropský literární klub, 1947.

————. "Los misioneros de los países checos que en los siglos XVII y XVIII actuaban en América Latina." *Ibero-Americana Pragensia* 11 (1968): 117–61.

Kantorowicz, Ernst H. *The King's Two Bodies.* Princeton: Princeton University Press, 1957.

Kašpar, Oldrich. *Los jesuitas checos en la Nueva España 1678–1767.* Mexico: Universidad Iberoamericana, Departamento de Historia, 1991.

————, and Anna Fechtnerová. "Checos, moravos, silesios en el Nuevo Mundo en los siglos XVII y XVIII. Registro Bio-Bibliográfico." *Annals of the Náprstek Museum* 15 (1988): 165–204.

Kaufmann, Thomas DaCosta. *Central European Drawings, 1680–1800: A Selection from American Collections.* Princeton: Princeton University Press, 1989.

————. "East and West: Jesuit Art and Artists in Central Europe, and Central European Art in the Americas." In *The Jesuits: Cultures, Sciences, and the Arts, 1540–1773*, edited by John W. O'Malley, Gauvin Alexander Bailey, Steven J. Harris, and T. Frank Kennedy, 274–304. Toronto: University of Toronto Press, 1999.

Kerber, Bernhard. *Andrea Pozzo*. Beitrage zur Kunstgeschichte 6. Berlin: de Gruyter, 1971.

Kino, Eusebio Francisco. *Cartas a la Procura de Misiones*, edited by Manuel Igancio Pérez Alonso. Mexico: Universidad Iberoamericana, 1987.

⸻. *Crónica de la Pimería Alta: Favores Celestiales*. Hermosillo: Gobierno del Estado de Sonora, 1985, 1913.

⸻. *Kino's Historical Memoir of Pimería Alta. A Contemporary Account of the Beginnings of California, Sonora, and Arizona, by Father Eusebio Francisco Kino, S. J., Pioneer Missionary Explorer, Cartographer, and Ranchman. 1683–1711*. 2 vols., edited by Herbert Eugene Bolton. Spain and the West 3–4, Semicentennial Publications of the University of California. Cleveland: The Arthur H. Clark Company, 1919.

Kircher, Athanasius. *China monumentis, qua sacris, quà profanis, nec non variis naturae & artis spectaculis, aliarumque rerum memorabilium argumentis illustrata*. Amsterdam: Joannem Janssonium à Waesberge & Elizeum Weyerstraet, 1667.

Klopp, Onno, ed. *Die Werke von Leibniz gemäß seinem handschriftlichen Nachlasse in der königlichen Bibliothek zu Hannover*. Hannover: Klindworth, 1864–84.

Knipping, John Baptist. *Iconography of the Counter Reformation in the Netherlands: Heaven on Earth*. 2 vols. Nieuwkoop: De Graff, 1974.

Kolakowski, Leszek. "Quietism." *Encyclopedia of Religion*, vol. 12, 153–55. New York: Macmillan, 1987.

Konrad, Herman W. *A Jesuit Hacienda in Colonial Mexico: Santa Lucía, 1576–1767*. Stanford: Stanford University Press, 1980.

Kowalsky, N., and J. J. Metzler. *Inventory of the Historical Archives of the Congregation for the Evangelization of Peoples or De Propaganda Fide*. 3rd ed. Rome: Pontificia Universitas Urbaniana, 1988.

Kramm, Heinrich. *Deutsche bibliotheken unter dem einfluss von humanismus und reformation; ein beitrag zur deutschen bildungsgeschichte*. Beiheft . . . zum Zentralblatt für Bibliothekswesen 70. Leipzig: O. Harrassowitz, 1938.

Kreutzer, E. "Erdteile." In *Lexikon der christlichen Ikonographie*, edited by Engelbert Kirschbaum, I.661–64. Rome: Herder, 1968.

Kroess, A. *Geschichte der böhmischen Provinz der Gesellschaft Jesu*. 2 vols. Vienna: Nachfolger, 1910–27.

Kropf, Francis Xavier. *Historia Provinciae Societatis Jesu Germaniae Superioris*. Vol. 4. Munich: Joannis Jacobi Vötter, 1746.

Lach, Donald. *The Preface to Leibniz "Novissima Sinica."* Honolulu: University of Hawaii, 1957.

⸻, and Edwin J. Van Kley. "Asia in the Eyes of Europe in the Seventeenth Century." *The Seventeenth Century* V (1990): 93–109.

⸻. *Asia in the Making of Europe*. Chicago: University of Chicago, 1965-.

Lacouture, Jean. *Jesuits: A Multibiography*, translated by Jeremy Leggatt. Washington, D.C.: Counterpoint, 1995.

Lamalle, Edmond. "La propaganda du P. Nicolas Trigault en faveur des missions de Chine (1616)." *Archivum Historicum Societatis Iesu* 9 (1940): 49–120.

⸻. "L'archivio di un grande ordine religioso: L'Archivio Generale della Compagnia di Gesu." *Archiva ecclesiae* 24–25 (1981–82): 89–120.

Lamb, Ursula. "Religious Conflicts in the Conquest of Mexico." *Journal of the History of Ideas* 17 (1956): 526–39.

Lancre, Pierre de. *Tableau de l'inconstance des mauvais Anges et Demons, où il est amplement traicté des Sorciers et de la Sorcelerie [Paris, 1612]*, ed. Nicole Jacques-Chaquin. Paris: n.p., 1982.

Latourette, Kenneth S. *A History of Christian Missions in China*. New York: Macmillan, 1929.

———. *A History of the Expansion of Christianity*. 7 vols. New York: Harper & Bros., 1937–45.

Lázaro de Aspurz, P. *La aportación extranjera a las misiones españolas del Patronato Regio*. Madrid: Consejo de la Hispanidad, 1946.

Leão, Francisco G. Cunha, ed. *Jesuítas na Ásia: Catálogo e guia*, 2 vols. Lisbon and Macao: Insituto Cultural de Macau/Instituto Português do Património Arquitectónico/Biblioteca de Ajuda, 1998.

Leibniz, Gottfried Wilhelm. *Writings on China*, edited by Daniel J. Cook and Henry Rosemont. Chicago: Open Court, 1994.

Leidinger, Georg. "Herzog Wilhelm V. von Bayern und die Jesuitenmissionen in China." In *Forschungen zur Geschichte Bayerns* 12 (1904): 171–75.

Leite, Serafim. *História de Companhia de Jesus no Brasil*. Lisbon: Livraria Portugalia, 1938–50.

———, ed. *Monumenta Brasiliae*. Monumenta historica Societatis Iesu, 79–81, 87, 99. Monumenta Missionum Societatis Iesu, 10–12, 17. Rome: "Monumenta Historcia Societatis Iesu," 1956–.

León, Nicolas. *Catarina de San Juan y la China Poblana*. 5th edition. Puebla: Ediciones Altiplano, 1971.

Leturia, Pietro de. "Perchè la nascente Chiesa ispano-americana non fu rappresentata a Trento." In *Il Concilio di Trento I*, 35–43. Trent: 1942.

Lewy, G. "The Struggle for Constitutional Government in the Early Years of the Society of Jesus." *Church History* 39 (1960): 141–60.

Li Yan and Du Shiran. *Chinese Mathematics: A Concise History*, translated by John N. Crossley and Anthony W.-C. Lun. Oxford: Clarendon Press, 1987.

Li Yuzhong 李毓中. "Xibanya Saiweiya Yindu zongdang'an guannei suocang youguan Zhongguo shiliao jianmu chubian." 西班牙塞維亞印度總檔案館內所藏有關中國史料簡目初編. *Hanxue yanjiu tongxun* 漢學研究通訊 64 (1997): 476–84.

Li Zhizao, 李之藻, ed. *Tianxue chuhan* 天學初函. Taibei, 1965.

Liberius Candidus [Henri de Saint Ignace]. *Tuba magna mirum clangens sonum ad Sanctissimum D. N. Papam Clementem XI*. Argentina: 1713.

Lieberman, Victor. "Transcending East-West Dichotomies: State and Culture Formation in Six Ostensibly Disparate Areas." *Modern Asian Studies* 31 (1997): 463–546.

Lipowsky, Felix Joseph. *Geschichte der Jesuiten in Bayern*. Munich: J. Giel, 1816.

Lohfink, Norbert. "Zum Zion: Das Heilige Land und die Erkenntnis des Willens Gottes." In *Ignatius von Loyola und die Gesellschaft Jesu 1491–1556*, edited by Andreas Falkner and Paul Imhof, 71–75. Würzburg: Echter, 1990.

Lopetegui, León. *El padre José de Acosta, S. I., y las misiones.* Madrid: Consejo Superior de Investigaciones Científicas, Instituto Gonzalo Fernández de Oviedo, 1942.

López de Gómara, Francisco. *Historia general de las Indias.* Lima: Comision Nacional del V Centenario del Descubrimiento de America Encuentro de Dos Mundos, 1993.

López-Gay, J. "Evolución histórica del concepto de 'Evangelización.'" In *Evangelisation*, edited by Mariasusai Dhavamony, 161–90. Documenta Missionalia 9. Rome: Gregorian University, 1975.

Lo-shu Fu, ed. *A Documentary Chronicle of Sino-Western Relations, 1644–1820.* Monographs and papers, Association for Asian Studies, no. 22. 2 vols. Tucson: University of Arizona Press, 1966.

Lucas, Thomas M. *Landmarking: City, Church, and Jesuit Urban Strategy.* Chicago: Loyola Press, 1997.

Lugar, Catherine. "The History of the Manila Galleon Trade." In *Archaeological Report: The Recovery of the Manila Galleon Nuestra Señora de la Concepción*, edited by William M. Mathers, Henry S. Parker III, and Katherine A. Copus, 3–81. Sutton, Vermont: Pacific Sea Resources, 1990.

Lumnius, Joannes Fredericus. *De extremo Dei iudicio et Indorum vocatione libri duo.* Antwerp: Tilenium Brechtanum, 1567.

Maas, Otto. "Die Stiftung Ferdinands von Fürstenbergs zum Besten der ostasiatischen Missionen." *Theologie und Glaube* 25 (1933): 701–10.

Macaulay, Thomas Babington. *The History of England from the Accession of James II.* 5 vols. London: Macmillan, 1913–15.

——. "Ranke's History of the Popes." In *Reviews, Essays, and Poems*, 548–67. London: Ward, Lock, 1890.

MacCormack, Sabine. "Limits of Understanding: Perceptions of Greco-Roman and Amerindian Paganism in Early Modern Europe." In *America in European Consciousness, 1493–1750*, edited by Karen Ordahl Kupperman, 79–129. Chapel Hill: University of North Carolina, 1995.

Machilek, F. "Reformorden und Ordensreformen in den böhmischen Ländern von 10.-18. Jahrhundert." In *Bohemia Sacra: Das Christentum in Böhmen 973–1973*, edited by Ferdinand Seibt, 63–81. Düsseldorf: 1974.

Madariaga, José García. "¿Entra la materia doctrinal como objectivo proprio del 4° Voto (y II)?" *Manresa* 49 (1977): 215–28 and 53 (1981): 227–55.

Maffei, Giovanni Pietro. *Historiarum indicarum libri XVI.* 2 vols. Cologne: in officina Birckmannica, sumptibus Arnoldi Mylij, 1590.

Maggs Bros. *Bibliotheca Asiatica Part II: The Catholic Missions in India, China, Japan, Siam, and the Far East, in a Series of Autograph Letters of the Seventeenth Century.* London: Maggs Bros., 1924.

Mâle, Emile. *L'art religieux de la fin du xvie siècle du XVIIe siecle et du XVIIIe siecle; etude sur l'iconographie apres le Concile de Trente, Italie-France-Espagne-Flandres.* 2d ed. Paris: A. Colin, 1951.

Mali, Anya. "Strange Encounters: Missionary Activity and Mystical Thought in Seventeenth Century New France." *History of European Ideas* 22 (1996): 67–92.

Mancker, Andreas. "Schreiben eines österreichischen Jesuitenmissionärs an den Probst zu Pöllau betreffs seiner Reise nach Mexico und seiner Erfahrung daselbt," edited by Josef von Zahn. *Steiermärkische Geschichtsblätter* 1 (1880): 29–40.

Margiotti, Fortunato. *Il Cattolicismo nello Shansi dalle origini al 1738*. Rome: Edizioni 'Sinica Franciscana,' 1958.

Mariana, Juan de. *Discurso de las enfermedades de la Compañia: Con una disertacion sobre el autor y la legitimad de la obra y un apendice de varios testimonios de Jesuitas Espanolas que concuerdan con Mariana*. Madrid: Imprenta de D. Gabriel Ramirez, 1768.

Marquis, André-Jean. "Le traité missionaire 'Quod Reminiscentur' de Tommaso Campanella." *Neue Zeitschrift für Missionswissenschaft* (Supplementa) 17 (1971): 331–60.

Marriott, Brandon. "The Rebirth of Hope in a Time of Upheaval: An Analysis of Early-Modern Millennial Movements Across the Abrahamic Tradition." *World History Bulletin* 23 (2007): 26–30.

Martin, A. Lynn. *The Jesuit Mind: the Mentality of an Elite in Early Modern France*. Ithaca: Cornell University Press, 1988.

_____. "The Jesuit Mystique." *The Sixteenth Century Journal* 4.1 (1973): 31–40.

Martini, Martinus. *De bello Tartarico historia, in qua, quo pacto Tartari hac nostra aetate Sinicum imperium invaserint, ac fere totum occuparint, narratur, eorumque mores breviter describuntur*. Antwerp: ex off. Plantiniana Balthasaris Moreti, 1654.

_____. *Novus atlas sinensis*. Amsterdam: J. Blaeu, 1655; reprint, Trent: Comitato per la celebrazioni di Martino Martini, 1981.

Mateos, F. "Sobre misioneros extranjeros en Ultramar." *Missionalia Hispanica* 15 (1958): 245–51.

Matthei, Mauro. "Los primeros jesuitas germanos en Chile (1686–1722)." *Boletín de la Academia Chilena de la Historia* 34, Nr. 77 (1967): 147–89.

Maurice, Klaus. "Propagatio fidei per scientias: Uhrengeschenke der Jesuiten an den chinesischen Hof." In *Die Welt als Uhr: Deutsche Uhren und Automaten, 1550–1650*, edited by Klaus Maurice und Otto Mayr, 30–38. Munich: Deutscher Kunstverlag, 1980.

McCusker, John J. *Money and Exchange in Europe and America, 1600–1775: A Handbook*. Chapel Hill, N.C.: University of North Carolina Press, 1978.

McGrath, Tom. *MTV: The Making of a Revolution*. Philadelphia: Running Press, 1996.

McLachlan, R. "A Sixteenth-Century Account of China." *Papers of Far Eastern History* Canberra 12 (1975): 71–86.

Meier, Johannes. "Die Orden in Lateinamerika: Historischer Überblick." In *Conquista und Evangelisation: 500 Jahre Orden in Lateinamerika*, edited by Michael Sievernich, Arnulf Camps, Andreas Müller, and Walter Sennerr, 12–33. Mainz: Matthias-Grünewald, 1992.

Mejer, Otto. *Die Propaganda, ihre Provinzen und ihr Recht. Mit besonderer Rücksicht auf Deutschland*. Zweiter Teil. Göttingen and Leipzig: Dieterischen Buchhandlung, 1853.

Mendieta, Gerónimo de. *Historia eclesiástica indiana, obra escrita á fines del siglo XVI por fray Gerónimo de Mendieta, de la Orden de San Francisco; la pública por primera vez Joaquín García Icazbalceta*. México: Antigua librería [Impr. por F. Diaz de Leon y S. White], 1870.

Menegon, Eugenio. "Yang Guangxian's Opposition to Johann Adam Schall: Christianity and Western Science in his Work *Budeyi*." In *Western Learning and Christianity in China: The Contribution and Impact of Johann Adam Schall von Bell, S. J. (1592–1666)*, Vol. 1, edited by Roman Malek, 311–38. St. Augustin: Institut Monumenta Serica, 1998.

Merkel, Franz Rudolf. *G. W. von Leibniz und die Chinamission: Eine Untersuchung über die Anfänge der protestantischen Missionsbewegung*. Missionswissenchaftliche Forschungen 1. Leipzig: Hinrichs, 1920.

Merriman, Roger Bigelow. *The Rise of the Spanish Empire in the Old World and in the New*. 4 vols. New York: Cooper Square Publishers, 1962.

Metzler, Johannes. *Die Apostolischen Vikariate des Nordens*. Paderborn: Drucku Verlag der Bonifacius, 1919.

Metzler, Josef, ed. *America Pontificia: documenta pontificia ex registris et minutis praesertim in Archivo secreto vaticano existentibus*. 3 vols. Atti e documenti / Pontificio Comitato di scienze storiche 3. Vatican City: Libreria editrice vaticana, 1991–95.

———. "Foundation of the Congregation 'de Propaganda Fide' by Gregory XV," translated by George F. Heinzmann. In *Sacrae Congregationis de Propaganda Fide Memoria rerum*, vol. I/1, 79–111. Rome: Herder, 1971–76.

———. "Wegbereiter und Vorläufer der Kongregation: Vorschläge und erste Fründungsversuche einer römischen Missionszentrale." In *Sacrae Congregationis de Propaganda Fide Memoria rerum*, vol. I/1, 38–78. Rome: Herder, 1971–76.

Micus, F. J., ed. *Denkmale des Landes Paderborn*. Paderborn: Junfermann'sche Buchhandlung und Buchdruckerei, 1844.

Miesen, Karl-Jürgen. *Friedrich Spee: Pater, Dichter, Hexen-Anwalt*. Düsseldorf: Droste, 1987.

Millward, J. A. "'Coming onto the Map': 'Western Religions,' Geography and Cartographic Nomenclature in the Making of Chinese Empire in Xinjiang." *Late Imperial China* 20.2 (1999): 61–98.

Montalto, Lina. "Andrea Pozzo nella chiesa di Sant'Ignazio al Collegio Romano." *Studi romani* 6 (1958): 668–79.

Motolinía [Toribio de Benavente]. *Historia de los Indios de la Nueva España*. Barcelona: Herederos de J. Gili, 1914.

Moya, Rafael. "Hacia una participación fructosa de los religiosos en las misiones de Propaganda." In *Sacrae Congregationis de Propaganda Fide Memoria rerum*, vol. I/1 439–64. Rome: Herder, 1971–76.

Müller, Claudius C. "400 Jahre Sammeln und Reisen der Wittelsbacher." In *Wittelsbach und Bayern: 400 Jahre Sammeln und Reisen –außereuropäische Kulturen*, 11–33. Austellung of the Dresdener Bank and the Staatlichen Museums für Völkerkunde München. Munich: Hirmer Verlag, 1980.

Müller, Karl. "Katholische Missionsgescichtsschreibung seit dem 16. Jahrhundert." In *Einleitung in die Missionsgeschichte: Tradition, Situation und Dynamik des Christentums*, edited by Karl Müller and Werner Ustorf, 27–49. Stuttgart: Kohlhammer, 1995.

Müller, Rainer A. "Schul- und Bildungsorganisation im 16. Jahrhundert: Die Canisianische Kolegienpolitik." In *Petrus Canisius SJ (1521–1597) Humanist und Europäer*, edited by Rainer Berndt, 259–74. Berlin: Akademie Verlag, 2000.

Mullett, Michael A. *The Catholic Reformation*. London: Routledge, 1999.

Mundwiler, J. B. "Deutsche Jesuiten in spanischen Gefängnissen im 18. Jahrhundert." *Zeitschrift für katholische Theologie* XXVI (1902): 621–72.

Mungello, David E. *Curious Land: Jesuit Accommodation and the Origins of Sinology*. Honolulu: University of Hawaii Press, 1985.

———. *The Great Encounter of China and the West, 1500–1800*. Lanham, Md.: Rowman & Littlefield Publishers, 1999.

Münsterberg, Oskar. "Bayern und Asien im XVI., XVII. und XVIII. Jahrhundert: Ein Beitrag zur Geschichte des ostasiatischen Kunstgewerbes in seinen Beziehungen zu Europa." *Zeitschrift der Münchener Altertumsvereins* N. F. 6 (1894): 12–37.

Murphy, Paul V. "'God's Porters': The Jesuit Vocation According to Francisco Suárez." *Archivum Historicum Societatis Iesu* 70 (2001): 3–28.

Murr, Christoph Gottlieb von. *Nachrichten von verschiedenen Landern des Spanischen Amerika*. Halle: J. C. Hendel, 1809–1811.

Muzhang'a 穆彰阿. Da Qing Yitong Zhi 大清一統志. Taibei: 藝文印書館, 196-?.

Nadal, Hieronymus. *Epistolae et Monumenta P. Hieronymi Nadal*. 6 vols. Monumenta historica Societatis Iesu 13, 15, 21, 27, 90. Rome: Monumenta Historica Soc. Iesu, 1900–.

Nagel, Ernest. *The Structure of Science: Problems in the Logic of Scientific Explanation*. London: Routledge & Kegan Paul, 1961.

Napoli, Giovanni di. "Ecumenismo e missionarismo in Tommaso Campanella." *Euntes docete* 22 (1969): 265–308.

Navarrete, Domingo Fernández. *Controversias antiguas, y modernas de la mission de la gran China* [partially printed in Madrid, 1679].

———. *Tratados históricos, políticos, ethicos, y religiosos de la Monarchia de China*. 2 vols. Madrid: 1676–79.

Nebgen, Christoph. "... dahin zillet mein verlangen und begierd. Epistolae Indipetarum der Deutschen Assistenz SJ als Quellengattung. In *Sendung – Eroberung – Begegnung: Franz Xaver, die Gesellschaft Jesu und die Katholische Weitkirche im Zeitalter des Barock*, edited by Johannes Meier, 67–97. Wiesbaden: Harrassowitz, 2005.

Needham, Joseph. *Science and Civilisation in China*. 7 vols. Cambridge: Cambridge University Press, 1954.

———. "Time and Eastern Man." In *The Grand Titration: Science and Society in East and West*, 218–98. Toronto: University of Toronto Press, 1969.

Neill, Stephen. *A History of Christian Missions*. Penguin History of the Church 6. New York: Penguin, 1986.

Newton, Isaac. *Mathematical Principles of Natural Philosophy*, edited by Andrew Motte and Florian Cajori. Great Books of the Western World 34. Chicago: Encyclopaedia Britannica, 1955.

Ninness, Richard. "Gegenreformatorische Fürstbischöfe und ihr Dilemma." Paper presented at the Ninth Transatlantic Doctoral Seminar in German History. Washington, D.C., April 2003.

Noreen, Kirstin. "*Ecclesiae militantis triumphi*: Jesuit Iconography and the Counter-Reformation." *Sixteenth Century Journal* 29 (1998): 689–715.

O'Connell, Marvin R. *The Counter-Reformation 1559–1610*. The Rise of Modern Europe 4. New York: Harper & Row, 1974.

O'Malley, John W. *The First Jesuits*. Cambridge, Mass.: Harvard University Press, 1993.

———. *The Fourth Vow in Its Ignatian Context: A Historical Study*. Studies of the Spirituality of Jesuits 15.1. St. Louis: American Assistancy Seminar on Jesuit Spirituality, 1983.

———. "Mission and the Early Jesuits." *Ignatian Spirituality and Mission. The Way* Supplement 79 (Spring 1994): 3–10.

———. *To Travel to Any Part of the World: Jerónimo Nadal and the Jesuit Vocation*. Studies in the Spirituality of Jesuits 16.2. St. Louis: American Assistancy Seminar on Jesuit Spirituality, 1984.

———. *Trent and All That: Renaming Catholicism in the Early Modern Era*. Harvard: Harvard University Press, 2000.

Oberman, Heiko A. *Luther: Man between God and the Devil*, translated by Eileen Walliser-Schwarzbart. New Haven: Yale University Press, 1989.

Odlozilík, Otokar. "Czech Missionaries in New Spain." *Hispanic American Historical Review* 25 (1945): 428–54.

———. "Missioneros checos en México." *Boletín de la Sociedad Mexicana de Geografía y Estadística* 60 (1945): 423–36.

Olin, John C. "The Idea of Pilgrimage in the Experience of Ignatius Loyola." *Church History* 48 (1979): 395–6.

Oorschot, Theo G. M. van. "Friedrich Spees Rolle und Schicksal bei der Rekatholisierung von Peine in den Jahren 1628–1629." In *Friedrich Spee im Licht der Wissenschaften*, edited by Anton Arens, 21–35. Mainz: Gesellschaft für Mittelrheinische Kirchengeschichte, 1984.

Osswald, M. C. "Die Entstehung einer Ikonographie des Franz Xaver im Kontext seiner kultischen Verehrung in den Jahren von 1552 bis 1640." In *Franz Xaver, Patron der Missionen*, edited by R. Haub and J. Oswald, 60–80. Regensburg: Schnell + Steiner, 2002.

Ostler, Nicholas. *Empires of the Word: A Language History of the World*. New York: HarperCollins, 2005.

Pachtler, Georg M., ed. *Ratio Studiorum et institutiones scholasticae Societatis Jesu per Germaniam olim vigentes collectae concinnatae dilucidatae*. Vol. 3. Monumenta Germaniae Paedagogica IX. Berlin: Hofmann, 1890.

Padberg, John W. *The General Congregations of the Society of Jesus: A Brief Survey of Their History*. Studies in the Spirituality of Jesuits 6. St. Louis: Institute of Jesuit Sources, 1974.

Pagden, Anthony. "Dispossessing the Barbarian: The Language of Spanish Thomism and the Debate over the Property Rights of the American Indians." In *The Languages of Political Theory in Early-modern Europe*, 79–98. New York: Cambridge University Press, 1987.

_____. *The Fall of Natural Man: The American Indian and the Origins of Comparative Ethnology.* Cambridge Iberian and Latin American studies. Cambridge: Cambridge University Press, 1982.

_____. "The School of Salamanca and the 'Affairs of the Indies.'" *History of Universities* 1 (1981): 71–112.

Palafox y Mendoza, Juan de. *Carta del Illmo. y venerable siervo de Dios Don Juan de Palafox, obispo de Puebla, al santisimo papa Inocencio X, sobre los asuntos que tuvo con los jesuitas.* Mexico: V. G. Torres, 1841.

_____. "Histoire de la conquête de la Chine par les Tartares." *Recueil de voyages au nord*(Amsterdam, [1731]), VI.119–462. In *The Making of the Modern World*, Thomson Gale (2006), Simon Fraser University (02 August 2006) http://galenet.galegroup.com.proxy.lib.sfu.ca/servlet/MOME?af = RN&ae = U107642310&srchtp = a&ste = 14.

_____. *History of the Conquest of China.* New Delhi: Deep & Deep Publications, 1978.

_____. *Obras del ilustrissimo, excelentissimo y venerable siervo de Dios, don Juan Palafox y Mendoza.* 13 vols. Madrid: Imprenta de Gabriel Ramirez, 1762.

Parker, T. M. "The Papacy, Catholic Reform, and the Christian Missions." In *The Counter Reformation and Price Revolution, 1559–1610.* Volume 8 of *The New Cambridge Modern History*, edited by R. B. Wernham, 44–71. Cambridge: Cambridge UP, 1968.

Parry, John Horace. *The Spanish Seaborne Empire.* New York: Knopf, 1966.

_____. "Transport and Trade Routes." In the *Cambridge Economic History of Europe*, II.155–219. Cambridge: Cambridge University Press, 1966-.

Parsons, James B. "Overtones of Religion and Superstition in the Rebellion of Chang Hsien-chung." *Sinologica* 4 (1956): 170–77.

Pastor, Ludwig. *The History of the Popes: From the Close of the Middle Ages*, translated by Ralph Francis Kerr. 40 vols. Nendeln, Liechtenstein: Kraus, 1968–69.

Pérez de Ribas, Andrés. *Historia de los triumphos de nuestra Santa Fe entre gentes de las más bárbaras y fieras del nuevo obre: conseguidos por los soldados de la milicia de la Compañia de Jesús en las misiones de Nueva España.* Madrid: Alo[n]so de Paredes, 1645.

Petech, Luciano. "Les marchands italiens dans l'empire mongol." *Journal asiatique* 250,4 (1962): 549–74. Reprinted in *Selected Papers on Asian History*, 161–86. Rome: ISMEO, 1988.

Pfister, Louis. *Notices biographiques et bibliographiques sur les Jésuites de l'ancienne mission de Chine. 1552–1773.* Vol. 1. Wiesbaden: Kraus, 1971.

Phelan, John L. *The Millennial Kingdom of the Franciscans in the New World.* Berkeley: University of California Press, 1970.

Pizzorusso, Giovanni. "Le choix indifferent: mentalités et attentes des Jésuites aspirants missionnaires dans l'Amérique française au XVIIe siècle." In *Mélanges de l'Ecole Française de Rome Italie et Méditerranée* 109 (1997): 881–94.

Plattner, Felix Alfred. *Deutsche Meister des Barock in Südamerika im 17. und 18. Jahrhundert.* Freiburg: Herder, 1960.

Platzweg, Carl. *Lebensbilder deutscher Jesuiten in auswärtigen Missionen.* Paderborn: Funtermann'schen, 1882.

Poirier, Sylvie. "'Nomadic' Rituals: Networks of Ritual Exchange Between Women of the Australian Western Desert." *Man*, New Series 27 (1992): 757–74.

Pollen J. H. "History of the Jesuits Before the 1773 Suppression." *The Catholic Encyclopedia*, September 15, 2003. http://www.newadvent.org/cathen/14086a.htm/.

Polzer, Charles W. "The Evolution of the Jesuit Mission System in Colonial New Spain, 1600–1767." Ph.D. diss., University of Arizona, 1972.

———. *Rules and Precepts of the Jesuit Missions of Northwestern New Spain*. Tucson: University of Arizona, 1976.

Pope, Robert. *The Half-Way Covenant: Church Membership in Puritan New England*. Princeton: Princeton University Press, 1969.

Prodi, Paolo. *The Papal Prince: One Body and Two Souls: The Papal Monarchy in Early Modern Europe*. Translated by Susan Haskins. Cambridge: Cambridge University Press, 1987.

Prosperi, Adriano. "America e Apocalisse." *Critica storica* XIII (1976): 1–67.

———. "Catholic Reformation," translated by Robert E. Shillenn. *The Oxford Encyclopedia of the Reformation*, edited by Hans J. Hillerbrand, 287–93. New York: Oxford University Press, 1996.

———. "L'Europa cristiana e il mondo: alle origini dell'idea di missione." *Dimensioni e problemi della ricerca storica* 2 (1992): 189–220.

Prpić, George J. "Rev. Juan M. Ratkay S. I., First Croatian Missionary in America (1647–1683)." *Radovi Hrvatskoga povijesnog instituta u Rimu* 3–4 (1971): 179–221.

Rabinowitz, L. *Jewish Merchant Adventurers: A Study of the Radanites*. London: Edward Goldston, 1948.

Ramos, Alonso. *Prodigios de la omnipotencia y milagros de la gracia en la vida de la venerable sierva de Dios Catharina de S. Joan . . .* Puebla: Imprenta plantiniana de D. Fernandez de Leon, 1689.

Ranger, Terrence. "The Local and the Global in Southern African Religious History." *Conversion to Christianity: Historical and Anthropological Perspectives on a Great Transformation*, edited by Robert W. Hefner, 65–98. Berkeley: University of California Press, 1993.

Ranke, Leopold von. *The History of the Popes During the Last Four Centuries*. 3 vols. Bohn's Popular Library. London: G. Bell and Sons, 1913.

Recopilación de leyes de los Reynos de las Indias. Prólogo por Ramón Menéndez y Pidal, estudio preliminar de Juan Manzano Manzanos. 4 vols. Madrid: Ediciones Cultura Hispánica, 1973.

Redden, Andrew, and Luke Clossey. "Global Cult of Mary." *World History Encyclopedia*, edited by Alfred Andrea. Santa Barbara: ABC-Clio, in press.

Reichert, Folkert. "Chinas Beitrag zum Weltbild der Europäer. Zur Rezeption der Fernostkenntnisse im 13. und 14. Jahrhundert." In *Das geographische Weltbild um 1300*, edited by Peter Moraw, 33–57. Berlin: 1989.

Reinhard, Wolfgang. "The Idea of Early-Modern History." In *Companion to Historiography*, edited by Michael Bentley, 281–92. London: Routledge, 1997.

———. "Pressure towards Confessionalization? Prolegomena to a Theory of the Confessional Age." In *The German Reformation: The Essential Readings*, edited by C. Scott Dixon, 172–92. Oxford: Blackwell, 1999.

Reinhardt, Rudolf. "Kontinuität und Diskontinuität. Zum Problem der Koad-jutorie mit dem Recht der Nachfolge in der neuzeitlichen Germania Sacra." In *Der dynastische Fürstenstaat: zur Bedeutung von Sukzessionsordnungen fur die Entstehung des frühmodernen Staat*, edited by Johannes Kunisch, 119–51. Historische Forschungen 21. Berlin: Duncker & Humblot, 1982.

Renger, Konrad. "Ruben's Bavarian Altarpieces and Counter Reformation Propaganda." *Rubens dall'Italia all'Europa*, 21–30. Vicenza: Neri Pozza, 1992.

Reparaz Ruiz, Gonzalo de. *Os portugueses no Vice-Reinado do Peru: (séculos XVI e XVII)*. Lisbon: Instituto de Alta Cultura, 1976.

Rey, José del. "Los jesuitas extranjeros que trabajaron en las misiones venezolanas." *Boletín de la Academia Nacional de la Historia [Venezuela]* 53 (1970): 91–125.

Ricard, Robert. *The Spiritual Conquest of Mexico*, translated by Lesley Byrd Simpson. Berkeley: University of California Press, 1966.

Ricci, Matteo. *Fonti Ricciane: documenti originali concernenti Matteo Ricci e la storia delle prime relazioni tra l'Europa e la Cia 1579–1615*, edited by Pasquale d'Elia. 3 vols. Rome: La Libreria dello Stato, 1942–49.

Rice, Eugene J., Jr., and Anthony Grafton. *The Foundations of Early Modern Europe, 1460–1559*. 2nd ed. New York: Norton, 1994.

Richard, Jean. *La Papauté et les missions d'Orient au Moyen Age (XIIIe–XVe siècles)*. Collection de l'École française de Rome 33. Rome: École française de Rome, 1977.

Richards, John F. "Early Modern India and World History." *Journal of World History* 8 (1997): 197–209.

———. *The Unending Frontier: An Environmental History of the Early Modern World*. California World History Library 1. Berkeley: University of California Press, 2003.

Richler, Mordecai. *The Best of Modern Humor*. New York: Alfred A. Knopf, 1983.

Rienstra, M. Howard, ed. and trans. *Jesuit Letters from China 1583–84*. Minneapolis: University of Minnesota Press, 1982.

Ripa, Cesare. *Iconologia; overo descrittione di diverse imagini cavate dall'antichita, e di propria inventione [by] Cesare Ripa*. Hildesheim, New York: G. Olms, 1970.

Riva Palacio, Vicente, ed. *México a través de los siglos: Historia general y completa del desenvolvimiento social, político, religioso, militar, artístico, científico y literario de México desde la antigüedad más remota hasta la época actual* . . . Mexico: Ballescá y comp.a, 1887.

Robertson, Hector Menteith. *Aspects of the Rise of Economic Individualism: A Criticism of Max Weber and His School*. Cambridge: Cambridge University Press, 1935.

Robertson, Roland. "Economics and Religion." *Encyclopedia of Religion*, vol. 5, 1–11. New York: Macmillan, 1987.

Rochemonteix, Camille de. *Les Jésuites et la Nouvelle-France au xvne siècle d'après beaucoup de documents inédits*. Paris: Letouzey et Ané, 1895–96.

Rodrigues, Francisco. *História da companhia de Jesus na assistência de Portugal*. 7 vols. Porto: 1931–50.

Roedl, Bohumír. "La Historia de José Neumann sobre la sublevación de los Tarahumaras como fuente historiográfica," translated by Bohumil Zavadil. *Ibero-Americana Pragensia* 10 (1976): 197–209.

Rogers, Francis M. "Celestial Navigation: From Local Systems to a Global Conception." In *First Images of America: The Impact of the New World on the Old*, edited by Fredi Chiapelli, 687–704. 2 vols. Berkeley: University of California Press, 1976.

Romeo, Rosario. "Le scoperte americane nella coscienza italiana del cinquecento." *Revista Storica Italiana* 65 (1953): 222–57 and 326–79.

Rooses, Max. *L'œuvre de P. P. Rubens; histoire et description de ses tableaux et dessins.* 5 vols. Anvers: J. Maes, 1886–92.

Rosenfeld, Emmy. *Friedrich Spee von Langenfeld: Eine Stimme in der Wüste.* Quellen und Forschungen zur Sprach- und Kulturgeschichte der germanischen Völker 2 (126). Berlin: Walter de Gruyter & Co., 1958.

Rouleau, Francis A. "The First Chinese Priest of the Society of Jesus, Emmanuel de Siqueira, 1633–1673." *Archivum Historicum Societatis Iesu* 28 (1959): 3–50.

Rubial García, Antonio. *La santidad controvertida: hagiografía y conciencia criolla alrededor de los venerables no canonizados de Nueva España.* Mexico: UNAM, 1999.

Ruiz-de-Medina, Juan. "'El Trato de la seda' en Japon y los jesuitas." In *Ecclesiae Memoria: Miscellanea in onore del R. P. Josef Metzle O. M. I. Prefetto dell'Archivo Segreto Vaticano*, edited by Willi Henkel, 307–18. Rome: Herder, 1991.

Rule, Paul A. "Jesuit Sources." In *Essays on the Sources for Chinese History*, edited by Donald Daniel Leslie, 176–87. Canberra: Australian National University Press, 1973.

Ryneš, Václav. "Jesuitas bohémicos trabajando en las misiones de América Latina después de 1620," translated by Antonín Vaculík. *Ibero-Americana Pragensia* 5 (1971): 193–201.

Sacchini, Francesco. *Historiæ Soc. Jesu pars secunda*, Cologne: 1621; *quinta*, Rome: 1661.

Sachs, Hannelore, Ernst Badstübner, and Helga Neumann. *Christliche Ikonographie in Stichworten.* 7th ed. Munich: Koehler & Amelang, 1998.

Sackur, Ernst. *Sibyllinische Texte und Forschungen: Pseudomethodius Adso und die tiburtinische Sibylle.* Halle: M. Niemeyer, 1898.

Sahagún, Bernardino de. *Historia General de las cosas de Nueva España*, edited by Angel María Garibay. 4 vols. Mexico: Porrua, 1956.

Sánchez, Joseph P. *Spanish Bluecoats: The Catalonian Volunteers in Northwestern New Spain, 1767–1810.* Albuquerque: University of New Mexico Press, 1990.

Sauer, Sabine. *Gottes streitbare Diener für Amerika: Missionsresien im Spiegel der ersten Briefe niederländischer Jesuiten (1616–1618).* Weltbild und Kulturbegegnung 4. Pfaffenweiler: Centaurus-Verlagsgesellschaft, 1992.

Scaduto, Mario. "La strada e i primi Gesuiti." *Archivum Historicum Societatis Iesu* 40 (1971): 323–90.

Schadt, Hermann. "Andrea Pozzos Langhausfresko in Sant' Ignzaio Rom. Zur Thementradition der barocken Heiligenglorie." *Das Münster* XXIV (1971): 153–60.

Schall von Bell, Johann Adam. *Historica narratio de initio et progressu missionis Societatis Jesu apud chinenses, ac praesertim in regia pequinensis.* Vienna: M. Cosmerovij, 1665.

———. *Lettres et Mémoires d'Adam Schall, S. J.: Relation Historique*, edited by Henri Bernard, translated by Paul Bornet. Tientsin: Hautes études, 1942.

Scheele, Paul-Werner. "'In Spe spes': Friedrich Spees frühe Dichtungen als Hoff-nungsimpulse." In *Friedrich von Spee: Priester, Poet, Prophet*, edited by Michael Sievernich, 65–82. Frankfurt am Main: Josef Knecht, 1986.

Schiller, Gertrud. *Ikonographie der christlichen Kunst*. Gutersloh: G. Mohn, 1966.

Schivelbusch, Wolfgang. *The Railway Journey: The Industrialization of Time and Space in the 19th Century*. Berkeley: University of California Press, 1986.

Schneller, Hermann. "Bayerische Legate für die Jesuitenmissionen in China." *Zeitschrift für Missionswissenschaft und Religionswissenschaft* 4 (1914): 176–89.

Schreiber, Georg. *Deutschland und Spanien: volkskundliche und kulturkundliche Beziehungen, zusammenhange abendlandischer und ibero-amerikanischer Sakralkultur*. Dusseldorf: L. Schwann, 1936.

Schurhammer, Georg. *Francis Xavier: His Life, His Times*, translated by M. Joseph Costelloe. Rome: Jesuit Historical Institute, 1973–82.

Schütte, Josef Franz. *Documentos del 'Archivo del Japón' en el Archivo Histórico Nacional de Madrid*. Madrid: Raycar S. A., 1978–79.

———. "Wiederentdeckung des Makao-Archivs: Wichtige Bestände des alten Fernost-archivs der Jesuiten, heute in Madrid." *Archivum Historicum Societatis Iesu* 30 (1961): 90–124.

———. *Valignano's Mission Principles for Japan*, translated by John J. Coyne. Modern scholarly studies about the Jesuits, in English translations 3. St. Louis: Institute of Jesuit Sources, 1980–85.

Schwager, Friedrich. *Die katholische Heidenmission der Gegenwart im Zusammenhang mit ihrer grossen Vergangenheit*. Steyl: Missionsdruckerei, 1907.

Scribner, Robert. "Cosmic Order and Daily Life: Sacred and Secular in Pre-Industrial German Society." In *Popular Culture and Popular Movements in Reformation Germany*, 1–16. London: Hambledon, 1988.

Sebes, Joseph. "Jesuit Attempts to Establish an Overland Route to China." *The Canada-Mongolia Review* 5 (1979): 51–67.

———. "Philippine Jesuits in the Middle Kingdom in the 17th Century." *Philippine Studies* 26 (1978): 192–208.

Seibert, Jutta, ed. *Lexikon christlicher Kunst: Themen, Gestalten, Symbole*. Freiburg: Herder, 1980.

Selwyn, Jennifer D. *A Paradise Inhabited by Devils: The Jesuits' Civilizing Mission in Early Modern Naples*. Ashgate: Aldershot/Hants England, 2004.

Sepp, Anton. *An Account of a Voyage from Spain to Paraquaria, Perform'd by the Reverend Fathers, Anthony Sepp and Anthony Behme*. [Translation of *Reissbeschreibung* (Nuremburg: 1697)]. London: J. Walthoe [etc.], 1752.

Serrure, Constant-Philippe, ed. *Het leven van Pater Petrus Thomas van Hamme, missionaris in Mexico en in China (1651–1727)*. Gent: C. Annoot-Braeckman, 1871.

Shiels, W. Eugene. *King and Church: The Rise and Fall of the Patronato Real*. Chicago: Loyola University Press, 1961.

Shirodkar, P. P. "Records on Jesuits in Goa Archives." In *Jesuits in India: In Historical Perspective*, edited by Teotonio R. De Souza and Charles J. Borges, 21–34. Macao: Instituto Cultural de Macau, 1992.

Sierra, Vincente D. *Los Jesuitas Germanos en la conquista espiritual de Hispano-America*. Institucion Cultural Argentino-Germana 15. Buenos Aires: n.p., 1944.

————. *El sentido misional de la conquista de América*. Madrid: Consejo de la Hispanidad, 1944.

Sievernich, Michael. "Die Mission und die Missionen der Gesellschaft Jesu." In *Sendung – Eroberung – Begegnung: Franz Xaver, die Gesellschaft Jesu und die katholische Weltkirche im Zeitalter des Barock*, edited by Johannes Meier, 7–30. Wiesbaden: Harrassowitz, 2005.

————. "Vision und Mission der Neuen Welt Amerika bei José de Acosta." In *Ignatianisch: Eigenart und Methode der Gesellschaft Jesu*, edited by Michael Sievernich and Günter Switek, 293–313. Freiburg: Herder, 1990.

Simmons, Charles E. "Palafox and His Critics: Reappraising a Controversy." *The Hispanic American Historical Review* 46 (1966): 394–408.

Smith, Jeffrey Chipps. "The Art of Salvation in Bavaria." In *The Jesuits: Cultures, Sciences, and the Arts, 1540–1773*, edited by John W. O'Malley, Gauvin Alexander Bailey, Steven J. Harris, and T. Frank Kennedy, 568–99. Toronto: University of Toronto Press, 1999.

Solís, Antonio de. *Istoria della conquista del Messico della popolazione, e de' progressi nell' America Settentrionale Conosciuta sotto nome di Nouva Spagna scritta in Castigliano da Don Antonio de Solis . . . e tradotta in Toscano da un'Accademico della Crusca*. Florence: Stamperia di S.A.S. per G.F. Cecchi, 1699.

Sonkeikaku Library—Maeda Ikutoku Kai Foundation, eds. *Jesuit Missions in Japan: Original Letters and Reports 1663–1688*. 2 vols. Tokyo: Yushodo, 1975.

"Soul." *Oxford English Dictionary Online*, 2nd edition. 1989. www.oed.com.

South China in the Sixteenth Century, Being the Narratives of Galiote Pereira, Fr. Gaspar da Cruz, O. P., Fr. Martin de Rada OESA, translated by Charles R. Boxer. London: Printed for the Hakluyt Society, 1953.

Souza, George B. *The Survival of Empire: Portuguese Trade and Society in China and the South China Sea 1630–1754*. Cambridge: Cambridge University Press, 1986.

Specker, J. "Missionarische Motive im Entdeckungszeitalter." In *Mission, Präsenz, Verkündigungs, Bekehrung?*, edited by Horst Rzepkowski, 80–91. Studia Instituti Missiologici Societatis Verbi Divini 13. St. Augustin: Steyler, 1974.

Spee von Langenfeld, Friedrich. *Güldenes Tugend-Buch*, edited by Theo G. M. van Oorschot. Friedrich Spee Sämtliche Schriften II. Munich: Kösel, 1968.

————. *Trutz-Nachtigal*, edited by Theo G. M. van Oorschot. Friedrich Spee Sämtliche Schriften I. Bern: Francke, 1985.

Spohnholz, Jesse. "Strangers and Neighbors: The Tactics of Toleration in the Dutch Exile Community of Wesel, 1550–1590." PhD dissertation, University of Iowa, 2004.

Stackhouse, Max L. "Missionary Activity." *Encyclopedia of Religion*, vol. 9, 563–67. New York: Macmillan, 1987.

Stadiensis, Albertus. *Historiographia Alberti Abbatis Stadensis, a condito orbe usque ad auctoris aetatem, id est, annum Iesu Christi M.CC.LVI. deducta & nunc primum evulgata*. Wittenberg: Clemens Berger, 1608.

Stalla, Gerhard. *Bibliographie der Ingolstädter Drucker des 16. Jahrhunderts*. Baden-Baden: Koerner, 1977.

Standaert, Nicolas, ed. *Handbook of Christianity in China*. Handbuch der Orientalistik: Vierte Abteilung, China, 15. Vol. 1. Leiden: Brill, 2001.

Stanonik, Janez. "Letters of Marcus Antonius Kappus from colonial America." *Acta Neophilologica* 19 (1986): 33–56; 20 (1987): 25–38; 21 (1988): 3–9; 22 (1989): 39–50; 23 (1990): 27–37.

Starn, Randolph. "The Early Modern Muddle." *Journal of Early Modern History* 6.3 (2002): 296–307.

Steiner, Peter. "Der erhaltene Kirchenschatz von St. Michael." In *St. Michael in München: Festschrift zum 400. Jahrestag der Grundsteinlegung und zum Abschluß des Weideraufbaus*, edited by Karl Wagner and Albert Keller, 136–63. Munich: Schnell & Steiner, 1983.

Steininger, Hans. "Roman Catholic Missionary Activities Emanating from Würzburg/Bavaria." In 紀念利瑪竇來華四百週年中西文化交流國際學術會議論文集, *731–42*. 臺北縣新莊市: 輔仁大學出版社, 民國 72 [1983].

Štěpánek, Pavel. "Simón de Castro—Simon Boruhradský: un arquitecto checo del siglo XVI en Nueva España—México." *Ibero-Americana Pragensia* 20 (1968): 159–74.

Stephens, Walter. *Demon Lovers: Witchcraft, Sex, and the Crisis of Belief*. Chicago: University of Chicago Press, 2002.

Stillig, Jürgen. *Jesuiten, Ketzer, und Konvertiten in Niedersachsen: Untersuchungen zum Religions- und Bildungswesen im Hochstift Hildesheim in der Frühen Neuzeit*. Hildesheim: Bernward, 1993.

Stitz, Peter. "Deutsche Jesuiten als Geographen in Niederkalifornien und Nordmexiko im 17. und 18. Jahrhundert." M.S. thesis, Jena, 1930.

———. "Kalifornische Briefe des P. Eusebio Francsico Kino (= Chini) nach der oberdeutschen Provinz, 1683–5." *Archivum Historicum Societatis Iesu* 3 (1934): 108–28.

Stockbauer, Jacob. *Die Kunstbestrebungen am Bayerischen Hofe unter Albrecht V. und seinem Nachfolger Wilhelm V.* Quellenschriften für Kunstgeschichte 8. Vienna: W. Braunmuller, 1874.

Stöcklein, Joseph, Peter Probst, and Franz Keller, eds. *Der Neue Welt-Bott. Allerhand so Lehr- als Geistriche Briefe, Schriften, und Reise-Beschreibungen, welche von denen Missionariis der Gesellschaft Jesu aus Beyden Indien und anderen Uber Meer gelegenen Ländern [. . .] in Europa angelangt seynd*. 5 vols. Augsburg, Graz: Philipp, Martin, und Johann Veith seel. Erben, 1726–55.

Strasser, Ulrike. "A Case of Empire Envy? German Jesuits Meet an Asian Mystic in Spanish America." *Journal of Global History* 2 (2007): 23–40.

———. *State of Virginity: Gender, Religion, and Politics in an Early Modern Catholic State*. Ann Arbor: University of Michigan Press, 2004.

Streit, Robert, and Johannes Dindinger. *Bibliotheca Missionum*. vols. 4, 5, 7. Aachen: Franziskus Xaverius Missionsverein, 1928–31; Rome: Herder, 1965–.

Strenski, Ivan. "The Religion in Globalization." *Journal of the American Academy of Religion* 72 (2004): 631–52.

Stroni, Hugo. *Catálogo de los Jesuitas de la Provincia del Paraguay (Cuenca del Río de la Plata) 1585–1767*. Subsidia ad Historiam S.I. 9. Rome: Institutum Historicum S.I., 1980.

Su Jiyu 蘇及寓. "Xiedu Shiju" 邪毒實據. In *Changzhi Xu* 徐昌治, ed., Po Xie Ji 破邪集. 水戶市 :弘道館, 安政乙卯, 1855.

Subrahmanyam, Sanjay. "Connected Histories: Notes towards a Reconfiguration of Early Modern Eurasia." *Modern Asian Studies* 31 (1997): 735–62.

————. *The Portuguese Empire in Asia, 1550–1700: A Political and Economic History.* London: Longman, 1993.

Sullivan, Richard E. "The Papacy and Missionary Activity in the Early Middle Ages." *Mediaeval Studies* XVII (1955): 46–106.

Sylvest, E. E. *Motifs of Franciscan Mission Theory in Sixteenth Century New Spain.* Washington, D. C.: Academy of American Franciscan History, 1975.

Tacchi Venturi, Pietro. "Nuove lettere inedite del P. Eusebio Francesco Chino d. l. C. d. G." In *Archivum Historicum Societatis Iesu* 3 (1934): 248–64.

————. "Sei lettere inedite del P. Eusebio Chino al P. Gian Paolo Oliva Gen. d. C. d. G." *Studi Trentini di Scienze storiche* 11 (1930): 3–17.

————. *Storia della Compagnia di Gesù in Italia.* 4 vols. in 2. Rome: Civiltà cattolica, 1930–51.

Teggart, Frederick. *Rome and China: A Study of Correlations in Historical Events.* Berkeley: University of California Press, 1939.

Teixeira, Manuel. *Luís de Almeida, S. J., Surgeon, Merchant, and Missionary in Japan.* 1970–1976[?].

Tenri University Library, ed. *The Far Eastern Catholic Missions 1663–1711: The Original Papers of the Duchess of d'Aveiro.* 3 vols. Tokyo: Yushudo, 1975.

Tercero Cathecismo y exposición de la doctrina christiana por sermones, para que los curas y otros ministros prediquen y enseñen a los indios y a otras personas [Lima: 1585]. In *Doctrina christiana y catecismo para instruccion de los indios.* Corpus Hispanorum de Pace XXVI-2. Madrid: Consejo Superior de Investigaciones cientificas, 1985.

The Constitutions of the Society of Jesus. Edited and translated by George E. Ganss. St. Louis: Institute of Jesuit Sources, 1970.

"The One Where Pooh Goes to Sweden: Anti-Americanism and Television." April 3, 2003. *Economist.com.* http://www.economist.com/business/displayStory.cfm?story_id = 1682750.

Thomas á Jesu. *De procuranda salute omnium gentium.* Rome: Collegio Internazionale S. Teresa, 1940.

Tibesar, A. S., P. Borges, E. J. Burrus. "Missions in Colonial America I." In *The Catholic Encyclopedia*, IX.944–64. New York: Gilmary Society, 1951.

Tietze, Hans. "Andrea Pozzo und die Fürsten von Liechtenstein." *Jahrbuch für Landeskunde von Niederösterreich*, new series. 13–14 (1914–15): 432–46.

Tillich, Paul. *Christianity and the Encounter of the World Religions.* Bampton lectures in America 14. New York: Columbia University Press, 1964.

Tintelnot, Hans. *Die barocke Freskomalerei in Deutschland: Ihre Entwicklung und europäische Wirkung.* Munich: F. Bruckman, 1951.

Tishken, Joel. "Lies Teachers Teach about World Religious History." *World History Bulletin* 23 (2007): 14–18.

Tobar, Balthasar de. *Compendio bulario indico.* Edited by Manuel Gutierrez de Arce. Escuela de Estudios Hispano-Americanos (Consejo Superior de

Investigaciones Cientificas). Publicaciones 82. Seville: [Escuela de Estudios Hispano-Americanos], 1954.

Torquemada, Juan de. *Monarquia indiana.* Biblioteca Porrua 41–43. Mexico: Editorial Porrua, 1969.

Treffer, G. "Iter Sinese: Ingolstadio-Pekinum. Ingolstädter Jesuitenmissionare in China." *Ingolstädter Heitmatblätter* 52 (1989): 1–4, 11.

Treutlein, Theodore Edward. "Jesuit Travel to New Spain (1678–1756)." *Mid-America* 19 (1937): 104–23.

————. "Non-Spanish Jesuits in Spain's American colonies." In *Greater America: Essays in honor of H. E. Bolton,* 219–42. Berkeley: University of California Press, 1945.

Trigault, Nicholas, ed. *De Christiana Expeditione apvd Sinas svspecta ab Societate Jesv ex P. Matthai Ricij eiusdem Societatis com[m]entarijs.* Augsburg: Christoph. Mangium, 1615.

Valades, Diego. *Rhetorica christiana: ad concionandi et orandi vsvm accommodata, vtrivsq facvltatis exemplis svo loco insertis.* Perugia: Petrumiacobum Petrutium, 1579.

Valentin, Jean-Marie. *Le Theatre des Jésuites dans les pays de langue allemande (1554–1680).* 3 vols. Bern: Peter Lang, 1978.

Van de Vorst, Charles. "La Compagnie de Jesús et le passage à l'ordre des Chartreuz (1540–1694)." *Archivum Historicum Societatis Iesu* 23 (1954): 3–34.

Van Hagen, Victor Wolfgang. *Der Ruf der Neuen Welt: Deutsche bauen Amerika.* Munich: Droemer Knaur, 1970.

Väth, Alfons. *Johann Adam Schall von Bell, S. J.* Nettetal: Steyler, 1991.

Vega, Garcilaso de la. *Los comentarios reales de los Incas.* Lima: Gil, 1941–46.

Vercruysse, Joseph E. "Jesuit Contribution to Church Unity: A Historical Overview." *CIS: News, Documentation, Abstracts, Bibliography* 20 (1989): 15–40.

Verhaeren, Hubert. *Catalogue de la Bibliothèque du Pé-t'ang.* Peking: Mission catholique des Lazaristes, 1949.

Villey, Michel. *La croisade: essai sur la formation d'une théorie juridique.* L'Eglise et l'etat au moyen age 6. Paris: J. Vrin, 1942.

Vitoria, Franciscus de. *De Indis et de iure belli relectiones,* edited by Ernest Nys. Classics in International Law. New York: Oceana, 1964.

Von Glahn, Richard. *Fountain of Fortune: Money and Monetary Policy in China, 1000–1700.* Berkeley: University of California Press, 1996.

Wallis, Helen M. and E. D. Grinstead. "A Chinese Terrestrial Globe A.D. 1623." *British Museum Quarterly* 25 (1962): 83–91 and plates 34–36.

Walravens, Hartmut. *China Illustrata. Das europäische Chinaverständnis im Spiegel des 16. bis 18. Jahrhunderts.* Weinheim: VCH, 1987.

Walsh, Walter. *The Jesuits in Great Britain: An Historical Inquiry into Their Political Influence.* London: G. Routledge & Sons, 1903.

Warszawski, Joseph. *Unicus Universae Societatis Iesu Vocationum Liber Autobiographicus Poloniae Provinciae Proprius (1574–1580).* Rome: 1966.

Weber, Max. *The Protestant Ethic and the Spirit of Capitalism,* translated by Talcott Parsons. Routledge: London, 1992.

————. *Sociology of Religion,* translated by Ephraim Fischoff. Boston: Beacon, 1963.

Weckmann, Lewis. "The Middle Ages in the Conquest of America." *Speculum* 26 (1951): 130–41.

Wei Jun 魏濬. "Li Shuo Huangtang Huoshi" 利說荒唐惑世. In *Po Xie Ji* 破邪集, edited by Changzhi Xu 徐昌治. 水戶市：弘道館, 安政乙卯, 1855.

Wei-hua, Chang. "A Commentary of the Four Chapters on Portugal, Spain, Holland, and Italy in the History of the Ming Dynasty." *Yenching Journal of Chinese Studies* 7 (1934): 161–62.

Wessels, C. "New Documents Relating to the Journey of Fr. John Grueber." *Archivum Historicum Societatis Iesu* 9 (1940): 281–302.

Wicki, Josef. "Der älteste deutsche Druck eines Xaverius-briefes aus dem Jahre 1545, ehemals in Besitz des Basler Humanisten Lepusculus." *Neue Zeitschrift für Missionswissenschaft* IV (1948): 105–9.

————. "Die Anfange der Missionsprokur der Jesuiten in Lisabon bis 1580." *Archivum Historicum Societatis Iesu* 40 (Jan.–June 1971): 246–322.

————. "Die ersten offiziellen mündlichen Berichterstattungen in Europa aus den überseeischen Missionsgebieten der Gesellschaft Jesu (ca. 1553–1577)" *Neue Zeitschrift für Missionswissenschaft* 14 (1958): 253–65.

————. "Die unmittelbaren Auswirkungen des Konzils von Trient auf Indien (ca. 1565–1585)." In *Missionskirche im Orient,* 213–29. Neue Zeitschrift für Missionswissenschaft. Supplementa 24. Immensee: Neue Zeitschrift für Missionswissenschaft, 1976.

————, ed. *Documenta indica.* Monumenta historica Societatis Iesu 70, 72, 74, 78, 83, 86, 9, 91, 94, 98, 103, 105, 113, 118, 123, 127, 132, 133. Monumenta historica Societatis Iesu. 4–6, 9, 14, 16, 19–21, 25, 28, 30, 35, 38, 42, 44, 47, 48. Rome: Apud "Monumenta Historica Soc. Iesu," 1948–.

————. "Liste der Jesuiten-Indienfahrer, 1541–1758." In *Portugiesische Forschungen der Görresgesellschaft,* 252–450. Aufsätze zur portugiesischen Kulturgeschichte 7. Münster: Aschendorffsche Verlagsbuchhandlung, 1967.

Widmaier, Rita, ed. *Leibniz korrespondiert mit China: der Briefwechsel mit den Jesuitenmissionaren (1689–1714).* Veroffentlichungen des Leibniz-Archivs 11. Frankfurt am Main: V. Klostermann, 1990.

Wigen, Kären. "Japanese Perspectives on the Time/Space of 'Early Modernity.'" Paper for the XIX International Congress of Historical Sciences, Oslo, Norway, August 7, 2000. www.oslo2000.uio.no/program/papers/m1a/M1a-wigen.pdf/.

Wilberg-Vignau, P. *Andrea Pozzos Deckenfresko in S. Ignazio: mit einem Anhang: Archivalische Quellen zu den Werken Pozzos.* Munich: Uni-Druck, 1970.

Wilczek, Gerhard. "Ingoldstadt-Macao-Peking: Die Jesuiten und die Chinamission." *Sammelblatt des Historischen Vereins Ingolstadt* 102/103 (1993/1994): 405–38.

Wilkinson, Endymion. *Chinese History: A Manual.* Rev. ed. Harvard-Yenching Institute Monograph Series 52. Cambridge, Mass.: Harvard UP, 2000.

Willard, Alice. "Gold, Islam, and Camels: The Transformative Effects of Trade and Ideology." *Comparative Civilizations Review* 28 (1993): 80–105.

Willeke, Bernward H. "Würzburg und die Chinamission im 17. und 18. Jahrhundert." *Reformation und Gegenreformation.* Festschrift für Theobald Freudenberger. *Würzburger Diözesangeschichtsblätter* 35/36 (1974): 417–29.

Williams, Paul. *Mahayana Buddhism: The Doctrinal Foundations*. London: Routledge, 1989.

Witek, John W. *Controversial ideas in China and in Europe: A Biography of Jean-Francois Foucquet, S.J. (1665–1741)*. Bibliotheca Instituti Historici S.I. vol. 43. Rome: Institutum Historicum S.I., 1982.

Wittmann, Patrizius. *Die Herrlichkeit der Kirche in ihren Missionen*. Augsburg, 1841.

Woodward, David. "Maps and the Rationalization of Space." In *Circa 1492: Art in the Age of Exploration*, edited by Jay A. Levenson, 83–87. Washington, D. C.: National Gallery of Art; New Haven: Yale University Press, 1991.

Wright, A. D. *The Counter-Reformation: Catholic Europe and the Non-Christian World*. New York: St. Martin's, 1982.

Young, John T. "An Early Confucian Attack on Christianity: Yang Kuang-Hsien and his Pu-te-i." *Journal of the Chinese University of Hong Kong* 3 (1975): 173–74.

Zambrano, Francisco, and José Gutierrez Casillas. *Diccionario Bio-Bibliográfico de la Compañía de Jesús en México*. 14 vols. Mexico: Editorial Jus, 1961–77.

Zempliner, Arthur. "Abhandlung über die chinesische Philosophie." *Studia Leibnitiana* II.3 (1970): 223–31.

Zhang Tingyu 張廷玉. *Ming Shi* 明史. Beijing: 中華書局: 新華書店北京發行所發行, 1974.

Zubillaga, Félix. "El procurador de las Indias Occidentales de la Compañía de Jesús (1574)." *Archivum Historicum Societatis Iesu* 22 (1953): 367–417.

_____. *La Florida: la mision jesuitica (1566–1572) y la colonizacion española*. Bibliotheca Instituti Historici S. I., v. 1. Rome: Institutum Historicum S. I., [1941].

_____. "Mexico." In *Diccionario histórico de la Compañía de Jesús: biográfico-temático*. Rome: Institutum Historicum, 2001.

_____. *Monumenta Antiquae Floridae (1566–1572)*. Rome: Apud "Monumenta Historica Soc. Iesu," 1946.

_____. *Monumenta Mexicana*. 6 vols. Rome: Apud "Monumenta Historica Soc. Iesu," 1956–76.

Index

Pamplona, 88
pantometry. *See* measuring
papacy, 11, 20, 28, 29, 45, 50, 52–53, 64,
    65, 66, 83, 84, 97, 101, 102, 107,
    126, 142, 146, 152, 156, 158, 168,
    179, 220, 233, 245, 246, 251
Paraguay, 115, 129, 150, 202
Paris, 195
Parma, 63
Parras o La Laguna, Misión de, 40
partido, 39
Paspuly, 171
Pastor, Juan, 150
Pastor, Ludwig, 11
Patrick, saint, 109
patronage, 80, 84, 92, 205, 212–215, 221
patronato, 12, 15, 21, 38–39, 58, 67, 107,
    142, 163–165, 227
Patute, 46
Pátzcuaro, 38
Paul III, pope, 14, 15, 22, 235
Paul IV, pope, 59, 242
Paul V, pope, 42, 76, 100, 157
Paul, saint, 131
Peine, 119
Peres, Manuel Baptista, 22
Pérez, Jacinto, 61, 150
Pernambuco, 21
Persia and Persians, 84, 203, 211, 216,
    250
Perspectiva pictorum et architectorum. See
    Pozzo, Andrea
Peru, 22, 101, 151, 217
Perugia, 60
Peter II, king of Portugal, 157
Petty, William, 91
Phelan, John, 9
Philip II, king of Spain, 38, 39, 54, 92,
    146, 154, 163, 166
Philip III, king of Portugal. *See* Philip IV,
    king of Spain
Philip III, king of Spain, 149, 156, 167,
    172
Philip IV, king of Spain, 52, 107, 150, 167,
    180, 215
Philip V, king of Spain, 92, 153
Philip William, elector palatinate, 185
Philippines, 12, 21, 38, 39, 48, 92, 93,
    105, 111, 112, 141, 144, 159, 187,
    203
Philosophical Transactions. See Royal Society
    of London
Piccolomini, Francesco, 46
Piertz, Leonard, 139
pilgrimage, 10, 13, 70, 139

Pimería Alta, 73
Pious Fund of California, 166
piracy, 40, 49, 145, 155, 170
Pius IV, pope, 59
Pius V, pope, 126, 127
plague, 31, 40, 155, 177, 208, 238
Plata, Río de la, 150
Pláticas. See Sahagún
Plato and Platonism, 226, 253
Platzweg, C., 4
Pliny the Elder, 45
pluralitas mundium, 69
poetry, 117–118
Polanco, Juan Alfonso de, 30, 67, 198, 221
Poland, 115, 119, 212, 218
Polish language, 201
Pöllau, 116
Polo, Marco, 94
Pondicherry, 210
Poor Clares, 16
porcelain, 179, 191
Porto, 21
Portocarrero Lazo de la Vega, Melchor
    Antonio, 151
Portugal and the Portuguese, 5, 11, 21, 59,
    61, 62, 95, 98, 112, 149, 154, 158,
    159, 168, 171, 172
Portuguese language, 19
Possevino, Antonio, 68
postal systems, 46–49, 53, 195, 210
potentia dei, 69
Pozzo, Andrea, 78, 85–88
Prague, 31, 35, 84, 89, 230
prayer, 81, 109, 126, 128, 140, 142, 159,
    217–220, 234
predestination, 229
Prester John, 234
Primum Mobile, 69
probabilism, 243
professors, 76, 83, 119, 128, 136, 166,
    212
Propagation of the Faith, Sacred
    Congregation for the, 13, 15, 65, 139,
    233, 236
prophecy, 97, 98, 100
Prosperi, Adriano, 97
Protestants, 14, 15, 18, 62, 66, 70, 79, 80,
    82, 92, 100, 107, 119, 150, 163, 174,
    185, 199, 209, 212, 221, 222,
    229–231, 235, 239–242, 243, 245
Prpić, G., 5
Prussia, 244
Pseudo-Methodius, 94
Ptolemy, 69, 71
Puebla, 38, 105, 149

Santo Domingo, 148, 221
Santo Stefano Rotondo, 82
Santos Mártires del Japón, 40
Sardinia, 149
Satan. *See* devil
Savignano, Andalo de, 251
Savoy, 64, 85
Saxe-Eisenach, 32
Saxony, 33
Schall von Bell, Adam, 35, 46, 51, 66, 112,
    116, 123, 172, 188, 190, 203, 213
Scheffler, Christoph Thomas, 88
Scheffler, Felix Anton, 88
Scherer, Heinrich, 76
Schilling, Heinz, 241
Schivelbuch, Wolfgang, 90
Schneller, H., 4
Schöpfl, Johann Adam, 89
Schreck, Johann Terrenz, 46, 49, 184, 185,
    197, 203, 209, 222, 229, 237
Schwerin, 32
Scotland, 252
Scribner, Robert, 162
Sebastian, king of Portugal, 154
secular clergy, 18, 65, 96, 141, 166
Segno, 35
Sem, 77
Semedo, Álvaro, 58
Sendschreiben und warhaffte Zeytungen,
    198
Sepp von Reinegg, Anton, 151
sermons, 14, 32, 64, 96, 127, 129, 194,
    229, 232, 234
Serrão, Jorge, 60
Seven Years' War, 47
Seville, 21, 26, 130, 146, 148, 150, 164,
    201
Shimabara Rebellion, 170
Shundi 順帝 emperor, 251
Siam, 203
Siberia, 212
Sicily, 63, 149, 233
Siebert, Johann, 46
Sierra, V., 5
Silesia, 5, 33, 88
silk, 45, 158, 170, 171, 176
silver, 22, 168, 170, 171, 189, 223,
    252
Simancas, 120
Simon Magus, 81
Sinaloa, 39, 40
Siqueira, Emmanuel de, 43
Sisoguíchic, 123
Sixtus V, pope, 54
Skarga, Piotr, 233

Smogulecki, [Jan] Mikołaj, 43
Smyrna, 63
social disciplining, 244–245
Society of Jesus, 16, 142, 162, 173, 256
    age of members, 136, 160
    as a "modern" institution, 120, 242–243
    as military order, 22, 50
    assistancy, 23, 24
    China, 40–44, 154–159
    constitutional crisis, 53–55
    Constitutions, 14, 22, 45, 50, 52, 56,
        57, 105, 141, 162, 202, 218
    consultor, 24
    disobedience, 58
    finances, 162–188
    Fourth Vow, 28–29, 50, 97
    general congregation, 23, 54, 55, 64,
        182, 193, 215, 218
    general superior, 23, 26, 29, 42, 50,
        53–55, 56, 126, 143, 147, 157, 172,
        177, 186, 195
    Germany, 30–37, 137–142, 163
    joining, 27, 119–130
    Mexico, 37–40, 142–153, 166
    mobility of, 97
    monogram, 76, 80, 83, 86, 88, 103
    name, 14, 22
    periodization, 18
    procurator, 25, 26–27, 56, 57, 61, 146,
        149, 156, 165, 173, 179, 187, 195,
        217
    provinces and provincials, 24, 25
    provincial, 24, 57
    provincial congregations, 23, 24, 38, 55,
        144, 160
    spiritual formed coadjutor, 27
    suppression of, 18, 59, 62, 183
    temporal formed coadjutor, 27
    third catalogue, 25
    visitor, 25, 39, 158, 173
Socotra, 155
Sollingen, 32
Sonnenberg, Walter, 33
Sonora, 40, 47, 153
Sophie Charlotte of Brandenburg, 210
Sophie of Hanover, 212
soteriology, 94, 108, 134, 225–237
Souza, Federico Guilherme de, 221
Spain and Spaniards, 11, 18, 21, 55, 60,
    61, 62, 64, 85, 95, 101, 103, 112,
    120, 121, 128, 142–153, 154, 158,
    168, 186, 204, 212, 256
Spanish language, 18, 200, 205
Spee von Langenfeld, Friedrich, 117–119
Speyer, 209